FAMILY ABUSE AND ITS CONSEQUENCES

NEW DIRECTIONS IN RESEARCH

Gerald T. Hotaling
David Finkelhor
John T. Kirkpatrick
Murray A. Straus

editors

SAGE PUBLICATIONS
The Publishers of Professional Social Science
Newbury Park   Beverly Hills   London   New Delhi

For information address:

SAGE Publications, Inc.
2111 West Hillcrest Drive
Newbury Park, California 91320

SAGE Publications Inc.   SAGE Publications Ltd.
275 South Beverly Drive   28 Banner Street
Beverly Hills   London EC1Y 8QE
California 90212   England

SAGE PUBLICATIONS India Pvt. Ltd.
M-32 Market
Greater Kailash I
New Delhi 110 048 India

Printed in the United States of America

Library of Congress Cataloging-in-Publication Data

Main entry under title:

Family abuse and its consequences.

    Bibliography: p.
      1. Family violence—United States—Congresses.
  I. Hotaling, Gerald T.
HQ809.3.U5F33   1988   362.8'2   88-1976
ISBN 0-8039-2720-7
ISBN 0-8039-2721-5 (pbk.)

FIRST PRINTING 1988

FAMILY ABUSE
AND ITS
CONSEQUENCES

Contents

Preface

This book contains 21 articles that were originally presented at the Second National Conference for Family Violence Researchers held at the University of New Hampshire. Over 160 papers were presented at that conference and we wish more of them could have been included here. Because of space limitations and the desire to organize the book along certain lines, many fine articles were not included. In one sense, however, this book reflects the voices of all conference participants. The high level of enthusiasm that marked the conference are truly a part of the final products that make up this book. A well-deserved thank you is in order to all the participants of the conference.

Several people contributed a great deal of their time and energy to make possible both the conference and this manuscript. Richard Gelles provided the original idea to convene a conference every three years geared specifically to the needs of researchers. He played a key role in the planning and design of the conference and this book.

The day-to-day problems of organizing a conference for 350 people and the endless paperwork involved in preparing manuscripts for final publication required a dedicated staff of people. No one could have handled these jobs better than Kathy Cole, Sieglinda Fizz, Heidi Gerhardt, Charlene Hodgdon, Ruth Miller, and Donna Wilson. The staff at Sage Publications, especially Terry Hendrix, deserve much credit for their understanding and patience. Financial assistance for the conference and book came from the Undesignated Gifts Fund of the University of New Hampshire. The University of New Hampshire has encouraged family violence research over the years through a variety of avenues and their support is greatly appreciated.

Introduction

Each year the amount of research on forms of family violence and abuse seems to grow geometrically. The recent introduction of three new journals as outlets for this scholarship stands as testimony to our ever expanding knowledge base. This collection of articles represents another forum for this research and contains some of the newest research on the prevalence, risk factors, and consequences of family violence and abuse.

The chapters in this volume have been organized into the three major areas of physical child abuse, dating abuse, and elder abuse. This style of classification belies the fact that there are a number of common themes, issues, and controversies that cut across each of these forms of violence and abuse. Also, the chapters in this volume point to a number of emerging strengths in the research on all forms of violence and abuse. First of all, compared to research in past years there is greater attention being paid to theoretical integration and theory borrowing from more developed areas. This is particularly evident in the work of Burgess and Youngblade (Chapter 2), Bolton (Chapter 3), Howes (Chapter 6), and Ferraro (Chapter 8). Second, there is more evidence of a concern with classification and measurement issues. For example, O'Leary and Arias (Chapter 15) are concerned with the reliability of self-report data in studies of spouse abuse, while Finkelhor and Pillemer (Chapter 17) attempt to make conceptual sense of elder abuse through typology construction and an exploration of the relationship of elder abuse to other forms of family violence and abuse.

Perhaps the most optimistic indicator of the growing sophistication of family violence and abuse research is the large number of empirical reports that have used case control designs. Fully 75 percent of the empirical chapters in this volume use a case control or multiple case control design. These designs allow for a comparison between violent or victimized groups and at least one other nonviolent or nonvictimized group in order to assess the ability of variables of interest to discriminate between groups. This type of research design is essential to the assessment of risk factors and consequences of family violence and abuse and to the development of sound theory. It is a tribute to researchers in this area that these designs have become the norm, considering that only six years ago the case control design was a rare exception.

In addition to methodological advances in research on family violence, there are at least three major issues debated by the contributors to this volume that continues traditional directions of inquiry. These issues, in the form of questions, are:

(1) how much violence and abuse occurs in familial and close relationships?
(2) what are the consequences of violence and abuse on victims and society-at-large?
(3) what do we really know about the perpetrators of violence and abuse?

How Much Violence and Abuse Occurs in Familial and Close Relationships?

Although estimates of the incidence and prevalence of family violence and abuse are no longer necessary to persuade people of the existence of this problem, they are extremely important for understanding the nature of the problem and for the development of effective public policy. Straus and Gelles (Chapter 1) present the results of the 1986 National Family Violence Resurvey on incidence rates of physical child abuse and wife abuse. They compare their findings to a number of other national and local estimates of the incidence of family violence. Their conclusions are controversial, but one thing is certain: The reader will be surprised by the sheer number of attempts in the last decade to estimate the scope of family violence and the growing sophistication of these efforts.

What Are the Consequences of Violence and Abuse on Victims and Society-at-Large?

Almost half of the chapters in this volume are concerned in one way or another with the consequences of family violence and abuse. These chapters contribute in an important way to the victimology of violence and abuse by making us come to grips with the pain, suffering, and long-term adjustment problems suffered by many in family and family-like relationships. As several of the chapters in this collection make clear; society also suffers in myriad ways.

The chapters can be divided roughly into three categories of consequences: (1) the consequences of violence on adult women; (2) the consequences of sexual abuse on children and adult women; and (3) the consequences of experiencing and witnessing parental violence on children. Taken together, they comprise the clearest and most direct evidence yet for the viability of a public health approach to family violence and abuse. Both Walker (Chapter 9) and Makepeace (Chapter 21) chronicle the physical and psychological effects of violence on women and its implications for policy concerning protection, treatment, and compensation for injuries.

The effects of sexual abuse are the focus of a growing research concern represented here by four chapters. Finkelhor and Browne (Chapter 19) present an exhaustive review of the short- and long-term affects of sexual abuse on children. Their findings pose a challenge to professionals concerned with the identification and assessment of child sexual abuse. Two chapters examine sexual abuse among adolescent and adult females. Murphy (Chapter 20) discusses the impact of date rape, while Shields and Hanneke (Chapter 18) explore the implications of marital rape and other forms of sexual violence on social and psychological functioning. Shields and Hanneke also examine the processes of victimization that seem to place incest victims at greater risk to marital rape.

Perhaps no other issue about family violence produces more controversy than that concerning the role of witnessing and experiencing parental violence on children's attitudes and behavior. Four chapters look at this relationship, each in a different way. Burgess and Youngblade (Chapter 2) attempt to understand why child maltreatment gets repeated in one generation after another. Their intriguing chapter will surely spark renewed empirical research interest on the intergenerational hypothesis. Adult aggressiveness outside of the family also seems firmly rooted in a history of child maltreatment. McCord (Chapter 5) in her analysis of longitudinal data on men first studied 40 years ago shows a strong relationship between adult aggressiveness and exposure to aggressive parental models as children. Along these lines, Gray (Chapter 7) presents an extensive review of the link between child maltreatment and juvenile delinquency using the most current research.

The consequences on children exposed to parental aggression and violence are not limited to long-term behavioral effects. Wolfe and his colleagues (Chapter 16) demonstrate in a case-control study that witnessing parental violence may be causally linked to a variety of child adjustment problems.

Research on Perpetrators

A number of assumptions have guided much of the research on wife abuse during the past 15 years. None has been so futile as the search for characteristics of victims in order to explain the violent behavior of men. Studying men, however, especially men who have been criminally violent, is not an easy task. But this is not the only reason for this glaring omission. Ptacek (Chapter 10) lays bare some of the assumptions that have steered researchers away from confronting an obvious fact: in order to understand male violence, one should study violent men. Three chapters in this volume do exactly that. Dutton and Browning (Chapter 11), Rouse (Chapter 12), and Johnston (Chapter 13) all demonstrate that not only can violent men be studied directly but that there are a number of common factors associated with men who batter. Taken together, they point to the need for the development of theory to help interpret the role of several important risk factors associated with the use of violence by males.

Although more is known about violence against children than about violence toward wives, Coontz and Martin (Chapter 4) make clear that much is to be gained by studying the explanations given by parents to account for their use of corporal punishment. Their chapter reveals important differences among mothers and fathers as well as important similarities in their justifications for their own violent behavior.

The chapters in this volume are proof of the genuine maturing of family violence and abuse research. New research on the short- and long-term consequences of abusive behavior and research on offender characteristics fills a sizable gap in our understanding of abusive dynamics.

More than the expansion of research into new areas defines the character of this volume. The growing methodological and conceptual skill evidenced by these chapters is truly noteworthy. The use of case-control designs, the selection of nonclinical samples, and more concise theory are becoming normative features of family violence and abuse research.

This state-of-affairs bodes well for our knowledge and response to the problem of abusive and violent behavior in families.

PART I

The Prevalence of Family Violence

1

How Violent Are American Families?
Estimates from the National Family
Violence Resurvey and Other Studies

Murray A. Straus
Richard J. Gelles

Eighteen years after statistics on the incidence of child abuse cases started being collected (Gil, 1970), and fifteen years after such data were first reported for spouse abuse (Straus, 1973), the question of how much violence occurs in American families remains controversial. However, a considerable body of evidence is now available, including studies reported in this book. In addition, data are available from a 1985 replication of the 1975 National Family Violence Survey (Gelles & Straus, 1988; Straus & Gelles, 1986; Straus Gelles, & Steinmetz, 1980). The purposes of this chapter are to present the rates from the 1985 national survey and to compare those rates to the rates from other epidemiological research on family violence.

Definition and Measurement
of Violence and Abuse

The focus of this chapter is not on all the "abuse" or "violence" that can go on within the family, but on *physical violence* as one type of abuse. Moreover, even restricting the focus to physical violence leaves important

AUTHORS' NOTE: This report is a publication of the Family Violence Research Program, University of New Hampshire, Durham, NH 03824. A bibliography listing other papers available for distribution is available on request. We are pleased to acknowledge the help of Diane Cyr Carmody and Barbara A. Wauchope in locating and summarizing the many studies that have used the Conflict Tactics Scales. We are also pleased to acknowledge the financial support provided by National Institute of Mental Health, grant MH40027. Several other organizations have supported the larger research program of which this project is a part, including a "training grant" (T32 MH15161) from the National Institute of Mental Health, and ongoing support by the Graduate School of the University of New Hampshire.

issues unresolved. For children, the line between "physical punishment" and "physical abuse" is a matter of controversy (Gelles, 1985). In view of these issues it is essential to begin with a definition, and to describe the way we operationalized this concept.

Violence is defined as an act carried out with the intention, or perceived intention, of causing physical pain or injury to another person.[1] This definition is synonymous with the legal concept of "assault" and the concept of "physical aggression" used in social psychology.

Operationalizing Violence and Abuse

The Conflict Tactics Scales (Straus, 1979, 1987, 1988) was used to measure violence. This instrument has been employed, not only in our own research, but by more than 40 other investigators (e.g., Allen & Straus, 1980; Cate, Henton, Joval, Christopher, & Lloyd, 1982; Henton, Cate, Koval, Lloyd, & Christopher, 1983; Giles-Sims, 1983; Hornung, McCullough, & Sugimoto, 1981; Jouriles & O'Leary, 1985; Jorgensen, 1977; Straus, 1974; Steinmetz, 1977). Four different studies have established that the Conflict Tactics Scales (CTS) measures three factorially separate variables: reasoning, verbal aggression, and violence or physical aggression (Barling, O'Leary, Jouriles, Vivian, & MacEwen, 1987; Jorgensen, 1977; Schumm, Martin, Bollman, & Jurich, 1982; Straus, 1979). The violence index and the subindexes used as the measures of child abuse and spouse abuse are described below.[2]

Format of the CTS. The introduction to the Conflict Tactics Scales asks respondents to think of situations in the past year when they had a disagreement or were angry with a specified family member and to indicate how often they engaged in each of the acts included in the CTS. The instrument is designed so that it can be replicated for any role relationship, such as parent-to-child, child-to-parent, sibling-to-sibling, husband-to-wife, wife-to-husband. The 1975 version of the CTS consisted of 19 items, eight of which refer to acts of violence. The 1985 version (used for this chapter) is identical except that "scalding or burning" was added to the list for parent-to-child violence and "choking" was added to the spouse violence list.[3]

Violent acts. The violent acts included in the 1985 version of the CTS used for this chapter are: threw something at the other; pushed, grabbed, or shoved; slapped or spanked; kicked, bit, or hit with a fist; hit or tried to hit with something; beat up the other; burned or scalded (for children) or choked (for spouses); threatened with knife or gun; used a knife or gun.

Violence indexes. The violent acts included in the CTS can be combined to form a number of different violence indexes. The following measures are used in this chapter:

Overall violence. This measure indicates the proportion (stated as a rate per 1,000) of parents or spouses who used *any* of the violent acts included in the CTS during the year covered by the study.[4]

Severe violence. For purposes of this study, "severe violence" was defined as acts that have a relatively high probability of causing an injury. Thus kicking is classified as severe violence because kicking a child or a spouse has a much greater potential for producing an injury than an act of "minor violence" such as spanking or slapping.[5] The acts making up the severe violence index are kicked, bit, punched, hit with an object, beat up, choked, threatened with a knife or gun, and used a knife or gun.

Child abuse. What constitutes abuse is, to a considerable extent, a matter of social norms. Spanking or slapping a child, or even hitting a child with an object such as stick, hair brush, or belt, is not "abuse" according to either the legal or informal norms of American society, although it is in Sweden and several other countries (Haeuser, 1985). Our operationalization of child abuse attempts to take such normative factors into consideration. It is the use by a parent of any of the acts of violence in the Severe Violence Index (see list above), except that "burned or scalded the child" was used instead of "choked" and that, to be consistent with current legal and informal norms, hitting or trying to hit with an object such as a stick or belt is *not* included.[6]

Spouse violence. The problem of terminology and norms is even greater for violence between spouse than for violence by parents. Although occasionally slapping a child is not usually considered abuse (or even "violence"), our perception is that the same act is often considered to be violence if done to a spouse. Thus in the case of violence between spouses, the "overall violence" rate is more important than is overall violence by parents.

Wife beating. Because of the greater average size and strength of men, the acts in the Severe Violence list are likely to be more damaging when the assailant is the husband. Consequently, to facilitate focusing on the rate of Severe Violence by husbands, the term *wife beating* will be used to refer to that rate.

The 1985 National Family Violence Resurvey

The incidence rates for family violence to be presented are based on interviews with a national probability sample of 6,002 households. To be eligible for inclusion, a household had to include (1) two adults, a male and female, 18 years of age or older, who were presently married, or (2) presently living as a male-female couple; or a household might include one adult 18 years of age or older who was either (3) divorced or separated within the last two years, or (4) a single parent living with a child under the age of 18. When more than one eligible adult was in the household, a random procedure was used to select the gender and marital status of the respondent. When more than one child under the age of 18 was in the household, a random procedure was used to select the "referent child" as the focus of the parent-to-child violence questions.

The sample was selected by "random digit dialing" and the interviews were conducted by telephone. The total sample of 6,002 cases combines four parts: a national probability sample of 4,032 households and three oversamples to ensure enough black families, Hispanic families, and enough cases from the smaller states to permit separate analyses of these ethnic groups and to produce certain state-by-state data. The rates to be reported in this chapter were computed by weighting each of the four components so as to make the total sample representative of the United States.

Interviews lasted an average of 35 minutes. The response rate, calculated as "completes as a proportion of eligibles" was 84%. A detailed report on the methodology of the study is available from the authors.

Violence Between Spouses

1985 National Survey Rates[7]

Couple violence. The rate of 161 in the first row of Table 1.1 indicates that just over 16%, or one out of six American couples, experienced an incident involving a physical assault during 1985.[8] Applying this rate to the approximately 54 million couples in the United States that year, results in an estimate of about 8.7 million couples who experienced at least one assault during the year.

Most of those assaults were relatively minor—pushing, slapping, shoving, or throwing things. However, the Severe Violence rate of 61 (see second row of Table 1.1) indicates that a substantial part were serious assaults such as kicking, punching, biting, or choking. Thus the figure in the column headed "Number Assaulted" indicates that, of the 8.7 million households where such violence occurred, 3.4 million were instances in which the violence had a relatively high risk of causing injury.

Husband-to-wife violence.[9] The middle two rows of Part A of Table 1.1 focus on assaults by husbands. The rate of 116 per 1,000 couples shows that almost one out of eight husbands carried out one or more violent acts during the year of this study. The most important statistic, however, is in the row labeled "severe violence by the husband." This is the measure we use as the indicator of "wife beating." It shows that more than 3 out of every 100 women were severely assaulted by their partners in 1985. If this rate is correct, it means that about 1.8 million women were beaten by their partners that year. However, the rate of 34 per 1,000 wives, along with all the other rates shown in Table 1.1, must be regarded as an underestimate. There are a number of reasons for this (see Straus et al., 1980, p. 35), including the virtual certainty that not every respondent was completely

TABLE 1.1

Annual Incidence Rates for Family Violence and
Estimated Number of Cases Based on These Rates

Type of Intrafamily Violence[a]	Rate per 1,000 Couples or Children	Number Assaulted[b]
A. Violence between husband and wife		
any violence during the year (slap, push, etc.)	161	8,700,000
severe violence (kick, punch, stab, etc.)	63	3,400,000
any violence by the husband	116	6,250,000
severe violence by the husband ("wife beating")	34	1,800,000
any violence by the wife	124	6,800,000
severe violence by the wife	48	2,600,000
B. Violence by parents–child age 0-17		
any hitting of child during the year	Near 100% for young child[c]	
very severe violence (Child Abuse-1)[d]	23	1,500,000
severe violence (Child Abuse-2)	110	6,900,000
C. Violence by parents–child age 15-17		
any violence against 15-17-year-olds	340	3,800,000
severe violence against 15-17-year-olds	70	800,000
very severe violence against 15-17-year-olds	21	235,000
D. Violence by children age 3-17 (1975-76 sample)		
any violence against a brother or sister	800	50,400,000
severe violence against a brother or sister	530	33,300,000
any violence against a parent	180	9,700,000
severe violence against a parent	90	4,800,000
E. Violence by children age 15-17 (1975-76 sample)		
any violence against a brother or sister	640	7,200,000
severe violence against a brother or sister	360	4,000,000
any violence against a parent	100	1,100,000
severe violence against a parent	35	400,000

SOURCE: Data from the 1985 and 1975 National Family Violence Survey.
a. Section A rates are based on a nationally representative sample of 6,002 currently married or cohabiting couples interviewed in 1985. The rates in Section A differ from those in Straus and Gelles (1986) because the rates in that paper are computed in a way that enabled the 1985 rates to be compared with the more restricted sample and more restricted version of the Conflict Tactics Scale used in the 1975 study. Section B rates are based on the 1985 sample of 3,232 households with a child age 17 and under. The rates shown in Section B differs from those in Straus and Gelles (1986) for the reasons given for Section A. Section C and D rates are based on the 1975-76 study because data on violence by children was not collected in the 1985 survey.

Notes for Table 1.1 continued:

b. The column giving the "Number Assaulted" was computed by multiplying the rates in this table by the 1984 population figures as given in the 1986 Statistical Abstract of the United States. The population figures (rounded to millions) are 54 million couples, and 63 million children age 0-17. The number of children 15-17 was estimated as 11.23 million. This was done by taking .75 of the number age 14-17, as given in Statistical Abstract Table 29.

c. The rate for 3-year-old children in the 1975 survey was 97%. See Straus (1983), and Wauchope and Straus (in press) for age-specific rates through age 17.

d. See "Definition and Measurement" section for an explanation of the difference between Child Abuse-1 and Child Abuse-2.

frank in describing violent incidents. The true rates could be as much as double those shown in Table 1.1.

Wife-to-husband violence. The last two rows of Part A show the rates for assaults *by* wives. Comparison of these two rows with the rates for husband-to-wife assaults in the previous two rows shows that the rates for violence by wives are remarkably similar to the rates for violence by husbands. The fact that women are so violent within the family is inconsistent with the extremely low rate of assault by women outside the family, but consistent with our 1975 national survey (Straus et al., 1980) and with a number of other studies, such as Lane and Gwartney-Gibbs (1985), Laner and Thompson (1982), Steinmetz (1977-1978).

Although the studies cited above and the studies to be reviewed later leave little doubt about the high frequency of wife-to-husband assault, the meaning and consequences of that violence is easily misunderstood. For one thing, as pointed out elsewhere (Straus, 1977; Straus et al., 1980, p. 43), the greater average size and strength of men, and their greater aggressiveness, means that the same act (for example, a punch) is likely to be very different in the amount of pain or injury inflicted (see also Greenblat, 1983).

To understand the high rate of intrafamily violence by women, it is also important to realize that many of the assaults by women against their husbands are acts of retaliation or self-defense (Straus, 1980). One of the most fundamental reasons why women are violent within the family (but rarely outside the family) is that, for a typical American woman, her home is the location where there is the most serious risk of assault. The rates of husband-to-wife assault just presented are many times the female assault victimization rate outside the family. The high risk of being assaulted at home relative to outside the home is also shown by statistics on homicide. The homicide victimization rates in Plass and Straus (1987, Table 1.2) show that women are seldom murder victims outside the family: 21% of stranger homicide victims but 76% of spouse murder victims. Since women are so often the victims of murderous assault within the family, it is not surprising that women, who commit only about a tenth of the nonspouse murders in the United States, commit nearly half (48%) of the murders of spouses (see Plass & Straus, 1987; Straus, 1986 for the rates; and Browne, 1987 for case examples).

**Couple Violence Rates from
Studies Using Other Methods**

Although we believe that the rates just presented provide the best estimate currently available of the incidence of physical violence in American families, there is always the possibility of some unknown error or bias. It is therefore important to also have information from other sources. Most of these studies also used the CTS to measure violence. However, before turning to those studies, this section presents incidence rates from three studies that used other techniques.

National Crime Survey. This survey provides the most extensive data available because it is based on a sample of approximately 60,000 households and is repeated annually. It is also an extremely carefully conducted survey. Nevertheless, the National Crime Survey rate is a drastically lower rate of spouse abuse than that found by the National Family Violence Resurvey: 2.2 per 1,000 (Gaquin, 1977-1978). By comparison, the National Family Violence Resurvey rate of 116 is more than 50 times higher.

The huge discrepancy between the National Crime Survey (NCS) rate of 2.1 and the National Family Violence Survey rate of 161 (and also the rates to be presented in the next section) raises the question of why the NCS rate is so low. The most likely reason for the tremendous discrepancy lies in differences between the context of the NCS versus the other studies. The NCS is presented to respondents as a study of crime, whereas the others are presented as studies of family problems. The difficulty with a "crime survey" as the context for determining incidence rates of intrafamily violence is that most people think of being kicked by their spouses as wrong, but not a "crime" in the legal sense. Thus only a minute proportion of assaults by spouses are reported in the National Crime Survey.

Scanzoni (1978) studied a sample of 321 women. Violence was measured by response to a question that asked what they did in cases of persistent conflict. In all, 16% (160 per 1,000) reported trying to hit the husband—a figure that is well with the range of rates obtained by studies using the CTS (see Table 1.2).

Fergusson, Horwood, Kershaw, and Shannon (1986, p. 409) interviewed 960 mothers of a birth cohort of New Zealand children, for a six year period starting in the first year of the child's life. The mothers were asked if their husbands (legal or de facto) had assaulted them during the previous year. The rate for the first year was 34 and the cumulative rate for the six-year period was 85. The U.S. rate of 116 per 1,000, shown in Table 1.1, is almost three and a half times greater. This is not surprising considering the much higher rates of other types of violence in the United States. For example, in 1980 the U.S. homicide mortality rate was 105, which is eight times greater than the New Zealand rate for that year.

Couple Violence Rates from
Other Studies Using the CTS

Over 40 different investigators have used the CTS in addition to the studies done with data from the two National Family Violence Surveys. A number of these studies present incidence rates that were computed by roughly the same method as the rates from the National Family Violence Resurvey in Table 1.1. The right column of Table 1.2 lists the rates that have so far been located in ascending order. The underlined rate is the rate from National Family Violence Resurvey.

Couple violence. Part A of Table 1.2 gives the rates for 12 studies. The range is from 121 per 1,000 couples to 510 per 1,000 couples. The National Family Violence Resurvey rate of 161 is close to the median of 159. The rate of 510 is for assaults experienced by a sample of battered wives when they were dating.

There are too few studies in Part B to generalize about the severe violence for couples.

Husband-to-wife violence. The largest number of studies have investigated assaults by husbands. The rates in Part C show a tremendous range, in part because the studies with high rates are of populations at high risk of violence, such as blacks and couples in therapy for marital conflict.

There is also a large range when severe assaults are considered (Part D of Table 1.2). The lowest rate (8 per 1,000) is only one third as high as the next lowest rate. For this type of violence, as for the others discussed so far, there are special characteristics of the populations that account for outliers at the low and high ends. The rate of 8 per 1,000 might suggest that the other rates are erroneously high. Rather, it probably reflects the fact that the sample for this study were Quakers, a pacifist denomination. Similarly, the scores at the high end are based on samples of students describing dating relationships. This fits the fact that youth tend to be the most violent age group, and dating and cohabiting couples therefore tend to have much higher violence rates than do married couples (Stets & Straus, in press; Yllö & Straus, 1981).

Wife-to-husband violence. The most important aspect of Parts E and F of Table 1.2 is the extent to which the rates parallel the rates for husband-to-wife assault. The repeated finding that the rate of assault by women is similar to the rate by their male partners is an important and distressing aspect of violence in American families. It contrasts markedly to the behavior of women outside the family. It shows that, within the family or in dating and cohabiting relationships, women are about as violent as men. This highly controversial finding of the 1975 study is confirmed by the 1985 study, and also by the rates found by other investigators listed in Table 1.2.

The importance of intrafamily violence by women should not be dismissed because men are larger and heavier and can inflict more serious

TABLE 1.2
Marital Violence Rates from CTS Studies by Other Investigators

Study	Sample	Comments*	Rate per Thousand
A. Any violence between husband and wife			
Henton, Cate, Koval, Lloyd, & Christopher (1983)	volunteer (N = 644)	1, 2b, 3b	121
Legg, Olday, Wesley (1984)	volunteer (N = 1,465)	1, 2a, 3a	134
Brutz & Allen (1986)	volunteer (N = 289)	3c	149
Kennedy & Dutton (1987)	probability (N = 708)		151
Hornung, McCullough, & Sugimoto (1981)	probability (N = 1,553)		157
Straus & Gelles	probability (N = 6,002)		161
Murphy (1984)	probability (N = 485)	1, 3a	191
Cate, Henton, Koval, Christopher, & Lloyd (1982)	volunteer (N = 355)	1, 2b	223
Sack, Keller, & Howard (1982)	volunteer (N = 211)	3a	240
Meredith, Abbott, & Adams (1986)	probability (N = 304)		250
Margolin (1984)	volunteer (N = 45)		290
Gully, Dengerink, Pepping, & Bergstrom (1981)	volunteer (N = 335)		322
Szinovacz (1983)	volunteer (N = 103)	1	360
Roscoe & Benaske (1985)	volunteer (N = 82)	1, 2b, 3d	510
B. Severe violence between husband and wife			
Hornung, McCullough & Sugimoto (1981)	probability (N = 1,553)		287
Kennedy & Dutton (1987)	probability (N = 708)		550

TABLE 1.2 Continued

Study	Sample	Comments*	Rate per Thousand
Straus & Gelles	probability (N = 3,520)		630
C. Any violence by the husband			
Rouse (1984)	probability (N = 120)	3m	108
Kennedy & Dutton (1987)	probability (N = 708)		112
Straus & Gelles	probability (N = 6,002)		116
Makepeace (1983)	volunteer (N = 244)	1, 2a, 3a	137
Brutz & Ingoldsby (1984)	volunteer (N = 288)	3c	146
Dutton (1986)	volunteer (N = 75)	3e	183
Makepeace (1981)	probability (N = 2,338)	1, 2b, 3a	206
Smith (1986)	probability (N = 315)	2b	206
Meredith, Abbott, & Adams (1986)	probability (N = 304)		220
O'Leary, Barling, Arias, Rosenbaum, Malone, & Tyree (1987)	volunteer (N = 393)		240
Szinovacz (1983)	volunteer (N = 103)		260
O'Leary, Barling, Arias, Rosenbaum, Malone, & Tyree (1987)	volunteer (N = 393)		270
Clarke (1987)	volunteer (N = 318)	3k	274
O'Leary, Barling, Arias, Rosenbaum, Malone, & Tyree (1987)	volunteer (N = 393)	1	340
Lockhart (1987)	volunteer (N = 307)	3f	355
Barling, O'Leary, Jouriles, Vivian, & MacEwen (1987)	therapy (N = 187)	2a	740

(continued)

TABLE 1.2 Continued

Study	Sample	Comments*	Rate per Thousand
D. Severe violence by husband			
Brutz & Ingoldsby (1984)	volunteer (N = 288)	3c	8
Kennedy & Dutton (1987)	probability (N = 708)		23
Straus & Gelles	probability (N = 6,002)		34
Meredith, Abbott, & Adams (1986)	probability (N = 304)		60
Schulman (1979)	probability (N = 1,793)		87
Makepeace (1983)	volunteer (N = 244)	1, 2a, 3c	93
Clarke (1987)	probability (N = 318)	1, 2a, 3k	102
E. Any violence by the wife			
Makepeace (1983)	volunteer (N = 244)	1, 2a, 3a	93
Makepeace (1981)	probability (N = 2,338)	1, 2b, 3a	120
Straus & Gelles	probability (N = 6,002		124
Brutz & Ingoldsby (1984)	volunteer (N = 288)	3c	152
Meredith, Abbott, & Adams (1986)	probability (N = 304)		180
Szinovacz (1983)	volunteer (N = 103)		300
O'Leary, Barling, Arias, Rosenbaum, Malone, & Tyree (1987)	volunteer (N = 393)		310
O'Leary, Barling, Arias, Rosenbaum, Malone, & Tyree (1987)	volunteer (N = 393)		330
O'Leary, Barling, Arias, Rosenbaum, Malone, & Tyree (1987)	volunteer (N = 393)	1	420
Barling, O'Leary, Jouriles, Vivian, & MacEwen (1987)	therapy (N = 187)	2a	730

TABLE 1.2 Continued

Study	Sample	Comments*	Rate per Thousand
F. Severe violence by the wife			
Brutz & Ingoldsby (1984)	volunteer (N = 288)	3c	25
Straus & Gelles	probability (N = 6,002)		48
Meredith, Abbott, & Adams (1986)	probability (N = 304)		50
Makepeace (1981)	volunteer (N = 244)	1, 2a, 3c	59

*Key to comments:

1. = Dating couples
2. = CTS rates are for acts that occur over the previous year unless noted below:
   a. study did not report whether rates were for previous year or for "ever"
   b. study reports rates for acts occurring "ever"
3. = additional sample information

a. college students	h. rural mothers
b. high school students	i. urban fathers
c. Quakers	j. rural fathers
d. battered women	k. women
e. batterers	m. men
f. half-black/half-white	n. mothers
g. urban mothers	p. fathers
	q. delinquents

4. = rates reported as a range
   a. low end
   b. high end

injury. Nor should it be dismissed on the grounds that it is in self-defense or in retaliation, as is true of a substantial part of wife-to-husband violence. In the 1985 survey, we asked who hit first. According to the husbands, they struck the first blow in 44% of the cases, the wives in 45% of the cases, and the husband could not remember or disentangle it in the remaining 11% of cases. According to the wives, husbands struck the first blow in 53% of the cases, wives in 42% of the cases, and the remaining 5% of wives could not disentangle who hit first (see also Straus, 1980).

Violence by women is a critically important issue for the safety and well-being *of women*. Let us assume that most of the assaults by women are of the "slap the cad" genre and are not intended to and do not physically injure the husband (Greenblatt, 1983). The danger to women of such behavior is that it sets the stage for the husband to assault her. Sometimes this is immediate and severe retaliation. But regardless of whether that occurs, the fact that she slapped him provides the precedent and justification for him to hit her when *she* is being obstinate, "bitchy," or "not

130,575

listening to reason" as he sees it. Unless women also forsake violence in their relationships with male partners and children, they cannot expect to be free of assault. Women must insist as much on nonviolence by their sisters as they rightfully insist on it by men. That is beginning to happen. After years of denial, shelters for battered women are confronting this problem. Almost all shelters now have policies designed to deal with the high rate of child abuse, and some are also facing up to the problem of wife-to-husband violence.[10]

Violence Against Children and by Children

National Family Violence Survey Rates

Overall violence rate. No rates or numbers are shown in the first row of Part B of Table 1.1 because statistics on whether *any* violence is used are almost meaningless unless one takes into account the age of the child. For children age 3 and under, the true figure is close to 100%. For example, 97% and 90% of the parents of 3-year-olds in the 1975 and 1985 surveys reported one or more times during the year when they had hit the child (Straus, 1983, Figure 1; Wauchope & Straus, in press), which is a rate of 997 or 990 per 1,000. For children age 15 and over, the rate of 340 per 1,000 in the first row of Part C of Table 1.1 shows that the rate is much lower, but it nonetheless means that about a third of 15- to 17-year-olds were hit by a parent during the year of the study.

The most important data in Part B are the statistics on "very severe" and "severe" violence. These are alternative measures of child abuse. The first (as noted earlier) omits hitting the child with an object such as a stick or belt, and will be called "Child Abuse 1." The second, which will be called the "Child Abuse 2" rate, adds hitting with an object on the grounds that hitting with an object carries a relatively greater risk of injury than spanking or slapping with the hand. For this reason we think that the more inclusive measure (Child Abuse 2) is the better indicator of the extent of physical abuse of children.

Child Abuse 1. The rate of such indubitably abusive violence was 23 per 1,000 children in 1985. If this rate is correct, it means a minimum of 1.5 million children are seriously assaulted per year. As in the case of the estimated number of beaten wives, the actual rate and the actual number is almost certainly greater because not all parents were willing to tell us about instances in which they kicked or punched a child.

Child Abuse 2. The third row of Part B shows that, in 1985, 110 out of every 1,000 children were assaulted by a parent in a way that we regard as "abuse." When this rate is applied to the 63 million children living in the United States in 1985, it results in an estimate of 6.9 million abused children per year.

Abuse of children age 15-17. Although infants and young children experience the highest rates of child abuse, teenagers are by no means immune. About one out of three parents of a child age 15 through 17 reported having physically assaulted the child at least once during 1985. This was usually one of the acts of "minor violence" such as slapping. However, serious assaults were far from absent. In fact, Part C of Table 1.1 shows that 70 out of every 1,000 children this age were victims of a serious assault by one of their parents, including 340 per 1,000 who were victims of very serious assaults.

Violence by Children

Children age 3-17. The first row of section D in Table 1.1 reveals that children are the most violent people of all in American families. The rates are extremely high for violence against a sibling—800 out of 1,000 had hit a brother or sister, and more than half had engaged in one of the acts in the CTS "severe violence" list. This came as a surprise, even though it should not have. Had we analyzed the issue theoretically beforehand, it would have been an obvious prediction because of the well-known tendency for children to imitate and exaggerate the behavioral patterns of parents, and because there are implicit norms that permit violence between siblings, exemplified by phrases such as "kids will fight."

The rate of assault against parents is much lower, as might be expected, perhaps because of the strong norms against hitting one's father or mother. However, the rate is still substantial and is not confined to minor violence: 90 per 1,000 children severely assaulted a parent during the year of this survey.

Children ages 15-17. There is a vast difference between being punched by a 5-year-old and being punched by a 15-year-old—at least in respect to the pain or injury that can result. Consequently, we computed separate rates for assaults by 15- to 17-year-olds. The first row in Part E of Table 1.1 shows that even in their late teens, two thirds of American children assault a sibling at least once during the course of a year, and in over a third of these cases the assault involved an act with a relatively high probability of causing injury (kicking, punching, biting, choking, attacks with a knife or gun, and so on). These incredible rates of intrafamily violence by teenagers make the high rates of violence by their parents seem modest by comparison.

Finally, the last two rows in Table 1.1 show that teenagers attack their parents about as often as the parents attack each other. The overall violence rate is slightly lower (100 per 1,000 children this age versus 113 per 1,000 husbands and 121 per 1,000 wives), and the rate of severe violence against a parent (35 per 1,000 children) is midway between the rate of severe husband-to-wife violence (32) and severe wife-to-husband violence (45).

Parent-Child Violence Rates from
Studies Using Other Methods

There are two major sources of data on physical child abuse in addition to the rates produced by studies using the CTS. However, both of these are measures of *intervention* or treatment rather than *incidence* rates (see Straus & Gelles, 1986 for further explanation). They are presented here because they are probably the most widely known and cited statistics on intrafamily violence in the United States, and therefore need to be evaluated in relation to other measures of child abuse.

CPS rate. Annual statistics are compiled on the number of child abuse cases reported to the Child Protective Services (CPS) under the mandatory reporting laws that are in effect in all the states. The 1984 rate was 27.3 per 1,000 children (American Association for Protecting Children, 1986). However, the CPS rate covers not only physical abuse, but also sexual abuse, and neglect. Other information in the report indicates that about one quarter of these cases involved physical abuse. If this interpretation is correct, the incidence rate is approximately 6.8 per 1,000. By contrast, the National Family Violence Resurvey rates in Table 1.1 is 23 per 1,000 for "Child Abuse 1" and 110 per 1,000 for when using the "Child Abuse 2" measure. Thus the survey rate for the more severe assaults on children is 3.4 times greater than the CPS rate, and the survey rate for the more inclusive measure of physical abuse is 16 times greater than the CPS. We think that the best way to interpret these differences is to say that comparison of the CPS rate with the rate obtained in the National Family Violence Resurvey shows that there are from 3.4 to 16 times more physically abused children in the United States than are publicly recognized.

National Incidence Study. This study attempted to find out about all known cases of child abuse in a sample of 26 counties surveyed in 1980 (National Center on Child Abuse and Neglect, 1981). The procedure went beyond the official reporting system described above by also collecting data on cases known to personnel in community institutions (schools, hospitals, police, courts), regardless of whether the cases had been officially reported. It produced a rate of 5.7 per 1,000 children. This figure is about 26% higher than the rate of officially reported cases of physical abuse in *1980* (the CPS rate has gone up tremendously since then because the new attention to sexual abuse has produced an influx of cases), but is still much lower than the incidence rate obtained by either the 1975 or the 1985 National Family Violence Survey.

Parental Violence Rates from
Other Studies Using the CTS

Table 1.3 summarizes the incidence rates for physical violence against children from studies that used approximately the same method of

TABLE 1.3
Parent-to-Child Violence Rates from CTS Studies
by Other Investigators

Study	Sample	Comments*	Rate per Thousand
A. Any hitting of child			
Schumm, Martin, Bollman, & Jurich (1982)	probability (N = 98)	3i	322
Schumm, Martin, Bollman, & Jurich (1982)	probability (N = 83)	3h	338
Schumm, Martin, Bollman, & Jurich (1982)	probability (N = 98)	3j	352
Schumm, Martin, Bollman, & Jurich (1982)	probability (N = 83)	3g	390
Meredith, Abbott, & Adams (1986)	probability (N = 304)	3n	500
Meredith, Abbott, & Adams (1986)	probability (N = 304)	3p	580
Gelles & Straus	probability (N = 3,232)		<u>620</u>
Brutz & Ingoldsby (1984)	volunteer (N = 288)	3p	689
Brutz & Ingoldsby (1984)	volunteer (N = 288)	3n	742
Giles-Sims (1985)	volunteer (N = 27)	3d	908
B. Severe violence—"child abuse-2" (ages vary)			
Brutz & Ingoldsby (1984)	volunteer (N = 288)	3p	88
Gelles & Straus	probability (N = 3,232)		<u>110</u>
Brutz & Ingoldsby (1984)	volunteer (N = 288)	3n	113
Meredith, Abbott, & Adams (1986)	probability (N = 304)	3n	170
Meredith, Abbott, & Adams (1986)	probability (N = 304)	3p	211

(continued)

TABLE 1.3 Continued

Study	Sample	Comments*	Rate per Thousand
Dembo, Bertke, LaVoie, Borders, Washburn, & Schneidler (1987)	volunteer (N = 145)	2a, eq, 4a	460
Giles-Sims (1985)	volunteer (N = 27)	3d	593
Dembo, Bertke, LaVoie, Borders, Washburn & Schneidler (1987)	volunteer (N = 145)	2a, e1, 4b	680

*See key to comments in Table 1.2.

computing the rate as was used in the National Family Violence Resurvey.

Any violence. It is difficult to interpret the distribution of rates shown in Part A of Table 1.3 because "any violence" includes ordinary physical punishment, and because physical punishment declines sharply with each year after age 6 (Straus, 1983; Wauchope & Straus, in press). Thus the rates at the low end are for hitting adolescents. A second problem is that some of the studies combined rates for violence by the father and by the mother, and some used only the rate of hitting by one or the other parent. Finally, as in the case of the other rows in the table, the nature of the sample affects the rate. This is shown by the fact that the rate of 908 per 1,000 is for the children of a sample of battered women.

Severe violence. We have so far not located any other study using the Child Abuse 1 measure, which focuses on the most severe and dangerous assaults on children. However, Part B of Table 1.3 allows comparison of the National Survey rate with several other studies that used the Child Abuse 2 measure. At first it seems as though the National Survey rate is unusually low. However, the difference is not that great because the three highest rates are for samples from high violence populations—battered women and delinquent children.

Summary and Conclusions

This chapter presented the rates of spouse abuse and child abuse from the 1985 National Family Violence Resurvey and compared those rates with estimates from other studies. We found that:

- Overall, 161 out of every 1,000 couples experienced one or more physical assaults on a partner during the year of the study.

- Attacks by husbands on wives that were serious enough to warrant the term "wife beating" (because they involved dangerous forms of assault, such as punching, biting, kicking, choking) were experienced by 34 per 1,000 American wives. If this rate is correct, it means that about 1.8 million women were severely assaulted by their partners in 1985.
- Assaults by women on their male partners occur at about the same rate as assaults by men on their female partners, and women initiate such violence about as often as men.
- Two estimates of child abuse were computed. The first is based on whether the child was kicked, bitten, punched, beaten up, burned or scalded, or was threatened or attacked with a knife or gun. Using this measure, we found an abuse rate of 24 per 1,000 children. If this rate is correct, it means that about 1.5 million children are physically abused each year.
- The second child abuse measure adds hitting the child with an object to the above list. This measure results in a rate of 110 per 1,000 children, which if it is correct, means that about 6.9 million children are severely assaulted each year.
- Children are the most violent persons in American families. Almost all young children hit a sibling, and more than one out of five hit a parent. The intrafamily violence rate for children in their late teens (15-17) is much lower, but still substantial: about two-thirds hit a sibling, and 10% hit a parent.

We also compared these rates with data from other studies, both studies using similar survey methodology and studies using different methods.

- The rate of assault between spouses from the National Family Violence Survey is more than 50 times greater than the rate based on the National Crime Survey, the only other national survey. The difference probably results from the fact that most people consider hitting a spouse wrong, but not a crime in the legal sense.
- Comparison of the National Family Violence Resurvey rates for child abuse with the rates for child abuse cases known to the Child Protective Services (CPS) of each state shows that the incidence rate found by this survey is about three and half times greater than the rate of physical abuse cases known to CPS. If child abuse is defined to include hitting a child with an object, then the survey rate is about 16 times greater than the number of cases reported to protective service agencies in 1985.
- A number of other studies have used the Conflict Tactics Scales to measure intrafamily violence. Some of these studies resulted in rates that are much higher and some much lower than those reported in this chapter. However, these differences seem to be owing to differences in the composition of the samples used in those studies, and differences in certain other factors such as the age of the children in studies of child abuse.

A previous analysis comparing the two national family violence surveys (Gelles & Straus, 1988; Straus & Gelles, 1986) suggested that there have been substantial reductions in the rates of child abuse and wife beating. Despite these reductions, it is obvious from the rates reported in this chapter that the incidence of intrafamily violence is extremely high. American society still has a long way to go before a typical citizen is as safe in his or her own home as on the streets or in a workplace.

Notes

1. See Gelles, 1985 for an analysis of the ambiguity of the terms *abuse* and *violence*. As pointed out in a previous theoretical article (Gelles & Straus, 1979), the fact of a physical assault having taken place is not sufficient for understanding violence. Several other dimensions also need to be considered. However, it is also important that each of these other dimensions be measured separately so that the causes and consequences and joint effects can be investigated. Among the other dimensions are the seriousness of the assault (which can range from a slap to stabbing and shooting), whether a physical injury was produced (which can range from none to death), the motivation (which might range from a concern for a person's safety, as when a child is spanked for going into the street, to hostility so intense that the death of the person is desired), and whether the act of violence is normatively legitimate (as in the case of slapping a child) or illegitimate (as in the case of slapping a spouse), and which set of norms are applicable (legal, ethnic or class norms, couple norms, and so on). See also Straus and Lincoln (1985) for an analysis of the "criminalization" of family violence.

2. The construct validity, reliability, and independence from social desirability response set effects has been demonstrated by many studies in the years since the first publication using this instrument in 1973. See Straus (1979, in press) for additional evidence, for alternative scoring methods, and for discussions of the limitations of the instrument.

3. In addition, the 1985 CTS was supplemented by questions intended to assess the consequences or outcomes of acts of violence. We added a series of questions that asked whether an act of violence produced an injury that required medical attention—either seeing a doctor or overnight hospitalization, and also questions on depression and other possible mental health effects. These data are reported in Straus and Gelles (in press).

4. A rate per 1,000 cases is used so as facilitate comparison with the rates from other major surveys such as the National Crime survey and the annual tabulation of cases reported to Child Protective Services in each of the states. For a more detailed explanation of this and other reasons for using a rate per 1,000, see footnote 9 in Straus and Gelles, 1986.

5. It should be recognized that in most instances, the outcome from being kicked, although painful, does *not* result in an injury. However, absence of injury does not make it less of an abusive act. Our distinction between minor and severe violence parallels the legal distinction between a "simple assault" and an "aggravated assault." An aggravated assault is an attack that is likely to cause grave bodily harm, such as an attack with a knife or gun, irrespective of whether the object of the attack was actually injured.

6. From a scientific perspective it would be preferable to avoid the term *abuse* because of the definitional problems just mentioned and because it is a political and administrative term. Despite this, we will use *abuse* for two reasons. First, it is less awkward than *Very Severe Violence Index*. Second, it is such a widely used term that avoiding it creates communication difficulties.

7. The rates to be reported here are higher than those in the paper comparing violence rates in 1985 with those found in the 1975-76 (Straus & Gelles, 1986) because the need for comparability meant that the analysis could not use the 1985 additions to the CTS list of violent acts (described earlier), and also could not use the 1985 additions to the sample

(children under three, single parents, and information about marriages that had recently been terminated).

8. The term *couple violence* in this context refers to whether *either* partner was violent, and not necessarily that both were violent. Of the couples in which either was violent, in about half the cases both were violent, about one quarter were cases in which the husband was violent but not the wife, and in the remaining one quarter the wife was violent but not the husband.

9. For convenience and economy of wording, terms such as *marital*, and *spouse*, and *wife*, and *husband* are used to refer to couples, irrespective of whether they are a married or a nonmarried cohabiting couple. For an analysis of differences and similarities between married and cohabiting couples in the 1975-1976 study, see Yllö, 1978; Yllö and Straus, 1981.

10. This will not be easy to accomplish, in part because, as we noted in an earlier article (Straus & Gelles, 1986), the cost of giving publicity to violence by wives is that it will be used to defend male violence. Our 1975 data, for example, have been used against battered women in court cases, and also to minimize the need for shelters for battered women. However, the cost of failing to attend to this problem will ultimately block the goal of being free from violence by men. There may be costs associated with acknowledging the fact of female domestic violence, but the cost of denial and suppression is even greater. Rather than attempting to deny the existence of such violence (see Pleck et al., 1977 for an example and the reply by Steinmetz, 1978), a more productive solution is to confront the issue and work toward eliminating violence by women. The achievements of the 20 year effort to reduce child abuse and the 10 year effort to reduce wife beating (see Straus & Gelles, 1986) suggest this is a realistic goal.

References

Allen, C. M., & Straus, M. A. (1980). Resources, power, and husband-wife violence. In M. A. Straus & G. T. Hotaling (Eds.), *The social causes of husband-wife violence*. Minneapolis: University of Minnesota Press.

American Association for Protecting Children (1986). *Highlights of official child neglect and abuse reporting, 1984*. Denver, CO: Author.

Barling, J., O'Leary, K. D., Jouriles, E., Vivian, N. D., & MacEwen, K. E. (1987). Factor similarity of the conflict tactics scales across samples, spouses, and sites: Issues and implications. *Journal of Family Violence, 2*, 37-55.

Browne, A. (1987). *When battered women kill*. New York: Free Press.

Brutz, J., & Ingoldsby, B. B. (1984, February). Conflict resolution in Quaker families. *Journal of Marriage and the Family*, 21-26.

Brutz, J. L., & Allen, C. M. (1986). Religious commitment, peace activism, and marital violence in Quaker families. *Journal of Marriage and the Family, 48*, 491-502.

Cate, R. M., Henton, J. M., Joval, K., Christopher, F. S., & Lloyd, S. (1982). Premarital abuse: A social psychological perspective. *Journal of Family Issues, 3*, 79-90.

Clarke, C. (1987). *Domestic violence: A community survey*. Department of Psychology, University of Illinois. Unpublished manuscript.

Dembo, R., Dertke, M., La Voie, L., Borders, S., Washburn, M., & Schmeidler, J. (1987). Physical abuse, sexual victimization and illicit drug use: A structural analysis among high risk adolescents. *Journal of Adolescence*.

Dutton, D. G. (1986). Wife assaulters' explanations for assault: The neutralization of self-punishment. *Canadian Journal of Behavioral Science, 18*, 381-390.

Fergusson, D. M., Horwood, L. J., Kershaw, K. L., & Shannon, F. T. (1986). Factors associated with reports of wife assault in New Zealand. *Journal of Marriage and the Family, 48,* 407-412.

Gaquin, D. A. (1977-78). Spouse abuse: Data from the National Crime Survey. *Victimology, 2,* 632-643.

Gelles, R. J. (1985). Family violence. *Annual Review of Sociology, 11,* 347-367.

Gelles, R. J., & Straus, M. A. (1988). *Intimate violence.* New York: Simon & Schuster.

Gelles, R. J., & Straus, M. A. (1987). Is violence toward children increasing? A comparison of 1975 and 1985 national survey rates. *Journal of Interpersonal Violence, 2,* 212-222.

Gelles, R. J., & Straus, M. A. (1979). Determinants of violence in the family: Toward a theoretical integration, pp. 549-581. In W. R. Burr, R. Hill, F. I. Nye, & I. L. Reiss (Eds.), *Contemporary theories about the family.* New York: Free Press.

Gil, D. G. (1970). *Violence against children: Physical child abuse in the United States.* Cambridge, MA: Harvard University Press.

Giles-Sims, J. (1985). A longitudinal study of battered children of battered wives. *Family Relations, 34,* 205-210.

Giles-Sims, J. (1983). *Wife battering: A systems theory approach.* New York: Guilford.

Greenblat, C. S. (1983). A hit is a hit is a hit ... or is it? Approval and tolerance of the use of physical force by spouses. In D. Finkelhor, R. J. Gelles, G. T. Hotaling, & M. A. Straus (Eds.), *The dark side of families: Current family violence research.* Beverly Hills, CA: Sage.

Gully, K. J., Dengerink, H. A., Pepping, M., & Bergstrom, D. (1981). Research note: Sibling contribution to violence behavior. *Journal of Marriage and the Family, 43,* 333-337.

Haeuser, A. A. (1985, June). *Social control over parents' use of physical punishment: Issues for cross-national child abuse research.* Paper presented at the United States-Sweden Joint Seminary on Physical and Sexual Abuse of Children, Satra Books, Sweden.

Henton, J., Cate, R., Koval, J., Lloyd, S., & Christopher, S. (1983). Romance and violence in dating relationships. *Journal of Family Issues, 4,* 467-482.

Hornung, C. A., McCullough, B. C., & Sugimoto, T. (1981). Status relationships in marriage: Risk factors in spouse abuse. *Journal of Marriage and the Family, 43,* 675-692.

Jorgensen, S. R. (1977). Societal class heterogamy, status striving, and perception of marital conflict: A partial replication and revision of Pearlin's Contingency Hypothesis. *Journal of Marriage and the Family, 39,* 653-689.

Jouriles, E. N., & O'Leary, K. D. (1985). Interspousal reliability of reports of marital violence. *Journal of Consulting and Clinical Psychology, 53,* 419-421.

Kennedy, L. W., & Dutton, D. G. (1987). *Edmonton area series report no. 53: The incidence of wife assault in Alberta.* Edmonton: University of Alberta, Population Research Laboratory.

Lane, K. E., & Gwartney-Gibbs, P. A. (1985). Violence in the context of dating and sex. *Journal of Family Issues, 6,* 45-59.

Laner, M. R., & Thompson, J. (1982). Abuse and aggression in courting couples. *Deviant Behavior: An Interdisciplinary Journal, 3,* 229-244.

Legg, J., Olday, D. E., & Wesley, B. (1984). *Why do females remain in violent dating relationships?* Paper presented at the Second National Family Violence Research Conference, University of New Hampshire.

Lockhart, L. L. (1987). A reexamination of the effects of race and social class on the incidence of marital violence: A search for reliable differences. *Journal of Marriage and the Family, 49,* 603-610.

Makepeace, J. M. (1983). Life events stress and courtship violence. *Family Relations, 32,* 101-109.

Makepeace, J. M. (1981). Courtship violence among college students. *Family Relations, 30*(1) 97-102.

Meredith, W. H., Abbott, D. A., & Adams, S. L. (1986). Family violence: Its relation to marital and parental satisfaction and family strengths. *Journal of Family Violence, 1,* 299-305.

National Center on Child Abuse and Neglect (NCCAN). (1981). *Study findings: National study of incidence and severity of child abuse and neglect.* Department of Health, Education & Welfare. Washington, DC: Government Printing Office.

O'Leary, K. D., Barling, J., Arias, I., Rosenbaum, A., Malone, J., & Tyree, A. (1987). Prevalence and stability of spousal aggression. *Journal of Consulting & Clinical Psychology.*

Plass, P., & Straus, M. A. (1987). *Intrafamily homicide in the United States: Incidence rates, trends, and differences by region, race, and gender.* Paper presented at the Third National Family Violence Research Conference, University of New Hampshire, Family Research Laboratory, Durham.

Pleck, E., Pleck, J. H., Grossman, M., & Bart, P. B. (1977). The battered data syndrome: A comment on Steinmetz' article. *Victimology: An International Journal, 2,* 680-683.

Roscoe, B., & Benaske, N. (1985). Courtship violence experienced by abused wives: Similarities in patterns of abuse. *Family Relations, 34,* 419-424.

Sack, A. R., Keller, J. F., & Howard, R. D. (1982). Conflict tactics and violence in dating situations. *International Journal of Sociology of the Family, 12,* 89-100.

Scanzoni, J. (1978). *Sex roles, women's work, and marital conflict.* Lexington, MA: Lexington Books.

Schulman, M. A. (1979). *A survey of spousal violence against women in Kentucky.* Law Enforcement Assistance Administration, Study No. 792701. Washington, DC: Government Printing Office.

Schumm, W. R., Martin, M. J., Bollman, S. R., & Jurich, A. P. (1982). Classifying family violence: Whither the woozle? *Journal of Family Issues, 3,* 319-340.

Smith, M. D. (1986). Effects of question format on the reporting of woman abuse: A telephone survey experiment. *Victimology.*

Steinmetz, S. K. (1978). Services to battered women: Our greatest need. A reply to Field and Kirchner. *Victimology: An International Journal, 3,* 222-226.

Steinmetz, S. K. (1977-78). The battered husband syndrome. *Victimology, 2,*(3-4): 499-509.

Steinmetz, S. K. (1977). *The cycle of violence: Assertive, aggressive, and abusive family interaction.* New York: Praeger.

Stets, J. E., & Straus, M. A. (in press). The marriage license as a hitting license: A comparison of dating, cohabiting, and married couples. In M. A. Straus & R. J. Gelles (Eds.), *Physical violence in American families: Risk factors and adaptations to violence in 8,145 families.* New Brunswick, NJ: Transaction Press.

Straus, M. A. (1988). *Measuring physical and emotional abuse of children with the conflict tactics scales.* Durham, NH: Family Research Laboratory, University of New Hampshire.

Straus, M. A. (in press). The conflict tactics scales and its critics. In M. A. Straus & R. J. Gelles (Eds.), *Physical violence in American families: Risk factors and adaptations to violence in 8,145 families.* New Brunswick, NJ: Transaction Press.

Straus, M. A. (1986). Domestic violence and homicide antecedents. *Bulletin of the New York Academy of Medicine, 62,* 446-465.

Straus, M. A. (1983). Ordinary violence versus child abuse and wife beating: What do they have in common? In D. Finkelhor, G. T. Hotaling, R. J. Gelles, & M. A. Straus (Eds.), *The dark side of families: Current family violence research.* Beverly Hills, CA: Sage.

Straus, M. A. (1980). Victims and aggressors in marital violence. *American Behavioral Scientist, 23,* (May/June): 681-704.

Straus, M. A. (1979). Measuring intrafamily conflict and violence: The conflict tactics (CT) scales. *Journal of Marriage and the Family, 41,* 75-88.

Straus, M. A. (1977). Wife-Beating: How common, and why? *Victimology, 2,* 443-458. (Reprinted in Straus & Hotaling, 1980)

Straus, M. A. (1974). Leveling, civility, and violence in the family. *Journal of Marriage and the Family, 36,* 13-29.

Straus, M. A. (1973, June). A general systems theory approach to a theory of violence between family members. *Social Science Information, 12,* 105-125.

Straus, M. A., & Gelles, R. J. (1986). Societal change and change in family violence from 1975 to 1985 as revealed by two national surveys. *Journal of Marriage and the Family, 48,* 465-479.

Straus, M. A., & Gelles, R. J. (Eds.). (in press). *Physical violence in American families: Risk factors and adaptations to violence in 8,145 families.* New Brunswick, NJ: Transaction Press.

Straus, M. A., Gelles, R. J., & Steinmetz, S. K. (1980). *Behind closed doors: Violence in the American family.* New York: Anchor/Doubleday.

Straus, M. A., & Lincoln, A. J. (1985). A conceptual framework for understanding crime and the family, pp. 5-23. In A. J. Lincoln & M. A. Straus (Eds.), *Crime and the family.* Springfield, IL: Charles C Thomas.

Szinovacz, M. (1983, August). Using couple data as a methodological tool: The case of marital violence. *Journal of Marriage and the Family,* 633-644.

Wauchope, B. A., & Straus, M. A. (in press). Age, gender, and class differences in physical punishment and physical abuse of American children. In M. A. Straus & R. J. Gelles (Eds.), *Physical violence in American families: Risk factors and adaptations to violence in 8,145 families.* New Brunswick, NJ: Transaction Press.

Yllö, K. (1978). Nonmarital cohabitation: Beyond the college campus. *Alternative Lifestyles, 1,* 37-54.

Yllö, K. A., & Straus, M. A. (1981, July). Interpersonal violence among married and cohabiting couples. *Family Coordinator, 30,* 339-345.

PART II

Physical Violence Against Children

2

Social Incompetence and the Intergenerational Transmission of Abusive Parental Practices

Robert L. Burgess
Lise M. Youngblade

onventional wisdom suggests that abusive parents were themselves maltreated as children. Not only does this assertion pervade common knowledge, but this "fact" is mentioned and seemingly without disagreement in most child abuse publications (see Blumberg, 1974; Helfer, 1980). It is also assumed that the basic mechanisms of transmission are well-known. Attachment-based research has suggested that the insecure attachment an infant forms with its mother sets the infant at risk for later maltreatment (Egeland & Brunquell, 1977; Egeland & Sroufe, 1981; Lamb, Greensbauer, Malkin, & Shultz, 1985). To the extent that an infant internalizes the insecure attachment as a subsequent working model of relationships, the wheel is set in motion for the maltreatment of the next generation. Similarly, social learning research (Burgess, 1979; Gelles & Straus, 1979; Patterson, 1982a) has suggested that the lessons a child learns at home, whether they be through modeling or reinforcement contingencies, play a significant role as mechanisms of transmission; in effect, "teaching" this child to use violence and probably maltreat a child later. It is worth noting, however, that there are important differences between these two theoretical positions—attachment theory and social learning theory—in terms of the emphasis they give to early experience. Early experience plays a more critical role in attachment theory (see Ainsworth & Wittig, 1969), whereas it may (Bijou & Baer, 1961) or may not (Burgess & Bushell, 1969) be emphasized in social learning approaches to behavior change.

AUTHORS' NOTE: We would like to thank Beverly Fagot, Richard Gelles, James G. Kelly, Michael Lamb, and Gerald R. Patterson for their helpful feedback on an earlier draft of this chapter.

These theoretical differences aside, the actual empirical evidence in support of the intergenerational transmission of abusive parental practices is less than convincing. The most commonly cited studies are largely selected case histories, and in some instances, the data reported by Curtis (1963), Kempe, Silverman, Steele, Droegmueller, and Silver (1962), Silver, Dublin, and Lourie (1969), and Gibbens and Walker (1956) have been misinterpreted or misrepresented (Potts, Herzberger, & Holland, 1979). In perhaps one of the best studies (Straus, Gelles, & Steinmetz, 1978), only a minority, *less than 15%*, of abused parents were themselves found to be abusive toward their own children. Similarly, Knutson, Mehm, and Berger (1984) reported data supportive of the intergenerational hypothesis but for this pattern to occur both the mother *and* the father must have experienced abuse. In addition, Elder, Caspi, and Downey (1986) have presented evidence suggestive of the intergenerational transmission of, what they call, explosive personalities.

Another approach to the exploration of intergenerational continuity is represented by studies examining the relationship between experiencing violence in the home and violent forms of delinquent activity. These studies, too, are equivocal (Fagan & Wexler, 1984; Koski, 1984). In particular, Fagan and Wexler (1984) point out that not only is the link tenuous between experiencing violence in the home and violent forms of delinquency, but there also are several equally likely alternative explanations explaining this apparent link. They hypothesize, for example, that delinquent youths may learn aggressive and deviant behaviors as a function of the peers they associate with and, in turn, they bring these lessons back to the family.

Thus an impartial assessment of this literature leads to the conclusion that the transmission of abusive behavior patterns across generations is by no means an inevitable consequence of having been maltreated (see also Cicchetti & Rizley, 1981). Clearly, more work is needed in this area, not only to understand the general processes involved in intergenerational transmission, but also to explore the possibility that these processes might very well translate into different developmental trajectories and outcomes for boys and girls (see Baumrind, 1971).

In this chapter, we shall present a position that is rather different from that taken by previous researchers (e.g., Elder, Caspi, & Downey, 1986; Knutson, Mehm, & Berger, 1984). In particular, we will emphasize four major points. One, we need to redirect our attention from simply trying to determine whether violence in the family is passed from generation to generation to specifying the conditions under which it is or is not. Two, in addressing the question of what exactly is being transmitted intergenerationally, we need to distinguish between marker and process variables. By failing to distinguish between these two types of variables they are often treated as being of equal importance. Three, we shall argue that it is important to conceptualize parental behavior in such a way that it is assessed as one exemplar of a person's general interpersonal style. Four, we will take the position that to understand the general processes involved in intergenerational transmission, we need to look at socialization influences outside the family as well as those within the family.

A Model of Intergenerational Transmission

The first question we must address in delineating a model of intergenerational transmission is: What, in fact, is being transmitted? Obvious candidates include the documented correlates or predictors of child maltreatment. It may be, for example, that family contexts are passed from generation to generation. Low SES and single parenthood are contextual factors that have been implicated in child maltreatment (Burgess, Anderson, Schellenbach, & Conger, 1981; Straus, Gelles, & Steinmetz, 1980). Any observed linkage between generational patterns of abusive behavior, then, may be owed to the tendency for adult children to replicate the social class level of their parents and its accompanying life-style. Alternatively, perhaps styles of interpersonal interaction are passed from generation to generation. Or, perhaps both factors are at work. To begin to answer this question, it is necessary to look more closely at the correlates of maltreatment.

Marker Variables

Research into the major predictors of maltreatment has led to a lengthy list of *marker variables* operating at different levels of analysis. Marker variables, a term from biological and medical research, serve the function of telling us where to look for probable causal processes. These markers (e.g., low SES, large family size, social isolation), singly and in combination, may be conceptualized as indicators of *ecological instability* or *social insularity*. Bigelow (1969) used the concept of ecological instability in noting that during times of rapid population growth and shifting populations, both intergroup and intragroup violence are likely. The argument is that as the balance of resources to stressors in a given ecology shifts to favor stressors, aggression and violence become more probable. Analogously, a family can be conceptualized as an ecosystem. Here we use the term *ecosystem* in the sense with which it is usually defined: a community together with its habitat. In other words, an ecosystem is an interacting environmental and biotic system. Under normal conditions, we assume that an ecosystem will be in a state of dynamic equilibrium, such that there is an equal balance (or, possibly an excess) of resources to stressors. To the extent that the resources a family can marshal decrease in proportion to the stressors with which it must cope, conflict and violence may become more likely.

The concept of social insularity has been used by Wahler (1980) to describe how macro social structural variables can impinge on an individual parent and, in some cases, lead to abuse. For example, there are studies that indicate that higher rates of abuse are found in poor, blue-collar, less well-educated families (Straus, Gelles, & Steinmetz, 1980). Or, at a somewhat different analytic level, we have learned that parents isolated from important social support systems in their neighborhoods and elsewhere are more likely to become abusive toward their children (Garbarino & Crouter, 1978). Other research has documented the importance of the social structure of the family itself. Thus large family size and single- and stepparenthood are associated with maltreatment (Friedman, 1976; Light, 1973; Richardson, Burgess, & Burgess, 1984). Given these research findings, the concept of social insularity alerts us to the fact that the conditions outlined above increase the likelihood that a person will have frequent and intensive aversive exchanges with others and will experience high levels of stress. For example, the day-to-day demands and pressures of family life become greater when there are more children to deal with, particularly in families in which economic resources are limited. Similarly, the contacts an abusive parent has with relatives, friends, neighbors, and the larger community or its agencies may often be aversive. Wahler and Hahn (1984) have shown that, rather than interacting with people who form a social support network and who provide assistance, empathy, and problem-solving help, abusive parents often interact with others who are in similar situations to themselves. The outcome is that instead of helping each other they often simply match "war stories," thus exacerbating, rather than ameliorating, the aversive nature of the extra-familial interactions they have. On the other hand, the interactions a nonabusive parent has with the outside world tend to serve as social support as well as monitoring mechanisms for socially appropriate parenting behavior. To the extent that these interactions are aversive for the abusive parent, the parent eventually will tend to avoid them, perhaps interacting only under duress. In this way, the abusive parent becomes more and more isolated from social supports and monitoring mechanisms, and violence becomes more likely.

Apart from social structural correlates of maltreatment, research has identified factors operating on a microlevel of analysis. Several characteristics of abusive parents themselves have been found to be associated with maltreatment rates, including emotional disturbances (Elmer, 1967), difficulty in dealing with aggressive impulses (Wasserman, 1967), a rigid and domineering personality (Johnson & Morse, 1968), alcoholism (Blumberg, 1974), depression and anxiety (Wolfe, 1984), and autonomic hyperreactivity (Vasta, 1982). A variety of child characteristics have also been identified, including developmental problems such as poor speech, physical deformities, and handicaps (Johnson & Morse, 1968), mental retardation (Martin, Beezley, Conway, & Kempe, 1974; Sandgrund, Gaines, & Green, 1974), a difficult temperament (Frodi, 1981; Johnson & Morse, 1968), and prematurity (Klaus & Kennell, 1976).

To expand further on the possible significance of the concept of ecological instability, we may hypothesize that these microlevel variables operating at the level of the individual may be reactions to sudden or chronic ecological instability. For example, alcoholism (Blumberg, 1974) or depression and anxiety (Wolfe, 1984) may be reactions to stress to the family, such as loss of employment, excessive financial debt, or chronic "insularity" (Wahler, 1980). Similarly, violence to the child may be a possible reaction to sudden or chronic ecological instability, whether as a direct result, or as mediated through these personal-characteristic variables. Thus there is the intriguing possibility that these personal characteristics, which have been previously assumed to precede abusive incidents, may actually be the result of the same factors that lead to family violence itself. In all likelihood, under theoretically specifiable conditions, both possibilities may occur.

Although the marker variable research described above has stimulated the search for possibly important causal processes, there are several limitations to this line of research. If we are not careful, an overemphasis upon the identification of marker variables can divert us from the more important task of discovering the actual processes responsible for the linkage between the markers and the phenomenon to be explained. By emphasizing marker variables we also tend to overlook the fact that these variables often are very weakly related to child maltreatment, explaining only small proportions of the variance. In addition, a focus on marker variables can lead us to ignore the conditionality of most relationships. Certainly, we recognize that not all people who are poor, undereducated, or socially isolated abuse their children.

Yet, with these caveats in mind, we should not ignore the strengths of marker variable research. One, it may tell us where to look for possibly important process variables that, we hope, will help us to identify the conditions under which these marker variables do and do not lead to the actual maltreatment of children. And, two, the transmission of these marker variables across generations may increase the risk of child maltreatment. In other words, these variables may represent stressors that exhaust family resources, thereby increasing the likelihood of child maltreatment.

Process Variables

In recent years, increasing attention has been given to addressing the questions of how, and under what circumstances, conditions indicative of ecological instability lead to the maltreatment of children. Consistent with Wahler's (1980) concept of social insularity, researchers began by trying to see whether there were certain styles of interaction that seem to culminate in violence and other forms of child maltreatment. The initial hypothesis was that the fundamental determinants of child abuse were to be found in day-to-day transactions between parents and their children (Burgess, 1979). The products of this initial effort have been published in several articles (e.g., Burgess & Conger, 1978; Conger, Burgess, & Barrett, 1979; Lightcap, Kurland, & Burgess, 1982), and chapters (e.g., Burgess, 1979, 1980; Burgess, Anderson, Schellenbach, & Conger, 1981; Burgess & Garbarino, 1983; Burgess, Garbarino, & Gilstrap, 1983; Burgess & Richardson, 1984a, 1984b).

This research, as well as that from other investigators, has given us an increasingly detailed picture of the dynamics of child abuse. We have discovered, for example, that abusive parents are often very poor observers of their children's behavior (Burgess et al., 1981). This lack of effective and accurate monitoring may be a result of either the parents' lack of skills (Patterson, 1980; 1985) or resources (Wolfe, 1985), or both. In either case, one outcome of poor observing skills is that such parents tend to respond to their children in ways that are functionally noncontingent (Dumas & Wahler, 1985; Patterson, 1979; Wahler & Hann, 1984). Apart from making life rather unpredictable for children, this circumstance has serious consequences for the parent-child relationship. Rewards that are consistently provided on a noncontingent basis may eventually lose whatever ability they had to function as positive reinforcers (Bijou & Baer, 1961). Imagine, for example, a family in which the parents, perhaps owing to their failure to track their child's behavior accurately, are just as likely to give their approval when their child has misbehaved as when the child has behaved properly. Later on, any attempt; to use their approval in a deliberate effort to regulate the child's behavior will probably fail. Under these circumstances, their approval is not functioning as a positive reinforcer for their child. Because of this, parents who respond noncontingently to their children are, thereby, depriving themselves of one major source of influence over their children: the use of positive incentives (Burgess & Richardson, 1984a). This may account for the fact that abusive parents exhibit lower frequencies of positive behavior toward their children than do nonabusive parents (Burgess & Conger, 1978; Lahey et al., 1984). In other words, their efforts to use positive behaviors to control their child's behavior may have been weakened as a result of lack of success. This history of ineffective child management may also account for the finding that abusive parents view children and child-related activities less positively than do nonabusive parents (Disbrow, Doerr, & Caulfield, 1977). These parental views are not without meaning. Patterson (1982b), for example, found a close relationship between a mother's labeling of her child as deviant and her rejection of the child. Such rejection makes the child a more likely target for abuse (Burgess & Garbarino, 1983; Burgess, Garbarino, & Gilstrap, 1983).

Given the normal conflicts of interest that characterize family life, and a low rate of positive reinforcement, parents inevitably must turn to other measures. This may explain the higher frequency of aversive (punitive) behavior directed by abusive parents to their children. Reid (1984) reports, for example, that abusive mothers display approximately twice the rate of aversive behavior of nonabusive parents with child management problems and nearly four times the rate found in nondistressed families. Other investigators have found a similar pattern (e.g., Bousha & Twentyman, 1984).

Interestingly, there is evidence that an abusive parent's use of punishment is often a function of events other than the child's behavior. For instance, Dumas and Wahler (1985) have shown that higher rates of aversive behavior are especially common when the parent has had negative interactions with social agencies or neighbors and is especially irritable. The parent at these times is more likely to exhibit high rates of aversive behavior, perhaps even abusive behavior, toward the child regardless of what the child is doing. It is important to note that punishment that is provided noncontingently becomes increasingly ineffective, at least at levels acceptable to society (Parke, Deur, & Saivin, 1970). Thus at those times when the parent is very irritable, matters can quickly get out of hand. This would be particularly likely if the child reciprocates the parent's abusive behavior, or if there is a flare-up in fighting among siblings. Both possibilities are more common in abusive families (Burgess & Conger, 1978; Burgess et al., 1981; Reid, Taplin, & Loeber, 1981).

As exchanges within the family become increasingly negative, emotions flare (Vasta, 1982) and it becomes more and more difficult to terminate the aversive interchanges. The evidence shows that abusive mothers are much less successful in their child-management efforts than are nonabusive mothers. In one study, it was reported that nondistressed mothers were successful in 86% of their discipline attempts; nonabusive mothers with child-management problems were successful 65% of the time; abusive mothers, on the other hand, were effective in only 46% of their discipline attempts (Reid et al., 1981). These abusive parents were also less likely to use positive acts such as teasing or humor and more likely to use physical coercion in their attempts at discipline.

Over time, then, interactions within the family become less and less positive, and more negative. Indeed, there is growing evidence of a significant relationship between the frequency of mildly aversive interchanges and the rate of intensely aversive interchanges between parents and children (e.g., Reid, 1984). The more often a parent exhibits mild forms of aversive behavior, the more likely it is that significantly abusive behavior will occur. Consequently, violent attacks may not necessarily be the result of especially strong situational or personal stress, but the outcome of progressively aversive exchanges between a child and a parent who is frequently and easily irritated and unskilled in quickly resolving conflicts of interest and discipline confrontations. It is possible, of course, that the probability of an abusive assault is greater on those days that aversive interchanges are highest and the parent's effectiveness at child management is lowest (Reid et al., 1982).

In any case, this tendency to be negative and hostile will, of course, contribute to the reduction of exchanges marked by positive affect. Because these exchanges become unpleasant, the impetus for family interaction becomes extinguished, except during occasions when contact is necessary. The overall effect, then, will be lowered frequencies of family interaction (Burgess & Conger, 1978).

One conclusion to be drawn from this line of research is that these coercive interpersonal contingencies are the principle causal processes linking the marker variables described earlier to actual occurrences of child maltreatment. One of two possibilities may be occurring. First, these interpersonal contingencies of reinforcement and punishment may be the links allowing us to specify when variables such as single parenthood, low income, or unemployment will result in family violence or not. It all depends on whether these coercive interpersonal contingencies have developed within the family (Burgess & Richardson, 1984a). It follows from this that child maltreatment may occur even in the absence of most or all of the marker variables so long as the interpersonal contingencies operating in the family have become progressively coercive. The second possibility is that the common marker variables denote circumstances that place parents at risk for maltreatment because they increase the likelihood of conditions that can lead to coercive interpersonal contingencies. Our guess is that both possibilities are at work. In either case, the effects of ecological instability on families are transmitted via these patterns of family interaction (Burgess, 1979).

From our perspective, the analysis we have described has a number of advantages over the typical ecological model whether it is applied to development, in general (Bronfenbrenner, 1977) or to child maltreatment, in particular (Belsky, 1980; Garbarino, 1976). In both of these cases, the ecological model describes nested levels of analysis: the family (micro-system), the community (exosystem), and the culture (macrosystem), such that variables at each level affect a person's development. In this way, the model has reminded us that development does not occur in a vacuum. The course that development takes is, at least in part, a function of the varying contexts people find themselves in. This represents an important contri-bution to our efforts to understand human behavior. But, as it is typically described and employed, the ecological perspective suffers from two defects. First, it can easily lead to the mistaken conclusion that these varying levels of analysis are of potentially equal causal importance (e.g., Bronfenbrenner, 1977). Second, in their enthusiasm to identify possibly critical contexts, its proponents have failed to give sufficient attention to the identification of the causal processes responsible for the impact of context on behavior (e.g., Bronfenbrenner & Crouter, 1982). The principal advantage of the approach we have taken is that we have attempted to specify the processes whereby macro- and microlevel marker variables can lead to child maltreatment. Another advantage to the process model we have described, so far as intergenerational continuity is concerned, is that it leads to the hypothesis that it may be these patterns of interaction that are transmitted from one generation to the next. The proximate causal mechanisms primarily responsible for transmission are postulated to be the interpersonal contingencies of reinforcement and punishment described above, along with associated modeling experiences (Burgess, 1979).

The Concept of Social Competence

In our examination of what is actually transmitted from one generation to the next, we have suggested two principal candidates. The first was the general class of social indicators associated with ecological instability. The second candidate consisted of those family interaction patterns marked by high levels of coercion. There is a third candidate that subsumes the other two. This third possibility is suggested by research findings that indicate that abusive parents may be incompetent in most social situations, not just in the home. For example, in one study it was found that mothers interact with their husbands, their relatives, their neighbors, friends, and coworkers in ways that are functionally similar to the way they interact with their children (Richardson & Burgess, 1985). Wahler (1980) reports data consistent with this finding. In other studies it has been reported that abusive parents are deficient in problem-solving skills (e.g., Reid et al., 1981; Wahler & Hann, 1984). In several studies it has been found that depression is characteristic of abusive mothers (Wolfe, 1985). Panaccione and Wahler (1986) found depression to be the most significant predictor of a mother's reports of her child's behavior, followed by her coercive encounters with other adults, her aversive behavior toward her child, and her child's actual behavior. Griest, Wells, and Forehand (1979) found that maternal depression contributed significantly more variance in mothers' reports than did actual child behavior. Drawing upon the depression literature, it may be predicted that depressed mothers will tend to underestimate the frequency of positive child behaviors and positive parent-child interactions (Lewinsohn, Mishel, Chaplin, & Barton, 1980; Roth & Rehm, 1980). Moreover, depressed mothers may more likely attend differentially to and recall negative events (Bower, 1981). For all of these reasons, then, child maltreatment may be a result not just of a deficiency in family management techniques, but also of a more general deficit in social skills (Burgess, 1979).

If there is merit to this argument, then it will be useful for us to consider patterns of family interaction within a broader conceptual framework. To accomplish this we will employ the concept of *social competence.* This term has been of considerable interest to psychologists and sociologists alike. Unfortunately, the literature on the topic is somewhat confused and uneven with such terms as *social competence, social skills, interpersonal functioning,* and *personal effectiveness* being used synonymously. Furthermore, researchers have operationalized these concepts in different ways. Some have focused on conversational skills, others on assertiveness, empathy, or problem-solving skills.

To bring some order to this conceptual morass, let us begin by assuming that sustained interaction, and the social relationships that follow therefrom, represent, in the most fundamental sense, the exchange of valued outcomes (Homans, 1974). From this theoretical perspective, the ability to initiate and sustain interaction depends on one's ability and willingness to reinforce others positively. Thus how reinforcing one is may be the most general indicator of one's interpersonal competence. This point of view is consistent with the theoretical literature, which, despite displaying diverse conceptualizations, seems to agree that the most basic element of social competence is the ability of people to reach mutually acceptable goals in ways that are socially valued (Combs & Slaby, 1977; Ellis & Whittington, 1981; Ford, 1982; White, 1959). Moreover, research by investigators such as Argyle and his associates (Argyle, Graham, Campbell, & White, 1979) indicates that the one general rule for social interaction is to sustain levels of reward sufficiently high to keep each of the actors involved with one another.

Less abstractly, differing circumstances may require different manifestations of interpersonal positiveness. For example, one situation might call for showing respect for and empathy toward another person's opinion, while a different situation might require a display of leadership in encouraging potential competitors to set aside their differences in order to work toward a common goal. In both cases, however, the underlying element is the ability to mediate positive outcomes for others. In order to be rewarding, however, the specific response should be appropriate to the situation. The situation, in turn, would include the needs or goals of the exchange partner(s), the roles each is performing, and so on (Richardson, 1984). For example, a 3-year-old may ask for help tying her shoes. To the extent that the mother complies with this request in a supportive manner, the exchange is rewarding for the child. To the extent that the child smiles at or is appreciative of the mother's efforts, the exchange may be rewarding for the mother as well. Thus for the exchange situation to be rewarding for both participants, the responses generated by both must be consistent with the needs and goals of the other, as well as the role each is playing. Ultimately then, interpersonal positiveness, like positive reinforcement generally, must be defined functionally. Therefore, in addition to having a capacity for displaying interpersonal positiveness, a second major skill is the ability to observe a situation accurately, including one's own as well as the other person's behavior. Third, a socially competent person must be able to match his or her skills to an accurate perception of the situation (Richardson, 1984). For our purposes, then, *social competence* shall be defined as the *appropriate application of interpersonal skills to meet the demands of a situation and provide positive outcomes for the actors involved in that situation* (Burgess, 1986).

We have already seen evidence that abusive parents typically behave in less than competent ways toward their children. They are poor observers, they respond noncontingently, and they are less positive and more negative than nonabusing parents. Moreover, general social incompetence (as reflected by a style of interpersonal coerciveness) may not only lead to abuse but also to many of the correlates of abuse, such as poor work histories, low income and education, and social isolation. In other words, social incompetence may be the theoretical thread tying together all of these various indicators or markers of child maltreatment. If this is a reasonable hypothesis, then it may be argued further that varying levels of competence/incompetence can be transmitted from one generation to another, and the process variables described earlier comprise some of the many concrete behavioral manifestations of social competence. To the extent that this is so, our next task is to identify the socialization experiences that affect a person's developing competence.

The Family as a Primary Socialization Agent

It is axiomatic that the family of orientation is a primary learning environment for the acquisition of one's social behavior. Here we use the adjective "primary" in the same way C. H. Cooley did when he discussed the "primary group" (Cooley, 1902). In other words, it is primary in the sense that the mother-infant attachment bond normally is the very first social relationship we have. The theories of Bowlby (1969) and Ainsworth (Ainsworth & Wittig, 1969) argue that antecedent maternal behaviors are responsible for producing differential attachment patterns, which, in turn, influence the way infants respond to important others in their environments. For example, Sroufe and Waters (1977) suggest that children who show an insecure attachment to their mothers will transfer their avoidance and social hesitancy to their interactions with others. However, in an excellent and exhaustive review of the attachment literature and the Strange Situation paradigm that is typically used to assess the infant-mother dyad, Lamb et al. (1984) point out that, so far, we have little reliable evidence about the specific dimensions of parental behavior that lead to secure or insecure attachment. The most we can possibly say is that an infant's maltreatment may lead to insecure attachment. Importantly, however, Lamb et al. (1984) report that temporal stability in security of attachment is high only when there is stability or consistency in family and caretaking circumstances. Relationships between early experiences and later outcomes have been demonstrated only when there is continuity in the situations that apparently produce the outcomes in question. This suggests that early experiences per se may not be critical determinants, and that future attempts to study the effects of early experiences must also consider more carefully the occurrence of concomitant and subsequent events that may ameliorate, accentuate, or maintain the "effects" of early experiences (Lamb et al., 1984, p. 129).

We already do know, of course, that parent-child relations continue well beyond infancy. This evolving, perhaps ever-changing, set of relationships obviously has important implications for a child's developing competence. Thus the child who is exposed consistently to the coercive patterns of parent-child interactions found in abusive homes (Burgess & Conger, 1978; Reid, Patterson, & Loeber, 1982; Wahler, 1980) will have reduced access to socially competent models. There will be fewer opportunities for this child to imitate socially skillful adults and to practice increasingly sophisticated interpersonal behaviors. In addition, this child will less likely be exposed to a history of differential reinforcement for prosocial behavior. Evidence for this is suggested by several studies (George & Main, 1979; Hoffman-Plotkin & Twentyman, 1984; Kinard, 1980; Reidy, 1977). For example, Burgess et al. (1981) observed higher rates of coercive interaction between abused siblings than between siblings in nonabusive families. Moreover, they also found a greater tendency on the part of abused siblings to reciprocate aversive behaviors rather than positive behaviors. In contrast, children from nonabusive families were more likely to reciprocate positive acts. Thus these children appear to be reproducing the interaction styles typically displayed by their parents.

In addition, over time, not only may the child's deviant behavior be the outcome of exposure to coercive interaction patterns, but the child's parents' also may come to reject the antisocial child (Patterson, 1982b). We must not overlook the possibility that a child's temperament may play a significant role in setting the stage for the development of increasingly coercive parental behavior (Frodi, 1981; Johnson & Morse, 1968). Whichever is the case, Patterson (1982b) provides evidence consistent with the hypothesis that parental rejection covaries with measures of antisocial child behavior, both within the family and with peers. Consistent bouts of coercive interchanges between parent and child can lead to active parental rejection of the child.

There are, of course, other possibly important role models and significant socialization agents. For example, relatives, such as a favorite grandparent or aunt, may be especially salient to a growing child. Similarly, we may expect to find significant role models in friends of the family, teachers, a particular coach, neighbors, or parents of peers. In fact, one may even use parents as negative role models. That is, having experienced pain and rejection, one may deliberately select other role models, or be particularly sensitive to the pain of aversive interaction, thus becoming especially sensitive to others. The point we wish to emphasize here is that a thorough understanding of intergenerational relations and the occurrence of behavioral continuity and discontinuity across generations requires that we look at socialization pressures outside as well as within the family. One especially significant site of social control overlooked by most students of intergenerational relations is the child's peer group.

Peers as Socializing Agents

Although our family has the first and, under certain conditions, an enduring effect on our social development, with increasing age, school, the neighborhood, and peers become increasingly important (Burgess & Richardson, 1984b; Hartup, 1983). In fact, some interesting evidence from the nonhuman primate literature suggests that parents and peers may contribute independently to the development of socially competent behavior (e.g., Suomi & Harlow, 1975). Of course, it is also quite likely that our initial encounters with peers may be influenced by our earlier experiences at home. Those of us fortunate to have socially competent models (e.g., parents, older siblings, close relatives) will have a head start. Those of us who suffer the misfortune of having unskilled or highly coercive parents will be handicapped. Moreover, parents can influence their children's peer relationships in many ways (Rubin & Sloman, 1984). Initially, they set the stage by deciding what neighborhood to live in, what day care or school setting to place the child in, and, in effect, by defining who the child's pool of potential playmates will be. Similarly, parents arrange social contacts by suggesting and scheduling visits by playmates, chauffeuring the child from place to place, and by enrolling the child in organized activities, such as Little League. Parents may also give direct advice and guidance to their children, approving or positively reinforcing certain actions and not others, expressing disapproval, and giving information. Parents also serve as role models via their own friendship network, such that parents' friends may become important as models, as well as the parents themselves. And, parents function as a secure home-base for their children's exploration of peer relationships.

There is some empirical evidence supportive of the notion that our initial encounters with peers may be significantly influenced by our earlier experiences at home. Berg and Medrich (1980) have explored the impact of neighborhoods on children's social relationships and parents' formal and informal interactional styles as contacts for modeling, thus suggesting that the influence of parents and home environments on children's social relationships is quite significant. The possibility exists that a history of coercive exchanges between a parent and a child may lead not only to parental rejection (Patterson, 1982b), but also to the child bringing this same style of interaction to the school setting, which, in turn, may lead to the child being promptly rejected by peers because of the high rate of aversive behavior. George and Main (1979) report data from observations of abused and nonabused toddlers in a play group setting. The abused children were more likely to respond antisocially than were nonabused toddlers. For example, they were not just more aggressive, but also were more ready to respond negatively to friendly overtures than were matched controls. Reidy (1977) reported that abused children were judged by teachers to be significantly more aggressive than matched nonabused children. Hoffman-Plotkin and Twentyman (1984) found that abused children had high rates of aggression and were disciplined more often than either neglected or comparison children. As noted above, the socialization effects of parents may be transmitted via sibling interactions. In effect, the interactions one has with one's siblings may be a "training ground" for later peer interactions. This becomes especially salient if one considers the effects of family size. That is, the larger the family, the more widely parents must spread their time and energy among family members (Richardson, Burgess, & Burgess, 1984). Thus one might suppose that in large families a child has even a greater opportunity to be exposed to the socialization effects of siblings.

Whether the impact of peer relations on a child's developing competence is direct or indirect (via the child's previous experiences in the home), the fact is that poor peer relations are associated with problems later in childhood, adolescence, and early adulthood. The argument we would like to make is that the quality of an abused child's peer relations can function to determine whether that child continues to exhibit higher rates of coercive behavior than other children or, instead, comes to behave in more socially accepted ways. In short, peer relations may function as an important causal pathway, in some cases linking a history of abuse with becoming an abusive parent and, in other cases, breaking the intergenerational cycle of abuse. This argument gains cogency when we examine carefully the literature on peer maladjustment.

Evidence has been accumulating that peer social maladjustment is associated with many problems in later life: dropping out of school (Ullman, 1957); delinquency (Roff, Sells, & Golden, 1972); being arrested (Kupersmidt, 1983); mental health problems in later childhood and adolescence (Cowen, Pederson, Babigian, Izzo, & Trost, 1973); and psychoses (Kohn & Clausen, 1955). Recent studies indicate that it is peer dislike, that is, being actively rejected, rather than simply not having friends, that is predictive of such disorders (e.g., Coie, Dodge, &

Coppotelli, 1982; Kupersmidt, 1983). The behavioral correlates of peer rejection include inept group entry techniques (Dodge, 1983), which are indicative of poor timing and poor observing skills. Similarly, rejected children take offense too easily and are more likely to draw hostile inferences about the intentions of others (e.g., Coie & Kupersmidt, 1983; Dodge, 1980; Dodge & Frame, 1982). Several researchers, for example, Keane and Tryon (1984) and Asher and Renshaw (1981) have concluded that inept self-monitoring may be one of the factors that characterizes unpopular children. Other studies indicate that these rejected children experience difficulty in negotiating the use of valued objects, are unable to control their anger, and are more aggressive (Coie et al., 1982; Dodge, Coie, & Brakke, 1982; Putallaz & Gottman, 1983).

These studies, taken together, indicate that there are topographic, as well as functional, similarities between the interpersonal styles of abusive parents and children who are rejected by their peers. Elder, Caspi, and Downey (1986) note that when a stable disposition underlies different behavioral manifestations the process is generally described as heterotypic continuity. For both abusive parents and rejected children there is evidence of poor observing skills, the tendency to react noncontingently, lower frequencies of positive behavior, and higher frequencies of aversive, aggressive behavior. This may be a case of heterotypic continuity, with the underlying disposition being social incompetence. Moreover, unlike many childhood disorders, antisocial behavior tends to be relatively stable over time (Graham & Rutter, 1973; Olweus, 1980; Robins, 1966) and predicts problems in adulthood including poor work histories, alcoholism, substance abuse, and criminal behavior (e.g., Robins, 1978; Wolfgang, Figlio, & Sellin, 1972).

Conclusions

The goal of this chapter has been to present a process model that we hope will allow us to understand better the conditions under which a pattern of child maltreatment will be repeated in one generation after another. Evidence was presented showing that abusive parents typically rely upon coercive patterns of family interaction. Drawing upon an exchange theory perspective, coercion was seen to be indicative of interpersonal incompetence or a lack of social skills. We then examined the kinds of life circumstances that can affect a person's developing social competence. The emphasis was upon the specific socialization experiences encountered in the family and in the peer group. A unique feature of the model we have proposed is that a child's peer relations may function as an important causal pathway in determining whether coercive behaviors that are observed in the home as a child are carried on into adulthood. That is, adverse peer relations may contribute to the crystallization of a child's social incompetence, thereby setting up a vicious cycle of rejection, depression, low self-esteem, and so forth. In a similar way, the abused child's relationships with a variety of "significant others" may strengthen the child's early experiences at home. To the extent that the contacts the abused child has with others serve to reinforce incompetence, these maladaptive interpersonal skills will be carried through the life course and eventually passed on to the next generation. On the other hand, should significant others outside the family contribute positively to the child's developing competence, the developmental trajectory would be marked by peer acceptance, increasing social competence, social support, and a discontinuation of the intergenerational cycle of abuse.

In either case, then, by determining the direction development will take, the person's level of interpersonal competence/incompetence may be the principal medium through which intergenerational transmission occurs. A similar argument has been presented by Elder et al. (1986), who assert that unstable, explosive personalities and unstable family relations represent mutually reinforcing dynamics across the life span and persist from one generation to the next. One important difference between our approach and that of Elder et al. (1986) is that we have taken the position that any comprehensive effort to chart and understand continuity and discontinuity across generations will require the examination of socialization experiences outside the family as well as within it.

The model we have suggested has implications not only for theory but also for empirical investigation and practice. The best research direction to take, of course, would be to design and implement a prospective, longitudinal study addressing the issues of intrafamilial development of child maltreatment patterns, the extent to which these interpersonal patterns are indicative of more generalized forms of social incompetence, and what forms of social and peer support are available or unavailable to the abused child, followed through the life course into the second and third generations. A more circumspect first step, however, would be to examine the nature of the peer relationships that abused children form to see how they might function to produce continuity and discontinuity across generations. Some of the testable hypotheses that follow from our model are:

(1) siblings in abusive families will be more coercive toward one another than are children from nonabusive families;
(2) children from abusive families are more likely to be coercive toward peers than are children from nonabusive families;
(3) children from abusive families are more likely to be rejected by normal peers than are children from nonabusive families;
(4) noncoercive abused children are less likely to be rejected than are coercive children.

There are other implications that follow from our model. We need to determine, for example, the extent to which social competence is trans-situational. In other words, does a person's level of social competence function like a trait or does it vary significantly across contexts? Some evidence exists that rejected children may join with other rejected children, forming deviant peer groups. This implies, however, that socially incompetent children have some social skills, and this, in turn, leads to important questions about the outcome of deviant peer group membership and later development. Does having at least some basic skills for joining and maintaining membership in deviant groups translate into the competence necessary to be a nonabusive parent? Or does being part of a delinquent peer group exacerbate coercive interpersonal patterns?

Similar concerns are evident in thinking about treatment and intervention with abusive families and abused children. "Relief nurseries" are implemented in some cities as a free community service for stressed parents. That is, parents may bring their preschool children to these nurseries when they feel sufficiently unable to cope with their children. This "time out" for parents was designed as a child abuse prevention measure. Although this service is highly beneficial for parents, concern should be raised regarding the child's outcome. What are the effects of grouping possibly socially unskilled children together? Do they learn some forms of social skill and competence as a function of being so grouped, or do they reinforce and crystallize each other's incompetence? Would it be more effective to "mainstream" these children with "normal" peers in hopes that they would glean some basic elements of social competence from their more skilled counterparts? Or, again, would mainstreaming lead to a vicious cycle of rejection, low self-esteem, and so forth?

Although answers to these questions are imperative, for both theory and for practice, the literature is, unfortunately, lacking even in beginning to address the issues we have raised. Thus, although we have come a long way from simply documenting important molar correlates of child maltreatment, we have a long way to go before understanding the developmental outcomes and trajectories of abused children, and the transmission of these patterns across generations.

References

Ainsworth, M. D., & Wittig, B. A. (1969). Attachment and exploratory behavior of one-year-olds in a strange situation. In B. M. Foss (Ed.), *Determinants of infant behavior* (Vol. 4). London: Methuen.

Arend, R., Gove, F. L., & Sroufe, L. A. (1979). Continuity of individual adaptation from infancy to kindergarten: A predictive study of ego-resiliency and curiosity in preschoolers. *Child Development, 50,* 950-959.

Argyle, M., Graham, J. A., Campbell, A., & White, P. (1979). The rules of different situations. *New Zealand Psychologist, 8,* 13-22.

Asher, S. R., & Renshaw, P. D. (1981). Children without friends: Social knowledge and social skill training. In S. R. Asher & J. M. Gottman (Eds.), *The development of children's friendships.* New York: Cambridge University Press.

Baumrind, D. (1971). Current patterns of parental authority. *Developmental Psychology,* (Monograph 4).

Belsky, J. (1980). Child maltreatment: An ecological integration. *American Psychologist, 35,* 320-335.

Berg, M., & Medrich, E. A. (1980). Children in four neighborhoods: The physical environment and its effect on play and play patterns. *Environment and Behavior, 12,* 320-348.

Bigelow, R. (1969). *The dawn warriors: Man's evolution toward peace.* New York: Little Brown.

Bijou, S. W., & Baer, D. M. (1961). *Child development: Vol. 1. A systematic and empirical theory.* New York: Appleton-Century-Crofts.

Blumberg, M. L. (1974). Psychopathology of the abusing parent. *American Journal of Psychotherapy, 28,* 21-29.

Bousha, D. M., & Twentyman, C. T. (1984). Mother-Child interactional style in abuse, neglect, and control groups: Naturalistic observations in the home. *Journal of Abnormal Psychology, 93,* 106-114.

Bower, G. H. (1981). Mood and memory. *American Psychologist, 36*(2), 129-148.

Bowlby, J. (1969). *Attachment and loss: Vol. 1. Attachment.* New York: Basic Books.

Bronfenbrenner, U. (1977). Toward an experimental ecology of human development. *American Psychologist, 32,* 513-531.

Bronfenbrenner, U., & Crouter, A. C. (1982). Work and family through time and space. Chapter in S. B. Kamerman & C. D. Hayes (Eds.), *Families that work: Children in a changing world* (pp. 39-83). Washington, DC: National Academy of Sciences.

Burgess, R. L. (1979). Child abuse: A social interactional analysis. In B. B. Lahey & A. E. Kazdin (Eds.), *Advances in clinical child psychology.* New York; Plenum.

Burgess, R. L. (1980). Family violence: Some implications from evolutionary biology. In T. Hirschi & M. Gottfredson (Eds.), *Understanding crime: Current theory and research* (pp. 91-99). Beverly Hills, CA: Sage.

Burgess, R. L. (1986). Social incompetence as a precipitant to and consequence of child maltreatment. *Victimology: An International Journal, 10,* 72-86.

Burgess, R. L., Anderson, E. A., Schellenbach, C. J., & Conger, R. (1981). A social interactional approach to the study of abusive families. In J. P. Vincent (Ed.), *Advances in family intervention, assessment, and theory: An annual compilation of research* (Vol. 2, pp. 1-46). Greenwich, CT: JAI.

Burgess, R. L., & Bushell, D., Jr. (1969). *Behavioral sociology: The experimental analysis of social process.* New York: Columbia University Press.

Burgess, R. L., & Conger, R. D. (1978). Family interaction in abusive, neglectful, and normal families. *Child Development, 49,* 1163-1173.

Burgess, R. L., & Garbarino, J. (1983). Doing what comes naturally? An evolutionary perspective on child abuse. In D. Finkelhor, R. J. Gelles, G. T. Hotaling, & M. A. Straus (Eds.), *The dark side of families: Current family violence research* (pp. 88-101). Beverly Hills, CA: Sage.

Burgess, R. L., Garbarino, J., & Gilstrap, B. (1983). Violence to the family. In E. J. Callahan & K. McCluskey (Eds.), *Life span development psychology: Non-normative life events.* New York: Academic Press.

Burgess, R. L., & Richardson, R. A. (1984a). Coercive interpersonal contingencies as a determinant of child abuse: Implications for treatment and prevention. In R. F. Dangel & A. Polster (Eds.), *Behavioral parent training: Issues in research and practice* (pp. 239-259). New York: Guilford.

Burgess, R. L., & Richardson, R. A. (1984b). Child abuse during adolescence. In R. M. Lerner & N. Galambos (Eds.), *Experiencing adolescence: A sourcebook for parents, teachers, and teens* (pp. 119-151). New York: Garland.

Cicchetti, D., & Rizley, R. (1981). Developmental perspectives on the etiology, intergenerational transmission, and sequelae of child maltreatment. In D. Cicchetti & R. Rizley (Eds.), *New directions for child development: Developmental perspectives on child maltreatment*. San Francisco: Jossey-Bass.

Coie, J. D., Dodge, K. A., & Coppotelli, H. (1982). Dimensions and types of social status: Across-age perspective. *Developmental Psychology, 18,* 557-570.

Coie, J. D., & Kupersmidt, J. B. (1983). A behavioral analysis of emerging social status in boys groups. *Child Development, 54,* 1400-1416.

Combs, M. L., & Slaby, D. A. (1977). Social skills training with children. In B. B. Lahey & A. E. Kazdin (Eds.), *Advances in clinical child psychology*. New York: Plenum.

Conger, R. D., Burgess, R. L., & Barrett, C. (1979). Child abuse related to life change and perceptions of illness: some preliminary findings. *The Family Coordinator, 28*(1), 74-78.

Cooley, C. H. (1902). *Social organization*. New York: Scribner's.

Cowen, E. L., Pederson, A., Babigian, H., Izzo, L. D., & Trost, M. (1973). Long-term follow-up of early detected vulnerable children. *Journal of Consulting and Clinical Psychology, 41*(3), 438-446.

Curtis, G. (1963). Violence breeds violence—perhaps. *American Journal of Psychiatry, 120,* 386-387.

Disbrow, M. A., Doerr, H. O., & Caulfield, C. (1977). *Measures to predict child abuse*. Project Report. Seattle: University of Washington.

Dodge, K. A. (1980). Social cognition and children's aggressive behavior. *Child Development, 51,* 162-170.

Dodge, K. A. (1983). Behavioral antecedents of peer social status. *Child Development, 54,* 1386-1399.

Dodge, K. A., Coie, J. D., & Brakke, N. P. (1982). Behavior patterns of socially rejected and neglected preadolescents: The roles of social approach and aggression. *Journal of Abnormal Child Psychology, 10,* 389-410.

Dodge, K. A., & Frame, C. L. (1982). Social cognition biases and deficits in aggressive boys. *Child Development, 53,* 620-635.

Dumas, J. E., & Wahler, R. G. (1985). Indiscriminate mothering as a contextual factor in aggressive-oppositional child behavior. *Journal of Abnormal Child Psychology, 13,* 1-17.

Egeland, B., & Brunquell, D. (1977). *An at-risk approach to the study of child abuse: Some preliminary findings*. University of Minnesota. Unpublished manuscript.

Egeland, B., & Sroufe, L. A. (1981). Attachment and early maltreatment. *Child Development, 52,* 44-52.

Elder, G. H., Jr., Caspi, A., & Downey, G. (1986). Problem behavior and family relationships: A multi-generational analysis. In A. Sorensen, F. Weinert, and L. Sherrod (Eds.), *Human development and the life course: Multidisciplinary perspectives*. Hillsdale, NJ: Lawrence Erlbaum.

Ellis, R., & Whittington, D. (1981). *A guide to social skill training*. London: Croom Helm.

Elmer, E. (1967). *Children in jeopardy: A study of abused minors and their families*. Pittsburgh: University of Pittsburgh Press.

Fagan, J. A., & Wexler, S. (1984, August). *Family origins of violent delinquents.* Paper presented at the second national conference for Family Violence Researchers, University of New Hampshire, Durham, New Hampshire.

Ford, M. E. (1982). Social cognition and social competence in adolescence. *Developmental Psychology, 18,* 323-340.

Friedman, R. (1976). Child abuse: A review of the psychosocial research. In Herner Co. (Eds.), *Four perspectives on the status of child abuse and neglect research.* Washington, DC: National Center on Child Abuse and Neglect.

Frodi, A. M. (1981). Contributions of infant characteristics to child abuse. *American Journal of Mental Deficiency, 85,* 341-349.

Garbarino, J. (1976). A preliminary study of some ecological correlates of child abuse: The impact of socioeconomic stress on mothers. *Child Development, 47,* 178-185.

Garbarino, J., & Crouter, A. (1978). Defining the community context of parent-child relations: The correlates of child maltreatment. *Child Development, 49,* 604-616.

Gelles, R. J., & Straus, M. A. (1979). Determinants of violence in the family: Toward a theoretical integration. In W. R. Burr, R. Hill, F. I. Nye, & I. L. Reiss (Eds.), *Contemporary theories about the family.* New York: Free Press.

George, C., & Main, M. (1979). Social interactions of young abused children: Approach, avoidance, and aggression. *Child Development, 50,* 306-318.

Gibbens, T.E.N., & Walker, A. (1956, April). Violent cruelty to children. *British Journal of Delinquency, 6,* 260-277.

Graham, P., & Rutter, M. (1973). Psychiatric disorder in the young adolescent: A follow-up study. *Proceedings of the Royal Society of Medicine, 66,* 1226-1229.

Griest, D. L., Wells, K. C., & Forehand, R. (1979). An examination of predictors of maternal perceptions of maladjustment in clinic-referred children. *Journal of Abnormal Psychology, 88,* 277-281.

Hartup, W. W. (1983). Peer relations. In E. M. Hetherington (Ed.), *Handbook of child psychology* (Vol. IV, pp. 103-196). New York: John Wiley & Sons.

Helfer, R. E. (1980). Developmental deficits which limit interpersonal skills. In C. H. Kempe & R. E. Helfer (Eds.), *The battered child* (3rd ed.). Chicago: University of Chicago Press.

Herrenkohl, R. C., Herrenkohl, E. C., & Egolf, B. P. (1983). Circumstances surrounding the occurrence of child maltreatment. *Journal of Consulting and Clinical Psychology, 51,* 424-431.

Hoffman-Plotkin, D., & Twentyman, C. T. (1984). A multimodal assessment of behavioral and cognitive deficits in abused and neglected preschoolers. *Child Development, 55,* 794-802.

Homans, G. C. (1974). *Social behavior: Its elementary forms.* New York: Harcourt Brace Jovanovich.

Johnson, B., & Morse, H. A. (1968). Injured children and their parents. *Children, 15,* 147-152.

Keane, S. P., & Tryon, A. S. (1984). *The relationship between self-efficacy and children's social status.* Paper presented at the annual convention of the American Association of Behavior Therapy, Philadelphia.

Kempe, C. H., Silverman, F. N., Steele, B. F., Droegmueller, W., & Silver, H. K. (1962). The battered child syndrome. *Journal of the American Medical Association, 181,* 17-24.

Kinard, E. M. (1980). Emotional development in physically abused children. *American Journal of Orthopsychiatry, 50,* 686-695.

Klaus, M. H., & Kennell, J. H. (1976). *Maternal-Infant bonding.* St. Louis: C.V. Mosby.

Knutson, J. F., Mehm, J. G., & Berger, A. M. (1984). *Is violence in the family passed from generation to generation?* Manuscript submitted for publication.

Kohn, M., & Clausen, J. (1955). Social isolation and schizophrenia. *American Sociological Review, 20,* 265-273.

Koski, P. (1984, August). *The effect of family violence on delinquency: Data questions and hypotheses.* Paper presented at the second Family Violence Research Conference, Durham, NH.

Kupersmidt, J. B. (1983). *Predicting delinquency and academic problems from childhood peer status.* Paper presented at the biennial meeting of the Society for Research in Child Development, Michigan.

Lahey, B. B., Conger, R. D., Atkeson, B. M., & Frieber, F. A. (1984). *Parenting behavior and emotional status of physically abusive mothers.* Manuscript submitted for publication.

Lamb, M. E., Gaensbauer, T. J., Malkin, C. M., & Shultz, L. (1985). The effects of child abuse and neglect on security of infant-adult attachment. *Infant Behavior and Development, 8*(1), 1-14.

Lamb, M. E., Thompson, R. A., Gardner, W. P., Charnov, E. L., & Estes, D. (1984). Security of infantile attachment as assessed in the "strange situation": Its study and biological interpretation. *Behavioral and Brain Sciences, 7*(1), 127-171.

Lewinsohn, P. M., Mishel, W., Chaplin, W., & Barton, R. (1980). Social competence and depression: The role of illusory self-perceptions. *Journal of Abnormal Psychology, 89,* 203-212.

Light, R. J. (1973). Abused and neglected children in America: A study of alternative policies. *Harvard Educational Review, 43,* 556-598.

Lightcap, J. L., Kurland, J. A., & Burgess, R. L. (1982). Child abuse: A test of some predictions from evolutionary theory. *Ethology and Sociobiology, 3,* 61-67.

Martin, H. P., Beezley, P., Conway, E. G., & Kempe, C. H. (1974). The development of abused children. *Advances in Pediatrics, 21,* 25-73.

Olweus, D. (1980). Familial and temperamental determinants of aggressive behavior in adolescent boys: A causal analysis. *Developmental Psychology, 16,* 644-660.

Panaccione, V. F., & Wahler, R. G. (1986). Child behavior, maternal depression, and social coercion as factors in the quality of child care. *Journal of Abnormal Child Psychology, 14*(2), 263-278.

Parke, R. D., Deur, J. L., & Saivin, M. (1970). The intermittent punishment effect in humans: Conditioning or adaptation. *Psychonomic Science, 18,* 193-194.

Patterson, G. R. (1979). A performance theory for coercive family interaction. In R. B. Cairns (Ed.), *The analysis of social interactions: Methods, issues, and illustrations.* Hillsdale, NJ: Lawrence Erlbaum.

Patterson, G. R. (1980). Mothers: The unacknowledged victims. *Monograph of the Society for Research on Child Development,* No. 186.

Patterson, G. R. (1982a). *Coercive family process.* Eugene, OR: Castalia.

Patterson, G. R. (1982b). The unattached mother: A process analysis. Prepared for W. Hartup & Z. Rubin (Eds.), *Social relationships: Their role in children's development.* Harwichport Conference, Harwichport, MA, June.

Patterson, G. R. (1985). Beyond technology: The next stage in the development of parent training. In L. Abate (Ed.), *Handbook of family psychology and psychotherapy.* New York: Dow-Jones-Irwin.

Patterson, G. R., Dishion, T. J., & Bank, L. (In press). Family interaction: A process model of deviancy training. (To appear in L. Eron (Ed.), special edition of *Aggressive Behavior.*)

Potts, D. A., Herzberger, S. D., & Holland, A. E. (1979). *Child abuse: A cross generational pattern of childrearing?* Paper presented at the Midwestern Psychological Association Convention, Chicago.

Putallaz, M., & Gottman, J. M. (1983). Social relationship problems in children: An approach to intervention. In B. B. Lahey & A. E. Kasdin (Eds.), *Advances in clinical child psychology* (Vol. 6). New York: Plenum.

Reid, J. B. (1984). Social-Interactional patterns in families of abused and nonabused children. In C. Zahn-Waxler, M. Cummings, & M. Radke-Yarrow (Eds.), *Social and biological origins of altruism and aggression.* Cambridge: University of Cambridge Press.

Reid, J. B., Patterson, G. R., & Loeber, R. (1982). The abused child: Victim, instigator, or innocent bystander? In D. J. Bernstein (Ed.), *Response structure and organization.* Lincoln: University of Nebraska Press.

Reid, J. B., Taplin, P. S., & Loeber, R. (1981). A social-interactional approach to the treatment of abusive families. In R. Stuart (Ed.), *Violent behavior: Social learning approaches to prediction, management, and treatment* (pp. 83-100). New York: Brunner/Mazel.

Reidy, T. (1977). The aggressive characteristics of abused and neglected children. *Journal of Clinical Psychology, 83*(4), 1140-1145.

Richardson, R. A. (1984). *Interpersonal competence as a determinant of parenting in its social context: Social network involvement in childrearing.* Ph.D. dissertation, Pennsylvania State University.

Richardson, R. A., Burgess, J. M., & Burgess, R. L. (1984). *Family size and age structure and the maltreatment of children: A social interaction analysis.* Unpublished manuscript[t]

Richardson, R. A., & Burgess, R. L. (1985). *Interpersonal competence, social support, and parental behavior.* Unpublished manuscript.

Robins, L. N. (1966). *Deviant children grow up: A sociological and psychiatric study of sociopathic personality.* Baltimore: Williams & Wilkins.

Robins, L. N. (1978). Study of childhood predictors of adult antisocial behavior: Replication from longitudinal studies. *Psychological Medicine, 8,* 611-622.

Roff, M., Sells, S. B., & Golden, M. M. (1972). *Social adjustment and personality development in children.* Minneapolis, MN: University of Minnesota Press.

Roth, D., & Rehm, L. P. (1980). Relationships among self-monitoring processes, memory, and depression. *Cognitive Therapy and Research, 4,* 149-157.

Rubin, Z., & Sloman, J. (1984). How parents influence their children's friendships. In M. Lewis (Ed.), *Beyond the dyad.* New York: Plenum.

Sandgrund, A. K., Gaines, R., & Green, A. (1974). Child abuse and mental retardation: A problem cause and effect. *American Journal of Mental Deficiency, 79,* 327-330.

Silver, L. B., Dublin, C. C., & Lourie, R. S. (1969). Does violence breed violence? *American Journal of Psychiatry, 126,* 404-407.

Sroufe, L. A., & Waters, E. (1977). Attachment as an organizational construct. *Child Development, 48,* 1148-1199.

Straus, M. A., Gelles, R. J., & Steinmetz, S. K. (1978). *Violence in the American family.* New York: Anchor/Doubleday.

Straus, M. A., Gelles, R. J., & Steinmetz, S. K. (1980). *Behind closed doors: Violence in the American family.* Garden City, NY: Anchor/Doubleday.

Suomi, S., & Harlow, H. (1975). The role and reason of peer relationships of Rhesus monkeys. In M. Lewis & L. A. Rosenblum (Eds.), *Friendship and peer relations* (pp. 153-183). New York: John Wiley.

Ullman, C. A. (1957). Teachers, peers, and tests as predictors of adjustment. *Journal of Educational Psychology, 48,* 257-267.

Vasta, R. (1982). Physical child abuse: A dual-component analysis. *Developmental Review, 2,* 125-149.

Wahler, R. G. (1980). The insular mother: Her problems in parent-child treatment. *Journal of Applied Behavior Analysis, 13,* 207-219.

Wahler, R. G., & Hann, D. M. (1984). The communication patterns of troubled mothers: In search of a keystone in the generalization of parenting skills. *Journal of Education and Treatment of Children, 7,* 335-350.

Wahler, R. G., & Dumas, J. E. (1986). Maintenance factors in coercive mother-child interactions: The compliance and uncertainty hypotheses. *Journal of Applied Behavior Analysis, 19,* 13-22.

Wasserman, S. (1967). The abused parent of the abused child. *Children, 14,* 175-179.

White, D. A. (1959). Motivation reconsidered: The concept of competence. *Psychological Review, 66,* 297-331.

Wolfe, D. A. (1984, August). *Behavioral distinctions between abusive and non-abusive parents: A review and critique.* Paper presented at the Second Family Violence Research Conference, University of New Hampshire.

Wolfe, D. A. (1985). Parental competence and child abuse prevention. In R. J. McMahon & R. Peters (Eds.), *Childhood disorders: Behavioral/developmental approaches.* New York: Brunner/Mazel.

Wolfgang, M. E., Figlio, R. M., & Sellin, T. (1972). *Delinquency in a birth cohort.* Chicago: University of Chicago Press.

3

"Normal" Violence in the Adult-Child Relationship: A Diathesis-Stress Approach to Child Maltreatment Within the Family

F. G. Bolton, Jr.

F ew contradictions are as great as that between the perception of childhood as a safe time of exploration and the record of adult violence directed against children. Contradictory or not, violence remains a reality for many children.

Two decades of child maltreatment research has produced wide speculation regarding the origins of adult violence toward children. Most difficult to understand is that violence perpetrated by parents toward their own offspring. The term *abusive parent* should be, in "normal" families, an oxymoron: "a combination of contradictory or incongruous words" (*Webster's Seventh New Collegiate Dictionary*, 1963). Yet the frequency with which violence toward children occurs at the hands of parents, suggests that the role of perpetrator of violence toward a child, and the role of parent are not mutually exclusive.

There has been a rush to establish some rationale for parental behavior that contradicts all that *parent* is thought to represent. This body of literature was described as early as 1973 as being repetitious and trapped in a circular examination of itself (Gelles, 1973). Recent methodological reviews describe continuing methodological problems (Bolton, Laner, Gai, & Kane, 1981) and its "primitive and rudimentary" nature (Gerbner, Ross, & Zeigler, 1980). It appears that conceptual and methodological obstacles have slowed our path toward understanding the behavioral contradictions in the role of "abusive parent."

If we recognize that some parents live within an environment that can clearly be described as "high risk," but do not engage in violence, and if we recognize that some parents live within a "low risk" environment, but engage in violence against children, we are left with two interdependent possibilities. It is possible that we have overstated the role of stress in the violent parent. It is possible that we have yet to identify that propensity (diathesis) in the violent parent that allows for violence to be rationalized as "normal."

Although a foreign possibility, it may well be that there is a choice to be made by a parent, conscious or not, as to whether he or she will engage in violence toward his or her child. If our early research has defined the stressors that hasten a parent toward a decision whether to be violent, there remains something that has not been defined. What has not been provided through child maltreatment research is an operational sense of the propensity (diathesis) held by the parent to respond to stress with violence toward their child. This chapter will offer a model that can initiate discussion of such a diathesis in the violent parent.

The development of a "diathesis-stress" model is illuminated by the application of three theoretical foundations heretofore seen as unique and freestanding contributions to parent-child relationships; attachment theory, sociobiology, and existing child maltreatment theory. Consider the following assumptions:

(1) Attachment theory. Humans are equipped at birth with a basic set of skills (attachment behaviors) that hold the capacity to initiate and develop a reciprocal relationship between adult and child. *It is this relationship that provides the child protection against all forms of violence, including that of parental violence* (Bowlby, 1969).

(2) Sociobiology. Behavior is purposeful and adaptive. Through behavioral choices, the individual will seek to maximize survival, increase the likelihood of offspring survival, support kin over others, and seek adaptation to the environment (Barash, 1979).

(3) Child maltreatment theory. Violence toward children is a shared potential and not an aberration that afflicts only a few "sick" individuals (Burgess, Anderson, Schellenback, & Conger, 1981). Adults at extreme risk for violence may initiate it when their sense of survival or self-esteem is threatened (Helfer, 1975).

Given these theoretical foundations, the adult at risk for making a decision to engage in a violent act toward a child would be an adult who (A) finds the attachment relationship between him- or herself and the child impaired for some reason or (B), finds the child to be a threat to self or kin. The model would appear graphically as:

_____

DIATHESIS _____ *STRESS*

This chapter offers that our slow path toward reaching a more solid understanding of parental violence toward children may be traced to two obstacles:

(1) The relationship established between parents and their children is believed to have a "natural" path with "normal" and predictable events. Violence would seem to exist outside the scope of that "normal" relationship rather than a genuine behavioral option. We have embraced nonviolence in the parent-child relationship, and have left no room for its opposite choice.

(2) Even as we come to accept the difficult reality of violence of parents toward children, we initiate our search for reason at the wrong point. With the assumption that all families, and by inference all parents, have an equal opportunity to engage in a "normally" nonviolent relationship with their children, we have charted our course too narrowly. If all parents share an equal likelihood of adopting nonviolent behavior, our search to describe violent parents must begin with specific stressors and precipitating events that generate what can only appear as a behavioral aberration. The problem remains that many parents and families live comfortably with the stressors our research indicates characterize those who engage in violence toward their children.

Impaired Parent-
    Child Attachment
	Emotional
	    Resource and

Sociobiological
    Pressures
    [Survival]
	Physical Resource
	    Limitations in the
	    Parent or Family

The parent's promise of protection to the child is balanced against the threat the child may represent to the adult's sense of self-survival (and survival of other kin). This is a balance that is influenced by the availability of emotional and physical resources in the environment. This resource availability defines the environment in which the parent-child relationship is intended to prosper. It is vitally important to understand that this prospering does not occur automatically. Insofar as the true power in the parent-child relationship rests within the parent, the choice as to whether the relationship will survive is theirs.

Mandates in the Parent-Child Partnership

The parent-child relationship demands partnership for survival. The child arrives unprotected and demanding. Physical and emotional resources that aid in the survival of both parent and child are finite. Since the child's capacity to sacrifice is limited, it is the parent who must hold the capacity to sacrifice both physical and emotional needs to assure protection for the child. In being asked, and even demanded, by the child to make this sacrifice, the parent may feel that his or her own real or perceived survival is threatened. It must be remembered that, for the parent, making a decision not to sacrifice for the sake of the child is a true option.

Robert L. Trivers (1974) has suggested that the key feature of the parent-child partnership is the level of "parental investment." Simply put, the adult is required to sacrifice immediate personal rewards in order to increase the chances of the child's adequate growth and survival. This expenditure of adult energy and resources must be drawn from other areas vital to the adult's life. This is an "investment" that provides a "return" only if the child moves (in the perception of the adult) from a helpless "taker" to a more independent and "giving" partner. This movement toward independence may be felt to be extremely slow moving in even the best of parent-child partnerships.

The child is not without weapons in this battle. The child is provided with the capacity to elicit "parental investment" through attachment behaviors (e.g., eye contact, helpless appearance, touching, and mimicking). If the parent holds complimentary skills in this area, the parental investment is offered, and a "reciprocal altruism" (Shapiro, 1978) is developed that sets the stage for the child's separation and individuation experiences. The potential for mismatching in these complimentary parent and child skill areas is high. This is a mismatch that weakens the ordinary protection offered the child by the parent (i.e. "normal parenting").

Weakening of parental protection and investment can occur if

(1) the child has difficulty in transmitting his or her attachment signals and cues
(2) the parent has difficulty in interpreting the child's attachment signals and cues
(3) restrictions in the environment force attention away from the parent-child communication in order to meet more pressing survival needs
(4) emotional limitations in either parent or child prevent full participation in the relationship

These are the problem areas that describe the parent-child relationship with a predisposition (diathesis) toward a reduction in protective mechanisms. It is this reduction that allows for the introduction of violence in the relationship as a response to external stressors. The key issue that remains is a suggestion as to how to identify such a propensity in the midst of many parent-child relationships that are facing seemingly incapacitating stress

Strengths and Weaknesses in Parent and Child

Table 3.1 provides an overview of the factors within the parent-child relationship that could mitigate *against* weakened protectiveness and violence as a parental option. If in evidence, a basic protectiveness should be present in the parent-child partnership.

Conversely, negative historical or behavioral factors in adult or child may suggest a predisposition *toward* a weakening of protective elements of the parent-child relationship. Some of these warning signals in the parent (Table 3.2) and the child (Table 3.3) may be manifested in the following: Through some combination or permutation of these risk factors in the parent-child relationship, three major risk patterns reveal themselves either separately or in juxtaposition. The first point of predisposition toward the selection of violence would be the parent who presents a competitive (for survival) pairing, in which attachment is tenuous at best. The need to compete, the need for the parent to see the child as an avenue to his or her own (the parent's) emotional survival, and the desperate attempt by the parent to view the relationship as the mechanism through which lifelong demons in the area of trust and self-esteem are purged presents a dangerous package.

As can be seen in Tables 3.2 and 3.3, purely mechanical failure of attachment's protection may flow from the parent's and child's physiological and neurological mismatching. Differences in stimulation threshold and needs, weakened physiology in either partner, birth-related problems in the child, and insufficient fund of knowledge in the parent may result in a series of unmet expectations that destroys hope in either partner.

Finally, and most critically, if this child, this parent, and the process of parent-child partnership is greatly divergent from that which the child has been biologically prepared to deal with, problems will arise. If the parent, as far too many have, has been led to believe that the parent-child relationship is "natural" and "instinctive" in its entirety, difficulty can be predicted. The net impact of this belief, as witnessed through the violent parent-child pairing, is competition for survival and a fruitless struggle to understand the failure of expectations.

Even with the weaknesses promised by the mismatching of parent and child described earlier, it is possible that violence will not be selected as a behavioral option by the parent. If stress from the environment does not shift the scales of reason in this tenuous attachment relationship, comparative safety may be maintained. If heavy environmental stressors are added to the negative warning signals from the assessment of the attachment relationship, the downward slide toward violence is more likely to occur. There are reasonably clear environmental warning signals to be drawn from earlier research in the child maltreatment area.

TABLE 3.1
Positive Protective Elements in the Parent-Child Relationship

---

(1) A functioning adult who holds the capacity to nurture and protect a child. (Barash, 1979)

(2) A child who holds the instinctive ability to elicit care-giving behaviors from the parent. (Bowlby, 1980)

(3) A parent who anticipates and receives the rewards of his/her relationship with the child in an altruistic manner. (Trivers, 1974)

(4) A parent and child who have a reciprocal reward system in which the behavior of one member can be perceived as rewarding by the other partner. (Grey et al., 1976)

(5) A combination of physical and emotional resources which do not interfere with the development of the parent-child relationship as a result of their scarcity. (Bolton, 1983)

Weaknesses in the Physical or Emotional Environments

Table 3.4 displays categories that generate concern when present in the environment of the parent-child pair. This is a concern that is increased if this pairing is attempting to develop a sense of protectiveness and sharing in the absence of a solid attachment.

The environment most predictive of violence potential between parent and child is that which is most scarce in the physical and emotional necessities. These elements may be thought of as necessities in that they contribute significantly to the survival of the individuals and the relationship between them. Any absence or constriction in the availability of these elements of the environment places the parent and child in competition. Although competition between parent and child is not often considered, it is a recurrent and genuine factor in the life of the parent and child who succumb to violence. It can be only a destructive force.

Problem areas that advance competitive potential between parent and child include the parent's relative youthfulness (as compared to other parents), the prematurely shortened educational career of the parent, and the underemployment or unemployment that predicts a difficulty in escaping such an environment. This is a world that demands competition between its inhabitants on a daily basis; any attempt to break clear of it is almost unthinkable.

The stresses of this competitive environment are increased as large numbers of children are born in close succession. This is particularly unfair, for this is a parent whose lack of knowledge about children (personal needs and development) already overwhelms his or her ability to form a

TABLE 3.2
Factors in the Parent Predicting Problems in Parent-Child Dyad

Historical Concerns	*Behavioral Concerns*
Missed or distorted attachments in childhood. (Ainsworth, 1980)	Denial of pregnancy through failures in prenatal care, failure to acquire knowledge or prepare environment. (Osofsky & Osofsky, 1980)
Impaired intellectual or emotional functioning. (Polansky et al., 1972)	
Childhood exposure to hostility, rejection, and deprivation. (Kempe & Helfer, 1972)	Distortion of pregnancy through absence of fantasy, rigid fantasy or seeing child as compensating for own childhood. (Grey et al., 1976)
Impaired relationship ability. (Steele, 1975)	Negative reaction to child or childbirth. (Hurd, 1975)
Self-imposed isolation or social withdrawal. (Helfer, 1975; Giovannoni & Billingsley, 1970)	Postnatal disappointment or depression. (Klaus et al., 1972)
Impaired ability to trust; propensity to externalize blame. (Spinetta & Rigler, 1972)	Rigid expectations of child. (Robson & Moss, 1970)
	Rejection of child-care tasks. (Bromwich, 1976)
Sense of personal inadequacy through low self-esteem and self-confidence; pervasive anxiety and insecurity. (Newberger & Newberger, 1978)	Perception of child as an extension of parent's self rather than as an individual. (Taylor, 1980)
Weakened self-control through poor frustration tolerance, inability to delay gratification, and poor impulse control. (Laury, 1970; Fontana, 1973)	Inability to perceive child's behavior as rewarding. (Emde, 1980)
	Absence of reciprocal interaction. (Brazelton et al., 1974)
Inability to ask for help through absence of available social support and poor use of support when available. (Garbarino & Gilliam, 1980)	Inability to interpret child's cues. (Ainsworth, 1970)
	Requiring child to play parental roles. (Helfer, 1975)
	Disallowing relationships between child and others. (Terr, 1970)
	Concentration on the external appearances of parenting only. (Parens, 1972)
	Failure to respond to separation from child. (Klaus and Kennell, 1970)

TABLE 3.3
Factors in the Child Predicting Problems in the Parent-Child Dyad

Historical Concerns	*Behavioral Concerns*
Product of a difficult pregnancy. (Osofsky & Osofsky, 1980; Cohen, 1980)	Failure to reciprocate parental actions. (Lynch & Roberts, 1977; Emde, 1980)
Product of a difficult delivery. (Grey et al., 1976)	Failure to seek parental attention, withdrawn, lethargic. (Solnit & Provence, 1979; Restak, 1979)
Congenital anomaly, prematurity, or low birth weight. (Milowe & Lourie, 1964; Drotar et al., 1975; Hunter et al., 1978)	Frightened, anxious, insecure. (Perry & Millemit, 1977)
Birth situation contributing to long separation. (Leifer et al., 1972; Seashore et al., 1973; Leiderman et al., 1975; Klaus & Kennell, 1976)	Over or under reactions to separation from parent. (Rutter, 1976)

Emotionally too adult for chronological age. (Elmer & Gregg, 1967) |
Difficulty in early care (e.g., neurological impairments). (Brown & Bakeman, 1977; Schwarzbeck, 1979)	Distortions in affection. (Kretchmer, 1973)
Distortions in growth and development (e.g., non-organic failure-to-thrive). (Golberg et al., 1980; Glaser et al., 1980)	Continuous seeking of parental approval. (Friedrich and Boriskin, 1976; Dunn & Richards, 1977)
Feeding difficulty. (Hansen, 1977; Kerr et al., 1978)	Justification of parental actions and acceptance of responsibility. (Bowlby, 1980)
Soothing difficulty. (Korner, 1974)	Impaired ability to trust. (Martin, 1976)
Perceived by parent as "different" or a "difficult child to care for." (Korner, 1973; Lozoff et al., 1977)	Impaired sense of self-esteem and self-confidence. (Court & Kerr, 1971; Steele, 1975)
Perceived by parent as having "something wrong" or not being "understandable." (Robson & Moss, 1970; Brazelton, 1980)	Waiting for own parenthood to "make things all right." (Sugarman, 1977)

relationship with the child(ren) in question. Large numbers of children contribute stress, lack of knowledge contributes stress, lack of resources necessary for survival contributes stress, and other adults in the environ-

TABLE 3.4
Environmental Stressors Present in the High-Risk
Parent-Child Relationship

Poverty or financial insecurity. (Gil, 1970; Pelton, 1978)	Unemployment or underemployment. (Straus, Gelles & Steinmetz, 1978)
Early marriage or marital distress. (Herzog, 1966; Helfer, 1975)	Ignorance of child development. (David & Appell, 1969; Heifer, 1978)
Early childbirth. (Bolton, 1980)	Ignorance of child-care techniques. (Fontana, 1973; Murphy & Moriarity, 1976)
Frequent childbirth in close succession. (Light, 1973)	
Remarriage that includes births in the second family. (Burgess et al., 1981)	Adequate child-care knowledge with refusal to apply such knowledge. (Williams, 1974; Bell, 1979)

ment contribute stress. This is a world inhabited by an endangered parent and child who have no personal support system available and are not competent at using the "official" support systems professionally designed to aid families under this sort of stress. There is little the parent can do in this environment other than learning to tolerate its frustrations.

Unfortunately, this is not an adult who is well suited to gaining control over impulses, waiting out frustration, and delaying gratification of their own needs for the sake of a child. This parent is a frightened, inadequate, insecure individual. Low frustration tolerance, poor impulse control, and fear of continued rejection collide directly with the child's needs as is evident by the parent's inability to respond to them correctly. Faced with just "one more" situation of not knowing how to respond appropriately, the decision to initiate violence against the child may seem rational to this parent attempting to escape his or her own limits and that of the environment.

Diathesis-Stress: The Interrelationship

There is no event, or series of predictable events, that directly lead to a violent confrontation between parent and child. Rather, the origins of this violence rest in the possibility of the existence of obstacles that impede the growth of a "naturally occurring" partnership between parent and child. The more obstacles that exist, the more risk for violence in the relationship is present. If barriers are in existence that reduce the protective promises assumed within the parent-child relationship, the selection of violence as the parent's behavior of choice may be their manifestation.

The abilities of both parent and child to demonstrate reciprocal attachment, historical factors and subsequent behavioral-choice restrictions, and the immediate physical and emotional environment in which this relationship is to be nurtured intertwine to reduce or enhance risk. The risk is not simply that violence will occur, as has been our assumption in the past. The true risk is that the protective mechanisms within a specific parent-child relationship that mitigate against violence toward the child will be rendered ineffective.

To achieve the "natural" level of protectiveness assumed to exist between parent and child, each must demonstrate a willingness and capacity to contribute to the other's ongoing survival and satisfaction. The child must instinctively stimulate in, and draw caregiving from, the parent. The parent must instinctively recognize the child's need for this care. Not only must this mutual giving be present, it must be present at little or no cost to the partner. We must learn better to assess those parent-child relationships in which these "musts" are not a reality.

The parent who had not been provided altruistic parenting (attachment) in his or her own childhood, it seems likely, will view the child as a tool to be used. The predominant expectation is that the child will bring that emotional comfort and safety the parent has been unable to experience in his or her own life. If, after entering a parent-child relationship, the parent does not find the rewards offered by the child (growth, development, and increasingly independent functioning) to be reinforcing, the complimentary motivations to give, communicate, and reciprocate the child's interactions will decline. A second stage will find them being experienced as an irritant. A final stage may find that parent electing to resort to violence to punish or even remove the irritant from his or her life.

Despite the need for the understanding of violence as a possibility in the parent-child relationship, it should not be assumed that violence between parents and children (at least a severe degree of violence) is an automatic element of such a relationship. In the absence of gross environmental deprivation of some duration, reduction in emotional capacity or functioning, or intellectual impairment, most adults hold the ability to attach to and protect a child. This is only a safe assumption, however, if the parent's own childhood was marked by the safety of a positive attachment and the environment does not generate competition for survival between parent and child.

The understanding that parents hold the capacity to reject even their own children must come to be accepted by those who hold to a "natural" view of the parent-child relationship. Some adults simply do not want their own or anyone else's children. Still other adults seek children for aberrant emotional reasons and reject the children when their needs go unmet. There are those adults whose world will just not support the weight of a child because of limited resources. Finally, there are adults who become parents only to learn that they are subject to more than one, or all, of these obstacles to a stereotypical parent-child relationship. The parent-child pairing is just not as naturally "infallible" as many of the pronatalists among us assume.

The time has come to seek an ability to measure the "diathesis" for violence in parents and families generally.

The "Measurement" of Diathesis for Parent-Child Violence

Gaining a sense of the stressors in the environment of a potentially violent parent-child pairing is not our most difficult task. Unlike many of the emotional constructs used to signify the lack of attachment between parent and child, environmental stressors are often visible inadequacies. Table 3.4 presented a clear sense of the objective and often measurable elements of the environment that increase stress for the parent-child relationship. Yet, until emotional elements such as attachment, history, and capacity are identified, we will not gain the possibility of determining who our highest risk parent-child pairs are. Child maltreatment writings have offered "history of deprivation" (Court & Kerr, 1971), "disturbed family background" and "absence of good enough mothering" (Steele, 1975) and "personal rearing deprivation and subsequently mistaken notions of childrearing" (Spinetta & Rigler, 1972) as impairments to the relationships between parent and child. One shorthand description of these experiences is that of attachment. It is offered here that the absence of such an experience in one's own childhood contributes mightily to an inability to establish such a relationship with a child of one's own.

If the parent is driven (by his or her unfulfilled attachment needs) to assume that the child will fulfill those needs, thoughts of the child begin and end with that need. The child, in this circumstance, is assumed to be a "giving" and not a "taking" element of the parent's life. As the relationship between parent and child is first initiated, pregnancy itself is not recognized as a shared time with another developing individual; it is merely a period of waiting until other needs can be met. Early contact with the infant is not engrossing but troubling; troubling because the helplessness of the child was unanticipated. The very real helplessness of the child does not engender altruistic care but a grudging acceptance of responsibilities accompanied by a sense of being taken advantage of by the child. The child is not rewarding because the long anticipated reward of unencumbered caring does not flow from the child. This is not a parent who can foresee the future gratification to be found in the child's normal growth. Ultimately, the critical communication links between parent and child are not developed. If this negative foundation is exacerbated through the presence of a child who is somehow impaired, the potential for negative effects is increased. Finally, if all of these variables occur within an environment filled with stress, the

TABLE 3.5
A Typology of Relationship Risk Levels

Risk Level	Description	Parent	Child	Environment
High (I)	total rejection	never experienced an attachment	physically or intellectually impaired	low resource availability, high competition between parent and child
High (II)	parental behavior self-rewarding	experienced distorted attachment	functional	adequate
Moderate	progressive risk increase	adequate attachment	impaired	adequate
Low (I)	average risk	adequate attachment	functional	high stress and crisis, low resource, high parent-child competition
Low (II)	possible drift into problems	inadequate knowledge	functional	adequate

suggestion of violence potential in the family becomes a near certainty.

In moving from theory to practice, it is the clinician's role to (1) attempt to grasp the parent's definition of the problem between him- or herself and the child, (2) evaluate that parental perception against the stresses of the environment and the parent's capacity for dealing with the environment, (3) make some estimate as to any positives in the parent's situation or understanding, and (4) place this parent-child relationship along some continuum of risk. Table 3.5 describes a sample typology in which different situational factors or misperceived roles demand different levels of risk assignment. The history of parental attachment experiences and impairments in the child are considered to be the highest risk-producing elements. It is confusion in these areas that contribute most to problems in parental investment. A second level of risk is represented by environmental or situational factors that may force a functional parent-child relationship into a resource-scarce competition for individual survival. Finally, deficits in parental knowledge are included as elements that may allow for a "drift" into violent confrontation through lack of understanding or skill. In this typology the highest-risk parent holds the clear capacity, if not the propensity, to reject parental mechanisms that would otherwise protect the child. At the other extreme, the lowest-risk parent may simply err into a violent act through a lack of understanding.

For too long, research has ignored the parent-child pair that exists between anger and ignorance. This is the parent who holds a propensity for problems through the diathesis provided by his or her own failed attachment experiences. This is a propensity that will not explode into violence until the child becomes a competitor in the parent's environment. If we come to accept the possibility of parental rejection of a child, the possibility of parent-child competition, and the contributions of scarce resources in the environment, we will soon find more constructive measures for reducing the likelihood of parental violence directed toward children.

References

Ainsworth, M.D.S. (1980). Attachment and child abuse. In G. Gerbner, C. Ross, & E. Zeigler (Eds.), *Child abuse: An agenda for action*. New York: Oxford University Press.

Ainsworth, M.D.S., & Bell, S. M. (1970). Attachment, exploration, and separation: Illustrated by the behavior of one-year-olds in a strange situation. *Child Development, 41,* 49-67.

Barash, D. P. (1979). *The whisperings within*. New York: Penguin.

Bell, R. Q. (1979). Parent, child, and reciprocal influences. *American Psychologist, 34*(10), 821-826.

Bolton, F. G., Jr. (1980). *The pregnant adolescent: Problems of premature parenthood*. Beverly Hills, CA: Sage.

Bolton, F. G., Jr., Laner, R. H., Gai, D. S., & Kane, S. P. (1981). The "study" of child maltreatment: When is research . . . research? *Journal of Family Issues, 3*(4), 531-539.

Bolton, F. G., Jr. (1983). *When bonding fails: Clinical assessment of high-risk families*. Beverly Hills, CA: Sage.

Bowlby, J. (1969). *Attachment and loss, Vol. I: Attachment*. New York: Basic Books.

Bowlby, J. (1980). *Attachment and loss, Vol. III: Sadness and depression*. New York: Basic Books.

Brazelton, T. B. (1980). Behavioral competence in the newborn infant. In P. M. Taylor (Ed.), *Parent-Infant relationships*. New York: Grune & Stratton.

Brazelton, T. B., Kowslowski, B., & Main, M. (1974). The origins of reciprocity: The early mother-infant interaction. In M. Lewis & L. Rosenbaum (Eds.), *The effect of the infant on its caregiver*. New York: John Wiley.

Bromwich, R. M. (1976). Focus on maternal behavior in infant intervention. *American Journal of Orthopsychiatry, 46*(3), 439-446.

Brown, J. V., & Bakeman, R. (1977). *Behavioral dialogues between mothers and infants: The effect of prematurity*. Paper presented at the American Pediatric Society and the Society for Pediatric Research, San Francisco, April.

Burgess, R. L., Anderson, E. A., Schellenbach, C. J., & Conger, R. D. (1981). A social-interactional approach to the study of abusive families. In J. P. Vincent (Ed.), *Advances in family intervention, assessment, and theory* (Vol 2, pp. 1-46). Greenwich, CT: JAI .

Cohen, R. L. (1980). Maladaption to pregnancy. In P. M. Taylor (Ed.), *Parent-Infant relationships*. New York: Grune & Stratton.

Court, J., & Kerr, A. (1971). The battered child syndrome-2: A preventable disease? *Nursing Times (London), 67*(23), 695-697.

David, M., & Appell, G. (1969). Mother-Child interaction and its impact on the child. In A. Ambrose (Ed.), *Stimulation in early infancy*. New York: Academic Press.

Drotar, D., Baskiewicz, A., Irvin, N., Kennell, J., & Klaus, M. (1975). The adaption of parents to the birth of an infant with a congenital malformation: A hypothetical model. *Case Western Reserve Pediatrics, 56*(5), 710-717.

Dunn, J. B., & Richards, M.P.M. (1977). Observations on the developing relationship between mother and baby in the neonatal period. In H. R. Schafer (Ed.), *The origins of human social relations.* New York: Academic Press.

Elmer, E., & Gregg, G. S. (1967). Developmental characteristics of abused children. *Pediatrics, 40,* 596-602.

Emde, R. N. (1980). Emotional availability: A reciprocal reward systems for infants and parents with implications for prevention of psycho-social disorders. In P. M. Taylor (Ed.), *Parent-Infant relationships.* New York: Grune & Stratton.

Fontana, V. (1973). *Somewhere a child is crying: Maltreatment causes and prevention.* New York: Macmillan.

Friedrich, W. N., & Boriskin, J. A. (1976). The role of the child in child abuse: A review of the literature. *American Journal of Orthopsychiatry, 46,* 580-590.

Garbarino, J., & Gilliam, G. (1980). *Understanding abusive families.* Lexington, MA: D.C. Heath.

Gelles, R. J. (1973). Child abuse as psychopathology: A sociological critique and reformulation. *American Journal of Orthopsychiatry, 43,* 611-621.

Gerbner, G., Ross, C. J., & Zeigler, E. (Eds). (1980). *Child abuse: An agenda for action.* New York: Oxford University Press.

Gil, D. G. (1970). Violence against children. Cambridge, MA: Harvard University Press.

Glaser, H. H., Heagarty, M. C., Bullard, D. M., & Pivchik, E. C. (1980). Physical and psychological development of children with early failure to thrive. *Journal of Pediatrics, 73*(5), 690-698.

Goldberg, S., Brachfeld, S., & Divitto, B. (1980). Feeding, fussing, and play: Parent-Infant interaction in the first year as function of early medical problems. In T. Field, S. Goldberg, D. Stern, & A. Sostek (Eds.), *High risk infants and children: Interactions with adults and peers.* New York: Academic Press.

Grey, J., Cutler, C., Dean J., & Kempe, C. H. (1976). Perinatal assessment of mother-baby interaction. In R. E. Helfer & C. H. Kempe (Eds.), *Child abuse and neglect: Family and community.* Cambridge, MA: Ballinger.

Hansen, C. M. (1977). *Failure-to-Thrive: A manual prepared for social workers.* Piscataway, NJ: Protective Services Resource Institute, Rutgers Medical School, Department of Pediatrics.

Helfer, R. E. (1975). *The diagnostic process and treatment programs.* (DHEW Publications No. OHDS) 75-69. Washington DC: U.S. Government Printing Office.

Helfer, R. E. (1978). *Childhood comes first: A crash course in childhood for parents.* East Lansing, MI: Author.

Herzog, E. (1966). Social and economic characteristics of high risk mothers. In F. Haselkorn (Ed.), *Mothers at risk.* Garden City, NY: Adelphi University Press.

Hunter, R. S., Kilstrom, N., Kraybill, E. N., & Loda, F. (1978). Antecedents of child abuse and neglect in premature infants: A prospective study in a newborn intensive care unit. *Pediatrics, 61*(4), 629-635.

Hurd, M. J. (1975). Assessing maternal attachment: First step toward prevention of child abuse. *Journal of Gynecological Nursing, 4*(4), 25-30.

Kempe, C. H., & Helfer, R. E. (1972). *The battered child* (2nd ed.). Chicago: University of Chicago Press.

Kempe, C. H., & Helfer, R. E. (1980). *The battered child* (3rd ed.). Chicago: University of Chicago Press.

Kerr, M.A.D., Bogues, J. L., & Kerr, D. S. (1978). Psychosocial functioning of mothers of malnourished children. *Pediatrics, 62*(5), 778-784.

Klaus, M. H., & Kennell, J. H. (1976). *Maternal-Infant bonding: The impact of early separation or loss on family development.* St. Louis: C.V. Mosby.

Klaus, M. H., Jerauld, R. Kreger, M. (1972). Maternal attachment: Importance of the first postpartum days. *New England Journal of Medicine, 286,* 460-463.

Klaus, M. H., Kennell, J. H., Plumb, N., & Zuehlke, S. (1970). Human maternal behavior at first contact with her young. *Pediatrics, 46*(2), 187-191.

Korner, A. F. (1973). Individual differences at birth: Implications for child care practice. In D. Bergsma (Ed.), *The infant at risk.* New York: Intercontinental Medical Book.

Korner, A. F. (1974). The effect of the infant's state, level of arousal, sex and ontogenetic stage on the caregiver. In M. Lewis & L. A. Rosenblum (Eds.), *The effect of the infant on its caregiver.* New York: John Wiley.

Kretchmer, N. (1973). Ecology of the newborn infant. In D. Bergsma (Ed.), *The infant at risk.* New York: Intercontinental Medical Book.

Laury, G. V. (1970). The battered child syndrome: Parental motivation, clinical aspects. *Bulletin of the New York Academy of Medicine, 46*(9), 676-685.

Leiderman, P. H., & Seashore, M. J. (1975). Mother-Infant separation: Some delayed consequences. In M. A. Hofer (Ed.), *Parent-Infant interaction.* Amsterdam: Elsevier.

Leifer, A. D., Leiderman, P. H., Barnett, C. R., & Williams, J. A. (1972). Effects of mother-infant separation on maternal attachment behavior. *Child Development, 43,* 1203-1218.

Light, R. L. (1973). Abused and neglected children in America: A study of alternative policies. *Harvard Educational Review, 43*(4), 556-598.

Lozoff, B., Brittenham, G. M., Trause, M. A., Kennell, J. H., & Klaus, M. (1977). The mother-newborn relationship: Limits of adaptability. *Journal of Pediatrics, 91*(1).

Lynch, M. A., & Roberts, J. (1977). Predicting child abuse: Signs of bonding failure in the maternity hospital. *British Medical Journal, 1,* 624-626.

Martin, H. P. (1976). *The abused child: A multidisciplinary approach to developmental issues and treatment.* Cambridge, MA: Ballinger.

Milowe, D., & Lourie, R. S. (1964). The child's role in the battered child syndrome. *Journal of Pediatrics, 65,* 1079-1081.

Murphy, L. B., & Moriarity, A. E. (1976). *Vulnerability, coping, and growth from infancy to adolescence.* New Haven, CT: Yale University Press.

Osofsky, H. J., & Osofsky, J. D. (1980). Normal adaptation to pregnancy and new parenthood. In P. M. Taylor (Ed.), *Parent-Infant relationships.* New York: Grune & Stratton.

Parens, H. (1972). Indices of the child's earliest attachment to his mother, applicable in routine pediatric examination. *Pediatrics, 49*(4), 600-603.

Pelton, L. H. (1978). Child abuse and neglect: The myth of classlessness. *American Journal of Orthopsychiatry, 48*(4), 608-617.

Perry, N., & Millemit, C. R. (1977). Child rearing antecedents of low and high anxiety eighth-grade children. In C. D. Spielberger & T. G. Sarason (Eds.), *Stress and anxiety.* Washington DC: Hemisphere.

Polansky, N., Borgman, D., & DeSaix, C. (1972). *Roots of futility.* San Francisco: Jossey-Bass.

Restak, R. M. (1979). *The brain: The last frontier.* New York: Warner.

Robson, K. S. (1967). The role of eye-to-eye contact in maternal-infant attachment. *Journal of Child Psychology and Psychiatry, 8,* 13.

Robson, K. S., & Moss, H. A. (1970). Patterns and determinants of maternal attachment. *Journal of Pediatrics, 77*(6), 976-985.

Rutter, M. (1976). Separation experiences: A new look at an old topic. *Journal of Pediatrics,*
    95(1), 147-154.
Schwarzbeck, R., III. (1979). Identification of infants at risk for child neglect: Observations
    and inferences in the examination of mother-infant dyad. In S. P. Hersch & K. Levin
    (Eds.), *Selected readings in mother-infant bonding.* (DHEW Publication No. OHDS
    79-30225). Washington DC: Government Printing Office.
Seashore, M. H., Leifer, A. D., Barnett, C. R., & Leiderman, P. H. (1973). The effects of
    denial of early mother-infant interactions on maternal self-confidence. *Journal of*
    Personality and Social Psychology, 26, 369-378.
Shapiro, M. (1978). *The sociobiology of homo sapiens.* Kansas City, MO. Pinecrest Fund.
Solnit, A. J., & Provence, S. (1979). Vulnerability and risk in early childhood. In J. D. Osofsky
    (Ed.), *Handbook of infant development.* New York: John Wiley.
Spinetta, J. J., & Rigler, D. (1972). The child-abusing parent: A psychological review.
    Psychological Bulletin, 4, 296-304.
Steele, B. F. (1975). *Working with abusive parents from a psychiatric point of view.* DHEW
    Publication No. OHD 75-70. Washington DC: Government Printing Office.
Straus, M. A. (1980). Stress and child abuse. In C. H. Kempe & R. E. Helfer (Eds.), *The*
    battered child (3rd ed.). Chicago: University of Chicago Press.
Straus, M. A., Gelles, R. J., & Steinmetz, S. K. (1980). *Behind closed doors: Violence in the*
    American family. New York: Anchor/Doubleday.
Sugarman, M. (1977). Paranatal influence on maternal-infant attachment. *Orthopsychiatry,*
    47(3), 407-421.
Taylor, P. M. (Ed.). (1980). *Parent-Infant relationships.* New York: Grune & Stratton.
Terr, L. C. (1970). A family study of child abuse. *American Journal of Psychiatry, 127*(5),
    665-671.
Trivers, R. L. (1974). Parent-Offspring conflict. *American Zoologist, 14,* 249-264.
Webster's seventh new collegiate dictionary. (1963). Springfield, MA: G. & C. Merriam.
Williams, T. M. (1974). Childrearing practices of young mothers: What we know, how it
    matters, why it's so little. *American Journal of Orthopsychiatry, 44*(1), 70-75.

4

Understanding Violent Mothers and Fathers: Assessing Explanations Offered by Mothers and Fathers for Their Use of Control Punishment

Phyllis D. Coontz
Judith A. Martin

Aggression is, for the most part, a male activity. As Maccoby and Jacklin (1974, p. 228) point out, "males do appear to be the more aggressive sex, not just under a restricted set of conditions but in a wide variety of settings and using a wide variety of behavioral idexes." Males are both more verbally and physically aggressive than females; they are more likely to be both perpetrators and victims of aggressive attacks. These gender differences are already evident at the age of two, and they persist throughout the adult years (Feshbach, 1970).

Physical maltreatment of children is one type of aggressive activity that does not follow this pattern. Men and women are equally likely to be participants in abusive interactions with their children. A recent national study (U.S. Department of Health & Human Services, 1981, p. 31) found the mother or mother substitute was the only involved parent in 24% of all child abuse cases; fathers or father substitutes were perpetrators in 22%; both parents participated in 41% of the cases. Although men and women do not differ in the extent of their involvement in abuse, in the methods used to maltreat the child, or in the extent they injure children (Kadushin & Martin, 1981), they may differ in the attitudes and values they espouse as they attempt to understand the event and their role in it. This chapter describes an exploratory study designed to examine three major questions:

- Do mothers and fathers differ in their beliefs about the utility of violence in disciplining children?

- Do mothers and fathers offer different types of justification for their violent behavior?
- Do mothers and fathers differ in their feelings, particularly in the degree they feel guilt, at the end of a violent episode?

Although some recent research has compared the characteristics of mothers and fathers who maltreat children, we know of no research that has examined gender differences in understanding and justifying the abuse event itself. To assist in the development of hypotheses for this study, we will draw on findings of developmental studies of maternal and paternal behavior and of normative attitudes toward discipline and its appropriate use with children.

It must be noted, however, that abusive families do differ from "normal" families who serve as participants in developmental research, both in their overall life circumstances and in specific characteristics of family members. Abusers are much more likely to be poor, to have large families, and to struggle to raise their children without the help of a coparent. Abusers also tend to be highly stressed and isolated people with a more limited array of coping skills and external resources than other parents (Parke, 1982). The impact of some of these special circumstances will also be considered in this research.

Gender Differences in Child Discipline

Two key assumptions guided the development of hypotheses tested in this study. We assume that social expectations concerning appropriate activities and attitudes of fathers and mothers do affect both the beliefs and behavior of parents in general and of abusers in particular. Two aspects of maternal and paternal roles are of particular importance; these concern different levels of power and of child-caring responsibility claimed for men and women in our society. Our second major assumption is that these different approaches to parenting are reinforced by actual differences in the amount of time men and women spend with their children. Mothers are intimately and extensively involved with their offspring, whereas fathers spend much more limited and circumscribed time with them. Mothers are, therefore, considered much more knowledgeable about both the needs of their children and effective techniques in dealing with them. Both of these perspectives were identified as significant aspects of parenting behavior in an extensive study of 22 middle-class couples in Scotland (Backett, 1982). General social expectations, reinforced by experience, have particularly powerful impact on the way adults understand and explain their child caring role (see also Horwitz, 1982).

Several years ago, Parsons and Bales articulated a now classic description of the differences between male and female parenting roles:

According to Parsons and Bales (1955), fathers' and mothers' roles, like masculine and feminine roles, are divided along instrumental and expressive lines. The father's role is instrumental, one of competence and mastery. The father is provider, judge, and ultimate disciplinarian. He is the child's model for planning ahead, delaying gratification, and interacting with the world outside the family. The mother, on the other hand, is expressive. She smooths over interpersonal relations and keeps the family functioning as a unit. She is affectionate, solicitous, conciliatory, and emotionally supportive. (Weinraub, 1978, p. 115)

Despite tendencies toward more diversified responsibilities for both parents, this division of labor is prevalent among many families today (Backett, 1982; Rapoport et al., 1977).

Differences in the degree of power invested in maternal and paternal roles are also evident to children. In a recent cross-national study of 838 children between the ages of 5 and 15, Goldman and Goldman (1983, p. 808) note, "Father is frequently seen as the family disciplinarian, and mother as more loving and accommodating in attitude" (p. 798). The father, they found, is considered the boss of the family. "The mother is rarely identified as either the authority or the leader in the family, and this is expressed by one or two children in various age groups almost as quirks of a particular family: 'Dad's hopeless with money, so mum looks after that side very well' (English boy, 13 years) and 'Ma organizes the holidays and outings. We never see much of Dad, he's always down at the boozer' (North American boy, 13 years)." (See also Weinraub, 1978.)

This variability in relative power suggests men and women may respond differently when their parental power is threatened. Most abusive parents perceive their maltreatment as a response to some serious misbehavior of the child. Most feel they had to take extreme disciplinary measures because the child challenged their authority directly and had to be controlled (Kadushin & Martin, 1981). Because they are expected to be both aggressive and in charge, fathers may be more likely to justify their use of violence by suggesting they have the right to use physical aggression as a control tactic. Pleck (1976, p. 156) states, "Males are expected to show greater emotional control than women, and are often described as being more alienated from their feelings; but at the same time, men appear to become angry or violent more easily than women and are often rewarded for doing so, covertly if not directly." The authority position of women in the family, in contrast, is not so clearly sanctioned, and their right to behave aggressively is much more circumscribed. When asked to justify their violent activity, therefore, we would expect them to refer to their nurturant and caretaking responsibilities and to be less likely to claim their "right" to physically punish the child.

The impact of social values on men and women are reinforced by differences in their daily experiences with children in the home. As Backett (1982) discovered, parents realize that a mother's disciplinary methods develop in a different context from those of a father. Her opportunity to interact intensively and repeatedly with her child allows her to develop a more extensive historical knowledge of both that child and of discipline that "works." She is also more likely to refer to that experience when justifying her disciplinary behavior (p. 168). Fathers, spending less intensive and repetitive time with their children, were likely to focus more rapidly and more powerfully on the child's misdeeds:

> Respondents frequently maintained, for example, that the mother had gradually become accustomed to not noticing every little 'misbehavior' of the child. They said that the mother simply did not have the time or the energy to deal with every issue. Many of the fathers were presented as more likely to focus on these "little things," and to take more forceful stands over issues which the mothers had decided to ignore. (Backett, 1982, pp. 169-170)

Weinraub (1978) reviewing an earlier study conducted by Osofsky and O'Connell, points out that fathers of these 4- to 6-year-old children "were also more action oriented, either jumping into or totally withdrawing from physically helping their daughters with the task, while mothers were more supportive and encouraged their daughters' efforts" (p. 117).

The effect of relative power invested in maternal/paternal roles and of the level of experience mothers and fathers have with their children are reflected in the following hypotheses:

- Hypothesis 1: Fathers are more likely than mothers to argue for the efficacy of physical punishment in child rearing.
- Hypothesis 2: Abusive mothers are more likely to describe themselves as using nonviolent disciplinary techniques prior to resorting to abuse than are their male counterparts.

Despite recent pressure on fathers to carry greater parenting and housekeeping burdens, mothers in our society continue to hold major responsibility for the well-being and healthy futures of their children. As Russo (1976) points out, motherhood is a mandated role for women but a voluntary role for men. In her study, Backett (1982) describes the women she interviewed as carrying this burden in the family. In order for these middle-class couples to develop what they considered a "fair" division of labor, Backett found they resorted to a variety of, and sometimes tenuous, coping strategies. Some argued that it was equitable for women to carry a disproportionate share of the load because their husbands *had* helped in the past; others referred to his willingness to help in a crisis if needed (pp. 78-79). These parents also noted, however, that husbands had a tendency to ignore tasks that obviously needed doing or did not know how to carry them out effectively.

The view that fathers are required to assist mothers only in emergency situations is reflected in findings of a study conducted by Marton et al. (1981). Exploring child care activities of fathers of premature infants, they found these men were extensively involved only so long as the child remained hospitalized. Once the child had gained weight and had been brought home, their caretaking activity decreased. Children are also fully aware that mothers are mainly responsible for their care. In the international study of children's views of mothers and fathers conducted by Goldman and Goldman (1983), only 3.8% of the sample mentioned responsibilities their parents shared. The authors comment, "There was little indication of awareness of roles in the family which could be shared by mothers and fathers, except where father takes over the cooking or washing or other domestic chores in an emergency when mother is sick or 'it's her evening at bingo' (English girl, 13 years)" (p. 808).

The following hypothesis reflects differential responsibility mothers and fathers hold for child rearing:

- Hypothesis 3: Abusive mothers are more likely to take personal responsibility for misbehavior of their abused children, while abusive fathers are more likely to blame other forces for the child's behavior.

As a result of this imbalance in relative responsibility, we also expect that abusive mothers and fathers will describe different affective responses to the incident. Because they take more personal responsibility for their child's actions, mothers should be more likely to describe themselves as feeling guilty. Fathers, on the other hand, should be more likely to maintain their feelings of anger and outrage because they feel less responsible than mothers do. This viewpoint is summarized in the following hypothesis:

- Hypothesis 4: Fathers will report stronger feelings of anger and outrage after engaging in abusive acts; mothers will report stronger feelings of guilt.

In her examination of parenting styles, Backett describes three different instances in which parental disciplinary behavior may be severe. Parents acknowledge the use of what she terms "disapproved expedients" at times when situational pressures are overwhelming or other priorities seem to necessitate such a response. She notes that parents tend to feel guilty after using such expedients, but she notes no gender differences in expression of this feeling (p. 94). She also cites a few instances in which parents felt their child was behaving in an extremely difficult but "incomprehensible" way. Parents, she notes, "related how they had been totally unable to remedy the situation, or had 'lost control' of their own tempers, since they could not understand the child. Subsequently, they expressed considerable feelings of mortification that they had been unable to cope, as the child's behavior had seemed so irrational" (p. 122). Some parents, in such circumstances, felt they were at fault, since they *should* have known what to do; others argued that nobody seemed to understand the child. Again, Backett does not comment on gender differences in these responses.

A number of studies indicate that women are more anxious about expressing aggression than men are; women are also aware that such behavior is less acceptable in the eyes of others than it is for males (Towson & Zanna, 1982). However, the literature does not indicate whether women feel greater guilt as a result of their participation in aggressive acts. Despite the lack of evidence, we have chosen to explore the hypothesis that abusive mothers do express such feelings more frequently. We are interested in discovering whether parents who perceive themselves as responsible for the problems their children exhibit also acknowledge feelings one would expect in such situations. Parents who take no such responsibility, on the other hand, should also have no reason to acknowledge guilt feelings.

Intervening Factors:
Social Class and Single Parent Status

We have argued that although mothers and fathers are equally likely to be involved in physical abuse, their attitudes, values, and ideas about its use will differ. In addition to different parental perceptions, based on sex-role expectations, we also recognize that physical abuse is not evenly distributed throughout society. It is more highly concentrated in specific socioeconomic groups and ecological areas. The highest rates of physical abuse are found among lower-class families living in urban areas (U.S. Department of Health & Human Services, 1981).

The differential distribution of the use of physical abuse suggests that the use of physical abuse is related to social class. Although not conclusive, there is evidence that working- and lower-class parents are more likely to use physical punishment, while middle-class parents are more likely to resort to psychological means of discipline (Bronfenbrenner, 1958; Kohn, 1963; Stark & McEvoy, 1970; Erlanger, 1984). In the recent National Study of the Incidence and Severity of Child Abuse and Neglect (U.S. Department of Health & Human Services, 1981), emotional abuse and neglect were recognized proportionately more often in families with incomes of $15,000 or more, while physical abuse and neglect were recognized in families with annual incomes of $15,000 or less.

We hypothesize that differences in the conditions of life enjoyed by members of different classes influence the behavior, attitudes, and values of those members. Members of different classes perceive the world differently by virtue of enjoying different styles and conditions of life, and thus come to develop different conceptions of social reality including values about what is appropriate and desirable. Conceptions of the desirable and the appropriate are what we mean by value. In this analysis we borrow the definition of *value* advanced by Clyde Kluckholm: "a conception, explicit or implicit, distinctive of an individual or characteristic of a group, of the desirable which influences the selection from available modes, means, and ends of action" (Parsons & Shils, 1951, p. 395). In other words, we are suggesting that class position shapes the values of members of that class, which include parental values, and that parental values are expressed in parent-child interaction. We further argue that lower-class families hold values that are consistent with the use of physical aggression. The decision to opt for the use of physical abuse among parents from a lower-class position is consistent with the general cultural pattern of lower-class life. This does not mean that physical abuse is confined to lower-class families, but that it is more prevalent there because it is a part of everyday life.

The use of physical punishment has been viewed as part of a general cultural pattern whereby violence is part of everyday life and is seen as the most expedient way to solve difficult problems and situations. This general pattern of physical aggression has been termed the "subculture of violence" by Wolfgang and Ferracuti (1967), who developed an interpretative framework to analyze the greater propensity toward violence among members of the lower class. Wolfgang and Ferracuti argue that the use of force or violence in interpersonal relationships is generally viewed as a reflection of basic values that are distinctive from the dominant "middle-class" culture.

Wolfgang and Ferracuti further hypothesize that the expression of violence is a part of a normative system that is reflected in the psychological traits of the subculture participants. Attitudes toward use of violence become interwoven with the personal identities and perceptions of social reality of members of the group. Wolfgang and Ferracuti (1967, pp. 158-161) put forth seven propositions defining the nature of the subculture of violence:

(1) No subculture can be totally different from or totally in conflict with the society of which it is a part.
(2) To establish the existence of a subculture of violence does not require that the actors sharing these basic value elements should express violence in all situations.
(3) The potential to resort or willingness to resort to violence in a variety of situations emphasizes the penetrating and diffusive character of this culture theme.
(4) The subcultural ethos of violence may be shared by all ages in a subsociety, but this ethos is most prominent in a limited age group, ranging from late adolescence to middle age.
(5) The counternorm is nonviolence.
(6) The development of favorable attitudes toward, and the use of, violence in a subculture usually involve learned behavior and a process of differential learning, association, or identification.

(7) The use of violence in a subculture is not necessarily viewed as illicit conduct and the users therefore do not have to deal with feelings of guilt about their aggression.

According to Wolfgang and Ferracuti's theory, lower-class families are influenced by the conditions of poverty and disorganization that surround them. Moreover, members of the lower-class learn violent behavior patterns and values that justify and sustain its continued use.

In his analysis of value differences among parents from different class backgrounds, Kohn (1963) offers some support for the Wolfgang and Ferracuti thesis. He found that working-class and middle-class parents expressed different values over the forms and expected consequences of discipline. Working-class parents were more likely to value the efficacy of imposing external proscriptions, that is, commands and rules, whereas middle-class parents were more likely to value self-discipline and control in relating to their children. Thus working-class children were expected to adhere to parentally imposed rules whereas middle-class children were expected to exercise self-control. Violations of these expectations resulted in perceived grounds for disciplining children. To the working-class parent, it was the overt act that mattered and the fact that the child did not defer to authority. Insubordination was to be dealt with through corporal discipline. To the middle-class parent, it was the child's motives and feelings that mattered. Intent was to be dealt with through rational and psychological appeals. Kohn also found that parental roles were perceived differently by middle-class and working-class parents. Among middle-class families, these roles were not as sharply differentiated as they were among working- and lower-class families.

Kohn's evaluation suggests that assessment of disciplinary practices in abusive families must focus on concrete behavior and violation of parental rules. Hypotheses outlined above reflect one's concern about the immediate form and consequences of behavior, rather than the child's motives.

Consideration of subculture-of-violence theory also suggests that different disciplinary processes may occur in middle-class families than in very poor abusive families. Unfortunately the lack of middle-class subjects in this study prevented us from evaluating the impact of different social class backgrounds on parental attitudes and beliefs. However, such an assessment needs to be undertaken. Because developmental research is based on evaluation of middle-class family life, study hypotheses may reflect differences in the behavior of such families but fail to clarify differences between those in poorer circumstances.

Wolfgang and Ferracuti's interpretive framework is heuristically valuable for examining physical abuse because it draws attention to the values and norms that are incongruous with those of the dominant culture. Given that physical abuse is more highly concentrated among lower-class families, it seems reasonable to us to examine the values and attitudes of lower-class parents regarding the grounds for and conditions under which they use physical punishment and how these differ from those employed by the dominant culture. Equally important is the need to examine the changing structure of middle-, working-, and lower-class families. Based upon decennial census trends, poverty is becoming "feminized." That is, the number of poverty-level households maintained by women is growing. According to recent census data, the proportion of the poverty population living in female-headed households has increased from 15% to 26% in the last two decades. (Data for blacks are even more striking. For example, in 1980, 59% of the black poverty population lived in female-headed families, U.S. Bureau of the Census, 1981a). Even with the recent popularized image of the single father, empirically this phenomenon is restricted to middle-class males. Although some working- and lower-class fathers seek and are awarded custody of their children, it is most often in the context of another marriage or two-parent arrangement. Thus the poverty rates among women heading households are *much* higher than for male heads of households and husband-wife families.

There are at least two serious facets of the "feminization" of poverty that affect the quality of life among lower-class families. Women generally earn much less than men, which means that they frequently do not have sufficient resources to support the needs of a family. Mothers raising children by themselves seldom receive compensatory funds from the absent father. Estimates are that only three-fifths of women with dependent children are awarded or have an agreement to receive child support. Of those, only one-half received the full amount awarded during 1978; another 28% received no payment at all (U.S. Bureau of the Census, 1981b).

These female heads of households must, as a consequence, assume the dual roles of mother and father without having access to either adequate economic or social support. We would further argue that the situation is exacerbated among working- and lower-class female headed households because parental roles are more sharply differentiated. That is, female heads of households are more likely to experience role conflict in parenting because they are assuming both the role of mother and father. Furthermore, single female heads are more likely to adhere to the values and norms of the subculture of violence while they struggle to fulfill the dual role expectations of mothering and fathering. We would, therefore, predict that our four previously stated hypotheses are more likely to apply to two-parent families than to single-parent female families.

Methodology

This pilot study reanalyzes data collected in 1977-1978 as part of a study of transactional patterns in maltreating families (Kadushin & Martin,

1981). In six of the most densely populated counties in Wisconsin, letters were sent to all parents who had been investigated by protective service agencies and had been considered confirmed abusers by those agencies during the study years. One-third of the eligible sample subjects agreed to participate in the study; 66 usable interviews were obtained from them.

Respondents were interviewed in their homes and were asked to describe the abuse event itself, the parent's understanding of why and how this event occurred, and his or her general life circumstances at the time of the incident. Respondents were also asked to discuss their previous experiences disciplining the abused child and to describe their child's birth and early history. An assessment of the reliability of parental responses, obtained through comparison of their statements with protective service records, yielded substantial agreement (Kadushin & Martin, 1981, pp. 101-103).

The final sample of 66 subjects was largely an urban one. In all, 79% of the families resided in a major metropolitan area. Two-thirds of the respondents were women. The median age of the abusive parents was 31. The children they maltreated were almost as likely to be boys (44%) as girls (56%). These children varied widely in age. Most of the families were poor. While 60% received money from wages, the remainder relied on welfare, social security, or other such sources for funds. One-third of the abusers had not completed high school.

These families are similar to most abusive families except to the extent that women are overrepresented. Abusers who had inflicted serious injury on the child were less likely to participate in this research.

Measures for the particular variables examined in this research were obtained through reassessment of responses to specific interview questions. They are summarized in Table 4.1. Difficulties emerged in substantiating the validity of these measures, similar to those found in other studies using preexisting records. Our future research in this area will require better developed measures tested on a new sample.

Results

Interestingly, the sample was evenly split between those parents who said they would again physically discipline their child (55%) and those who claim they would not (45%). However, men and women did not differ in this regard (see Table 4.2).

Although a number of parents reported having been severely disciplined or actually maltreated as children, two-thirds of those who responded to this question felt their own parents were justified in disciplining them in this way. These parents perceived their own misbehaviors as having warranted a physical response. A number also felt that corporal punishment helped them learn to conform. (Note, however, that 23 respondents, a third of the

TABLE 4.1
Measures Used in the Study

Variable	Interview Question Assessed
Efficacy of physical punishment	(1) "If you were to live the incident over again, what, if anything, would you do differently?" (Claimed would or would not use physical punishment.)
	(2) If physically disciplined by parents as a child, "How did you feel about the way your parents handled this?" (Parents did/did not have the right to use such punishment.)
Number of nonviolent disciplinary techniques	(1) Going back over the incident "step by step," abuser is asked to describe child's behavior and then, "What did you do about that?"
Personal responsibility for child's misbehavior	(1) "We know it's hard to understand why children do what they do, but I would like to know why you think your child did . . ." (Parent takes any responsibility for child's misbehavior or considers child or other factors responsible.)
Feelings after the incident	(1) "What were you feeling about the incident when it was all over?" (Parent felt angry, justified or guilty, remorseful, or combination of these.)

sample, did not answer this question.) Again, no significant male-female differences were found in these responses. Hypothesis I was not supported.

When parents were asked what actions they had taken in response to their child's misbehavior during the abuse incident, almost half (42%) reported that their only response was to maltreat the child. Most other parents (49%) stated that they had tried one nonviolent alternative before resorting to abuse. Only six individuals described repeated attempts to use such alternatives. Most of the parents (84%) who chose a nonviolent means of correction before resorting to abuse reported that they tried to reason with, yelled at, or threatened the child. Only one parent attempted to ignore the child's actions.

Significant differences did appear in the descriptions mothers and fathers offered of their abusive encounters. However, fathers were *more* likely than mothers to cite the use of nonviolent alternatives (Table 4.2).

TABLE 4.2
Results (N = 66)

	Mothers	Fathers	Significance Level
	(in percentages)		
Hypothesis 1:			
(a) would use physical punishment	55.8 (24)	54.5 (12)	NS
(b) parents had right to use physical punishment	71.4 (20)	53.3 (8)	NS
Hypothesis 2: did use nonviolent disciplinary techniques	47.7 (21)	77.3 (17)	$\chi^2 = 4.102$ $p = .04$
Hypothesis 3: parent takes responsibility	21.4 (9)	28.6 (6)	NS
Hypothesis 4: did feel guilt after the incident	62.5 (20)	63.2 (12)	NS

While half the women described their use, more than three-quarters of the fathers did so. These differences are in a direction opposite to that predicted in our hypothesis.

A minority of the parents in our study accepted any responsibility for their child's current conduct problems (24%). Almost half (46%) claimed the child deliberately chose to disobey ("He was just irresponsible"; "She just wanted her own way") or needed to do so ("Well, she's a teenager now and has to have her own way"). Another third blamed other people or forces, such as the school, peers, or the neighborhood, for influencing the child's actions. No differences were found in the responses of mothers and fathers on this item. Hypothesis 3 is rejected.

Almost two-thirds of the parents (63%) reported feeling some guilt at the close of the abuse incident. In several cases this affect was mixed with anger (18%) or feelings of justification (10%). A total of 18% of the parents said that they primarily felt angry after maltreating their child, and 20% primarily felt justified in their actions at the end of the abuse event. The predominant feeling during the incident was anger. Some 84% expressed this affect. Again, no male/female differences were observed.

When we examined results relative to married abusers, they paralleled those obtained for the sample as a whole. Only with respect to the second hypothesis did suggestive differences emerge. We were unable to assess gender differences in single parent families because only one single father participated in the study.

Implications

Despite the absence of significant findings in this study, we feel that continued investigation of maternal/paternal responses relative to gender role expectations is warranted. In particular, more carefully designed research, using valid and reliable measures, and controlling for significant factors such as social class and family structure is required.

One possible explanation for the results we obtained rests in the low social class status of most participants in this study. Despite Kohn's (1963) assertion that gender roles are more differentiated among such families, poor men and women may be more likely to *share* common attitudes about disciplining children. Inclusion of families from a range of socioeconomic backgrounds would allow us to test this hypothesis.

After reviewing explanations offered for their actions, we also feel that examination of discreet aspects of abuse events may not prove as fruitful as consideration of maltreaters' more general orientations toward the incident. It is our observation that attitudes, values, and rationalizations reported by these individuals tend to fall into a limited number of categories. These include, for example, "the angry woman" and the "bewildered father." Delineation of these more global orientations may be a necessary prerequisite for further study of gender differences.

References

Backett, K. (1982). *Mothers and fathers.* New York: St. Martin's Press.

Bronfenbrenner, U. (1958). Socialization and social class through time and space. In E. Maccoby, T. Newcomb & E. Hartley (Eds.), *Readings in social psychology.* New York: Holt, Rinehart & Winston.

Erlanger, H. (1984). Social class and corporal punishment in childrearing: A reassessment. *American Sociological Review, 39,* 68-85.

Feshbach, S. (1970). Aggression. In P. Mussen (Ed.), *Carmichael's manual of child psychology* (Vol. 2, pp. 159-245). New York: John Wiley.

Gold, M. (1958). Suicide, homicide, and the socialization of aggression. *American Journal of Sociology, 63,* 651-661.

Goldman, J., & Goldman, R. (1983). Children's perceptions of parents and their roles: A cross-national study in Australia, England, North America, and Sweden. *Sex Roles, 9*(7), 791-812.

Horwitz, A. (1982). Sex-Role expectations, power, and psychological distress. *Sex Roles, 9*(7), 607-623.

Kadushin, A., & Martin, J. (1981). *Child abuse: An interactional event.* New York: Columbia University Press.

Kohn, M. (1963). Social class and parent-child relationships: An interpretation. *American Journal of Sociology, 68,* 421-480.

Maccoby, E., & Jacklin, C. (1974). *The psychology of sex differences.* Stanford, CA: Stanford University Press.

Marton, P. et al. (1981). The role of the father for the infant at risk. *American Journal of Orthopsychiatry, 51*, 672-679.

Parke, R. (1982). Theoretical models of child abuse: Their implications for prediction, prevention, and modification. In R. Starr (Ed.), *Child abuse prediction: Policy implications (pp. 31-66)*. Cambridge: Ballinger.

Parsons, T., & Shils, E. (1951). *Toward a general theory of action*. Cambridge: Harvard University Press.

Pleck, J. (1976). The male sex role: Definitions, problems, and sources of change. *Journal of Social Issues, 32*, 155-164.

Rapoport, R., et al. (1977). *Fathers, mothers and society*. New York: Basic Books.

Russo, N. (1976). The motherhood mandate. *Journal of Social Issues, 32*, 143-153.

Stark, R., & McEvoy, J. (1970). Middle-Class violence. *Psychology Today*, Vol. 4, pp. 52-65.

Towson, S., & Zanna, M. (1982). Toward a situational analysis of gender differences in aggression. *Sex Roles, 8*, 903-914.

U.S. Bureau of the Census (1981a). *Household and family characteristics*. Current Population Reports, Series P-20, No. 366. Washington, DC: Government Printing Office.

U.S. Bureau of the Census. (1981b). *Child support and alimony: 1978*. Current Populations Reports, Special Studies. Series P-23, No. 112. Washington, DC: Government Printing Office.

U.S. Department of Health & Human Services (1981). *National study of the incidence and severity of child abuse and neglect*. Washington, DC: Government Printing Office.

Weinraub, M. (1978). Fatherhood: The myth of the second-class parent. In J. Stevens, Jr., & M. Mathews (Eds.), *Relationships* (pp. 109-133). Washington, DC: National Association for the Education for Young Children.

Wolfgang, M., & Ferracuti, F. (1967). *The subculture of violence*. London: Tavistock.

5

Parental Aggressiveness
and Physical Punishment
in Long-Term Perspective

Joan McCord

An ample literature shows that aggressive parents tend to produce aggressive children (e.g., Bandura & Walters, 1959; Egeland & Sroufe, 1981; Eron, Walder, & Lefkowitz, 1971; Lewis, Shanok, Pincus, & Glaser, 1979; Main & Goldwyn, 1984). Yet little is known about the process of transmission. Evidence in studies by Straus and his coworkers suggests that parental aggression generates norms supporting violence for enforcing a moral order (Steinmetz & Straus, 1974; Straus, Gelles, & Steinmetz, 1980; Owens & Straus, 1975). White and Straus (1981, p. 265) have suggested that physical punishment "lays the groundwork for the normative legitimacy of all types of violence." White and Straus supported their position with evidence from two sources. Among a national sample of families, those who were most likely to report arrests "for something serious" also reported severe spousal abuse. And among a sample of college students, those who were most likely to report committing crimes also reported experiencing violence in their families of orientation. Because reporting biases tend to create similarities between descriptions of oneself and descriptions of others (Hastorf, Richardson, & Dornbusch, 1958), evidence less subject to these biases would be desirable.

Research designs that gather information about parents from sources different from those used to gather information about children reduce perceptual bias. A handful of longitudinal studies have used independent sources for information about child-rearing environments and subsequent behavior. These studies have not emphasized effects of physical discipline or parental aggression, although their results suggest that parental aggressiveness has an important impact on personality (Block, 1971;

Farrington & West, 1981; McCord, 1979; Olweus, 1980; Pulkkinen, 1983).

The purpose of the present study is to examine effects of parental aggression, using a longitudinal design in which evidence about the family during childhood was gathered without knowledge about how the individual would develop. Following the suggestion of Straus and his coworkers, the study considers effects of witnessing aggression as potentially different from effects of being trained through use of physical punishment. White and Straus (1981) propose three unintended "lessons of physical punishment": the lesson that violence is associated with love, the lesson that violence is associated with virtue, and the lesson that violence can be justified when it serves to enforce an important choice. The present research is designed to consider a fourth lesson: physical punishment teaches the association of choice with self-interest.

Method

Subjects in the present study had participated in a delinquency prevention program, which, to avoid stigmatizing, included boys considered to be "average" as well as those considered to be "difficult." At the time of their referral to the program, the subjects ranged in age from 5 to 13 (M = 10.5, S.D. = 1.6). Between 1939 and 1945, counselors assisted 253 boys and their families in a variety of ways, both inside and outside the home.[1] Most families were assigned more than one counselor who, after each encounter, filed a detailed report of conversations and behavior. Covering a span of more than five years, the counselors' case records reveal the texture of life among families living in deteriorated urban areas of eastern Massachusetts.

In 1957, coders read the case records, transcribing information into categorical scales. Since the coders had no access to information about the subjects other than what was contained in the case records, the scales are uncontaminated by retrospective bias.

Variables used in the present study describe the social setting of the home, family structure, after-school supervision, parental affection for the child, family aggression, and disciplinary techniques used by the parents.[2] In 1938 and 1939, the social settings in which the boys resided had been evaluated. Neighborhoods were rated in terms of delinquency rates, availability of recreational facilities, and proximity to bars, railroads, and junkyards. Supervision was rated on the basis of whether or not a child's activities outside of school were governed by an adult. A parent who seemed pleased with the boy and concerned for his welfare was considered affectionate.

The family was classified as generally aggressive if there was considerable parental conflict or if either parent was aggressive. Raters looked for conflicts between the parents about values, money, alcohol, religion, or about the child. A parent who typically yelled, threw things, or attempted to injure someone when frustrated or annoyed, was counted as aggressive.

Raters coded a parent as punitive if corporal punishments formed a basis for the parent's attempt to control the boy.

Family structure was considered unified or broken. If at least one of the boy's parents was not living with the boy for a period of six months, his family was classified as broken. To avoid confounding effects of broken homes with those of parental aggression, only men reared in intact families were included in the analyses. To justify treating the men as independent when testing hypothesized relationships, only one man from a family was included. After eliminating men from broken homes, and brothers, 130 men remained.

The study compares men reared in three types of intact homes: those in which the parents were generally aggressive, those in which parents were nonaggressive, and those in which the parents were not generally aggressive although they used physical punishment in their child rearing. The *aggressive families* (N = 40) were those in which at least one parent was aggressive or there was considerable conflict. The *nonaggressive families* (N = 31) were those in which neither parent was aggressive; the parents were not in frequent, open conflict; and discipline did not depend on physical punishment. The *punitive families* (N = 59) were those in which neither parent was generally aggressive and the parents were not in open conflict, yet at least one of the parents used physical punishments.

To check the possibility that family aggressiveness was confounded with other social factors that could account for differences in aggression among the men, the three types of homes were compared regarding their social settings, parental affection, and supervision. None of the comparisons revealed reliable differences. Similar proportions of boys from the three types of families lived in the worst neighborhoods: 38% of those from aggressive families, 32% of those from nonaggressive families, and 27% of those from punitive families. Approximately equal proportions had affectionate parents: 48% of those from aggressive families, 58% of those from nonaggressive families, and 59% of those from punitive families. And approximately equal proportions were supervised after school: 55% of those from aggressive families, 74% of those from nonaggressive families, and 71% of those from punitive families.

The present follow-up began in 1975, when the boys had become middle-aged men. Their names and pseudonyms were checked through courts, mental hospitals, alcohol treatment centers, and the department of vital statistics in Massachusetts. Records were supplemented by information from the states to which some of the men had moved. Information for the follow-up was collected and coded by a staff unfamiliar with the records gathered during childhood.

Men who had been convicted for larceny, auto theft, burglary, assault, attempted rape, rape, kidnapping, attempted murder, or murder, were considered criminals.

The men were asked to respond to a written questionnaire and to consent to an interview. A male interviewer, blind to other information about them, spent between one and three hours with the men discussing their lives. His records of the structured interviews were coded by a staff who had no access to other records.

The men discussed their homes, families, jobs, and educational histories. To measure the subjective sense of achievement, they were asked to look back on life and describe some of the things that stand out. Answers were coded as positive (reflecting pride, sense of achievement, good fortune, or pleasure) versus neutral or negative.

During the interview, the men described the sorts of things that annoyed them. As a measure of tolerance for frustration, each was then asked: "About how often does this (do these things) happen?"

Both the questionnaire and the interview included four questions designed to detect alcoholism (Mayfield, McLeod, & Hall, 1974). These questions asked whether the men had ever felt annoyed by criticism of their drinking or felt guilty about drinking, whether they had tried to cut down on drinking, and whether they had ever taken a morning eye-opener. A man was considered an alcoholic if he gave an affirmative answer to more than two of these questions. He was also considered alcoholic if he described himself as an alcoholic, if he had received treatment for alcoholism in a hospital or clinic, or if he had been convicted at least three times for drunkenness or driving while intoxicated.

Both interviews and questionnaires asked about health. Arthritis, gout, emphysema, depression, high blood pressure, asthma, ulcers, heart trouble, and allergies were considered psychosomatic.

Several questions in the interview yielded information about a man's relationship with his wife. Men were asked what sort of things they did with their wives and whether their wives knew most of their friends. Men were free to include their wives in responses to questions about what makes a good marriage, about what they generally do when stuck by a decision, about the sorts of things that annoy or anger them, about people they admire and people who have made a difference in the way their lives have turned out. After reading these responses and the notes describing interaction during the interview, coders indicated whether the respondent demonstrated warmth toward his current wife.

After the interview, each man was offered $20 for his time. Many of the men refused the money, often explaining that they were happy to contribute their time. Since this action constituted refusal of a benefit that they could have taken, it provided evidence of altruism.

Results

Comparison of criminal records showed that the men who had been exposed to aggressive parents were most likely to become criminals, $\chi^2(2) = 10.38$, p = .006. Almost one third (30%) had been convicted for serious crimes as juveniles and an additional 18% were convicted for index crimes as adults. Men disciplined punitively whose parents had not been generally aggressive were less likely to become criminals than those reared by aggressive parents; 15% were convicted as juveniles and an additional 12% were convicted for index crimes as adults. The men reared by nonaggressive parents were least likely to become criminals; 13% were convicted for index crimes, half as juveniles, and the remainder only as adults.

As can be seen in Table 5.1, aggressive parents appeared to generate aggressive antisocial behavior. It is important to note, however, that men reared in generally aggressive families were not particularly likely to become alcoholics or psychotics. Nor were they particularly prone to develop psychosomatic disorders. Parental aggression apparently had effects related specifically to aggression rather than to more general personality dysfunctions.

Aggressiveness is sometimes linked to an orientation toward high achievement. Both education and occupational status were used to reflect achievement motivation. Neither measure showed evidence that parental aggression affected achievement. Approximately equal proportions of each group had graduated from high school, and approximately equal proportions had white collar positions of managerial or professional status (see Table 5.2).

Differences in the lives of the men suggested that norms of aggressiveness had indeed been communicated to the men reared in aggressive households. In addition to the heightened probability of criminality, men reared in aggressive households were more likely to be annoyed, $\chi^2(2) = 6.01$, p < .05. They were less likely than those from nonaggressive households to be married, but if they were married, they were more likely to express affection for their wives, $\chi^2(2) = 6.42$, p < .05.

Men who had been reared by punitive parents who were otherwise not aggressive were more likely than men in the other two groups to express pride and pleasure in their accomplishments $\chi^2(2) = 6.09$, p < .05. They were the least likely of the three groups to show altruism $\chi^2(2) = 8.26$, p < .02.

Summary and Discussion

Men who had been part of a youth study active between 1939 and 1945 were subjects for investigating the impact of parental aggression. Case

TABLE 5.1
Problems

(Percent of each type for which description was true)

Variable	Aggressive (N = 40)	Nonaggressive (N = 31)	Punitive (N = 59)
Criminal (not alcoholic)	23	0	19
Criminal and alcoholic	25	13	8
Alcoholic (not criminal)	8	16	15
Other problems (only)*	10	26	25
None of the above	35	45	32

*Died before age 35; psychotic; psychosomatic.

TABLE 5.2
Current Lives

(Percent of each type for which description was true)

Variable	Aggressive (N = 32)[a]	Nonaggressive (N = 23)[a]	Punitive (N = 36)[a]
High school graduate	47	40	47
Managers, professionals, etc.	15	23	23
Currently married*	54	70	47
Showed warmth to wife*	62	24	35
Memories: pride/pleasure*	55	56	82
Frequently annoyed*	59	22	44
Showed altruism*	24	30	3

a. Numbers vary somewhat for different measures.
*$p < .05$.

records of social workers who had regularly visited 130 intact families provided descriptions of the youngsters and their parents. Some 30 years after these descriptions were written, the men were retraced.

To focus on effects of parental aggression, the study compared three groups of men: Those whose parents had been openly aggressive toward one another; those whose parents, though apparently not generally aggressive, used physical punishment in their child rearing; and those whose parents were neither generally aggressive nor users of physical punishments. The three groups were similar in terms of the proportions whose families lived in deteriorated areas, whose parents supervised their after-school activities, and whose parents displayed affection and concern for their welfare.

Men reared by generally aggressive parents appear to have become aggressive and expressive adults. Over half had records for committing serious crimes. The combination of affection and annoyance found among these men suggests that they had learned, as White and Straus (1981) suggested, to link violence with affection.

Among men reared by generally nonaggressive parents, those who had received punitive discipline appeared to be self-centered. They were likely to take pride in their accomplishments and they were unlikely to contribute their time for the benefit of others. It seems reasonable to conclude that punishment had taught these men that actions are good or bad depending on their consequences for themselves.

The study provides evidence that transmission of aggression is promoted through the example of parents whose conflict and injurious behavior seems to serve as a model for their children. Parental aggression that is focused on the child appears to teach the child to be concerned about himself—and thus, indirectly, to be less concerned with others.

Notes

1. The project included a control group. This group was matched to the boys in the treatment group on variables believed to influence criminality. Since they had not been visited by counselors, information about them and their families was based on intake interviews, supplemented by teachers' reports and official records. With such limited grounds for evaluating family interactions, the control group could not be used for the present analyses. Originally, 325 boys were included in each group. By January 1942, 253 boys remained in each group. (See Powers & Witmer, 1951, for details regarding selection of cases and a description of the treatment program.)

2. See McCord (1979) for a more complete description of the scales.

References

Bandura, A., & Walters, R. H. (1959). *Adolescent aggression.* New York: Ronald.

Block, J. (1971). *Lives through time.* Berkeley: Bancroft.

Egeland, B., & Sroufe, A. (1981). Developmental sequelae of maltreatment in infancy. In R. Rizley & D. Cicchetti (Eds.), *Developmental perspectives on child maltreatment.* San Francisco: Jossey-Bass.

Eron, L., Walder, L. O., & Lefkowitz, M. M. (1971). *Learning aggression in children.* Boston: Little Brown.

Farrington, D. P., & West, D. J. (1981). The Cambridge study in delinquent development (United Kingdom). In S. A. Mednick & A. E. Baert (Eds.), *Prospective longitudinal research: An empirical basis for primary prevention.* Oxford: Oxford University Press.

Hastorf, A. H., Richardson, S. A., & Dornbusch, S. M. (1958). The problem of relevance in the study of person perception. In R. Tagiuri & L. Petrullo (Eds.), *Person perception and interpersonal behavior.* Stanford, CA: Stanford University Press.

Lewis, D. O., Shanok, S. S., Pincus, J., & Glaser, G. H. (1979). Violent juvenile delinquents. *Journal of the American Academy of Child Psychiatry, 18*(2), 307-319.

Main, M., & Goldwyn, R. (1984). Predicting rejection of her infant from mother's representation of her own experience: Implications for the abused-abusing intergenerational cycle. *Child Abuse & Neglect, 8,*(2), 203-217.

Mayfield, D., McLeod, G., & Hall, P. (1974). The CAGE questionnaire: Validation of a new alcoholism screening instrument. *American Journal of Psychiatry, 131,* 1121-1123.

McCord, J. (1979). Some childrearing antecedents of criminal behavior in adult men. *Journal of Personality and Social Psychology, 37,*(9), 1477-1486.

Olweus, D. (1980). Familial and temperamental determinants of aggressive behavior in adolescent boys: A causal analysis. *Developmental Psychology, 16,* 644-660.

Owens, D. J., & Straus, M. A. (1975). The social structure of violence and approval of violence as an adult. *Aggressive Behavior, 1,* 193-211.

Powers, E., & Witmer, H. (1951). *An experiment in the prevention of delinquency: The Cambridge-Somerville Youth Study.* New York: Columbia University Press.

Pulkkinen, L. (1983). Search for alternatives to aggression in Finland. In A. P. Goldstein & M. Segall (Eds.), *Aggression in global perspective.* Elmsford, NY: Pergamon.

Steinmetz, S. K., & Straus, M. A. (1974). General introduction: Social myth and social system in the study of intra-family violence. In S. K. Steinmetz & M. A. Straus (Eds.), *Violence in the family.* New York: Dodd, Mead.

Straus, M. A., Gelles, R. J., & Steinmetz, S. K. (1980). *Behind closed doors: Violence in the American family.* New York: Anchor/Doubleday.

White, S. O., & Straus M. A. (1981). The implications of family violence for rehabilitation strategies. In S. E. Martin, L. B. Sechrest, & R. Redner (Eds.), *New directions in the rehabilitation of criminal offenders.* Washington, DC: National Academy Press.

6

Abused and Neglected Children with Their Peers

Carollee Howes

I n the past two decades child abuse has become a serious social problem. Several million children experience abuse each year. The magnitude of the social problem of abuse has led to an increase in research on the subject. This research has tended to focus on etiology, prevention, and treatment of the abusers rather than on the psychological consequences of the abuse for the child (see Belsky, 1978 for a review of this literature). However, from several theoretical perspectives, abused children may be particularly at risk in the area of peer relationships. Furthermore recent observational studies suggest that peer interactions of abused children are maladaptive. Therefore the purpose of this chapter is to examine the relationship between child abuse and subsequent peer interactions and relationships. Theoretical perspectives on the relationship between adult child interactions and relationships and peer interaction and relationships will be presented. Empirical evidence for the social relationships of abused children with their peers will then be discussed with particular attention to research completed as part of the University of California, Los Angeles research project on sociomoral development in abusing and nonabusing families. Finally implications for intervention and treatment of abused children will be presented.

AUTHOR'S NOTE: This chapter was written with support by grants from Child Help Incorporated and from the William Keck Foundation. The research could not have been accomplished without the support and encouragement of Dr. Norma Feshbach, Codirector of the University of California, Los Angeles research project on sociomoral development in abusing and nonabusing families; the assistance of Robert Eldredge, Michael Espinosa, and Jon Schlichting; and the cooperation of the children and their parents and their caregivers. Reprint requests should be sent to Carollee Howes, Graduate School of Education, University of California, Los Angeles, CA 90024.

Why Should Abused Children Be at Risk
for Maladaptive Peer Relationships:
Theoretical Perspectives

Three major child development theories; attachment theory, social learning theory, and social network theory, each suggest that because of disturbances in the family environment, the abused child is at risk for maladaptive peer relationships. Attachment theory (Bowlby, 1979; Sroufe, 1983) argues that the child's formation of an attachment or affective bond with the mother or primary adult caregiver is a critical developmental issue in the first year of life, that the quality of the attachment is related to the child's later ability to form relationships with peers, that this is a critical development issue in the first year of life, and that the quality of the attachment is related to the child's later ability to form relationships with peers. Pastor (1981) and Sroufe (1983) have demonstrated that less securely attached infants have more difficulty than securely attached infants in forming peer relationships as preschoolers. Of particular importance for abused children is the finding that maltreatment is associated with the formation of less than secure attachment relationships (Egeland & Sroufe, 1981). Therefore, attachment theory predicts that maltreated children would have difficulties in forming relationships with peers because of their problematic relationship with their mothers or other primary caregivers. By extension, the theory would suggest that if maltreated children had the opportunity to form a secure attachment relationship with an alternative caregiver, such as in an intervention program, then that child would also be able to form relationships with peers.

Social network theory (Lewis, 1982) assumes that the social systems of parent-child relationships and peer relationships are overlapping but not dependent systems. The quality of relationships in one system may influence, but does not determine, the quality of relationships in the other system. From this perspective the maladaptive parent-child relationship of the maltreated child does not determine that the child will have difficulty in forming relationships with peers. This point is supported by a Lewis and Schaeffer (1981) study that found no differences between the peer relationships of maltreated and normal children. Unfortunately, as will be discussed later, Lewis and Schaeffer's results are confounded by grouping together physically abused and neglected children and by the possible effects of intervention.

Social network theory further suggests that the isolated quality of abusing parents' relationships with other adults, their isolation from social networks, may be detrimental to the abused child's relationships with peers. Several studies have reported that abusing parents are isolated from social contacts (Barbarino & Sherman, 1980). The isolated parent provides the child with fewer opportunities to engage with others, to learn alternative styles of social interaction, and to learn to trust that others will provide emotional or physical support than does a parent who is integrated into a social support system (Cochran & Brassare, 1981; Lewis, Feiring, & Kotsonis, 1984). Several studies of peer interaction suggest that it is experience with peers that predicts competent peer interaction (Mueller & Brenner, 1977; Howes, 1980). If isolated abusing parents are not providing their children with experiences with peers, then their children may be less able to form relationships with peers. The treatment implications of this theory are programs that foster and facilitate peer relationships.

Social learning theory suggests that by observing the aggressive or abusive behavior of adults the child learns to respond to frustration, anger, or fear in an aggressive manner (Bandura, 1973). In a test of this hypothesis Fairchild and Erwin (1977) report that boys who watched a punitive parent-child interaction were more often physically aggressive. Thus an abused child is expected to have a limited behavior repertoire so that his or her response to frustration, fear, or anger with peers is to become aggressive. Aggressive responses to peers are often maladaptive responses. Normative research on peer interaction suggests that children are liked by peers when they respond to their overtures with positive and neutral behaviors (Hartup, Glazer, & Charlesworth, 1967). If the maltreated child responds negatively to prosocial overtures as well as aggressive overtures, that child has a decreased probability of establishing positive peer relationships. Social learning theory would suggest that within an intervention program adults could model appropriate social behaviors between peers. With alternative adult models of social behaviors the abused children would learn more appropriate behaviors. Appolloni and Cook (1975) and Furman, Rahe, and Hartup (1979) have extended the idea of adult models to include peer models of appropriate social behaviors. These studies suggest that integrating abused children into peer programs with normal children could then serve as models for the abused children.

A transactional model of development (Sameroff & Chandler, 1975) suggests that abuse may result from the mismatch between characteristics of the child and the caregiver. The child with behavioral characteristics such as abnormal cries or unattractive physical characteristics may be a particularly difficult child to engage in social interaction (Frodi, 1981). A less than optimally empathetic and sensitive caregiving adult may respond to a difficult child with abuse. This same characteristic that contributed to the child's becoming a victim of abuse may also contribute to maladaptive peer relationships. Several studies suggest that physical attractiveness may partially determine children's responses to peers (Hartup, 1983).

Social Relationships of Abused Children:
Observational Studies

Until recently information on the social development of abused children was drawn from case histories and studies that did not include control groups of other than abused children. These studies concluded that abused children were deficient in emotional and social development (Elmer & Gregg, 1967; Martin, Beezley, Conway & Kempe, 1974; Morse, Sahleer & Friedman, 1981). Recently, three observational studies have compared the peer behaviors of abused children to control children. George and Main (1979) compared the peer interactions of toddler-aged abused children and well matched controls. The abused and control children attended different day care centers and observers were aware of the classification of subjects. Abused children avoided peers four times as often as the control children and they behaved aggressively toward peers twice as often as the controls. Lewis & Schaeffer (1981) also studies peer interaction in day care settings. This sample was composed of toddler-aged abused and neglected children and control children who attended the same day care center as the maltreated children. No differences were found between the two samples of children.

Finally, Hoffman-Plotkin and Twentyman (1984) observed preschool age children with histories of abuse, neglect, or no maltreatment. The three groups of children were observed by observers blind to subject classification in day care centers that integrated maltreated children into the regular classrooms. Neglected children were less likely than abused or control children to interact with peers. The abused children were more likely than the neglected or control children to engage in aggressive behaviors with peers. These three studies have all observed maltreated children enrolled in day care intervention programs. Unfortunately none of the studies attempted to examine the effects of intervention itself, length of intervention, or type of intervention program on the peer interaction of the children. For example, studies of peer interaction when handicapped children are mainstreaming into regular classrooms have produced different results depending on the preparation given the children, the length of the intervention and so forth (see Field, Roopnarine, & Segal, 1984).

Furthermore these observational studies of abused children's peer interactions have examined only frequencies of behaviors. Comparing frequencies of behavior categories does not provide information on the relationship of the behavior of the maltreated child to the behavior of the peer partner. Frequency analysis cannot, for example, differentiate between an aggressive response to an aggressive overture and an aggressive response to a prosocial overture. In the first case aggression may be appropriate, in the second case it is unlikely to be appropriate. Finally, previous studies of abused children's peer interactions have examined social behaviors only between peer nonpeer relationships. Peer relationships or friendships that are developed over the course of multiple interactions may be a better indicator of the child's ability to form future social relationships than that child's social interaction behaviors at a given time.

Peer Studies of the University of California
Research Project on Sociomoral Development
in Abusing and Nonabusing Families

Design. The peer studies of the University of California research project on sociomoral development in abusing and nonabusing families were designed to address these unanswered questions. Two samples of children were observed. One sample consisted of 59 children who were not enrolled in intervention programs and who were observed in newly formed groups. The second sample consisted of 18 children who were enrolled in a day care intervention program. The children ranged in age from 14 to 61 months. In all, 26 (5 in intervention) of the children had been subject to physical abuse. Four of the children (all in intervention) had been subject to parental neglect. A total of 21 of the children (all in newly formed groups) had been referred to a child guidance clinic because of abnormal behaviors. And 26 of the children (9 in intervention) were normal control children.

For the purposes of analysis the children were divided into three age groups: (1) 13 to 35 months; (2) 36 to 47 months; (3) 48 to 61 months. All of the children in the intervention program were in age group one. The sample was balanced for sex of child and heterogeneous across diagnostic and group formation (newly formed versus intervention) categories in terms of socioeconomic and racial composition. Children in the abused category were more likely than children in the other diagnostic categories to have a nonworking parent.

Each child was observed during free play with peers. The abused and clinic children in newly formed groups were observed in randomly established play groups as their parents completed study questionnaires. The control children in newly formed groups were observed during their first week in a day care center. Each child in the intervention sample was observed in two situations while the child was involved in classroom free play with children from all three diagnostic categories, and in a structured play situation.

Free play observations consisted of four five-minute observations on each child during the newly formed play groups or free play periods in the day care centers. The four observations were combined to make a single 20-minute long observation for each child. The children were observed in random order. Structured play observations were conducted on each possible dyad in the intervention sample. Each observation lasted 20 minutes and was conducted in a small play area within the day care center. A standard set of toys (two each of a bucket and shovel, small blocks, grip ball, small car, stacking rings), placed in a standard fashion, were provided for play. A familiar caregiver accompanied the children to the play room. The caregiver was instructed not to interact with the children and to redirect any of the children's initiations to the peer partner.

All observations were coded using a continuous coding procedure. The presence and order of occurrence of preselected social behaviors were recorded on coding sheets divided into intervals. Every five seconds the observer moved to the next interval. An initiating behavior was coded with (1); the next social behavior that occurred in the same subsequent interval was coded with a (2); and so on. A social behavior was considered an initiation if there was no social behavior from the partner in the same or previous interval. The behavior of both partners in the dyad was simultaneously recorded and ordered. For example both the sequence (1) child A vocalize, (2) child B smile; and the sequence (1) child A vocalize and (2) child a A smile, were recorded. If behaviors occurred simultaneously both behaviors were given the same order number. Order numbers continued until the interaction terminated. An interaction was considered terminated if there was no response from the partner in the same or subsequent five-second interval.

Results

Frequencies of Peer Interaction. Comparisons of free-play behaviors in newly formed groups and in the intervention programs suggested differences owing both to the nature of the peer group and to the diagnostic category of the children. In newly formed groups abused children and clinic children were less socially skilled than normal children. Abused and clinic children in newly formed groups expressed fewer positive emotions, directed fewer positive and negative behaviors to peers, initiated less social interaction and engaged in less complex play behaviors than did the normal children in newly formed groups (Howes & Espinosa, 1984). When only toddler-aged (age group one) children were compared, abused children in the intervention programs were more socially competent and more similar to normal control children than were abused children in newly formed groups (Howes & Espinosa, 1984).

Older abused children in newly formed groups expressed less positive emotion in peer interaction than the younger abused children. In contrast the normal children in newly formed groups increased their expression of positive emotion with age. The clinic children did not change their expression of positive emotion with age (Howes & Espinosa, 1984).

Comparisons of social behaviors within the structured play setting also suggested that within an intervention program abused toddlers' peer-directed behaviors are similar to those of normal children (Eldredge, 1984. However neglected toddlers in the intervention program were more passive than abused or normal children (Eldredge, 1984).

Responses to Peer Behaviors. The conditional probability of responses of the children in the intervention program to a partner's aggression, friendly social behaviors, and distress were examined (Howes & Eldredge, 1984). Responses to aggression included: aggression, resist a toy-take, and cry. In the free play situation, the abused children responded to aggression with resistance or by crying; the neglected children with resistance, and the nonmaltreated children by crying. In the structured play situation, the abused and neglected children responded to aggression with aggression or resistance, and the nonmaltreated children by resistance or crying.

Responses to friendly behavior included friendly behaviors, aggression, and resisting offers. In the free play situation, the abused, neglected, and nonmaltreated children responded to friendly behaviors with friendly behaviors. In the structured situation, the abused and neglected children resisted object offers as well as responded in a friendly fashion. The neglected children also failed to respond with aggression, and the nonmaltreated children responded with friendly behaviors.

Responses to the distress of peers included prosocial and aggressive responses. In the free play situation, abused children responded with aggression and nonmaltreated children with prosocial behaviors. In the structured situation, the abused children responded with aggression and failed to respond with prosocial behaviors, and the nonmaltreated children responded with prosocial behaviors.

Friendships. Friendships were identified within the intervention sample using a three part behavioral criteria for identifying friendships (Howes, 1983, Howes, 1984). Children were identified as friends if they exhibited mutual preference, mutual enjoyment, and the ability to engage in skillful peer interaction. In order to behaviorally identify friends, the 18 intervention subjects were observed weekly for 10 weeks. Each week at least one five-minute observation was completed on each child. The identity of the peer partner was recorded for each initiation and response. If at least 50% of the initiations made from a child to a partner received a response, and if the two children engaged in mutual activity with mutually expressed affect, and if the two children engaged in complementary and reciprocal or role reversal play (Howes, 1980), then the children were considered friends. Abused, neglected, and control children were equally likely to form friendships.

Summary and Implications for Intervention

Several studies suggest that abused children are more aggressive or avoidant with peers than are normal children (George & Main, 1979; Hoffman-Plotkin & Twentyman, 1984; Howes & Eldredge, 1984). A particularly interesting difference between abused and normal children is the abused child's aggressive response to a peer's distress. The abused child's response to the distress of peers is reminiscent of the behavior of some abusing parents who are unable to comfort their children.

Studies that have examined separately the behavior of neglected children suggest that neglected children are more reluctant than normal or abused children to engage with peers (Eldredge, 1984; Hoffman-Plotkin & Twentyman, 1984; Howes & Eldredge, 1984). These findings highlight the importance of treating abused and neglected children as separate groups for the purpose of research. There may also be different intervention implications for abused and neglected children. Although abused children appear to need help in finding alternatives to aggressive responses to peers, neglected children appear to need help in becoming engaged with peers.

Abused children enrolled in intervention programs with a peer component were more competent in engaging with peers than abused children who did not receive intervention. The abused children in intervention programs engaged in similar frequencies of positive social behaviors to normal children in the program, they responded to the friendly overtures of their peer partners with friendly responses and they formed friendships with the other children in the group (Howes, 1984; Howes & Eldredge, 1984; Howes & Espinosa, 1984). The abused children who were not in intervention programs decreased their positive emotional expressiveness with peers with age (Howes & Espinosa, 1984). These findings suggest the importance of peer-based intervention with abused children and further suggest that such intervention may optimally begin in the toddler period.

Research on the effects of day care on normal children suggests that day care can function as an alternative social support system for the enrolled child (Rubenstein, 1984). Specifically this research suggests that both caregivers (Cummings, 1980) and peers (Howes, 1983) can serve as alternative attachment figures for children in day care settings. Day care intervention for maltreated children may, through the formation of alternative attachments and through increasing the child's opportunities to engage with peers, facilitate the acquisition of competent peer interaction skills and the development of peer relationships.

Interventions for the abusing family that are designed to enhance the abusing parent's ability to parent the child may not be sufficient to promote normal social development in the abused child. In the Howes and Espinosa study (1984), all of the parents of children in the newly formed groups were in individual or group treatment. However, their children were less able to interact with peers than were the children in the intervention sample.

The peer interaction skills that the abused children acquired within the intervention problem may form the base for the children to form, as adolescents and adults, their own social support networks. It is hoped that such social support networks would be able to buffer these adults who were once abused children from the child rearing stresses experienced by their own parents.

References

Appolloni, T., & Cook, T.(1975). Peer behavior conceptualized as a variable influencing infant and toddler development. *American Journal Orthopsychiatry, 45,* 4-17.

Bandura, A. (1973). *Aggression: A social learning analysis.* Englewood Cliffs, NJ: Prentice Hall.

Barbarino, B., & Sherman, S. (1980). High risk neighborhoods and high risk families. *Child Development, 51,* 188-198.

Belsky, J. (1978). Three theoretical models of child abuse: A critical review. *Child Abuse and Neglect, 2,* 37-49.

Bowlby, J. (1979). *Attachment and loss.* New York: Basic Books.

Cummings, E. (1980). Caregiver stability and day care. *Developmental Psychology, 16,* 31-37.

Cochran, M., & Brassard, J. (1981). Child development and social networks. *Child Development, 50,* 601-616.

Egeland, B., & Sroufe, A. (1981). Attachment and early maltreatment. *Child Development, 52,* 44-52.

Eldredge, R. (1984). *Social and emotional behaviorals of abused, neglected, and normal toddlers in a day care setting.* Unpublished doctoral disssertation, University of California, Los Angeles.

Elmer, E., & Gregg, G. (1967). Developmental characteristics of abused children, *Pediatrics, 1*(40), 596-602.

Fairchild, L., & Erwin, W. (1977). Physical punishment by parent figures as a model of aggressive behavior in children. *The Journal of Genetic Psychology, 130,* 279-284.

Field, T., Roopnarine, J., & Segal, M. (1984). *Friendship in normal and handicapped children.* Norwood, NJ: Ablex.

Frodi, A. (1981). Contribution of infant characteristics to child abuse. *American Journal of Mental Deficiency, 85,* 341-349.

Furman, W., Rahe, D., & Hartup, W. (1979). Rehabil tation of socially withdrawn preschool children through mixed age and same age socialization. *Child Development, 50,* 915-922.

George, C., & Main, M. (1979). Social interaction of young abused children. *Child Development, 50,* 306-318.

Hartup, W., Glazer, J., & Charlesworth, R. (1967). Peer reinforcement and sociometric status. *Child Development, 38,* 1003-1016.

Hartup, W. (1983). The peer system. In P. Mussen (Ed.), *Handbook of child psychology* Vol. 4). New York: John Wiley.

Hoffman-Plotkin, D., & Twentyman, C. (1984). A multimodal assessment of behavioral and cognitive deficits in abused and neglected preschoolers. *Child Development, 55,* 784-802.

Howes, C. (1980). Peer play scale as an index of complexity of peer interaction. *Developmental Psychology, 16,* 371-372.

Howes, C. (1983). Patterns of friendship. *Child Development, 54,* 1041-1953.

Howes, C. (1984). Social interactions and patterns of friendships in normal and disturbed children. In T. Field, J. Roopnarine, & M. Segal (Eds.), *Friendships in normal and handicapped children.* Norwood, NJ: Ablex.

Howes, C., & Eldredge, R. (1985). Responses of abused, neglected, and nonmaltreated children to the behaviors of their peers. *Journal of Applied Developmental Psychology, 6,* 261-270.

Howes, C., & Espinosa, M. (1984). *The consequences of child abuse for the formation of relationships with peers.* Paper presented at the Second Conference on Family Violence, Durham, NH.

Lewis, M. (1982). The social networks systems model. In T. Field (Ed.), *Review of human development*. New York: Plenum.

Lewis, M., Feiring, C., & Kotsonis, M. (1984). The social network of the young child. In M. Lewis (Ed.), *Beyond the dyad*. New York: Plenum.

Lewis, M., & Schaeffer, S. (1981). Peer behavior and mother-infant interaction in maltreated children. In M. Lewis & L. Rosenblum (Eds.), *The uncommon child*. New York: Plenum.

Martin, H., Beezley, P., Conway, E., & Kempe, C. (1974). The development of abused children. *Advances in Pediatrics, 21,* 25-73.

Morse, C., Sahleer, O., & Friedman, S. (1981). A three-year follow-up study of abused and neglected children. *American Journal of Mental Deficiency, 79,* 327-330.

Mueller, E., & Brenner, J. (1977). The origins of social skills and interaction among playgroup toddlers. *Child Development, 48,* 854-861.

Pastor, D. (1981). The quality of mother-infant attachment and its relationship to toddler's initial sociability with peers. *Developmental Psychology, 17,* 326-335.

Rubenstein, J. (1984). The effects of maternal employment on young children. In F. Morrison, C. Lord & Keating (Eds.), *Advances in applied developmental psychology* (Vol. 2). New York: Academic Press.

Sameroff, A., & Chandler, M. (1975). Reproductive risk and the continuity of caregiving casualty. In F. D. Horowitz (Ed.), *Review of child development research* (Vol. 4). Chicago: University of Chicago Press.

Sroufe, A. (1983). Infant-caregiver attachment and patterns of adaptation in preschool. In M. Perlmuller (Ed.), *Minnesota symposium in child psychology*. Minneapolis: University of Minnesota Press.

7

The Link Between Child Abuse and Juvenile Delinquency: What We Know and Recommendations for Policy and Research

Ellen Gray

> We as a society can never achieve any meaningful success in the war on delinquency until we view the problem in its entire continuum. There is a continuum which initiates with brutality, confusion and withdrawal of love and finalizes in a person—either adolescent or adult—who is repressed, hostile and perhaps even violent. (Faherty, 1981, p. 30)

Child abuse, juvenile delinquency, and adult crime are arguably the most serious social problems in America today. Their causes and cures have been pondered and measured by some of our greatest researchers and theorists, giving rise to a host of explanations. But most of this work has been done in separate circles, using the tools and language of different disciplines, operating on different levels of abstraction, and disseminated to entirely different audiences.

It is now being considered that child abuse and delinquency may be points on a continuum rather than separate problems. At minimum, it would seem that there are many overlapping causes for child abuse, juvenile delinquency, and crime. At maximum, there may be a simple causal path: child abuse leads to juvenile delinquency. In the middle are reciprocal causality (child abuse can cause delinquency and delinquency can cause child abuse) and interaction effects (child abuse causes delinquency when other factors are present).

These possibilities and the empirical evidence available to support them were scrutinized closely by researchers, practitioners, and policymakers in the juvenile justice and child abuse fields when they gathered recently at the Wingspread Conference Center for the conference, Child Abuse: Prelude to Delinquency? Implications of this research both for future studies and national and local policy were sifted out and worked through by the 30 invited participants. The conference was convened by the National Committee for Prevention of Child Abuse with support from the federal Office of Juvenile Justice and Delinquency Prevention[1] and the Johnson Foundation.

Retrospective Analysis

Participants considered the several different avenues of demonstrating the link between the two phenomena.[2] One way of establishing an association is to show that juvenile delinquents have experienced maltreatment at a rate higher than that of the general population. The National Incidence Study on child abuse and neglect conducted for the National Center on Child Abuse and Neglect in 1982 estimated that each year in this country 3.4 children per thousand are known to suffer demonstrable physical harm at the hands of a parent or other in-home caretaker; 5.7 children per thousand are victims of some type of abuse—physical, sexual, or emotional; and 5.3 children per thousand endure physical, educational, or emotional neglect (pp. 1, 4). Among the low-income populations, the rate of abuse and neglect combined was estimated at 27 children per thousand (p. 10).

Nine studies of juveniles involved in delinquent acts were considered at this conference (Kratcoski, 1982; Mouzakitis, 1981; Alfaro, 1978, 1981; Shanok & Lewis, 1981; Steele, 1975; Steele, 1976; Weinbach, Adams, & Parker, 1981; and Lewis & Shanok, 1977). They all found that these juveniles have endured child abuse and neglect at far greater rates than the estimates for the general population established by the National Incidence Study, even when the per-year rates for the general population were adjusted for the number of years of having been at risk by the time one reaches the age of the delinquent juveniles. Most of these studies reported maltreatment rates higher than the estimate for low-income groups, but the extent of the difference in rate varied widely.

Prospective Analysis

Another way to demonstrate a link between maltreatment and delinquency examined at this conference is to show that victims of child maltreatment are involved in delinquency at a higher rate than age-mates from the general population. Estimates of the prevalence of delinquency vary dramatically by type of report—self or official reports—and by the breadth of the definition, ranging from the estimate that 34% of all youths are taken into police custody, to the estimate that 1.3% were being admitted annually to juvenile detention centers and adult jails (in the mid-1970s).

Prospective study, either in person or through agency records, of children who were maltreated has been conducted by many investigators (e.g., Baher, Hyman, Jones, Jones, Kerr, & Mitchell, 1976; Elmer, 1977; Farber & Joseph, 1985; Friedman & Morse, 1974; Herrenkohl & Herrenkohl, 1981; Kent, 1976; Lynch & Roberts, 1982; Martin & Beezley, 1977; Martin, Beezley, Conway, & Kempe, 1974; Morse, Sahler, & Friedman, 1970; Terr, 1970); but few follow-up studies have examined delinquency rates of abused children (see Kline, 1987). Only two of these include a comparison figure for the nonabused population. One is a study of eight New York counties (Alfaro, 1978, 1981) in which in one of the counties, almost 10% of the children who had been abused or neglected were later reported as delinquent or ungovernable, compared to the rate of 2% reported in these categories for all children in the county during the same period. Another is a study of a population of maltreated Utah youth aged between 12-17 years. Nearly 60% of the sample came to the attention of the court for at least one infraction of the law, as against 40% of the general population of 12-17 year olds (Kline, 1987).

The Cycle of Violence

The sensible hypothesis that experiencing physical abuse as a child relates particularly to delinquent behavior that involves violence has been tested. Some studies have found that violent delinquents are more likely to have experienced abuse than are nonviolent delinquents (Lewis, Shanok, Pincus, & Glaser, 1979; Lewis, Shanok, & Balla, 1979). A relationship between abuse and delinquent violence is indicated also by findings that delinquents who were abused or neglected are involved in violent offenses more often than are nonmaltreated delinquents (Alfaro, 1978, 1981; Bolton, Reich, & Gutierres, 1977; Gutierres & Reich, 1981; Lewis, Shanok, Grant, & Ritvo, 1984). It has also been tested whether being a victim of family violence decreases violent behavior and increases withdrawal, contributing instead to escape acts, such as truancy and running away. Empirical evidence for this theory is weak, however.

The above studies suggest an association between child maltreatment and juvenile delinquency in spite of the flaws and differences among them that make it difficult to state the connection unequivocally. The assertion that there are links between these two problems is not new, however. The more refined question is, what are those links? How is it that a child who is maltreated may be more likely to encounter the juvenile justice system than one who is not, or that a delinquent adolescent is more likely to have been abused or neglected than a nondelinquent adolescent?

Mechanisms of the Relationship

There is unlikely to be a simple cause-and-effect relationship between the two phenomena, considering that their separate etiologies are so complex in themselves. Intervening and confounding factors have to be considered, as do the different types of maltreatment and different types of delinquent behaviors, family and other social network variables, cultural factors, and individual differences. There is research to help us begin to specify some of the processes in the relationship between childhood abuse and adolescent delinquency, but only tentatively.

It may be, for instance, that severe physical punishment, even that which falls short of some definition of abuse, is linked to later delinquent behavior. Some studies have looked at the link between harsh discipline and delinquency, and found a striking correlation (Bandura & Walters, 1959; Welsh, 1976). The proposition that severe punishment is related not only to general delinquency but to violent juvenile offenses also has been supported somewhat by research (Farrington, 1978; West, 1969, 1982; West & Farrington, 1973, 1977; Welsh, 1976). These studies suggest that parental modeling of violence as a way to correct others' behavior or solve problems may be involved in this link.

There is evidence to buttress the theory that early trauma or congenital abnormality place the child at risk for subsequent maltreatment *and* delinquency (Elmer, 1977; Martin, 1972; Lewis, Shanok, Pincus, & Glaser, 1979). In this case, delinquency could be a direct result of the abnormality or of the abuse that intervened. However, the central nervous system and intellectual deficits noted can also be consequences of early maltreatment (see Starr, 1982).

Research to identify family situations or family characteristics that lead to both maltreatment and delinquent behavior is scarce. Many studies have examined the relationship between various family characteristics and child maltreatment, or the family variables related to delinquency, but do not look at both outcomes together. One study was found that integrates the two groups (Weinbach, Adams, Ishizuka, & Ishizuka, 1981). In their words, "the descriptive knowledge that had been compiled about conditions related to delinquency bore a startling resemblance to those which had been found to exist when the child abuse syndrome was present" (p. 162).

Some of the behavioral responses to maltreatment may either lead to delinquency or may be defined as delinquent. Many victims of maltreatment attempt to remedy their situation by retaliating or running away—both labeled delinquent behavior. While no studies have been found estimating the proportion of abused children who leave home while still under age, several studies indicate that a large proportion of this country's adolescent runaways have been abused (Cunningham, 1983; Farber, Kinast, McCoard, & Falkner, 1984; McCoard, 1983; Youth Development Bureau, 1978), and that many left home because of the abuse. Or, delinquency may put an adolescent at risk for abuse in the home, on the street, or in an institution, whether such abuse represents a new experience or the continuation of earlier maltreatment.

It is also possible that links between maltreatment and delinquency are created by juvenile justice practices that label and adjudicate maltreatment victims as juvenile offenders (Smith, Berkman, & Fraser, 1980). Related to this are assertions that child welfare and judicial systems are more likely to intervene with low-income parents and children than with families of greater financial means (Griffin & Griffin, 1978; Pagelow, 1982; Weinbach, Adams, Ishizuka, 1981), so that these systems not only create apparent links between maltreatment and delinquency, but do so disproportionately for youth from low-income backgrounds. The exact extent of the skew in maltreatment and delinquency rates among the low-income groups owing to this bias is still unclear.

As Garbarino and Plantz (1984) conclude in their literature review, it does appear that child maltreatment (particularly when defined broadly) is associated with juvenile delinquency (particularly when defined narrowly). The links may be causal in both directions, as well as being the result of common etiology in disrupted, ineffectual families, and culturally based practices that legitimate family violence, decrease social control in adolescence, and support institutional practices that respond punitively to adolescent reactions to family disruptions.

Recommendations for Future Research

A set of specific research and policy recommendations were drawn up given the review of the literature and based on discussions at the conference.[3] The research that was proposed would consider three aspects of the issue. The first is the nature and extent of the linkage. The second is intervention strategies. The third is the nature and effect of differing system responses to child abuse and delinquency.

Further research on the links between child abuse and juvenile delinquency would take four forms. The first category would consider the link between identified delinquent behavior and a prior history of abuse and neglect. This research would continue to look at the percentage of identified delinquents who were abused or neglected as children or adolescents compared to the general population of youth (see Alfaro, 1981; Lewis & Shanok, 1977; Mouzakitis, 1981). The research would also focus more on linking specific types of offenders—sex offenders, prostitutes, violent offenders, chronic offenders—with specific types of abuse and neglect backgrounds—sexual abuse, physical abuse, chronic abuse—(see Geller & Ford-Somma, 1984; Lewis, Shanok, Pincus, & Glaser, 1979;

James, 1980; Berdie, Berdie, Wexler, & Fisher, 1983; Wenet, Clark, & Hunner, 1981). Research would also include examining the link between status offense behavior such as running away and truancy, and prior abuse or neglect (Gullotta, 1977; McCoard, 1983; Youth Development Bureau, 1978).

Studies in the second category would look further at the connection between being identified as a victim of abuse and neglect and subsequent delinquency. This research (along the lines of Alfaro, 1981, and Bolton, Reich, & Gutierres, 1977) would follow a sample of identified victims of abuse and neglect prospectively through adolescence to determine what percentage become delinquent compared to the delinquency rates of the general population. The research might identify some contextual, environmental, and biological factors present in each case at the time the abuse and neglect became known, and look for patterns across cases. It might also look for patterns in the presence or absence of some specific intervening variables during the years subsequent to the abuse and neglect.

Research linking specific types of abuse and neglect to particular types of subsequent delinquent behavior was recommended. This research would also focus on a sample of identified abuse and neglect victims—but by specific type of abuse or neglect—and track these youth prospectively to document specific future delinquent behavior. Among the questions that might be explored in these studies are: Are victims of sexual abuse more likely to become prostitutes or sexual offenders? Are victims of physical abuse more likely to become violent juvenile offenders? Are victims of neglect more or less problematic (delinquent) than victims of abuse, or different in the types of delinquent behavior they become involved in?

Research was also advocated that would explore the connection between the severity and chronicity of the abuse and neglect, or the age of the victim at onset with specific subsequent delinquent behavior. Fisher (1984) makes the point that it appears that many clinicians identify severity, chronicity, and age of onset of abuse as more powerful predictors than type of abuse and neglect (e.g., Lourie, 1977). These variables should be examined in the context of future delinquency, both as independent factors and in conjunction with specific types of abuse.

An important recommendation emerging from this conference was that we conduct research to discover what the protectors and buffers are that help families avoid maltreatment even when predisposers are present, or that enable individuals to avoid becoming delinquent when they have been abused. This research would strengthen and refine our knowledge of the causal path between the two social problems, as well as indicating valuable prevention and treatment avenues.

In the category of research on intervention strategies, the effects of nonintervention versus intervention is an important question for research. Does intervention reduce or increase future delinquency? Does system identification as an abusing or neglecting family or child abuse or neglect victim increase stress, social isolation, and learned helplessness, and thereby increase the likelihood of future abuse and neglect or future delinquency?

The effects of child abuse prevention programs on delinquency rates would be most helpful to know. In communities where a system of child abuse prevention programs is functioning, is there a later reduction in delinquency? This question is researchable, although using whole communities as treatment and control subjects poses some problems. Epidemiology methods would be appropriate for assessing this impact.

High-risk indicators—what they are and how various settings, such as schools, could use them to select families for preventive services—was thought to be an important area for study. School failure, rejection by peers, severely withdrawn behavior, fearfulness around adults, and aggressiveness are examples of behaviors that might be considered high-risk indicators. Research is needed to identify the indicators, to produce reliable scales with which to measure the indicators, and to assess interventions based on these indicators.

It was suggested that we research alternative interventions with identified delinquents with abuse or neglect histories. If we identify juvenile delinquents who have abuse or neglect histories and treat them as victims rather than victimizers, can we reduce subsequent delinquency? What type of treatment programs will work best—individual, family or group therapy or counseling, natural helping networks, self-help groups, skills training—and with which types of delinquents?

Prospective research on intervention with identified abuse and neglect victims was considered to be important as well. This research strategy would identify specific, replicable intervention approaches for abuse and neglect victims and evaluate their long-term effectiveness in reducing future delinquency. The research might also monitor for other problematic behaviors such as depression and alcohol and drug abuse. Intervention strategies would include those focusing on family problem solving (family systems therapy), social isolation (natural helping networks for victim and family), and socialization (social skills training). Some treatment programs might be specific to types of abuse and neglect, for example, sex abuse programs focusing on sexuality issues (see Berkeley Planning Associates, 1980).

Intervention with whole families in identified cases of abuse and neglect and in cases of juvenile delinquency was specifically proposed as a subject of research. Is family-oriented intervention more likely to be successful than victim-oriented intervention? If so, in which cases? Short-term and long-term intervention should be assessed. Do cases of child abuse and neglect and juvenile delinquency with abuse and neglect backgrounds require long-term intervention?

"Coercive" versus "therapeutic" intervention should be looked at. This research would evaluate "coercive" intervention strategies compared to "voluntary" intervention, focusing on specific measures of clinical success or failure, including prevention of further abuse as well as reduction of future delinquency behavior by the victim.

The third proposed category of study is research on system responses. The first subarea that was identified was research on coordinated approaches. Many child abuse and neglect situations "fall through the cracks" between mandated service systems or directly enter the juvenile justice system, and are never identified as abuse and neglect. Some people believe teams and interagency protocols among the police, the protective service units, and the runaway shelters reduce these problems. Little research has been done in this area.

Research on the effects of various system responses is needed. Do particular responses increase child abuse and neglect or juvenile delinquency? Are abused or neglected youth who are placed in foster care, group homes, or institutions more likely to be reabused or become delinquent? Does testifying against the perpetrator of child abuse and neglect increase or decrease the likelihood of further victimization or subsequent delinquent behavior? Does the lack of group homes, independent living programs, and other support services for abused and neglected runaways increase their victimization by making them more vulnerable to prostitution, to street violence, or to delinquency?

Research on the "coercive system" versus the "therapeutic system" would step back from specific interventions and look at the two systems *in toto*. Research would help clarify the debate as to what is "coercive," and what is "therapeutic," and could begin to measure the effectiveness of each approach. "Effectiveness" in a system sense rather than clinical sense could include increased or decreased reporting, willingness to report, and delivery of services to abusing families and to victims. The juvenile justice system is currently moving away from a "rehabilitation" model toward a "punishment" or a "justice" model, and therefore, issues of coercion versus volition also exist in the area of delinquency. To the extent that states adopt a "justice" model (which sentences delinquents based on their offense rather than on their treatment needs), are child abuse and neglect services to delinquents commensurately cut?

Stepping back even further into the systems perspective, the issue of public awareness efforts and their effectiveness was thought to be in need of research. To what extent do the media help prevent or create an increase in delinquency? Violent behavior, attitude problems, and child maltreatment should be measured before and after definable media activities that may be construed as harmful or encouraging of violence. On the other side of the coin, how can the media and communications technology be best used to promote public awareness to reduce child abuse and delinquency? Again.

family violence and delinquency should be measured before and after media campaigns designed to reduce them. Market research techniques could be employed to test the effectiveness of certain messages.

Policy Recommendations

Policy recommendations were somewhat more difficult for the participants to devise, in part because recommendations depend on the outcome of the research that was suggested. In general, however, an incremental approach was advocated, whereby certain policy directions could be advocated now, in the hope that they will be refined with future research.

The first policy recommendation issuing from this conference was the promotion of interdisciplinary cooperation. There must be continuing interchange among agencies and professionals in the justice system, the child abuse and neglect system, schools, hospitals, and mental health. At present many sectors are dealing with a small piece of the same problem, but at different times or from varying vantage points. For instance, for many children the police provide the point of entry to the juvenile justice system. When they are deciding whether to book an adolescent for an infraction or a crime, such as truancy or running away or curfew violation, they could also be considering whether this might be an appropriate case for protective services. There would have to be cross-training and rich communication between systems for this to work.

Second, there should be specific and probing social history taking at intake for delinquency. Although family social histories are routinely required in juvenile court delinquency hearings, if not conducted correctly, they will not yield information about maltreatment that will help determine what intervention is recommended. Police and probation officers should be trained to ask a series of specific questions of a medical and nonmedical nature that lead into the issue of abuse, and together form a picture of what type of maltreatment the child has sustained, if any. For instance, the youth could be asked, "Have you ever been taken to the emergency room because of an accident or injury?" followed by more detailed questions if the answer is "yes." He could be asked, "Has a parent or caretaker ever hit you with a closed fist? (belt, board, heavy object, and so on)" followed by a probe about frequency and circumstances if the answer is affirmative. Such questions, in conjunction with others, give a much more complete picture of the youth's experience than "Have you ever been abused by your parents?" Information elicited from such interviews will help the judge and the other professionals make a more appropriate disposition and treatment plan than if it were based solely on the youth's offense.

A third recommendation was for educational strategies aimed at implementing change within certain systems so that they begin to recognize the youth as a victim in addition to being a perpetrator. This is different than saying the abused delinquent is a victim *instead* of a perpetrator. This latter formulation would serve neither public protection goals nor the specific clinical goals for the adolescent. Health systems, school systems, child welfare systems and, of course, juvenile justice systems would be the sites for such reeducation efforts.

A fourth policy statement made by participants in this conference is that when the young person who was or is abused is treated within the correctional system, there should be a specific and different treatment for him or her. Although new treatment approaches for abused delinquents are needed, and research must contribute to formulating these, there are statements that can be made about these treatments now. We know that treatment for the abused child is going to be a long-term affair. We also know that institutions that treat violent young people must use approaches that are nonforcing and nonviolent. Otherwise, institutional abuse is committed in addition to familial abuse.

A fifth broad policy goal that was suggested is the mobilization of citizens to help prevent child abuse and child victimization. This would be done in the first instance through public awareness efforts such as NCPCA's media campaign that would give messages about the link between abuse and delinquency, or encourage people to get help for themselves or others when stress nears the danger point. The next stage would be to support the use of paraprofessionals and volunteers in schools, hospitals, or police agencies to identify and assist juvenile victims of abuse and crime. Volunteers could be recruited from churches and the untapped resource of retired citizens.

Early intervention was recommended by this group as a sixth policy imperative. The earliest intervention would be with the young abused child and would keep him from becoming delinquent as a later reaction. Barring that, there are opportunities for early intervention when the young person comes to the attention of the court, before he becomes delinquent. Institutions that are in a position to do early intervention are health systems, courts, and schools.

Seventh, attractive, benign, broad-based intervention styles and services are needed—services that people will use without being identified as abusive, abused, or delinquent. Many of the efforts to strengthen families starting up now under the rubric of child abuse prevention are the type being advocated. In particular, the development and provision of services that could be called parent education were recommended. However, more specification was urged. Which parenting concepts and skills are most helpful at different stages of family development and in different family situations and crises needs to be spelled out and applied.

Eighth among the policy recommendations was that a broader selection of agencies and institutions must be enticed to service violent, abusive acting-out children in spite of the ability and propensity of these youth to elicit negative response from adults and authority figures. One means to this end is increasing public and professional awareness of the fact that most of these unpleasant youth are children who have been hurt. More concrete incentives such as funds for demonstration programs in nontraditional institutions are needed also.

Ninth, and finally, there should be some type of mandated interaction between policymakers and researchers. There are sometimes constraints on researchers. They are channeled toward more scholarly endeavors and not given encouragement, access, or time to deal with and participate in the policymaking process. Conversely, policymakers often must seize the appropriate moment to make an intuitively correct change, and cannot wait for research findings. The processes must be merged so that policy can take advantage of up-to-date learnings, and so that policymakers can inform those in the position to collect data on the questions they need answers to.

It will take time to reach this relationship, but exchange between these two groups produces a habit of thinking and a style of responding to specific events and opportunities that is constructive to both. Routine data collection for administrative purposes will begin to be altered in ways that will facilitate research when there is a habitual thinking about services as a potential source of research information. And research questions will come to be framed from the perspective of utilization when the policy implications of the research become clear to the investigators, and are recognized as serious.

Related to this is the responsibility of the researchers to make understandable and disseminate their work beyond the scholarly journals, and to work toward the use of their findings and against their misinterpretation and misuse. It was suggested that researchers and policymakers be trained in communications skills so that they can perform clearly and effectively with people they want to have an impact on.

Perhaps something should be said at this point about the level of intervention of the policy recommendations issued from this conference. It is obvious that structural changes in our society were largely bypassed in favor of systems-level interventions. This is not because the convened researchers and practitioners discounted the profound effect of structural inequities on family violence and juvenile delinquency. Quite the contrary, there was considerable recognition of the primacy of this explanation. The mandate from the funding source for this conference, however, and the goal of the National Committee for Prevention of Child Abuse for the conference, were to produce practical suggestions with some chance of being implemented in the short run. The changes in the structure of American society that are necessary to significantly and positively affect the rates of child abuse and juvenile delinquency and the mechanisms that link the two are immediately beyond the influence of those attending the conference and those they represent. However, these policy recommendations are made with support for any steps taken toward the alleviation of the macrolevel social problems such as poverty, racism, and condoning of violence that lead to the mid-range disorders of child abuse and delinquency that these prescriptions address.

Conclusion

Participants at this conference came up with new ideas, and looked at old ideas in a new way. They recommended a renewed commitment to services for children and youth that may not have worked perfectly in the past because they were not sufficiently or consistently supported (rather than because they are not effective services). They suggested broadened roles for the traditional formal institutions such as schools, juvenile courts, and churches, as well as researchers and policymakers. The conference highlighted the value of going back to the family and the community to look for intervention points. A commitment was made to the idea of prevention, so as to avoid needing so many rehabilitative services. There was a commitment to responsibly implement what is known, in spite of what is not known yet. The dialogue has begun; we have broadened our view of this dual problem of delinquency and child abuse, and focused our sense of what can be done about it.

Notes

1. Grant number 84-JN-AX-0001.

2. I am indebted to James Garbarino and Margaret Platz for their literature review, "Child Abuse and Delinquency: What are the Links?," prepared for this conference, and from which this discussion of the research literature is largely taken.

3. Many of these research recommendations were suggested or stimulated by Bruce Fisher in his working outline for the conference, others emerged from the conference process itself.

References

Alfaro, J. D. (1978). *Report on the relationship between child abuse and neglect and later socially deviant behavior*. Albany: New York State Assembly.

Alfaro, J. D. (1981). Report on the relationship between child abuse and neglect and later socially deviant behavior. In R. J. Hunner & Y. E. Walker (Eds.), *Exploring the relationship between child abuse and delinquency*. Montclair, NJ. Allanheld, Osmun.

Baher, E., Hyman, C., Jones, C., Jones, R., Kerr, A., & Mitchell, R. (1976). *At risk: An account of the work of the Battered Child Research Department*. NSPCC. London: Routledge and Kegan Paul.

Bandura, A., & Walters, R. H. (1959). *Adolescent aggression.* New York: Ronald.

Berdie, J., Berdie, M., Waxler, S., & Fisher, B. (1983). *An empirical study of families involved in adolescent maltreatment.* Final report, URSA Institute.

Berkeley Planning Associates (1980). *Abuse and neglect clinical demonstration program evaluation.* Final report. Berkeley, CA: Author (NTIS No. PB-278 439).

Bolton, F. G., Reich, J. W., & Gutierres, S. E. (1977). Delinquency patterns in maltreated children and siblings. *Victimology, 2,* 349-357.

Cunningham, S. (1983, December). Abused children more likely to become teenaged criminals. *APA Monitor,* 26-27.

Elmer, E. (1977). *Fragile families, troubled children,* Pittsburgh: University of Pittsburgh Press.

Faherty, V. (1981). National policies on child abuse and delinquency: Convergence or divergence? In R. J. Hunner and Y. E. Walker (Eds.), *Exploring the relationship between child abuse and delinquency.* Montclair, NJ: Allanheld, Osmun.

Farber, E. D., & Joseph, J. A. (1985). The maltreated adolescent: Patterns of physical abuse. *Child Abuse and Neglect, 9,* 210-216.

Farber, E. D., Kinast, C., McCoard, W. D., & Falkner, D. (1984). Violence in families of adolescent runaways. *Child Abuse and Neglect, 8,* 295-299.

Farrington, D. P. (1978). The family backgrounds of aggressive youths. In L. A. Hersov & M. Berger (Eds.), *Aggression and anti-social behaviour in childhood and adolescence.* Book supplement to Journal of Child Psychology and Psychiatry, No. 1. New York: Pergamon.

Fisher, B. (1984). Proposed research strategies on the links between child abuse and juvenile delinquency. Unpublished outline prepared for "Child Abuse: Prelude to Delinquency?" Conference, National Committee for Prevention of Child Abuse, Racine, WI.

Friedman, S. B., & Morse, C. W. (1974). Child abuse: A five-year follow-up of early case findings in the emergency department. *Pediatrics, 54,* 404-410.

Garbarino, J. (1981). Child abuse and juvenile delinquency. In R. H. Hunner & Y. E. Walker (Eds.), *Exploring the relationship between child abuse and delinquency.* Montclair, NJ: Allanheld, Osmun.

Garbarino, J., & Platz, M. (1984). Child abuse and delinquency: What are the links? In E. Gray (Ed.), *Child abuse: Prelude to delinquency?* Final report. Chicago: National Committee for Prevention of Child Abuse.

Geller, M., & Ford-Somma, L. (1984). *Violent homes, violent children: A study of violence in the families of juvenile offenders.* Trenton: The State of New Jersey, Department of Corrections, Division of Juvenile Services.

Gold, M., & Petronio, R. J. (1980). Delinquent behavior in adolescence. In J. Adelson (Ed.), *Handbook of adolescent psychology.* New York: Harper & Row.

Griffin, B. S., & Griffin, C. T. (1978). *Juvenile delinquency in perspective.* New York: Harper & Row.

Gullotta, T. P. (1977, November). *Runaway: Reality or myth?* Paper presented at the Annual Meeting of American Association of Psychiatric Services for Children, Washington, D. C.

Gutierres, S. E., & Reich, J. W. (1981). A developmental perspective on runaway behavior: Its relationship to child abuse. *Child Welfare, 60,* 89-94.

Herrenkohl, R. C., & Herrenkohl, E. C. (1981). Some antecedents and development consequences of child maltreatment. In R. Rixley & D. Cicchetti (Eds.), *New directions for child development, No. 11. Developmental perspectives on child maltreatment.* San Francisco: Jossey-Bass.

James, J. (1980). *Entrance into juvenile prostitution.* Washington, D.C.: National Institute of Mental Health.

Kent, J. (1976). A follow-up study of abused children. *Journal of Pediatric Psychology, 1,* 25-31.

Kline, D. F. (1987). *Long term impact of child maltreatment (abuse, neglect, and sexual abuse) on the victims as reflected in further contact with the Utah Juvenile Court and the Utah Department of Adult Corrections* (Grant No. 90-CA-1200-01). Logan, UT: Utah State University, Developmental Center for Handicapped Persons.

Kratcoski, P. C. (1982). Child abuse and violence against the family. *Child Welfare, 61,* 435-444.

Lewis, D. O., & Shanok, S. S. (1977). Medical histories of delinquent and non-delinquent children: An epidemiological study. *American Journal of Psychiatry, 134,* 1020-1025.

Lewis, D. O., Shanok, S. S., & Balla, D. A. (1979). Perinatal difficulties, head and face trauma, and child abuse in the medical histories of seriously delinquent children. *American Journal of Psychiatry, 136,* 419-423.

Lewis, D. O., Shanok, S. S., Grant, M., & Ritvo, E. (1984). Homicidally aggressive young children: Neuropsychiatric and experiential correlates. In R. A. Mathias, P. DeMuro, & R. S. Allinson (Eds.), *Violent juvenile offenders: An anthology.* San Francisco: National Council on Crime and Delinquency.

Lewis, D. O., Shanok, S. S., Pincus, J. H., & Glaser, G. H. (1979). Violent juvenile delinquents: Psychiatric, neurological, psychological, and abuse factors. *Journal of the American Academy of Child Psychiatry, 18,* 307-319.

Lourie, I. S. (1977). The phenomenon of the abused adolescent: A clinical study. *Victimology.*

Lynch, M. A., & Roberts, J. (1982). *Consequences of child abuse.* New York: Academic Press.

Martin, H. P., & Beezley, P. (1977). Behavioral observations of abused children. *Developmental Medicine and Child Neurology, 19,* 373-387.

Martin, H. P., Beezley, P., Conway, E. F., & Kempe, C. H. (1974). The development of abused children. In I. Schulman (Ed.), *Advances in pediatrics* (Vol. 21). Chicago: Year Book Medical.

Martin, N. (1972). The child and his development. In C. N. Kempe & R. E. Helfer (Eds.), *Helping the battered child and his family.* Philadelphia: J. B. Lippencott.

McCoard, W. D. (1983). Ohio project uncovers abuse/runaway links. *Midwest Parent-Child Review,* 8-9.

Morse, C. W., Shaler, O.J.Z., & Friedman, S. B. (1970). A three-year follow-up study of abused and neglected children. *American Journal of Diseases of Children, 120,* 439-446.

Mouzakitis, C. M. (1981). An inquiry into the problem of child abuse and juvenile delinquency. In R. J. Hunner & Y. E. Walker (Eds.), *Exploring the relationship between child abuse and delinquency.* Montclair, NJ: Allanheld/Osmun.

National Center on Child Abuse and Neglect (1982). *Executive Summary: National study of the incidence and severity of child abuse and neglect.* DHHS Publication No. OHDS 81-30329. Washington, DC: Government Printing Office.

Pagelow, M. D. (1982). *Exploring connections between childhood violence and later deviant behavior.* Paper presented at the Annual Meeting of the American Sociological Association, San Francisco.

Rhoades, P. W., & Parker, S. L. (1981, September). *The connections between youth problems and violence in the home.* (DHHS Grant No. 10-4-1—80101). Portland: Oregon Coalition Against Domestic and Sexual Violence.

Shanok, S. S., & Lewis, D. O. (1981). Medical histories of abused delinquents. *Child Psychiatry and Human Development, 11,* 222-231.

Smith, C. P., Berkman, D. J., & Fraser, W. M. (1980). *A preliminary national assessment of child abuse and neglect and the juvenile justice system: The shadows of distress.* GPO Report No. 1980-311-379:1371. Washington, DC: Office of Juvenile Justice and Delinquency Prevention.

Starr, R. H., Jr. (1982). A research-based approach to the prediction of child abuse. In R. H. Starr, Jr. (Ed.), *Child abuse predictions: Policy implications.* Cambridge, MA: Ballinger.

Steele, B. (1975). Child abuse: Its impact on society. *Journal of Indiana State Medical Association, 68,* 191-194.

Steele, B. (1976). Violence within the family. In R. E. Helfer & C. H. Kempe (Eds.), *Child abuse and neglect: The family and the community.* Cambridge, MA: Ballinger.

Terr, L. C. (1970). A family study of child abuse. *American Journal of Psychiatry, 127,* 665-671.

Weinbach, R. W., Adams, D. E., Ishizuka, H. A., & Ishizuka, K. I. (1981). Theoretical linkages between child abuse and juvenile delinquency. In R. J. Hunner & Y. E. Walker (Eds.), *Exploring the relationship between child abuse and delinquency.* Montclair, NJ: Allanheld/Osmun.

Welsh, R. S. (1976). Severe parental punishment and delinquency: A developmental theory. *Journal of Clinical Child Psychology, 5,* 17-21.

Wenet, G. A., Clark, T. R., & Hunner, R. (1981). Perspectives on the juvenile sex offender. In R. J. Hunner & Y. E. Walker (Eds.), *Exploring the relationship between child abuse and delinquency.* Montclair, NJ: Allenheld/Osmun.

West, D. J. (1969). *Present conduct and future delinquency: First report of the Cambridge Study in Delinquent Development.* New York: International Universities Press.

West, D. J. (1982). *Delinquency, its roots, careers, and prospects.* Cambridge, MA: Harvard University Press.

West, D. J., & Farrington, D. P. (1973). *Who becomes delinquent? Second report of the Cambridge Study in Delinquent Behavior.* London: Heinemann.

West, D. J., & Farrington, D. P. (1977). *The delinquent way of life.* London: Heinemann.

Youth Development Bureau (1978). *Runaway youth.* DHEW Publication No. OHDS 78-26054. Washington, DC: Government Printing Office.

PART III

Wife Abuse

8

An Existential Approach to Battering

Kathleen J. Ferraro

Attempts to explain violence directed at women by their lovers and husbands have focused on three major areas: the social system, political-historical relations, and individual characteristics. The purpose of this chapter is neither to review nor to critique contemporary theories of woman battering, but to offer an alternative perspective. This perspective is termed an existential approach to battering. The term *existential* appears in many disciplines, so it is important to specify its essential meaning for our purposes. Basic to the existential approach is the emphasis on the social meanings of actions, the image of humans as active agents in the creation of social reality (Douglas & Johnson, 1977; Kotarba, 1979). It represents an effort to tie together different levels of reality, from the individually interpreted meanings of face-to-face situations to the more objectified cultural and historical meanings. An existential approach gives primacy to the self and situations of interaction that the self confronts.

In the analyses of other substantive areas, the hallmark of an existential approach is its focus on the meanings of situations for the individuals involved. Accordingly, social reality can be understood only by focusing on the actors' perspectives. This is also true of the approach outlined here. But this focus does not preclude the recognition of influences beyond the immediate perceptual field of actors. Structural, economic, cultural, and political forces play a part in the perceptions of interacting individuals, even if their influence is not felt or known immediately. The meanings of actions reflect the boundaries imposed by the dominant discourse, as well as politically imposed material and relational boundaries. For example, a man who is angry that his wife does not have dinner on the table upon his return from work is creating meanings that reflect traditional assumptions

AUTHOR'S NOTE: I would like to acknowledge the helpful suggestions and criticisms contributed by Peg Bortner, John Johnson, and Rhonda Shapiro.

about the sexual division of labor, and the nuclear family. Whether that anger is expressed as violence or dialogue, or is internalized as resentment is also related to cultural expectations about the appropriate response to feelings of anger. A theoretical focus on the actor's perspective must also be cognizant of macro contexts that are elaborately, inseparably connected to the interactions of an intimate dyad. Empirical work on battering depends on an adequate portrayal of these contexts. The perception of threat to males in intimate dyads occurs within the context of patriarchal assumptions about appropriate male authority and dominance.

Dominance and Male Identity Under Patriarchy

A basic premise of patriarchy is that males are uniquely qualified to conduct the business of the civil society and to maintain order within the private realm. Patriarchal law, religion, philosophy, and morality stress the superiority of males and their consequent responsibility and right to control society and the women and children in their own families. Under patriarchy, women's obedience to male authority is exchanged for protection from other males, and material security (Coltheart, 1986).

The social stature of men is linked to their abilities to control those around them. Men who are leaders in the civil or economic realms are accorded higher esteem than men who have no subordinates. Thus the president of a corporation is more prestigious than a line worker in a factory. But even the line worker may achieve social status through the domination of a wife and children.

Under capitalist patriarchy, the opportunities to dominate are not equally distributed among men of different classes and races. But the ideology of male dominance is linked to the identity formation of all men. Men who do not control anyone else are likely to be perceived as boys rather than as adult men. For men who lack any control in the civil realm, dominance within the private realm of the home becomes their sole avenue for establishing a sense of self in control of others.

The structures of patriarchy have eroded over the past 20 years as they have been challenged and rejected by the women's rights movement. The ideology of male dominance, however, continues and remains an important aspect in the development of male identity. Social and self-esteem for males in the United States and most Western nations remains linked to the perception of control over at least one other.

Threat to the Self in the Intimate Dyad

For the purposes of this essay, the self is understood as the meaning of the individual's essential being to him- or herself, including those feelings and actions regarded as definitive for a particular point in time. A threat is anything that is disruptive to the sense of continuity and control of these meanings. Threats fall along a continuum with mild annoyance at one end to life-threatening events at the extreme. Life-threatening events are usually unexpected and consuming. They demand immediate attention, and usually, an all out effort to save the self. Natural disasters, life-threatening illnesses, attacks by strangers, and accidents all constitute life-threatening events. The physiological response to such threats is that of fight or flight. The choice of response will depend on one's strength and resources, past experiences, and cultural context. A violent fight is most likely to ensue when a specific opponent can be identified, the victim is of at least equal strength or has other resources at his or her disposal, and the attack occurs in a cultural context that encourages violence as a defensive tactic.

For men who batter their wives, most domestic violence is *not* a response to a life-threatening situation. They are not reacting to a sense that physical annihilation is imminent. For women who are the victims of brutal physical attacks in their marriages, the awareness of impending doom is often blocked by the enduring sense of trust and commitment that emerges in marriage (Ferraro & Johnson, 1983). The high percentage of female murders that occur within marriage attests to the failure to respond with fight or flight to threats from a violent husband. It is important to remember, however, that "flight" may be internal, through techniques of rationalization, or may be blocked through fear of retaliation and lack of resources.

The perception of threat to the self of violent husbands is more symbolic than are physical attacks. Batterers are usually not threatened with physical violence when they batter their wives. Their perception of threat is tied to the feelings, meanings, and actions that they regard as critical for continuity and survival of the self. Anything that an intimate other does or says that violates the batterer's expectations of allegiance and support of his sense of self is interpreted as a threat.

An individual is not cognizant of the totality of feelings and meanings that constitute a sense of self. Some actions are so threatening to one's sense of self that they are culturally, or subculturally, prohibited. But for the most part, the meanings that are most important to a sense of self remain undefined until they are threatened. One may be unaware of the centrality of dominance and control to their sense of self, yet become agitated and aggressive when those aspects of self are threatened. Perceptions of dominance and control are developed sequentially and symbolically within a cultural context that assigns significance to words and deeds. For example, turn taking in conversations, service of food, and seating arrangements may be implicated in displays of dominance or submission. Interpretation of behaviors is culturally and situationally specific. Thus a wide array of actions by others may be perceived as threatening, even if there is no intent to threaten.

There is an implicit expectation within marriage that one's spouse will support and nurture one's sense of self. Often, however, the needs of one partner impinge on the needs of the other. Therefore, tension is developed in the course of mediating acquiescence or resistance to the other's demands. Both partners are aware, at least subliminally, that allegiance to the other's self is strained and unnatural. The commitment of each partner is under scrutiny. The meanings of actions and words are open to negotiation and are potential symbols of allegiance or rejection. The conscious intent of the other is not important in the development of perceptions of threat. The individual perceives the other as threatening based on his or her own needs and ideas. When these are unarticulated, subterranean expectations, reactions to threat are particularly unpredictable and uncontrollable.

The Sequential Character of Threatening Categories

The perception of threat within marriage follows a developmental sequence. The meanings of a spouse's actions and words emerge over time as events gain symbolic significance. Discrete incidents, meaningless in themselves, are grouped into a perceptual category with loaded meaning. Each time similar events occur, they reinforce the perception of threat. Very minute, trivial incidents may be assigned to these perceptual categories and instigate a violent response, much to the bewilderment of the other.

This pattern is repeated over and over again in violent marriages. To outsiders, the violent response often seems unreasonable and unexplainable. Many have concluded that such men are sick, or that they have been programmed to respond violently through violence in their families of origin. But the response of "fight" makes sense if the perceptions of a violent man are taken seriously. His perceptions, regardless of their objective validity, are that his wife is bent on attacking him. His violent response is an effort to subdue the threat she represents. The response is not justified, but it is understandable *from his frame of reference.*

It is important to emphasize at this point that this approach is not an attempt to locate the cause of battering within the victim. On the contrary, the attempt to define dominance as central to masculine identity, and the consequent need for real and symbolic support of this identity, illustrates the untenable position battered women are in. The linkage of dominance over his wife to this basic sense of self results in the extension of control to almost every aspect of her behavior. And demonstrations of dominance, because they are symbolic, may become inaccessible to the wife. She may not even know what is threatening to him. As discussed below, even a woman who is intent on demonstrating subordination to her husband may be unable to meet ever-escalating demands or convince him of her loyalty.

While the concept of threat to the self situates battering within a meaningful context, it does not explain why some men respond with violence to this threat while others do not. Nor does it explain why most women do not use violence against men who denigrate them. In answer to why some, but not all, men physically batter their wives, it may be that other forms of violence serve to reestablish dominance. Emotional abuse, physical or emotional withdrawal, assaults against children, affairs with other women, or denial of money are all means of getting back at someone perceived as "disloyal," or "disobedient." It is also true that some men communicate feelings of betrayal directly to their wives. It may then be possible either to reduce that need to control or to renegotiate the meanings of actions that threaten the sense of control.

If the need to dominate and control lies behind men's violence toward wives, changing that need would be a prerequisite to eliminating violence. If only the expression of violence is prohibited (through punitive law or therapy), the threat to the dominating self remains a cause for cruelty.

Women generally do not respond to threats to their selves with violence toward their husbands for a variety of reasons. The lack of any form of resistance of women to oppression is a question of much interest and debate in contemporary feminist literature. Because of the power relations between men and women, women have much to lose through a violent response. They are generally physically weaker than their husbands, and are thus more likely to be injured in retaliation. They are also usually economically dependent on their husbands. Also, use of violence by a woman is inconsistent with the dominant ideology of both femininity and maternity. Violent women are likely to face criminal sanctions and loss of custody of their children in contested cases. On the other hand, Chesler (1986) found that even men who batter their wives got custody of their children when they wanted it in most cases. The use of violence by a subordinate group against a dominant group is strongly sanctioned. Thus even when women's sense of self is threatened by their husbands' words and deeds, they usually will not risk the consequences of responding violently.

The sequential quality of meanings is a key aspect of the existential approach. To view interactional events in isolation is to render them unintelligible, since the observer is denied access to the processes through which they have gained meaning in the intimate dyad. Perceptions of the other are rooted in prior experiences that give direction to development of meaning in the immediate situation. The threatening potential of any topic is known only through reflection on prior conflicts. The entire process may be hidden even to the violent man, since the development of meaning is gradual and unintended.

Characteristics of Violent Men

Preliminary data on violent men indicates that they are relatively unreflective about their feelings and needs.[1] They do not recognize stress or anger until it is out of control. They seldom discuss problems or feelings with others, and generally do not acknowledge feelings they define as socially unacceptable, such as sadness, fear, and loneliness. They also have difficulty acknowledging emotions that are not traditionally masculine, such as affection, dependency, joy, and silliness. Their notions about male and female roles in society tend to be traditional, particularly with regard to male strength, self-control, and dominance over others. These characteristics relate to the perception of threat to the self within marriage in two main ways. First, traditional beliefs about sex roles set up expectations for submissiveness on the part of their wives. Submissiveness does not relate only to acceptance of traditional domestic responsibilities, but more generally, to acceptance of the husband's definition of the relationship. His preferences of life-style, child rearing practices, sexual activities, and economic decisions take precedence. Second, the remoteness of feelings and needs results in ignorance of demands of the self. The perception of threat develops over time, but the violent man does not intervene early in the process largely because of a lack of awareness of feelings of betrayal. The accumulation of hurt feelings and resentments then becomes unmanageable. He is unable to know or express what is bothering him. Then a minor incident may trigger a violently angry response.

Threatening Actions and Words

It is not possible to specify the situations that will produce battering, because it is only the meaning of those situations to the violent man that lead to the perception of threat. These meanings are subjective and vary even within the individual over time. However, the themes of loyalty and control recur in scenarios of perceived threat.

Loyalty. The most general theme is loyalty. Loyalty is demonstrated through faithfulness and acceptance. Individuals vary in their needs for expressions of loyalty. The less certain one is of the loyalty of others, the more stringent his or her requirements for proof of its existence. Loyalty may be a demonstration of solidarity. When domination is desired, loyalty is required to ensure control. Political despots demand unquestioning allegiance, and severely punish expressions of uncertainty. So also do spouses who are insecure about the fidelity of their loved one develop excessive need of demonstrations.

Married individuals expect their spouses to express preference for them as lovers and as companions. They look for signs that demonstrate enjoyment in being together. The willingness to be physically close, to share feelings and ideas, and to do things together is a sign of loyalty. Refusal to talk, spend time with, or be intimate with a spouse is indicative of disloyalty. When suspicions of disloyalty emerge, demands for demonstrations of commitment increase. Demonstrations of loyalty become a focal concern and are monitored closely.

In a situation in which loyalty is uncertain, friendship and closeness with others becomes a threat. The more involved a spouse becomes with others, the more they give evidence of rejection. Therefore, friendships with outsiders or other family members become a point of contention. The extreme possessiveness of violent men has been noted by others (Dobash & Dobash, 1979; Pagelow, 1981). This possessiveness emerges in a context of uncertain loyalty in which time spent with others is viewed as a statement of preference for them over the husband. He will become sullen and irritable about her involvement with others. She, in turn, becomes exasperated by his possessiveness and begins to withdraw. He interprets this as further rejection and becomes more concerned about her loyalty and becomes more possessive. Eventually, her loyalty to him actually is undermined. His sense of threat is expanded, and he may become violent.

Even children may be viewed as threats to a wife's ultimate loyalty to her husband. Ironically, the husband desires children and is responsible for impregnation. Yet there is considerable evidence that the presence of a fetus coincides with the onset of violence (Dobash & Dobash, 1979; Gelles, 1974; Pagelow, 1981; Walker, 1979). Children do bring additional responsibilities that increase pressure on parents. But beatings directed at pregnant abdomens, especially when violence did not occur before pregnancy, seems to indicate resentment toward the fetal intruder. As one of Walker's informants explained:

> He didn't really start to beat me until I started showing how pregnant I was, until my belly started swelling. Then it was like he was jealous of that baby, before he was even born. He was jealous of my babies even when he went in the Navy. He would come home and beat them and beat me. (Walker, 1979, p. 119)

Other family members, especially the wife's relatives, may also be perceived as threats to her loyalty. Both partners, especially in youthful marriages, must move away from commitment to their families of origin to their families of procreation. Individuals demonstrate loyalty to their spouses by making decisions without the interference of in-laws, by not spending all free time with relatives, and by promoting the interests of their spouses while in the presence of parents. When a husband feels that his wife is more strongly attached to her own family than to him, his sense of loyalty is threatened. He will become jealous of time she spends with her family, and act in ways that alienate him from them. The allegiance of her family undermines his ability to control her.

Friends of the same age pose the greatest problems for a man unsure of his wife's loyalty. This group represents rivals for companionship and sexual involvement. Involvement with them is purely a matter of free choice, rather than family obligation. Time spent with friends is an expression of interest, and that interest may be threatening to a man needing constant reassurance of his wife's loyalty. Sexual jealously, a form of insecurity regarding a spouse's loyalty, is a common theme in the literature on violent marriages (Dobash & Dobash, 1979; Hilberman & Munson, 1978; Pagelow, 1981; Stacey & Shupe, 1983; Walker, 1979). Belief in a spouse's sexual fidelity is a vulnerable aspect of self to most members of Western society. Whitehurst's survey of 142 adult students and businessmen found 62% of the sample expressed the belief that acting violently in a situation involving a spouse's extramarital affair was justified (Whitehurst, 1971). Fear of a wife's promiscuity may be so strong that husbands fantasize lovers and develop paranoid perceptions of their wives' intentions. This leads to excessively controlling behavior. An extreme example from my research illustrates this point.

Sara[2] had a 3-year-old child from a prior relationship and was eight months pregnant with the child of her lover. He was so concerned about her sexual fidelity that he locked her in their small trailer each morning before leaving for work. The locked door and the small windows made her escape impossible, even if she had been interested in pursuing a sexual relationship. He nevertheless returned each day to accuse her of being unfaithful, and to beat her for her transgressions.

The need to ensure loyalty, including sexual fidelity, may become such a consuming concern that the man loses all sense of rationality, as in the example above. He may view the slightest indication of disloyalty as a vicious attack on his sense of self. An attempt to leave such a man only confirms his suspicions of disloyalty. He may respond with violence toward himself or his wife. The following example from a recent court case illustrates this process. Cindy's husband was violent for most of their nine-month marriage. He was extremely possessive and monitored her every move. He followed her around the house while she showered, dressed, or did housework. He listened in on all her phone calls. If she wanted to go to a convenience store to buy cigarettes after returning from her late shift job, he would get up from bed and ride with her. After several months of physical and psychological abuse, Cindy decided to leave him. She told a friend of her decision, and the friend relayed the information to Cindy's husband. That night while Cindy was asleep her husband came home in a rage. He took all the phones out of the house and put them on the porch. He kicked, beat, and threw Cindy against the wall. He told her she would never leave him. Finally, he got a loaded gun and told her he was going to kill her. He then placed the gun in her hands, pointed it at himself, and pulled the trigger. When the police arrived, Cindy was not believed, but was arrested and charged with murder.

These cases of severe, apparently senseless, violence point out the relationship between perceived threat to the self and violence. For these men, even the idea that their wives might be disloyal was an intolerable threat to their selves to which they responded with violence.

Control. Closely related to the theme of loyalty is that of control. In the cases above, loyalty was guarded through excessive possessiveness that often took the form of efforts to control women's movements and involvements. A sense of control as an aspect of self, however, is somewhat separate from the issue of loyalty. Control within the intimate dyad involves domination of the other's will. A sense of control as an aspect of the self is demonstrated not only through loyalty, but through obedience, conformity, and submissiveness.

Within the intimate dyad, decisions are made regarding life-style and routine. Patterns of sleeping, eating, working, recreation, and sexual activity are all negotiated in the intimate dyad. Most people bring expectations regarding these patterns to their marriages based on their childhoods. Every family develops its own solutions to the issues of how mundane living ought to be organized. For men whose selves are critically linked to a sense of control, these decisions are indicative of ability to dominate the family setting.

For violent men, decisions about how income is made and spent, how children are cared for, when and how often sexual relations occur, meal preparation, and leisure activities constitute occasions for asserting control. When wives question these activities, through words or actions, they threaten their mate's sense of self. Control and its manifestation take on a highly symbolic character in the intimate dyad, and have a sequential quality. Conflicts over trivial matters may be the battleground in which control is established, so that future violations of the male's expectations constitute a threat to control.

In her ground breaking work on woman battering, Del Martin pointed out the trivial nature of events preceding assaults on wives:

> Women reported these reasons: she prepared a casserole instead of fresh meat for dinner; she wore her hair in a pony tail; she mentioned that she didn't like the pattern on the wallpaper. (Martin, 1976, p. 49)

Such examples clearly indicate the lack of intentional provocation of abuse, which has been noted by others (Dobash & Dobash, 1979; Pagelow, 1981; Stacey & Shupe, 1983; Walker, 1979). Why would any sane person become violent for such innocuous actions? In each case, the wives' actions could be interpreted as threats to their husbands' control. The ability to determine what is served for dinner, how his wife wears her hair, and what wallpaper graces the walls establishes his control over the domestic sphere. The most casual remark may be interpreted as an intentional threat to the control that is so crucial to the husband's sense of self. His use of violence is based on the threat to his self, rather than the specific incident preceding the abuse.

The symbolic and developmental character of threats is exemplified by incidents of abuse triggered by the perception of threats to the husband's control. In Ellen's case, for example, the issue of clothes and makeup was symbolic of her husband's control over her. By insisting on plain, loose-fitting clothes and no use of makeup, Steven maintained a sense of control over other men. Steven used ridicule to enforce his view of how Ellen should dress. When she wore makeup he mocked her, and asked who she was trying to impress. He objected to her purchase of any new clothing, insisting that she wear only old blue jeans and loose fitting T-shirts. Ellen was fully aware of Steven's belief that he should control her physical appearance. She knew that anything she did to enhance her appearance, including tucking in her shirt instead of wearing it loose, constituted a threat to his authority. On her birthday, she received a blouse from her mother that she put on to wear to a meeting she was attending without Steven. He told her she could not wear the blouse, and after insisting that she would, Steven beat her. It was not only her insistence on wearing the blouse that evening that triggered Steven's abuse. It was the history of his symbolic control, through determining her appearance that was questioned by wearing the new blouse.

The Complex Pattern of Threats to the Self

The examples described above demonstrate that issues of loyalty, sexual fidelity, and control are intertwined. Perceptions of threat to the self involve complicated patterns that include a variety of issues coalescing to produce a threatening situation. For the individual actor, the sources of threat are not discrete and predictable. Women's attempts to prevent perceptions of threat, in order to avert violence, often fail because of the complexity of issues involved.

In most cases of abuse, men are responding to several issues simultaneously. In Ellen's case, Steven was confronted with a direct verbal rejection of his demands, an interference by his mother-in-law in the form of the blouse, and Ellen's preference for attending a meeting without him. Her birthday, a day that is usually celebrated as special, was an occasion for demonstrating his lack of concern with her preferences. Loyalty and control were both at issue, and Ellen's decision to choose her own clothing was the trigger to Steven's perception of threat.

The influences of stress on woman battering is often mentioned (Gelles, 1974; Straus, Gelles, & Steinmetz, 1980). Straus et al. (1980) indicate that their measures of stress and spouse abuse found a positive correlation. Straus et al. used an 18-item scale including problems related to work, family, money, and the legal system. Exactly how these factors contribute to increased rates of woman battering is not addressed. Focusing on the meaning of events to the actor, these background stress factors could be seen to weaken the sense of self. Unemployment, the death of a close relative, financial problems, all undermine confidence in the meanings that constitute the self. Insecurity engendered by stressful events paves the way for more critical evaluations of the intimate other. When the self is under attack from external sources, internal supports must be especially strong. The slightest deviation from complete support may be interpreted as a threat in a situation of instability.

Double Binding

In Denzin's (1984) phenomenological analysis of family violence, he calls attention to problems created by using violence as a response to perceived threats. According to Denzin,

> Contradictory negative and positive injunctions are repeatedly invoked in a field of experience that cannot be escaped. The family is trapped in its own negative field of violent experience. Families of violence are caught in double binding patterns of interaction that increase hostility, conflict and the collapse of the family as a unitary system of selves. (Denzin, 1984, p. 40)

For the abuser in violent families, his violent response to threats gains immediate compliance and triumph. But the long range consequences of violence are alienation and mistrust. The loyalty he seeks to ensure through violence is prohibited through his betrayal of trust in his use of violence. His wife can give only the appearance of loyalty, since she knows that, here, trust can be shattered by his violence. The husband senses his wife's hostility and becomes more needy of reassurance of her commitment to him. He scrutinizes her actions more closely, and finding them insufficient to prove her support, becomes violent. She is then even less capable of placing her trust in him, and the process intensifies.

The intimate dyad is caught in a double bind in which attempts to strengthen the sense of self produce more conflict and violence. Each partner seeks to reestablish the trust that existed prior to the abuse, but is confronted with the reality of betrayal. Attempts to convey confidence are viewed by the guilt-ridden abuser as necessarily inauthentic.

The ultimate example of the double bind is Eugene O'Neil's Hickey in *The Iceman Cometh*, who ultimately murders his wife because she is perpetually so understanding of his extramarital affairs!

> I couldn't forgive her for forgiving me. I even caught myself hating her for making me hate myself so much. (O'Neil, 1946, p. 239)

Gelles (1974), Pagelow (1981), and I (Ferraro, 1981) have all found that violence toward wives increases with the length of marriage. The cycle created by the double bind appears to lead to greater use of force.

Unfortunately, there is little information on couples who have resolved the issue of violence in their relationship. Researchers in the field and service providers are unable to produce more than one or two cases, at most, in which violence has ceased, once begun. Given the double binding that occurs in violent relationships, the prospects for eliminating abuse appear slim.

Methodological Issues

The existential approach attempts to understand violence from the actor's perspective. Yet all of our data on battering is retrospective. It has not been possible to observe battering first hand, and it is unlikely that such data could ever be collected. Even if specific violent events were witnessed, for example, through observation of police interventions, the continuing, ongoing dynamics of the intimate dyad would be lost.

We must, therefore, rely on retrospective accounts, with all of their shortcomings. We could, however, vastly improve the information we have on battering by increasing the number of accounts we have from batterers. Most of the information available is from the wives' point of view. This is unacceptable for a thorough existential analysis.

An existential approach to battering helps develop an appreciation for the complexity of the violent response. Threats to the self are subjective and context bound. Causal analyses that lump abstracted behaviors into independent variables in an attempt to explain violence will inevitably simplify and misrepresent the experience of these behaviors for the actors involved. The meanings of events cannot simply be added as one more variable in a regression equation. Rather, the process of developing meaning must be examined closely within the intimate dyad.

Toward the Elimination of Battering

Strategies for eliminating or reducing battering have ranged from the elimination of patriarchy to increased criminal sanctions for battering to pairing violent with nonviolent couples for advice. If it is true, as suggested here, that battering is a response to a perceived threat to the self, then that threat must be eliminated to stop violence. It has been argued that efforts by wives to nurture rather than threaten their husbands' sense of dominance will rarely succeed in fulfilling exaggerated needs. Most would agree that active participation in one's own domination is a high cost for the avoidance of violence even if it did work. The other alternative for eliminating threat, then, is to change men's need to dominate wives.

The goal of eliminating male dominance within marriage is a radical one that threatens the entire structure of capitalistic patriarchy. In fact, it is not likely to be achieved while domination continues to be the hallmark of masculine success in the public realm. While counseling, better law enforcement, and family planning will help reduce levels of male violence within the family, they will not alter the underlying cause. That will be accomplished only with the elimination of the need for domination that is so intimately linked with masculine identity in the ideology of capitalist patriarchy.

Notes

1. These data are part of a long-term research project being conducted by Practical Alternatives to Violence, Phoenix, Arizona.
2. Pseudonyms are used in all case descriptions to protect confidentiality.

References

Chesler, P. (1986). *Mothers on trial.* New York: McGraw-Hill.

Coltheart, L. (1986). Desire, consent and liberal theory. In C. Pateman and E. Gross (Eds.), *Feminist challenges* (pp. 112-123). Boston: Northeastern University.

Denzin, N. K. (1984). Towards a phenomenology of family violence. *American Journal of Sociology, 90,* 483-513.

Dobash, R. D., & Dobash, R. P. (1979). *Violence against wives.* New York: Free Press.

Douglas, J. D., & Johnson, J. M. (Eds.). (1977). *Existential sociology.* New York: Cambridge University Press.

Ferraro, K. (1981). *Battered women and the shelter movement.* Unpublished doctoral dissertation. Arizona State University, Tempe.

Ferraro, K., & Johnson, J. M. (1983). How women experience battering. *Social Problems, 30,* 325-339.

Gelles, R. J. (1974). *The violent home.* Beverly Hills, CA: Sage.

Gelles, R. J. (1979). *Family violence.* Beverly Hills, CA: Sage.

Hilberman, E., & Munson, K. (1978). Sixty battered women. *Victimology, 2,* 460-470.

Kotarba, J. A. (1979). Existential sociology. In Scott McNall (Ed.), *Theoretical perspectives in sociology.* (pp. 348-368). New York: St. Martin's Press.

Martin, D. (1976). *Battered wives.* San Francisco: Glide.

O'Neil, E. G. (1946). *The iceman cometh.* New York: Random House.

Pagelow, M. D. (1981). *Woman-battering.* Beverly Hills, CA: Sage.

Stacey, W. A., & Shupe, A. (1983). *The family secret.* Boston: Beacon.

Straus, M. A., Gelles, R. J., & Steinmetz, S. K. (1980). *Behind closed doors: Violence in the American family.* New York: Anchor/Doubleday.

Walker, L. E. (1979). *The battered woman.* New York: Harper & Row.

Whitehurst, R. N. (1971). Violence potential in extramarital sexual response. *Journal of Marriage and the Family, 33,* 683-691.

9

The Battered Woman Syndrome

Lenore E. Walker

The empirical and clinical data focusing on the various forms of family violence demonstrate that interpersonal violence is learned at home and passed down from one generation to another (see Finkelhor, Gelles, Hotaling, & Straus, 1983, for examples of such research). Although many of the theoretical models have attempted to explain domestic violence as attributable to the interactional aggression styles in families of origins, the issues raised by gender roles, which have not been as emphasized, may be even more significant. For example, Bandura's (1973) theory of modeling aggression is frequently cited to explain how individuals learn aggressive behavior from observing or experiencing such abuse in their own homes. Similarly, Berkowitz's (1983) social psychology explanations suggest that aggressive tendencies are stimulated or reinforced by the victim's responses. Yet, neither theory analyzes for the difference in aggressive patterns and responses by males and females. Given the knowledge that gender has major effects on mental health (Walker, 1984b), work roles (Sales & Frieze, 1984), marriage roles (Bernard, 1984) and, in fact, that girls and boys are socialized differently into "gender appropriate" role behaviors (Maccoby & Jacklin, 1974), it is reasonable to expect that male and female sex-role assignments are a mediating factor in passing on the skills permitting use of abusive rather than peaceful means to end family conflicts (Walker & Browne, in press).

The relationship between crime in the streets and criminal assault in the home has been demonstrated by data collected during this author's three-year study of battered women[1] (Walker, 1984a). The women we interviewed reported over twice as many arrests (71% to 34%) and convictions (34% to 19%) for the batterers as compared to nonbatterers with whom they had a relationship. In this study, only 20% of the batterers reportedly limited their violence to their wives. The other 80% also engaged in violent behavior toward other targets, such as child and parent abuse, incest, harming pets, destroying objects, and acting abusively toward other people. Children who live in abusive homes are at a higher risk to become adjudicated as delinquent; often accused of burglary, arson, forgery, prostitution, running away, drug charges, and other assaults. Research also shows that between 50% to 80% or more of incarcerated women have been battered. They are typically found guilty of property crimes, drug offenses, child abuse, and homicide. Although it is rarely part of their defense, most of these criminal acts are committed under duress from an abusive male partner, usually as a way of minimizing his violent behavior. These women are especially vulnerable to further extortion, rape, and physical abuse if confined to a correctional institution (Walker, 1983).

Patterns in Abusive Families

Patterson (1982) and his colleagues, Reid, Tapling, and Lorber (1981) have spent 15 years studying families with aggressive, delinquent boys. Observers, sent to these families' homes, recorded behavioral interactions between family members. They compared the observed behaviors with those collected in similar homes without an identified aggressive delinquent boy. Early in their work, they identified two family types, the nonviolent dysfunctional family and the abusive family that used physical violence. The ratio of positive to negative interactions observed between members of dysfunctional and abusive families differed significantly from "normal" families. More negative behavioral interactions were observed in homes with an aggressive delinquent boy, supporting the social learning theories. However, in abusive families, the negative interactions crossed gender lines. Being mean to females was approved behavior and was rewarded. This was especially true for interactions with the mother. Harshly blaming wives and mothers for all the family member's ills and misfortunes seems to be a norm in families as well as in the larger community. Despite the obvious suggestions from their data to explore the interaction effects of power relationships between men and women as well as other sex-role socialization patterns, the gender factors were largely left unexplored while other coercive family processes were analyzed. Reid (1984), however, is not attempting to understand this process, hypothesizing that their longitudinal data will reveal how those boys who have become sex offenders and spouse abusers learned their behavior.

The significant differences found between dysfunctional and abusive families with aggressive sons were in the performance patterns of negative acts. With dysfunctional and normal families, both positive and negative acts occurred in a fairly regular pattern. In abusive families, however, nasty acts seem to rapidly follow one another, as though they were beads on a chain. Then, there is a period of calm or absence of negative stimuli. Such chaining of negative acts seems to create what Patterson calls a "fogging" effect, making it difficult for the victim to respond effectively. This finding is consistent with battered women's reports of a three-phase cycle of violence; while the tension builds, women initially are likely to control the violence by making an effective response, later it builds to a rapid chaining of aversive acts producing the explosion, and, finally, a period of positive reinforcement, calm, or absence of tension. These patterns lead to an intensity in the relationship, with participants always expecting to be overwhelmed by the rapidity of abusive acts, yet also reinforced by the rewards in the third phase of the cycle.

Kelley (1983), studying child-abuse families, observed the violence in those families on a continuum. Nonviolent positive control of behavior is seen on one end, while an extremely punitive and controlling style is on the other. Psychologically coercive families that do not exhibit actual physical abuse toward the child also show such a wide behavioral control continuum. Social restraints, which often disguise or soften the punitive style outside the home, are not present within families. Parents transmit these standards of interactions, particularly the need for control at all costs, to their children, who in turn pass them on to the next generation, provided no other learning occurs to teach new behavior management skills.

Violent behavior against others tends to escalate as we found in our research of battering relationships (Walker, 1984a). Geen, Stonner, and Shope (1975) found that acts of aggression increased, rather than decreased, the likelihood of an individual being aggressive again. Tavris's (1983) review of the literature on the expression of anger came to a similar conclusion. Others such as Berkowitz (1983) suggest that aggressive tendencies may be stimulated and reinforced when the victim is compliant, passive, or evidences pain. Thus battered people may unwittingly reinforce and increase the pattern of violence by complying with the abuser's demands. Azrin, Holz. and Hake (1963) have demonstrated the escalation of violence because of the victim's tendency to acclimate to punishment. It appears that a batterer/battered person relationship follows its own rules and becomes quite difficult to terminate. And, gender appropriate behaviors of men and women almost guarantee the man will be the aggressive batterer while the woman becomes his victim.

Developmental Issues and Violent Men

The social learning theory explanation that violence is learned and reinforced by its social consequences is well accepted in the domestic violence literature (see for example Finkelhor, Gelles, Hotaling, & Straus, 1983). Sonkin and Durphy (1982) report that the violent men whom they've clinically treated continue to batter women because it works to control a situation and acts as a safe outlet for their feelings of frustration. Most batterers report that they would not have hurt the women they love had the women only done something to fix the situation. When further questioned, they actually mean that it is the woman's fault for not making them feel better. The data our research collected on their childhood homes indicates that their mothers were most likely to engage in both lenient and strict discipline, mostly in an attempt to shape their sons' behavior to avoid abuse from a harsh and punitive father. Perhaps inadvertently, they were taught to expect women to protect them from harm, including their own unpleasant feelings, and to react with rage when forced to do it themselves.

Abusers tend to respond to close personal interactions with an overabundance of negative acts and a deficit of positive behaviors. When analyzed over time, the batterers in our research study provided more behaviors in the tension building and acute battering incident phases than in the more positive loving-contrition stage. As is often found with abused children, batterers needs for attention and reassurance are extreme and their expectations for intimacy unrealistic. This can lead to angry and frustrated feelings when such expectations are not met. It is evidenced by their intrusive personal style, easily triggered responses of anger, pathological jealously, fears of abandonment, and violent outbursts in response to a threat of loss of control. These same behaviors are often used to describe the 2-year-old child's more age appropriate temper tantrums.

Ganley (1981) has suggested that violent men have a deficit in recognizing and differentiating their own emotional arousal cues. All unpleasant feelings tend to get perceived as the same, and therefore, all receive an angry response. Sex-role standards for little boys mandate that they respond to hurt feelings, sadness, fear, insecurity, and the like by turning it into anger and delivering an aggressive response (Pogrebin, 1982). It is entirely consistent to suggest that it is the interaction of sex-role socialization patterns along with socially learned aggressive responses that differentiate why some men who witness violence as children do not grow up to batter, while others who did not come from abusive backgrounds later turn to violence to control their wives and children.

Psychological Effects of Violence on Women

There has been a great deal written about the negative psychological effects living with violence has on women (Walker, 1979, 1981, 1984a; Martin, 1976; NiCarty, 1982; Giles-Sims, 1983; Browne, in press). Much of the literature supports the acceptance of an identifiable pattern of symptoms called Battered Woman Syndrome, and diagnosed in the ICD-9 as its own separate category and in DSM-III under the Post Traumatic

Stress Disorders (American Psychiatric Association, 1981). The clinical syndrome includes features of both anxiety and affective disorders, cognitive distortions including dissociation and memory loss, reexperiencing traumatic events from exposure to associated stimuli, disruption of interpersonal relationships, and psychophysiological disturbances. A hypersensitivity to potential violence occurs that creates an expectation of harm and a readiness to protect and defend oneself. If actual defense is seen as impossible, then the best coping skills are developed to keep the potential harm at a minimum level. For some, it is seen as an impossible task and a passive, helpless reaction is adopted. Such intense concentration on manipulating the environment to keep as safe as possible sets abused persons apart from others who believe their world is a relatively safe place.

The process of learned helplessness has been used to explain the cognitive, affective, and behavioral changes that occur when there is no faith that natural contingent outcomes will happen. It has been used to conceptualize battered women's reactions, or lack of reactions, to repeated physical, sexual, and psychological abuse. Typical battering episodes often involve a combination of physically assaultive behavior, threats, and destruction of property that occur in a rapid succession, similar to the "chaining" of nasty acts that Patterson observed. Women report feeling overwhelmed by the pattern of these acts, perhaps responding to the "fogging" effect observed, and thus reported difficulty in choosing any response other than just trying to wait out the storm. In the early laboratory experiments, Seligman's (1975) animals and human subjects developed the perceptual distortions if they couldn't predict whether their response would result in a successful outcome. It was the lack of prediction of success in managing the negative stimuli that seemed to produce the greatest psychological distress. This explains the battered woman's constant manipulation to control the level of abuse (perhaps to reduce the probability of "chaining" and "fogging") or the giving up of any hope of control; success, if redefined in a distorted but less psychologically destructive way. Some violence victims actually give up and wait to die, much like Seligman's treated rats who could have swum to stay alive when dropped in a tub of water, but instead, drowned almost immediately. Most, however, adapt to the change in their lives and change how they think, feel, and respond to conform to their newly necessary need to feel as safe as possible from a potential attack. This heightened expectation of future violence causes development of a single focus on survival.

Empirical data suggest that women have more training for learned helplessness than do men. The similarity to situational depression has been noted (Abramson, Seligman, & Teasdale, 1978) and women are more likely to be diagnosed with a depressive disorder (see for example, Brodsky & Hare-Mustin, 1980). Sex-role training that encourages girls to be more passive and dependent seems to exacerbate a tendency toward helplessness (Radloff & Rae, 1979; Radloff & Cox, 1981). Our data indicated that battered women perceived their fathers more likely to hold rigid stereotyped gender attitudes (mean = 27.06) as measured by the Attitudes Toward Women Scale (Spence & Helmrich, 1972). They also perceived such stereotyped traditional values in their batterer's attitudes toward women (mean = 25.67) (Walker, 1984a). Rosewater (1982) found that the battered women in her sample were less willing to conform to the rigid gender roles that were expected of them by their abusive mates. These findings suggest that batterers, like rapists, are expressing their rage toward women because the sex-role training women receive to be less powerful than men makes them an easy target victim. A similar analysis is appropriate with children.

Our research measured battered women's childhood experiences of aggression, sex-role attitudes, and other types of noncontingent expectancies. It was hypothesized that childhood experiences of victimization, so common in the histories of battered women, in combination with gender socialization into traditional feminine roles, would increase their later vulnerability to learned helplessness in a violent relationship. We also predicted that the psychological impact of living in an adult violent relationship would produce the same learned helplessness and further concluded that while early childhood experiences can cause such vulnerability, learned helplessness can also develop solely from the adult abusive relationship studied (Walker, 1984a, pp. 86-94). Thus the interaction of gender socialization with aggressive and other noncontingent behaviors can produce an expectancy that victimization is part of a woman's life and the best she can do is to survive with a minimum of harm.

Learned Helplessness Factors

The variables that were thought to measure items that could produce a learned helplessness response were subjected to statistical scaling techniques to see if they clustered into theoretically compatible factors. These are reported in detail elsewhere (Walker, 1984a). Five factors in childhood and seven from an adult battering relationship have been refined and now are used to measure the learned helplessness response in battered women. They can be found in Table 9.1. Further research is needed to quantify these factors but presence or absence gives a general assessment if other evidence of learned helplessness is owing to abuse in the individual's childhood or relationship. This helps support a diagnosis of Battered Woman Syndrome, especially in legal cases in which state of mind is important to determining level of intent, duress, self-defense, parenting ability, or injuries to be compensated.

TABLE 9.1
Learned Helplessness Factors

Childhood factors

_____ battering in home

_____ sexual assault or molestation

_____ critical periods of noncontingent control (i.e., moving, parent loss by death or divorce, alcoholic parent, sibling illness, school problems)

_____ rigid traditionality

_____ health problems

Relationship factors

_____ pattern or violent incidents (includes cycle pattern, frequency and severity of abuse, length of time in relationship)

_____ pathological jealousy, possessiveness, and isolation

_____ sexual assault and bizarre sexual requests and acts

_____ threats to kill (including previous use of a weapon)

_____ psychological torture—Amnesty International definition

  _____ isolation
  _____ induced debility (sleep and food deprivation)
  _____ monopolizing of perceptions
  _____ verbal degradation (name calling, denial of powers, humiliation)
  _____ hypnosis
  _____ drugs
  _____ threats to kill
  _____ occasional indulgences

_____ violence correlates such as cruel and violent acts against other people, child abuse, sexual abuse of children, violence against animals and inanimate objects

Conclusions

It is clear from our data that the psychological impact of living in violence is enormous. We found that over half of the batterers reportedly had abused their children and one-third threatened to do so during a violent episode. The battered women were eight times more likely to batter children when living with a batterer than with a nonbatterer. Almost one-half of our sample had been sexually assaulted as a child, four-fifths had been forced to have sex with their abuser when they said "no" (the definition of marital rape in some states). Much of the literature suggests that the battering is controlled by the abusive men. Rosenbaum and O'Leary (1981), for example, found that the differences between abusive and nonabusive couples were almost all accounted for by the men. Women's reactions to the violence seem to control how badly hurt they get, although our data suggest that the woman has more control during the early period of the tension building period than later on in the cycle.

Berkowitz's (1983) work would suggest that if women could be trained not to demonstrate pain from an attack, perhaps men might give up violence as a strategy. But Azrin et al.'s (1963) research assures us that men will increase the pain tactics, probably beyond the ability to withstand it despite any possible reciprocal pain control training. Patterson (1982) and Reid et al.'s (1981) findings that bursts of negative acts are experienced as more abusive than those that occur one at a time suggests that a new look be taken at what constitutes abuse. It is entirely possible that negative acts that wouldn't be defined as serious abuse if they occurred individually, become abusive stimuli when combined with others in a rapid chainlike delivery. Thus pattern and sequence of what we currently define as discipline needs to be reexamined. This notion also calls for a rethinking of conflict resolution tactics that teach people to look at each event discretely to measure its potential. It is obviously not discrete events but how they group together that has the greatest potential for conflict. Potential harm, then, needs to be calculated from the history of conflict and abuse, not just the single act.

A restructuring of cognitive ideas about traditional sex-role assignments to males and females is seen as critical in learning to raise peace loving people. Nonviolence is not enough, power differences between the sexes need to be eliminated. Our data suggest that it is the rigidity with which sex stereotyped attitudes are held that produces the negative effect. Women perceive that they must do the major amount of compromising when there are wide differences between their own and their partner's attitudes toward women's roles, especially in the home. Men and women must learn to nurture each other; and men can learn from women how to do so effectively.

Nonpunitive, nurturing child-raising techniques will be critical to any effort to make our families a peaceful place in which to live. Our data suggest that fathers' roles in both the batterers and battered women's homes were reportedly strict, punitive, and overly critical, even when they were rarely present. Boys need role models of men who can support and protect them so that they do not grow up to believe that this is a woman's role. Research on the family interactions in those homes where men and women are experimenting with equality should demonstrate a lower rate of coercive as well as sexist behaviors.

No-hitting rules are essential if we are to raise violence-free children. When we hit a child for discipline, we teach him or her that the person who loves you the most has the right to physically hurt you in the name of discipline. When batterers are asked why they abused the women they love, they often respond by saying they had to teach her a lesson or discipline her. As family violence researchers, it is our challenge to find a better way to develop mentally healthy, nonviolent, and nonsexist children.

Note

1. This study was funded by the National Institute of Mental Health, Grant No. R01MH30147, 1978-1981, Lenore E. Walker, Ed.D., principal investigator.

References

Abramson, L. Y., Seligman, M.E.P., & Teasdale, J. D. (1978). Learned helplessness in humans' critique and reformulations. *Journal of Abnormal Psychology, 87*(1), 49-74.

American Psychiatric Association (1981). *Diagnostic and statistical manual* (3rd ed.) (DSM-III). Washington: Author.

Azrin, N. H., Holz, W. C., & Hake, D. F. (1963). Fixed ratio punishment. *Journal of Experimental Analysis of Behavior, 6,* 141-148.

Bandura, A. (1973). *Aggression: A social learning analysis.* Englewood Cliffs, NJ: Prentice-Hall.

Berkowitz, L. (1983). The goals of aggression. In D. Finkelhor, R. Gelles, G. Hotaling, & M. Straus (Eds.), *The dark side of families* (pp. 197-212). Beverly Hills, CA: Sage.

Bernard, J. (1984). Mental health issues of women in a time of transition. In L.E.A. Walker (Ed.), *Women and mental health policy.* Beverly Hills, CA: Sage.

Brodsky, A., & Hare-Mustin, R. (Eds.). (1980). *Women and psychotherapy.* New York: Guilford.

Browne, A. (in press). Assault and homicide at home: When battered women kill. In L. Saxe & M. J. Saks (Eds.), *Advances in applied social psychology* Vol. 3. Hillsdale, NJ: Lawrence Erlbaum.

Finkelhor, D., Gelles, R., Hotaling, G., & Straus, M. (Eds.). (1983). *The dark side of families.* Beverly Hills, CA: Sage.

Ganley, A. (1981). *Participant and trainer's manual for working with men who batter.* (Available from: Center for Women Policy Studies, 2000 "P" Street, NW, Washington, DC, 20036)

Geen, R. G., Stonner, D., & Shope, G. L. (1975). The facilitation of aggression by aggression: Evidence against the catharsis hypothesis. *Journal of Personality and Social Psychology, 31,* 721-726.

Giles-Sims, J. (1983). *Wife battering: A systems theory approach.* New York: Guilford.

Kelley, J. A. (1983). *Treating child abusive families.* New York: Plenum.

Maccoby, E., & Jacklin, C. (1974). *The psychology of sex differences.* Stanford, CA: Stanford University Press.

Martin, D. (1976). *Battered wives.* San Francisco: Glide (now Volcano).

NiCarty, G. (1982). *Getting free.* Seattle: Seal.

Patterson, G. (1982). *Coercive family processes.* Eugene, OR: Castaglia.

Pogrebin, L. C. (1982). *Raising nonsexist children.* New York.

Radloff, L. S., & Rae, D. S. (1979). Susceptibility and precipitating factors in depression: Sex differences and similarities. *Journal of Abnormal Psychology, 88,* 174-181.

Radloff, L. S., & Cox, S. (1981). Sex differences in depression in relation to learned susceptibility. In S. Cox (Ed.), *Female psychology: The emerging self* (2nd ed.). New York: St. Martin's Press.

Reid, J. B., Taplin, P. S., & Lorber, R. (1981). A social interactional approach to the treatment of abusive families. In R. Stuart (Ed.), *Violent Behavior: Social learning approaches to prediction, management and treatment.* New York: Bruner/Mazel.

Rosenbaum, A., & O'Leary, D. K. (1981). Marital violence: Characteristics of abusive couples. *Journal of Consulting and Clinical Psychology, 49,* 63-71.

Rosewater, L. B. (1982). An MMPI profile for battered women. Ann Arbor: *Dissertation Abstracts.*

Rosewater, L. B., & Walker, L. E. (Eds.) (in press). *A handbook of feminist therapy: Women's issues on psychotherapy.* New York: Springer.

Sales, E., & Frieze, I. (1984). Women and careers. In Walker, L.E.A. (Ed.), *Women and mental health policy:* Beverly Hills, CA: Sage.

Seligman, M. (1975). *Helplessness: On depression, development, and death.* San Francisco: Freeman Press.

Sonkin, D., & Durphy, M. (1982). *Learning to live without violence: A handbook for men.* San Francisco: Volcano.

Spence, J. T., & Helmreich, R. (1972). The attitudes toward women scale. *JSAS, 2*(6), 1-51.

Walker, L. E. (1979). *The battered woman.* New York: Harper & Row.

Walker, L. E. (1981). Battered women: Sex roles and clinical issues. *Professional Psychology, 12*(1), 81-91.

Walker, L. E. (1983). *Battered women in the correctional system.* Paper presented at the American Correctional Association Annual Congress, Chicago.

Walker, L. E. (1984a). *The battered woman syndrome.* New York: Springer.

Walker, L. E. (Ed.). (1984b). *Women and mental health policy.* Beverly Hills, CA: Sage.

Walker, L. E. (1984c). Battered women, psychology and public policy. *The American Psychologist.*

Walker, L. E., & Browne, A. (in press). Gender & victimization by intimates. *Journal of Personality.*

10

The Clinical Literature on Men Who Batter: A Review and Critique

James Ptacek

I n the 10 years that wife beating has grown from a "domestic disturbance" to recognition as a social problem, battered wives' testimony has formed the cornerstone of feminist, sociological, and psychological literature on the subject. In contrast, studies of men who batter have appeared, until very recently, relatively infrequently. The most obvious reason for this is that battered women's testimony was seen by many as invaluable to raising the issue in public and providing women with resources. In addition, the shelter movement made it possible for researchers to locate battered women, and these women were more willing to tell their story than were their violent husbands.[1]

Paralleling the recent increase in social services for abusive husbands, a number of clinically oriented articles and books have begun to appear that deal specifically with the batterer. These articles and books are not based on formal empirical studies. Rather, they consist of reports and analyses based on clinical experience with wife beaters and battered women. They are written by social workers, psychologists, psychiatrists, and others in clinical services. The usual format includes a discussion of the characteristics of batterers, some analysis of the causes of the violence, and a recommendation for treatment.

Since there is such a practical need for an understanding of wife beating among those who treat its victims and perpetrators, one can only assume that these articles and books are widely read by social service workers. And since this literature is often so concretely prescriptive, it is probably far more powerful than the more academic research in affecting how clinicians respond to wife beating. Thus the clinical literature not only reflects, but also constructs the way that those in the human services view wife beating. For these reasons, the articles and books on men who batter merit close examination.

We know from research on battered women that, despite the best of intentions, the "helping professions" are not always helpful in meeting the needs of battered women. Hospitals and social service agencies have been criticized for being unprepared to provide meaningful aid to battered women (Gelles, 1976); for irresponsibly prescribing psychotropic drugs as a remedy (Dobash & Dobash, 1979); for blaming battered women for their own suffering (Stark, Flitcraft, & Frazier, 1979; Schechter, 1982); for a failure to see violence as the most important problem (Walker, 1979); and for making the preservation of the marriage a greater priority than the women's safety (Martin, 1976). This review will therefore be as concerned with what the literature reveals about the *clinical perspective* as with what it says about batterers. Three issues will be examined in the clinical literature: gender analysis; victims and victim-blaming; and psychopathology.

Gender Analysis

The relationship between violence against wives and the social structure of women's subordination would appear obvious. We live in a society in which the physical chastisement of wives was legal less than 100 years ago (Davidson, 1977); and in which the prosecution of wife beating as a crime was rare before 1970, and is still the exception today (Lehrman, 1981). Yet in the literature on men who batter, the importance of gender as a significant category of analysis is frequently overlooked, and in some cases, is denied completely.

A look at the language used in the literature to discuss wife beating reveals this lack of a gender analysis. The titles of three of the most recent books on wife beating fail to indicate gender at all (Maria Roy, editor, *The Abusive Partner: An Analysis of Domestic Battering,* 1982; William Stacey & Anson Shupe, *The Family Secret: Domestic Violence in America,* 1983; Jeanne P. Deschner, *The Hitting Habit: Anger Control for Battering Couples,* 1984). While child abuse receives minor treatment in the latter two books, wife beating is the primary focus of both.

Roy's book, which is concerned exclusively with men who batter, represents a dramatic shift from her earlier work (Maria Roy, editor, *Battered Women: A Psychosociological Study of Domestic Violence,* 1977). Gendered terms used in her earlier book have been replaced in her most recent work by gender-neutral terms. Compare these two paragraphs, the first from the 1977 book and the second from her 1982 publication:

Data on parental violence (Fig. 6) are based on each woman's reconstruction and recollection of the events of her own childhood. Information obtained concerning the history of violence was not elicited firsthand from the husbands, but rather from the information reported by the wives sampled. Most of the wives based their information on what their husbands told them over the years, and on the information garnered from their mothers or fathers-in-law. (Roy, 1977, p. 30)

Data on parental violence (Figs. 12A and 12B) are based primarily on the abused partner's reconstruction and recollection of the relevant events of their childhood. Information obtained concerning the abuser's childhood history of violence was not directly elicited from them in most cases, but rather from the information reported by the victim. Most victims garnered their information from their in-laws. (Roy, 1982, p. 29)

The intent of such gender-neutral usage is unclear. Yet the latter excerpt is representative of Roy's writing style in an article presenting data from 4,000 women.

Deschner states that "battered husbands" are very rare. But her most common terms for wife beating are *battering couples, battering adults,* and *consort battering.* Deschner states a preference for the latter term specifically because it is gender-neutral (Deschner, 1984, p. 3). And in an article on "spouse abuse" by Margolin, nearly 6 of 10 pages of text contain no reference to gender whatsoever, not even "husband" or "wife" (Margolin, 1979).

The rationales for such elaborate and linguistically awkward attempts to avoid reference to maleness or femaleness are not obvious. But the consequences of such choices are clear: Issues of gender and power are obscured and regarded as irrelevant to an understanding of wife beating.

There are a number of articles that do present a gender analysis of wife beating. For example, Adams and McCormick present their analysis in these terms:

The abuse of women is the man's problem; the woman is the victim. The use of violence as a method of solving problems and settling differences is a result of three interrelated forces: (1) the socialization of boys to be aggressive and dominant in their social relations; (2) the reinforcement of these values by parents, teachers, and social forces such as the media, television, films, and the use of violence by the police and military; (3) the social norms of patriarchal society which dictate that men are the dominant gender and are free to exercise this power in family life, social relationships, and in the institutions which direct our lives. (Adams & McCormick, 1982)

Other articles include sexism, men's "need" to control women in conjugal relationships, and adherence to traditional sex-role ideology in their analysis (Elbow, 1977; Coleman, 1980; Adams & Penn, 1981; Saunders, 1982a; Star, 1983; Harris, 1984).

Victims and Victim-Blaming

The question of who the victims of husband-wife violence are was made controversial with the publication of "The Battered Husband Syndrome" by Suzanne Steinmetz in 1978. That article, and the subsequent book by Straus, Gelles, and Steinmetz (1980) have been criticized for attempting to establish, on the basis of insufficient evidence, that women's violence against their husbands is extensive and serious enough to merit the label "husband-beating" (Pleck, Pleck, Grossman, & Bart, 1978; Dobash & Dobash, 1979; Gelles, 1979; Wardell, Gillespie, & Leffler, 1983; Breines & Gordon, 1983). At issue is not so much whether women are sometimes violent with men. The issue is whether men are sufficiently victimized by women to justify elevation to the level of a social problem "as a distinct parallel to wife beating" (Steinmetz, 1978, p. 504), as Steinmetz appears to argue. As the study on which the article and the following book were based did not ascertain the extent of self-defensive violence by women, and did not assess the consequences of violent actions (injuries), the evidence to substantiate that "husband-beating" is a widespread social problem is inadequate. Indeed, Gelles's own clarification of the data is titled "The Myth of Battered Husbands" (Gelles, 1979). But this controversy has contributed a notion of men as victims—of batterers as victims—to the clinical literature on men who batter.

An example is the article by Margolin (1979). It was mentioned that Margolin scrupulously avoids mention of gender throughout much of the article. The article begins with a reference to Steinmetz, and thereafter seems to conclude that since violence between husbands and wives is roughly equivalent, no gender distinction is necessary. This is only one way in which the literature on batterers minimizes and distorts women's victimization.

Another way that this occurs is in the equating of wife beating with nonphysical, nonviolent behavior by women. Lion writes:

> On examination, we find that husband battering occurs, too, though it is not often physical; more likely, it is emotional battering. One has only to study marriages in a clinical way to determine that some wives may hold great power over their husbands and manipulate them, exploit them, withhold sexual contact for long periods of time, and behave so as to keep their husbands dependent on them. Wives are usually physically weaker; and battering in its truest sense takes different forms among men and women; thus, men can batter their wives both physically and emotionally, and women can batter men emotionally. (Lion, 1977)

There are several things worth noting here. An assumption of male sexual entitlement is apparent, along with sweeping negative generalizations about women. Clearly, suffering is not limited to physical torment. But to suggest that men are emotionally victimized by women in a manner equivalent to physical beating is to trivialize physical abuse and deny the injustice of violence against wives. Such an analysis appears to have more in common with an age-old mistrust and dread of women than with the evidence of clinical study to which Lion refers.

One last way in which women's victimization is obscured involves the varied uses of the term *victim*. In the clinical literature, victim may refer to one who suffers physically (with the attendant psychological and social consequences), or to one whose suffering is essentially psychological. But it is also used in a third way to refer to a role in an interactional psychological drama. Deschner discusses wife beating in this sense:

> Another truncated cyclical pattern may result from spouses periodically trading victim and persecutor roles. A classic form of this marital game was described by Satir as a victim-persecutor-rescuer triangle. Often three family members play this deadly game, frequently switching roles. (Deschner, 1984, p. 19)

However valuable this conceptualization is for family therapy, there is danger in using "victim" too loosely in analyzing wife battering, in which women's suffering is palpable. A psychodramatic use of "victim" appears to equate physical violence with verbal behavior. In the example following Deschner's discussion above, it is not physical abuse that the batterer suffers, but "verbal persecutions," which Deschner also refers to as "nagging" (Deschner, 1984, p. 19). This psychodramatic sense of victimization is not limited to a discussion of "marital game" interactions in this book. Ostensibly speaking in a nonmarital game role sense, Deschner discusses the batterer as victim:

> Batterers are also victims part of the time. Partly because they fear their own loss of self-control, many behave submissively and tolerate verbal complaints and minor abuse out of fear that if they resist at all their anger will carry them too far. Most battering men seem less skilled at verbal warfare than their wives, so they endure losses in numerous verbal confrontations. In addition they are prey to lonely feelings as their battered partners pull away from them emotionally. Finally, batterers are especially vulnerable to that most painful of human emotions, jealousy. (Deschner, 1984, p. 21)

One may ask, how do loneliness, jealousy, and losing verbal confrontations make one a victim? Does the battered wife who complains and withdraws emotionally "victimize" the batterer? This seems absurd.

One of the consequences of seeing batterers as victims is that in the process, the abuser comes to be seen as less than responsible for the violence. As a result, battered women often absorb part of the blame. Margolin offers as an example of this:

Careful exploration of a couple's history with violence may reveal that both spouses have contributed to the escalation of anger with one spouse being the more verbally assaultive while the other is the more physically abusive. This places each partner in the role of both abuser and victim. The therapist can use this information to acknowledge each partner's pain and confusion as a victim as well as to help each partner accept responsibility for any actions that accelerated the abusiveness. The therapist can also reattribute the violence as a mutual problem rather than the fault of one partner. The goal of this reattribution is not to relieve either partner of responsibility for what has happened but to elicit both spouse's cooperation in seeing that the abusiveness is stopped. (Margolin, 1979, p. 16)

Regardless of the goal, would it be possible for a wife beater under this therapeutic intervention to *not* feel less responsible? Would it be possible for the battered woman to *not* feel blamed?

Other examples of analyses that blame the victim are not uncommon in the literature. Lion speaks of the battered women's "provocation," and states that "the victim may evoke violence in a vulnerable person" (Lion, 1977, p. 127). Faulk describes one type of battered woman as "querulous and demanding" (Faulk, 1977, p. 121). And Shainess begins with the assumption that "in most marriages, the partners are, in some way, psychologically and emotionally on the 'same level'" and constructs a contemporary version of the female masochistic personality (Shainess, 1977, p. 115).

There are a number of articles that dispute an emphasis on the battered woman's responsibility for the violence. In an article on counseling violent husbands, Saunders reviews studies of alleged masochistic behavior, women's psychological traits, and alleged verbal provocation and finds no support for the notion that women cause their own victimization (Saunder, 1982b). Others describe and challenge the batterer's tendency to blame the victim (Elbow, 1977; Adams & Penn, 1981; Harris, 1984).

Psychopathology

Fifteen years ago Richard Gelles published a critique of child abuse as psychopathology (Gelles, 1973). The dominant perception in the research on child abuse, Gelles indicated, was that of the abuser as psychopathological, as somehow mentally "sick." This is too narrow, he argued, because it seeks to explain child abuse with a single factor—psychopathology. It is further inconsistent with other assertions, often in the same articles, that the abuser is in many other ways normal, Gelles pointed out. The research on which the child abuse literature was based was unsound; and in these largely clinical articles, *descriptions* of violent behavior ("the abuser acts out impulsively") were transformed into *explanations* of violent behavior ("the violence arises from poor impulse control"), according to Gelles.

All of these observations are relevant to the literature on men who batter—the dominance of the psychopathological model, the narrowness, the inconsistencies, the inconclusive evidence, the confusion of description with explanation. Over the years, however, the pathological model has been transformed somewhat—disguised, perhaps—with respect to research on wife beaters.

In the earlier articles on men who batter, the references to psycho-pathology in the descriptions of the violence are explicit. Lion speaks of "paroxysmal rage attacks" and the "psychiatric abnormality" and the "mentally disturbed nature of the population" (Faulk, 1977, p. 121, 124). And Shainess refers to "irrational aggressive actions" among males who are "passively aggressive," "obsessive-compulsive" "sadistic," "paranoid," and "borderline" (Shainess, 1977, pp. 114-115).

Some of the more recent articles represent a complete break with the psychopathological model:

> Mental illness does not appear to be a factor in wife abuse. Symptoms of delusional jealously, paranoia, and severe depression may develop from the men's fear of losing their partners rather than from a severe mental disorder . . .

> The social and psychological theories can be integrated by hypothesizing a reciprocal causal relationship between low self-esteem in men and their cultural conditioning to be super achievers, emotionally tough, dominant over women, and possessive of people as well as things. Men who batter can be viewed as being on one end of a continuum of male socialization. To paraphrase one expert in the field, "men who batter are like all other men, only more so." (Saunders, 1982a, p. 2)

In articles such as this, male socialization rather than psychological abnormality is seen as the primary source of violence against wives (Adams & Penn, 1981; Adams & McCormick, 1982; Saunders, 1982a, 1982b; Brisson, 1982; Edelson, 1984; Harris, 1984).

In much of the recent literature examined, however, the overtly pathological language has been replaced by terminology only slightly less explicit. Variations on *impulsiveness* are frequently employed, such as "aggressive impulses," "poor impulse control," or "impulse to batter" (Geller & Walsh, 1978; Garnet & Moss, 1982; Geller, 1982; Star, 1983; Deschner, 1984; Goffman, 1984). Violence is also described in terms of "uncontrollable rage" or "uncontrollable aggression" (Walker, 1979; Geller, 1982; Deschner, 1984; Goffman, 1984). And *explosion* metaphors are often used, such as "violent eruptions," "temper outbursts," or "explosive rage" (Walker, 1979; Coleman, 1980; Pagelow, 1981; Weitzman & Dreen, 1982; Deschner, 1984; Goffman, 1984). Despite the variety of theoretical perspectives that inform these works, the notion that the batterer loses control over his behavior is a common assumption. For example, Geller (1982) uses a family systems perspective, and emphasizes that the batterer is solely responsible for the violence. Yet she speaks of "aggressive impulses," "violent impulses" (p. 202), and "uncontrollable aggression" (p. 200). Geller presents a case study of a couple in therapy in which she instructed the battered woman that "her husband could not continue to argue without hitting her when he needed a cooling off period" (p. 203). Apparently accepting that the batterer was unable to restrain himself, Geller urged the battered woman to mollify her behavior toward her husband in order to avoid further assaults. Goffman (1984), following a social learning approach, also emphasizes the batterer's responsibility. Yet he describes the violence in terms of a "battering impulse" (p. 16), "explosive and uncontrollable rage" (p. 13), and behavior that is "beyond the point of rational control" (p. 32). And Deschner (1984), whose analysis represents an unlikely combination of family systems theory, social learning theory, rational-emotive therapy, and instinct theory, talks of "criminal impulsivity" (p. 60), "uncontrolled and uncontrollable rage" (p. 14), and "instinctual aggressive reactions" (p. 51).

While these expressions suggest an implicit psychopathological model, this is generally accompanied by a denial that the abuser is mentally ill. There is an attempt made to normalize the batterer:

> The abusers who can be worked with within a psychotherapeutic model typically lead normal lives, and aside from the abuse inflicted upon their wives, show no other sign of deviant behavior. They conform to society's mores and values and they are usually good citizens. When they are not being abusive, they relate to their wives normally and most of these men are often good fathers. (Geller, 1982, p. 200)

> Few battering consorts and parents are full-time monsters deserving long prison sentences. Most are needy human beings who are often lovable and even loving. They have acquired a grievous habit of accessing their own primitive violence in order to get their way with family members, and their victims have inadvertently reinforced their attacks by submitting. But between attacks most of them are capable of behaving quite differently toward the victim as well as behaving normally toward other family members, work associates, and others. (Deschner, 1984, p. 21)

The wife beater is presented not as an abnormal individual, but as an unremarkable individual, who perhaps is subassertive and suffers from low self-esteem. His "explosiveness" is seen as anomalous to his general behavior. He is not sick: He has an "anger control problem." In fact, "anger control training" has become one of the more widely recommended strategies for treatment (Margolin, 1979; Deschner, 1984; Goffman, 1984). A survey of 90 agencies offering counseling for batterers indicates that this is one of the most frequently used methods (Deschner, 1984, p. 96).

But despite the apparent differences between the earlier psychopathological characterizations and some of the more recent descriptions of wife beaters, the notion that the batterer has lost control is central to both. In the early literature, the loss of control is organic or psychogenic in origin; the later emphasis is on an undefined impulsiveness, or on a learned response to stress that is so difficult to change that the abuser is seen as helpless. Indeed, there have been attempts to apply Walker's theory of learned helplessness to wife beaters (Ryan, 1981; Deschner, 1984). Regardless of the origin, the batterer is seen as not fully in control, and therefore as not fully responsible. The remedy is not punishment, but therapy. Conrad and Schneider regard this loss of control, which they speak of as "compulsiveness," as a predictable feature of the medicalization of deviance:

> When medical designations of deviance are proposed, they most likely will be based on the notion of "compulsivity." For most cases examined, definitive and uncontestable evidence of biophysiological causation does not exist. In lieu of such evidence, or in addition to ambiguous organic data, some type of "compulsivity" is proposed as the cause of the deviant behavior . . .
>
> Compulsivity denotes that the individual "cannot help it," since the behavior is caused by forces beyond his or her control. Compulsivity, in effect, removes motivation or cause from the will and locates it in the body or mind. (Conrad & Schneider, 1980, pp. 272-273)

This "compulsiveness" is easily recognized both in the pathological references to irrational attacks and in the more recent descriptions of impulsiveness, uncontrollable aggression, and explosiveness. And as the violence is seen as not entirely willed, it is therefore seen as not entirely the batterer's fault.

Perhaps the most critical difference between the earlier psychopathological model and the more recent transformation is that in the latter, the compulsiveness or loss of control is normalized, or more precisely, bracketed from the context of the wife beater's normal behavior. It is as though the perception of the batterer in much of the literature has shifted from one of sickness to one of temporary insanity. In this contemporary construction, the batterer's violence is perceived in terms of brief irrational episodes, a temporary loss of control. The batterer is not abnormal enough to be considered a psychopath, but is not responsible enough to be considered a criminal.

In regard to psychopathology, then, there are two main trends in the recent literature on wife beaters. On the one hand, there is a nonpsychopathological group of articles in which social and cultural determinants are emphasized over psychological abnormality; in which the terminology of psychopathology is abandoned, and the ambiguous language of impulsiveness, uncontrollable rage, and explosiveness is avoided; and in which the batterer's claim of "loss of control" is viewed primarily as an excuse, a way of avoiding responsibility for the violence. On the other hand, in much of the rest of the recent literature, despite the variety of seemingly nonpsychopathological approaches—social learning theory, family systems theory, rational-emotive therapy—there is a continuing and relatively unexamined assumption that the wife beater "loses control" over his behavior. This notion—that the batterer's will is somehow overpowered, that his violence lies outside of the realm of choice, that battering occurs during brief irrational episodes—is consistent with the psychopathological model. The postulate of abnormal psychological causation remains substantially unchallenged.

The notion of the batterer as victim complements this psychopathological theme. As has been shown, the abuser is not only portrayed as a victim of child abuse, but is often depicted as a victim of his wife's verbal and emotional abuse as well. Occasionally, he is seen as a victim of his wife's physical abuse. In some of the recent literature, he is also seen as a helpless victim of an impulse disorder. For example, Walker states that "unlike the psychopath, the batterer feels a sense of guilt and shame at his uncontrollable actions. If he were able to cease his violence, he would" (Walker, 1979, p. 26).

Why do so many recent articles and books appear to take the batterer's claim of "loss of control"—the classic excuse for avoiding responsibility—at face value? One answer may involve what Alan Stone calls therapeutic compassion:

> I have been enormously impressed by the ability of some psychiatrists to [treat] and to feel compassion not only for patients whose values and moral convictions are antithetical to their own, but also for patients who are morally terrible people by all conventional standards: drug pushers, rapists, child molesters, arsonists, etc. But one of the secrets of this therapeutic compassion is that the psychiatrist believes these patients are sick, and that successful treatment will reduce the patient's immoral behavior and alter his values. Therapeutic compassion is not necessarily forgiving, but it is premised on the psychiatrist's ability to believe that immorality is psychopathological. (Stone, 1984, p. 241)

In other words, Stone suggests that the case of a nonjudgmental stance is that the clinician will tend to see immoral behavior as a manifestation of psychological abnormality, as out of reach of the individual's rational control. Such a perspective is offered by Deschner:

> Blaming others must be replaced by a more realistic assessment of their frailties. In treating a battered wife, [rational-emotive therapist] Hauck insisted that she give up viewing her husband as "bad." People, he said,

transgress against others not because they are deliberately evil or obnoxious, but for one of just three reasons: They are ignorant of what they are doing; they are stupid; or they are emotionally disturbed. (Deschner, 1984, p. 82)

Few would deny that compassion is essential for therapeutic work. And such a stance as described by Stone and Deschner may likely facilitate cooperation on the part of batterers. But this kind of trade-off between clinician and batterer—the batterer's participation in counseling in exchange for a morally neutral, psychopathological explanation of his violent behavior—may also have harmful consequences.

From such a stance, the clinician may wittingly or unwittingly be validating the batterer's plea that he is not responsible for the violence, thus strengthening his rationalizations for beating his wife.

And finally, the position presented by Stone and Deschner may completely obscure the batterer's rational motives, and the benefits his violence secures. Physical abuse is often only one part of a pattern of threats, intimidation, coercion, and manipulation that the batterer employs to achieve dominance. In light of this, "anger control training" in and of itself may be an inadequate treatment. Such treatment assumes that the batterer has *lost* self-control; furthermore, the batterer's control over his wife may not necessarily be addressed. Some battered women's activists have asserted that if counseling for batterers succeeds only in teaching men how to control women in nonviolent ways, such programs will be of limited help to battered women.

Conclusion

The clinical literature on men who batter has grown with the increased visibility of batterers to social service workers. Several disturbing trends, however, have been noted. The significance of gender and power to an analysis of wife beating is ignored in some of the most recent literature. The confusion and ambiguity concerning issues of victimization and responsibility represents a related trend. Finally, the psychopathological underpinnings of much of the recent literature is evident in the shift from a notion of sickness to one of temporary insanity as an explanation of wife beating.

This characterization of the batterer as temporarily out of control is represented in these lyrics by Tom Waits:

We do crazy things when we're wounded
Everyone's a bit insane

Like many other of the batterer's rationalizations, however, this notion of loss of control must not be accepted at face value.

Note

1. The terms *battered wives, violence against wives, violent husbands,* and similar expressions will be used to refer to women and the men who abuse them regardless of whether they are actually married. This is done for convenience, but it is also appropriate because the status of women as *wives*—historically, as family members subordinate to their husbands—is one that affects women even if they are only cohabiting with men. This subordinate status is an essential part of the social phenomenon of wife beating (Dobash & Dobash, 1979).

References

Adams, D. C., & McCormick, A. J. (1982). Men unlearning violence: A group approach based on the collective model. In M. Roy (Ed.), *The abusive partner: An analysis of domestic battering.* New York: Van Nostrand Reinhold.

Adams, D. C., & Penn, I. (1981). *Men in groups: The socialization and resocialization of men who batter.* (Available from Emerge, 25 Huntington Avenue, Room 324, Boston, MA 02116)

Breines, W., & Gordon, L. (1983). The new scholarship on family violence. *Signs, 8,* 490-531.

Brisson, N. (1982, Spring). Helping men who batter women. *Public Welfare,* 29-34.

Coleman, K. H. (1980). Conjugal violence: What 33 men report. *Journal of Marital and Family Therapy, 6,* 207-213.

Conrad, P., & Schneider, J. W. (1980). *Deviance and medicalization: From badness to sickness.* St. Louis: C.V. Mosby.

Davidson, T. (1977). Wifebeating: a recurring phenomenon throughout history. In M. Roy (Ed.), *Battered women: A psychosociological study of domestic violence.* New York: Van Nostrand Reinhold.

Deschner, J. P. (1984). *The hitting habit: Anger control for battering couples.* New York: Free Press.

Dobash, R. E., & Dobash, R. (1979). *Violence against wives: A case against the patriarchy.* New York: Free Press.

Edelson, J. L. (1984, May-June). Working with men who batter. *Social Work,* 237-242.

Elbow, M. (1977, November). Theoretical considerations of violent marriages. *Social Casework,* 515-526.

Faulk, M. (1977). Men who assault their wives. In M. Roy (Ed.), *Battered women: A psychosociological study of domestic violence.* New York: Van Nostrand Reinhold.

Garnet, S., & Moss, D. (1982). How to set up a counseling program for self-referred batterers: The AWAIC model. In M. Roy (Ed.), *The abusive partner: An analysis of domestic battering.* New York: Van Nostrand Reinhold.

Geller, J. A. (1982). Conjoint therapy: Staff training and treatment of the abuser and the abused. In M. Roy (Ed.), *The abusive partner: An analysis of domestic battering.* New York: Van Nostrand Reinhold.

Geller, J. A., & Walsh, J. C. (1978). A treatment model for the abused spouse. *Victimology, 2*(3-4), 627-632.

Gelles, R. J. (1973). Child abuse as psychopathology: A sociological critique and reformation. *American Journal of Orthopsychiatry, 43,* 611-621.

Gelles, R. J. (1976). Abused wives: Why do they stay? *Journal of Marriage and the Family, 38,* 659-668.

Gelles, R. J. (1979, October). The myth of battered husbands and new facts about family violence. *Ms.*

Goffman, J. M. (1984). *Batterers anonymous: Self-help counseling for men who batter women.* (Avalilable from: B.A. Press, 1295 North "E" Street, San Bernadino, CA 93405)

Harris, R. N. (1984). *Violent love: The case of battering men.* (Available from R. N. Harris, Department of Sociology and Anthropology, St. John's University, Jamaica, NY 11439)

Lerman, L. G. (1981). Criminal prosecution of wife beaters. *Response to Violence in the Family, 4*(3).

Lion, J. R. (1977). Clinical aspects of wifebattering. In M. Roy (Ed.), *Battered women: A psychosociological study of domestic violence.* New York: Van Nostrand Reinhold.

Margolin, G. (1979). Conjoint marital therapy to enhance anger management and reduce spouse abuse. *American Journal of Family Therapy, 7*(2), 13-23.

Martin, D. (1976). *Battered wives.* New York: Pocket Books.

Pagelow, M. D. (1981). *Woman-battering: Victims and their experiences.* Beverly Hills, CA: Sage.

Pleck, E., Pleck, J. H., Grossman, M., & Bart, P. (1978). The battered data syndrome: A comment on Steinmetz's article. *Victimology, 2*(3-4).

Roy, M. (1977). *Battered women: A psychosociological study of domestic violence.* New York: Van Nostrand Reinhold.

Roy, M. (Ed.). (1982). *The abusive partner: An analysis of domestic battering.* New York: Van Nostrand Reinhold.

Ryan, D. M. (1981). Patterns of antecedents to husbands' battering behavior as detected by the use of the critical incident technique. *Dissertion Abstracts International.* (University Microfilms.)

Saunders, D. G. (1982a). *A model for a skills-oriented group for treating husband-wife violence.* (Available from the Family Violence Research Program, University of New Hampshire, Durham, NH 03824)

Saunders, D. G. (1982b). Counseling the violent husband. In P. A. Keller and L. G. Ritt (Eds.), *Innovations in clinical practice: A source book,* (Vol. I). Sarasota, FL: Professional Resource Exchange.

Schechter, S. (1982). *Women and male violence: The visions and struggles of the battered women's movement.* Boston: South End Press.

Shainess, N. (1977). Psychological aspects of wifebeating. In M. Roy (Ed.), *Battered women: A psychosociological study of domestic violence.* New York: Van Nostrand Reinhold.

Stacey, W., & Shupe, A. (1983). *The family secret: Domestic violence in America.* Boston: Beacon.

Star, B. (1983). *Helping the abuser: Intervening effectively in family violence.* (Available from: Family Service Association of America, 44 East 23rd Street, NY 10010)

Stark, E., & Flitcraft, A. (1983). Social knowledge, social policy, and the abuse of women: A case against patriarchal benevolence. In D. Finkelhor, R. J. Gelles, G. T. Hotaling, and M. A. Straus (Eds.), *The dark side of families: Current family violence research.* Beverly Hills, CA: Sage.

Stark, E., Flitcraft, A., & Frazier, W. (1979). Medicine and patriarchal violence: The social construction of a "private" event. *International Journal of Health Services, 9*(3), 461-493.

Steinmetz, S. K. (1978). The battered husband syndrome. *Victimology, 2*(3-4), 499-509.

Stone, A. A. (1984). *Law, psychiatry, and morality: Essays and analysis.* Washington, DC: American Psychiatric Press.

Straus, M. A., Gelles, R. J., & Steinmetz, S. K. (1980). *Behind closed doors: Violence in the American family.* New York: Anchor/Doubleday.

Walker, L. E. (1979). *The battered woman.* New York: Harper & Row.

Wardell, L., Gillespie, D. L., & Leffler, A. (1983). Science and violence against wives. In D. Finkelhor, R. J. Gelles, G. T. Hotaling, and M. A. Straus (Eds.), *The dark side of families: Current family violence research.* Beverly Hills, CA: Sage.

Weitzman, J., & Dreen, K. (1982, May). Wife beating: A view of the marital dyad. *Social Casework,* 259-265.

11

Concern for Power, Fear of Intimacy, and Aversive Stimuli for Wife Assault

Donald G. Dutton
James J. Browning

The literature on causative factors in wife assault has tended to be dominated by either psychological (Snell, Rosenwald, & Robey, 1964; Faulk, 1974; Scott, 1974; Elliott, 1977; Symonds, 1978) or sociological perspectives (Straus, 1973; Straus, Gelles, & Steinmetz, 1980; Straus & Hotaling, 1980). The former perspective treats wife assaulters as "abnormal" when victim surveys indicate otherwise (Schulman, 1979; Straus, Gelles, & Steinmetz, 1980). In doing so, they often fail to examine "normal" features of assaultive males' learning history that have contributed to his use of violence. The latter perspective is faced with the explanatory task of differentiating those males who are never assaultive from those who are repeatedly assaultive, since neither broad cultural norms nor subcultural norms effectively allow for such differentiation (Dutton, 1984).

Social psychological perspectives are especially well suited to the twin requirements of both locating a man's violence in the "normal" learning environment to which that man has been exposed and to differentiating assaultive from nonassaultive males on the basis of differences in the individual learning environment. Social learning theory (Bandura, 1979) for example, provides an analysis of the origins of aggression (i.e., observation of violence in family of origin, in subculture, on television, or reinforced performance of aggressive acts), and the instigators of aggression (i.e., aversive instigators, such as verbal insults; incentive instigators, such as anticipated benefits; and delusional instigators, such as bizarre belief systems). Both the origins and instigators of aggression provide a means for differentiating the learning and reinforcement milieus for assaultive and nonassaultive males. Furthermore the social learning perspective on the regulators of aggression with its emphasis on the function of aggression in generating reinforcers (such as gains in social power, and termination of aversive treatment) and the maintenance of aggression through "neutralization of self-punishment" (Bandura, 1979) is particularly applicable to wife assault. The neutralization of self-punishment refers to the variety of cognitive machinations that assaultive males may go through in order to justify (and maintain) a habit of wife assault. This would include the cognitive restructuring of their assaultive behavior in order to make it seem less reprehensible (through, for example, palliative comparison with someone worse, euphemistic labeling of the behavior, and so on) displacing responsibility for the behavior to alcohol or the victim herself, and minimizing the consequences of the behavior. Social learning analyses have had their greatest influence on the wife assault literature, not in the area of research on causes but in their contribution to a theoretical foundation for treatment of assaultive males (Ganley, 1981). Nevertheless, most professionals working with assaultive populations have witnessed the operation of delusional instigators, aversive instigators, and neutralization of self-punishment in the self-descriptive commentary of men in the groups. Just as clearly, however, what constitutes an "aversive instigator" for one man is not perceived as aversive by another man. In our own treatment groups, two particular dimensions repeatedly emerged in statements of the men in the groups that have directed our attempt to outline common sources of relationship-specific aversive instigators. These are (1) when the man feels he is losing power or control to the woman on an important issue and (2) in particular, when that important issue is the degree of intimacy or socioemotional distance in the relationship.

The selection of these particular concepts for research was based upon the frequency with which they were mentioned by wife assaulters in our own treatment groups, and by other clinicians working with wife assaulters (Ganley & Harris, 1978; Martin, 1977; Walker, 1979). Power issues were described through frequent mention of the need to control or dominate the female, descriptions of female independence as loss of male control, and by frequent attempts to persuade or coerce the female into adopting the male's definition of relationship structure and function.

Intimacy issues include sudden increases in the wife's demands for greater affection, attention, and emotional support and, at the other end of the continuum, increased demands for greater independence, or freedom from control by the male. Gelles (1975) and Rounsaville (1978) reported that for 40% of repeatedly assaulted wives, the onset of assault coincided with a sudden transition in intimacy such as marriage or pregnancy. Correspondingly, Daly, Wilson, & Weghorst (1982) describe sexual jealousy as an instigator of wife assault. Jealousy might be viewed as a reaction to perceived relationship loss. We propose that changes in socioemotional distance between the man and his wife can serve as aversive instigators of wife assault. Socioemotional distance can serve as a unifying concept to link reports of wife assault occurring in response to ostensibly opposite events, such as increases and decreases in intimacy. Our thesis is that an understanding of the interplay of power dynamics on issues of intimacy can provide an explanatory framework to deepen our understanding of relationship specific assault. As such, this explanation would seem most applicable to males who are violent in more than one relationship but not violent outside the relationship.

Power Issues

Although the consequences of the need for control and perception of control have been broadly researched (see, for example, Adler, 1966; Baum & Singer, 1980; Perlmuter & Monty, 1979; Bandura, 1977; Langer, 1983; Seligman, 1975), the need for control in primary relationships is not as thoroughly developed in the psychological literature.

McLelland's (1975) "Type III" power orientation describes men who satisfy their need for power through having impact on or control over another person. McLelland views power orientations as analogous to Freudian stages of psychosexual development, and accordingly views the Type III as phallically fixated. Winter (1973) applied McLelland's Type III typology to males who compulsively seduce and abandon women. The "Don Juan syndrome" as Winter described it, originated from twin motives to sexually conquer (have impact on) and flee from women. In such a transaction, a male purposively increases intimacy with a female up to the point of sexual seduction, and then decreases intimacy immediately after. Sexual and power motives are intertwined and ambivalence about intimacy produces a repeated approach-avoidance pattern on a continuum of socioemotional distance between the male and the objectified female. Dutton (1984) extended Winter's analysis to males in monogamous relationships, arguing that the same combination of strong power motivation and ambivalence would operate to create strong needs to control socioemotional distance in order to move alternatively closer (through courtship, conquest and impact) and further away (through emotional withdrawal, verbal criticism, extramarital affairs). Stewart and Rubin (1976) obtained data consistent with this analysis, finding that college-age males who scored high on Thematic Apperception Test measures of the need for power (n power) were more likely to dissolve premarital monogamous relationships than were males scoring low on n power. This dissolution was created by high n power males in two ways: first, through threatening the primary relationships by forming other romantic attachments (which fulfilled the need for new conquest) and second, through the generation of extreme control attempts in the primary relationship. These control attempts took the form of generating conflict through criticism of the female, and constant attempts to modify her attitudes and behavior, in order to have renewed, discernible impact on her. High scores on n power correlate significantly with frequency of arguments (McLelland, 1975) and with a variety of behavioral indicators of aggression, such as destroying furniture or glassware (Winter, 1973). Also, high scorers write stories with themes reflecting adversarial sexual beliefs (Slovin, 1972) that portray women as exploitive and destructive. Whether these beliefs are a cause or consequence of their adversarial behavioral tendencies toward women is not currently known. As we shall report further on, however, men in our own research who react with the greatest anger to scenes of husband-wife conflict, tend to be men who report high degrees of verbal and physical abuse from their mothers (but not from their fathers). Interestingly, Winter (1973) has proposed that men who developed the conquest-abandonment "Don Juan" syndrome did so in response to maternal mixed communications or double-bind communications (Bateson, 1972) in which maternal nurturance was mixed with hostility toward the son. This occurred, Winter speculated, in patriarchal societies where women were repressed and reacted with anger toward the only safe male target: their sons. The ambivalence from the mother created ambivalence toward women in the son. In the study we report next, self-reports of feelings of both anger and humiliation in response to watching videotaped husband-wife conflicts were significantly correlated to both verbal and physical abuse from the mother.

If a certain amount of transference occurs from the opposite-sex parent to one's spouse, then we might expect sons who were verbally or physically abused by their mothers to feel quite powerless in adult relationships. Male sex-role socialization, however, teaches men that powerlessness and vulnerability are unacceptable feelings and behaviors (Pleck, 1981). As a consequence, we might expect exaggerated power concerns in such men, along with mistrust of females and anxiety about intimacy with a female (except when the male feels in complete control over the extent of the intimacy—i.e., able to increase or decrease it as he pleases). Consequently, any perceived threats to male control over the amount of intimacy should produce exaggerated arousal and anxiety in such males. In short. such threat to control would constitute an aversive instigator.

Intimacy Anxiety

Pollack and Gilligan (1982) reported images of violence in TAT stories written by men in response to situations of affiliation. They suggest that, as "fear of success" scores demonstrate reliable gender differences with women scoring higher, fear of intimacy is a predominantly male anxiety and that males perceive intimate relationships to be dangerous. The working hypothesis we have adopted is that intimacy anxiety has both trait and state properties. The latter involve increases in response to sudden uncontrollable changes in the socioemotional distance between spouses. This distance we assume to be negotiated by both parties to a point that represents an optimal zone. An "optimal zone" for each person is that degree of emotional closeness or distance between themselves and their partner with which they feel comfortable at any given time. This comfort zone may be similar to optimal zones for interpersonal spacing (see Patterson, 1976) in that, as with interpersonal spacing zones, "invasions" (too much intimacy) or "evasions" (too little) may produce physiological arousal.

Such invasions by the female (from the male's perspective), we term *engulfments,* evasions are called *abandonments.* Fear of engulfment can be produced in three main ways: first by the female moving emotionally toward the male through increased demands for closeness, attention, and affection. Second, by the female remaining static and the male developing an increased need for greater distance than is currently provided. Ehrenreich (1983) has incisively described the sociological ramifications of the male "breadwinner" role and of male attempts to flee from the ensuing engulfment. Affective reactions to engulfment may vary but probably carry an admixture of repressed anxiety, and resentment, along with a vague sense of guilt. When coupled with a lack of verbal assertiveness to extricate himself from engulfment, the probability of aversive arousal increases.

Abandonment anxiety involves perceived uncontrollable increases in socioemotional distance from the male's perspective. Hence, it could be produced by (1) sexual threat or any other instance of the female moving emotionally further away (or reinvesting her energy outside the primary relationship), (2) the male developing an increasing need for intimacy but not successfully expressing it so that a "stationary" female stays at what was previously an optimal distance, but which is now too far. Also, formal redefinitions produce shifts in intimacy. For example, motherhood redirects female attention toward the child (while simultaneously increasing male "responsibility").

Finally, many clinical reports indicate that males exacerbate abandonment anxieties by behaving in such a way as to maximize the likelihood of abandonment by the female. Walker's (1979) description of the "battering cycle" describes a process whereby assaultive males, having gone through an "acute battering phase," experience guilt, remorse and anxiety that their wife will leave. If she moves to a new lodging, they put her under surveillance, obsess over her, try to convince her to return, and promise they will never be violent again. Men in therapeutic groups who are in an abandonment panic generally behave as though a life line were being cut off. They idealize the woman, obsess over her and their mistreatment of her. They reveal the exaggerated dependency they have on her, previously masked by their attempts to make her dependent on them, or by exaggerated control of her behavior.

Sexual jealousy, especially to the extent that it involves delusions or distortions may represent a form of chronic abandonment anxiety. Jealousy is mentioned frequently by battered women as an issue that incited violence (Rounsaville, 1978; Whitehurst, 1971; Roy, 1977; Daly, Wilson, & Weghorst, 1982). Recent studies (Murstein, 1978; Clanton & Smith, 1977; White, 1980) have viewed jealousy as a mediating construct, produced by anticipated relationship loss, and producing a range of behavioral responses (including aggression and increased vigilance), and affective reactions (including rage and depression).

In many relationships the degree of intimacy or socioemotional distance is a key structural variable that has dramatic impact on individuals in the relationship. Power and control over the degree of intimacy is especially important to the extent that (a) intimacy with one's spouse satisfies social needs unique to the primary relationship, (b) intimacy represents a major structural variable and (c) anxieties learned in the family of origin about intimacy transfer onto the spousal relationship. Perceived inability to homeostatically maintain the degree of intimacy within the optimal zone should produce arousal in males. Although this arousal may be clinically viewed as a component of state anxiety, a variety of mechanisms operate to induce males to experience the arousal as anger (Novaco, 1976; Dutton, Fehr, & McEwan, 1982). Male sex-role socialization is more compatible with expressions of anger than fear (Pleck, 1981; Fasteau, 1974). Feelings of agency, potency, expressiveness and determination accompany the expression of anger (but not fear) (Novaco, 1976). Dutton and Aron (in press) found that males viewing interpersonal conflict scenarios demonstrated significant positive correlations between self-reports of arousal and anger. Females demonstrated significant positive correlations between arousal and anxiety. Hence, the psychological step from aversive arousal to anger seems easier for males to take. Hence, one way that broad cultural norms may influence violence toward women is through shaping the interpretation of arousal states in males produced by loss of control over intimacy with their wives so that such states are experienced as anger.

In men who have poor communication skills, the anger may cue a prepotent response of aggression (Rule & Nesdale, 1976). Hence, we hypothesize that two trait factors: the need for power and intimacy anxiety may serve to produce extreme arousal states in some men in response to normal changes in relationship intimacy. Such arousal states should be interpreted as anger (following Novaco, 1976) and in men with poor verbal skills, may increase the likelihood of aggression.

If this is the case it is reasonable to expect that a physically assaultive population of men, all convicted of wife assault and with histories of repeated use of violence, may react with greater anger when they witness videotape scenarios portraying a couple conflict where the conflict issue is a change in intimacy. Furthermore, when the female member of the couple verbally dominates the male, a sense of uncontrollable intimacy change should produce the highest self-reports of anger in physically assaultive males compared to demographically matched controls without a history of wife assault.

Videotape Studies

Three groups of men were compared in this study. A Physically Aggressive (PA) group (n = 24) was made up of men who had been convicted of wife assault and were attending a treatment group for spousal violence; a Verbally Aggressive Group (VA) (n = 18) was made up of men attending counseling groups for marital conflict; a nonaggressive (NA) (n = 18) group was solicited through ads in local newspapers. All three groups were demographically similar (as measured by an index of socioeconomic status by Myers and Bean, 1968). The Status Conflict Tactics Scale Form N (Straus, 1979) was used to assess the men's means of dealing with conflict. Reports from each man and his wife were obtained. Table 11.1 lists the scores on each subscale of the CTS.

The physical subscale items measure physical actions directed toward the wife (e.g., Item 1—threw something at the other one, through Item S—used a knife or gun). Reports of 1 incident of any of these items receive a score of 1; reports of 2 incidents receive a score of 2; 3-5 incidents, a score of 3; 6-10 incidents, a score of 4; 11-20 incidents, a score of 5; and more than 20 incidents, a score of 6. Summary across items produces the total scores in Table 11.1. In this context, the wives' rating of physically assaultive males at 18.7 constitutes considerable violence directed toward them in the preceding year.

The videotape component of the project provided an examination of the emotional impact on wife assaulters on power and intimacy factors in conflict situations. The general strategy was to present the subject with a series of videotaped scenes depicting verbal conflict between a man and woman, encourage him to imagine himself actually being in the man's shoes, and take measures of arousal and experienced affect. The use of videotape was appealing in that the image could be presented vividly, while maintaining a relatively standard stimulus array across subjects. It also allowed the roles of both parties in the conflict to be manipulated, whereas such an aim would have been difficult or impossible using a role-play technique.

TABLE 11.1
Scores on Straus Conflict Tactics Scale by Group

		Reasoning Subscale	Verbal Subscale	Physical Subscale
PA Group				
(n = 24)	man's self-ratings	7.9	20.1	9.5
	wife's ratings of man	7.6	27.8	18.7
VA Group				
(n = 18)	man's self-ratings	9.6	15.7	0.7
	wife's ratings	7.7	13.4	0.9
NA Group				
(n = 18)	man's self-ratings	7.0	3.8	0.2
	wife's ratings	7.5	5.7	0.3

The videotape component employed a $3 \times 2 \times 3$ factorial design with three levels of subjects (PA, VSA, NA), two levels of power (male dominant, female dominant), and three levels of attempted intimacy change (abandonment, engulfment, neutral). Power and intimacy change were manipulated by varying the verbal content of the videotaped scene. The subjects in each group (PA, VSA, NA) were randomly assigned to viewing either male dominant scenes or female dominant scenes. Each subject then viewed three videotapes, each depicting a different intimacy condition. The order of presentation was counterbalanced.

The scenes were between five and seven minutes in duration, and involved the same man and woman arguing heatedly over an issue. The subjects were told that the man and woman were a couple who had been involved in an "in-depth" study of marriage at the university and had allowed a cameraman to film them at home. In fact, the couple were professional actors.

Relative power was manipulated by having either the man or the woman in the scene dominate the argument verbally. Family interaction researchers (see Mishler & Waxler, 1968; Jacob, 1975) have specified a number of discrete behaviors that seem to constitute verbal dominance, including greater talk time, successful interruptions, and winning acquiescence. This information was used to manipulate relative power.

Attempted intimacy change was manipulated by varying the issue discussed during the conflict. There were three issues, one for abandonment (woman attempting to move away from the man), engulfment (woman attempting to move closer to the man), and the neutral (no attempted movement) condition. It was decided to have the woman instigate this movement in the tapes (rather than the man) because the dynamic of interest here was the man's attempt to control the woman's behavior. Specifically, the abandonment issue involved the woman stating that she wished to become more independent, spend more time with her friends, and join a consciousness-raising group for women. The engulfment issue involved requests by the women that the man spend more time talking to her and that he be more open with his thoughts and feelings. Finally, the neutral scene involved an issue that is common to most couples, but does not *a priori* involve a change in intimacy. The couple argued over whether they would spend their vacation camping or in a city.

Generally, the taped scenes depicted a moderate to severe level of verbal conflict in a realistic home setting. The videotapes were pretested on a small number of married men in their late twenties to provide an estimate of the arousal-producing properties of the tapes as well as a rough check on the power and intimacy change manipulation.

Self-report measures of perceived affect and behavioral response probability were obtained immediately after each videotape scene. A series of 10 adjectives describing affective states were selected from a more extensive list compiled by Russell and Mehrabian (1974). Three of these adjectives (angry, hostile, and aggressive) have been used to assess anger by these authors (Russell & Mehrabian, 1974).

A three-way repeated measures unequal n ANOVA was performed on the men's ratings of their anger had they been the man in the scenario. This yielded a significant overall difference among groups ($F[2,54] = 5.07$, $p < .01$), which remained significant when the anger ratings were corrected for initial levels of anger by using preratings (taken prior to showing the scenes) as a covariate. Observation of the means suggests a linear relationship with the PA group rating the most anger and the NA group the least. Furthermore, Newman-Keuls comparisons indicated that the PA group reported significantly more anger to the abandonment scene than did the other two groups ($p < .01$). No main effect was found for male versus female dominance, the F score approached but did not attain the conventional (.05) level of significance.

Novaco's behavioral likelihood scales yielded consistent between-group differences with the PA group reporting the least amount of constructive reasoning ($F[2,54] = 9.02, p < .001$), the most verbal aggression ($F[2,54] = 8.82, p < .001$), and the most physical aggression ($F[2,54] = 10.3, p < .001$). Post hoc comparisons revealed the PA group to be significantly different from each of the other two groups on these measures. This was especially true for the abandonment scenes. Finally, the men were asked the relevance of the issues portrayed to their own relationships. The table of percentages generated by this question is contained in Table 11.2. An overall chi-square performed on these data was significant ($\chi^2 = 36.93, p < .0001$). It would appear from observation of the cell frequencies that the abandonment issue was the most relevant for the PA group and least relevant for the other groups.

To generate directions for future research, some "data snooping" techniques were performed. Specifically, an internal analysis was performed

TABLE 11.2
Scores by Group

| Group | Relevance of Intimacy Issue to Relationship (in percentages) | | | | Anger Self-Ratings | | |
	Abandonment	Engulfment	Neutral		Abandonment	Engulfment	Neutral
Physically aggressive	76	54	40	MD	20.0	16.2	19.6
				FD	25.5	17.4	18.3
					overall: 20.02		
Verbally aggressive	39	72	56	MD	17.1	18.4	19.6
				FD	14.4	14.3	16.1
					overall: 16.67		
Nonagressive	29	56	0	MD	12.3	17.2	18.7
				FD	10.9	10.2	12.9
					overall: 13.7		

NOTE: $X^2 = 36.93$, $df = 4$.
*$p < .001$.

that correlated all anger ratings collapsed across both subjects and videotapes. Composite self-report anger ratings correlated most highly with composite anxiety ratings (+.86, $p < .001$) and "humiliation" (+.60, $p < .001$). The emergence of humiliation as a key descriptor of affective reactions poses potential heuristic value. Self-reports of humiliation while watching the conflict scenarios correlated +.4, $p = .001$ with reports of being verbally abused by one's mother in the family of origin and .4, $p = .001$ with being physically abused by the mother. Correlations of humiliation with reports of verbal and physical abuse by the father however, were not significant. This finding suggests support for Winter's notion of maternal mixed messages contributing to men with strong ambivalence about intimacy and are, in our opinion, deserving of further study.

This study provided preliminary support for the hypothesis that assaultive males react more strongly to abandonment scenarios than do other males. Data bearing on anger, behavioral likelihood, and relevance to one's own relationship all indicated stronger reactions from this group. However, within groups variance was great and the sample size was small, hence our statistical tests lacked power. Our current work is aimed at both increasing the sample size and establishing more pertinent criteria for our PA group. To this end, men who are also violent outside their primary relationship will be screened out of the PA group, as their violence may be indicative of a broader learned pattern, whereas our research hypotheses pertain to violence that is relationship specific.

More work also needs to be done on the status of power-intimacy conjunctions as aversive instigators for assaultive males and the specific relationship of these instigators to behavioral repertoires with violence as a prepotent response. Our current working hypothesis is that perceived uncontrollable changes in socioemotional distance produces aversive arousal in males, which is "labeled" or interpreted as anger. Although anger increases the likelihood of aggression, it is not a sufficient cause (see Rule & Nesdale, 1976). However, when anger exists in conjunction with poor verbal and conflict resolution skills, the combination may further increase the likelihood of aggression. Among our current objectives is a further examination of the possibility that sex-role socialization can influence the basic experience of emotion in response to interpersonal conflict. If this proves to be the case it would suggest one direct means by which social norms influence individual experience in such a way as to increase the likelihood of aggression.

References

Adler, A. (1966). The psychology of power. *Journal of Individual Psychology, 22,* 166-172.
American Psychiatric Association. (1981). *Diagnostic and statistical manual of the mental disorders* (3rd ed.). Washington, DC: Author.

Bandura, A. (1977). Self-efficacy: Towards a unified theory of behavioral change. *Psychological Review, 84,* 191-215.

Bandura, A. (1979). The social learning perspective: Mechanisms of aggression. In H. Toch (Ed.), *Psychology of crime and criminal justice.* New York: Holt, Rinehart & Winston.

Bateson, G. (1972). *Steps to an ecology of mind.* New York: Ballantine.

Baum, A., & Singer, J. E. (1980). (Eds.). Applications of personal control. *Advances in Environmental Psychology* (Vol. 2). NJ: Lawrence Erlbaum.

Clanton, G., & Smith, L. (1977). *Jealousy.* Englewood Cliffs, NJ: Prentice-Hall.

Daly, M., Wilson, M., & Weghorst, S. J. (1982). Male sexual jealousy. *Ethology and Sociobiology, 3,* 11-27.

Dutton, D. G. (1984). A nested ecological theory of male violence towards intimates. In P. Caplan (Ed.), *Feminist psychology in transition.* Montreal: Eden.

Dutton, D. F., & Aron, A. (in press). Romantic attraction and generalized liking for others who are sources of conflict based arousal. *Canadian Journal of Behavioural Science.*

Dutton, D. F., Fehr, B., & McEwen, H. (1982). Severe wife battering as deindividuated violence. *Victimology: An International Journal, 7,* 13-23.

Ehrenreich, B. (1983). *The hearts of men.* Garden City, NJ: Anchor, Doubleday.

Elliot, F. (1977). The neurology of explosive rage: The episodic dyscontrol syndrome. In M. Roy (Ed.). *Battered women: A psychosociological study of domestic violence.* New York: Van Nostrand Reinhold.

Fasteau, M. F. (1974). *The male machine.* New York: McGraw-Hill.

Faulk, M. (1974). Men who assault their wives. *Medicine, Science and the Law, 14,* 180-183.

Ganley, A. (1981). *Court mandated therapy for men who batter: A three-day workshop for professionals.* Washington, DC: Center for Women Policy Studies.

Ganley, A., & Harris, L. (1988). *Domestic violence: Issues in designing and implementing programs for male batterers.* Paper presented at the 86th annual convention of the American Psychological Association, Toronto.

Gelles, R. (1975). Violence and pregnancy: A note on the extent of the problem and needed services. *The Family Co-ordinator, 24,* 81-86.

Jacob, N. (1975). Family interaction in disturbed and normal families: A methodological and substantive review. *Psychological Bulletin, 82,* 33-65.

Langer, E. (1983). *The psychology of control.* Beverly Hills, CA: Sage.

Martin, D. (1977). *Battered wives.* New York: Kangaroo Paperbacks.

McLelland, D. (1975). *Power: The inner experience.* New York: Halstead.

Mischler, N., & Waxler, N. (1968). *Interaction in families: An experimental study of family processes and schizophrenia.* New York: John Wiley.

Murstein, B. I. (1978). *Exploring intimate lifestyles.* New York: Springer.

Myers, J. K., & Bean, L. L. (1968). *A decade later: A follow-up of social class and mental illness.* New York: Wiley.

Novaco, R. (1976). The functions and regulation of the arousal of anger. *American Journal of Psychiatry,* 133:10, 11-24, 11-28.

Patterson, M. L. (1976). An arousal model of interpersonal intimacy. *Psychological Review,* 83(3), 235-245.

Perlmuter, L. C., & Monty, R. A. (1979). (Eds.). *Choice and perceived control.* Hillsdale, NJ: Lawrence Erlbaum.

Pizzey, E. (1974). *Scream quietly or the neighbours will hear.* London: Penguin.

Pleck, J. H. (1981). *The myth of masculinity.* Cambridge: MIT Press.

Pollack, S., & Gilligan, C. (1982). Images of violence in Thematic Apperception Test Stories. *Journal of Personality and Social Psychology, 42*(1), 159-167.

Rounsaville, N. (1978). Theories in marital violence: Evidence from a study of battered women. *Victimology, 3*(1-2), 11-31.

Roy, M. (1977). *Battered women: A psychosocial study of domestic violence.* New York: Van Nostrand.

Rule, B. G., & Nesdale, A. R. (1976). Emotional arousal and aggressive behavior. *Psychological Bulletin, 83,* 851-863.

Russell, D., & Mehrabian, N. (1974). Distinguishing anger and anxiety in terms of emotional response factors. *Journal of Counseling and Clinical Psychology, 42,* 79-83.

Schulman, M. (1979). *A survey of spousal violence against women in Kentucky.* U.S. Department of Justice, Law enforcement Assistance Administration. Washington, DC: Government Printing Office.

Scott, P. D. (1974). Battered wives. *British Journal of Psychiatry, 125,* 433-441.

Seligman, M. E. (1975). *Helplessness: On depression, development and death.* San Francisco: Freeman Press.

Slovin, M. (1972). *The theme of feminine evil: The image of women in male fantasy and its effects on attitudes and behavior.* Unpublished doctoral dissertation, Harvard University.

Snell, J. E., Rosenwald, P. J., & Robey, A. (1964). The wifebeater's wife. *Archives of General Psychiatry, 11,* 107-113.

Stewart, A., & Rubin, Z. (1976). The power motive in the dating couple. *Journal of Personality and Social Psychology, 34,* 305-309.

Straus, M. (1973). A general systems theory approach to a theory of violence between family members. *Social Science Information, 12*(3), 105-125.

Straus, M. (1979). Measuring intrafamily conflict and violence: The conflict tactics scale. *Journal of Marriage and the Family, 41,* 75-88.

Straus, M., Gelles, R. J., & Steinmetz, S. (1980). *Behind closed doors: Violence in the American family.* New York: Anchor/Doubleday.

Straus, M. A., & Hotaling, G. T. (1980). The social causes of husband-wife violence.

Symonds, M. (1978). The psychodynamics of violence-prone marriages. *American Journal of Psychoanalysis, 38,* 213.

U.S. Commission on Civil Rights. (1978). *Battered women: Issues of public policy.* Washington, DC: Government Printing Office.

Walker, L. (1979). *The battered woman.* New York: Harper & Row.

White, G. L. (1980). Inducing jealousy: A power perspective. *Personality and Social Psychology Bulletin, 6,* 222-227.

Whitehurst, R. N. (1971). Violence potential in extramarital sexual responses. *Journal of Marriage and the Family, 33,* 683-691.

Whitehurst, R. N. (1974). Violence in husband-wife interaction. In S. K. Steinmetz, & M. A. Straus (Eds.), *Violence in the family.* New York: Harper & Row.

Winter, D. G. (1973). *The power motive.* New York: Free Press.

12

Conflict Tactics Used by Men in Marital Disputes

Linda P. Rouse

Awareness of "wife beating" as a social problem has generated many questions about how violence comes to be a part of relationships between men and women. In every relationship there are stresses, conflicts, and differences of opinion: Why do some men react in a more abusive way than others toward their female partners? Do physically battering men tell us something about how men, generally, deal with conflict in intimate relationships? What can we learn from men's conflict styles that will help us understand, and change, the behavior of men who are physically or emotionally abusive toward their female partners? The research study that will be discussed in this chapter was designed to help answer such questions. Men in a random sample of households were asked how they handled conflicts during the past year in their relationship with a wife or girlfriend. They were also asked questions about some of the factors that may be related to men's conflict styles, factors such as age, stress, past exposure to use of physical force, family background, and sex-role orientation.

The Sample

In reading and interpreting the results of this study it is important to keep in mind that the findings do not necessarily apply to all men. The findings apply primarily to the kinds of men who received these questionnaires and took the trouble to fill them out. Questionnaires were mailed to 120 men in a computer-generated random sample of households from a current city listing of homeowners/property tax payers. A total of 65 completed questionnaires were returned, for a response rate of 54.2%.

The average age of respondents was 45. Nearly all identified their race as white. With only four exceptions, they were married to their current female partner. The average number of years they had been married was 20, but the range was from less than one year to almost 50 years. Two-fifths (40.0%) had children under 18 living at home. Most of the men (87.7%) were working full-time; none were unemployed; four (6.2%) were working part-time; four were retired (6.2%). Many of their female partners were also employed, either full-time (30.8%) or part-time (27.7%). About one-third of the female partners (35.4%) did not have jobs outside the home and were not looking for such work at this time. All the men had completed grade school and had gone on to high school; 26 (40.0%) had some college or a college degree; another 16 (24.6%) had some graduate education or a graduate degree. Finally, with respect to the men's satisfaction with their marital relationship, the majority (69.2%) reported feeling "very positive" or "somewhat positive"; only two (3.0%) expressed feeling "negative" about their relationship with the female partner overall.

Consider the types of persons who were not included in this sample. First, no questionnaires were sent to men who are not homeowners. No one living in an apartment rather than a house received a questionnaire. This means that the initial sample tended to leave out persons who are younger, poorer, and less "rooted" in favor of older, more middle-class, more permanent community residents. Second, not everyone who received a questionnaire completed and returned it. Who were the nonrespondents? Some were very elderly or persons in poor health during the time of the study. Some had moved out of Kalamazoo. Others were recently divorced or widowed, or still single and not dating one woman on a regular basis. Some men did not have enough schooling to be able to respond to a lengthy written questionnaire. Some men felt they were too busy to take time out to answer any questionnaire; others felt that the answers to these particular questions are nobody's business but their own. Significantly, the nonrespondents also include the most seriously abusive and battering men, who do not want to disclose their behavior.

The Conflict Tactics Scale

How men behave in conflicts with a wife or girlfriend is a central concern in this study. The Conflict Tactics Scale, developed by Straus (1979), is a measure of conflict behavior suitable for use with mailed questionnaires. It lists a set of actions (ranging from calm discussion to assault with a deadly weapon) that persons might use in a fight or argument with another family member. A modified version of the Conflict Tactics Scale was used in this study. Table 12.1 shows the specific items included, and how men in this sample described their own behavior in arguments with their female

TABLE 12.1

The Conflict Tactics Scale Items Means and Percentages

Items	Mean Frequency	Used Once or More in the Past Year Number (Percent)	Ever Used, "Yes" Number (Percent)
Discuss the issue or problem calmly	4.17	59 (90.8)	62 (95.4)
Get information to back up own side of things	1.87	33 (50.8)	44 (67.7)
Bring in or try to bring in someone to help settle things	.29	9 (13.8)	15 (23.1)
Insult or swear at the other person	1.57	30 (46.2)	36 (55.4)
Sulk or refuse to talk about it	2.25	42 (64.6)	50 (76.9)
Walk or stomp out of the room, leave the house	.83	21 (32.3)	35 (53.8)
Yell or shout	2.05	37 (56.9)	43 (66.2)
Do or say something to spite the other person	1.36	29 (44.6)	38 (58.5)
Threaten to hit or to throw something	.05	3 (4.6)	9 (13.8)
Actually throw or smash or hit or kick something	.15	5 (7.7)	8 (12.3)
Push, grab, or shove the other person	.16	7 (10.8)	13 (20.0)
Slap the other person	.06	1 (1.5)	7 (10.8)
Kick, bite, or hit the other with fist	.05	1 (1.5)	1 (1.5)
Hit the other with some object	.05	2 (3.0)	2 (3.0)
Beat up the other person	.00	0 (0.0)	0 (0.0)
Threaten with a knife or gun	.00	0 (0.0)	0 (0.0)
Use a knife or gun	.00	0 (0.0)	0 (0.0)

NOTE: Scoring: 0 = never; 1 = once; 2 = twice; 3 = 3-5 times; 4 = 6-10 times; 5 = 11-20 times; 6 = more than 20 times.

partners. The mean values presented in the first column in Table 12.1 represent the average frequency of occurrence, in the sample as a whole, of each conflict tactic (0 = never; 1 = once; 2 = twice; 3 = 3-5 times; 4 = 6-10 times; 5 = 11-20 times; and, 6 = more than 20 times). The middle columns in Table 12.1 show, for each item, the number and percentage of men who reported having used that particular conflict tactic at least once in the past year. The final columns in Table 12.1 refer to how many men in this sample have used a particular conflict tactic at least once in their relationship with their current female partner over the entire time they have been together.

Certain conflict tactics are considered to be more abusive than others. Insulting a person in an argument, for example, can be regarded as a verbal "attack," a form of emotional battering. Threats of violent or destructive behavior are also emotionally abusive, whether or not the threat is actually carried out in a particular confrontation. Beginning with pushing, grabbing, and shoving, direct use of physical force against the female partner is involved. In light of the potentially serious consequences of battering, any use of physical force during arguments in an intimate relationship can be regarded as an abusive conflict tactic. For this report, seven items from the Conflict Tactics Scale were combined to form an index of abusive conflict tactics: "insult or swear at the other"; "threaten to hit or throw something"; "actually throw or smash or hit or kick something"; "push, grab, or shove"; "slap the other person"; "kick, bite, or hit the other with fist"; and "hit the other with some object."

The abusive conflict tactics index scores for men in this sample ranged from 0 to 17, with a mean of 2.10. In all, 32 (49.2%) of the men in this sample reported using none of the behaviors that were included in the abusive conflict tactics index (during the past year). Considering only the direct use of physical force, 7 men (10.8%) reported using one or more conflict tactics, from pushing, grabbing, or shoving, at least once during the past year. Bear in mind, however, that even these men cannot be identified as "batterers" on the basis of this research. Questionnaires of the kind used in this study will not reveal the most serious cases of domestic assault. What these data do confirm is that many men sometimes use abusive conflict tactics in arguments with their wives or lovers, and for about 1 in 10 this will include use of physical force.

Factors Related to Use of Abusive Conflict Tactics

In the following sections, various factors will be examined in relation to the use of abusive conflict tactics.

Age is the most important general background characteristic related to reported use of abusive conflict tactics among men in this sample. The older a respondent, the less likely he is to report that he has used abusive conflict

tactics in a marital dispute during the past year. *Number of years married*
and *number of children under 18 living at home* also appear to be
connected to use of abusive conflict tactics (longer married, less abusive;
fewer children at home, less abusive) but this finding is basically a result of
the fact that the older men have been married longer and their children are
more likely to be grown.

It is sometimes suggested that abusive family relationships are more
characteristic of lower-class families than middle- or upper-class families.
Social class is typically measured by asking questions about income,
occupation, and education. In this study, no information on income or
occupation was requested from respondents but they did indicate their
highest grade or level of education completed. For men in this sample, *level
of education* was not related to use of abusive conflict tactics. These data do
not answer the question of whether there is a link between severe, repeated
domestic assault and social class, but do tell us that use of abusive conflict
tactics in this sample crosses over all levels of educational attainment.

Employment status has also been considered as a possible factor
connected with marital conflict. None of the men in this sample were
unemployed, so unemployment does not explain the variation among them
in use of abusive conflict tactics. The four retired men all reported using no
abusive conflict tactics in marital disputes, which again reflects the negative
relationship between age and use of force. Men who were employed
part-time showed the same overall pattern in use of abusive conflict tactics
as men who were working full-time.

Stress

Some theories of family violence point to stress as a factor that may
increase the use of abusive conflict tactics. Men in this study were asked to
fill in a "life events" type measure of stress. Presented with a list of 15 life
events that are generally experienced as "stressful," they simply checked off
any events that had happened to them in the past year, such as: troubles
with the boss at work; death of someone close; a lot worse off financially;
child having serious problems at school; and so on. Space was also
provided to fill in up to three significant stressful events not on the list that
had happened to them in the past year. Stress index scores are simply the
total number of events checked or filled in. One additional question asked
respondents how stressful, subjectively, they felt the past year had been for
them overall: not at all (0); somewhat (1); moderately (2); or, very (3). For
men in this sample, both measures of stress are significantly correlated with
greater use of abusive conflict tactics. The Pearson correlation coefficient
obtained for the relationship between number of stressful life events and use
of abusive conflict tactics was .30; between subjective feeling of stress and
abusive conflict tactics, .26.

Past Exposure to Use of Physical Force

Not all individuals react to stress in the same way. Social learning theory suggests that specific behaviors (such as the conflict tactics used in domestic disputes) are learned through past experience. If a person learns that violent or abusive behavior is appropriate when one is angry or frustrated, violence is more likely to occur as a reaction to stress in later life. Learning may take place as a result of direct experience or through observation of others. In this study, men were asked a series of questions about whether, as children and as teenagers, they had ever been: spanked; slapped; shoved; punched; kicked; choked; beaten up; or, threatened with a knife or gun. For each item, they simply answered "yes," "no," or "don't recall." In the same way, they were also questioned about whether they had ever seen anyone else spanked, slapped, shoved, and so on, and whether they had ever done any one of these things to someone else. Index scores for "victimization," "observation," and "commission," respectively, were then computed by adding up the number of "yes" answers in each series of questions.

Observing, committing, and being victimized by use of physical force "as a younger child, up to the age of 12" were not related to later use of abusive conflict tactics *for men in this sample.* Table 12.2 shows the Pearson correlation coefficients for each type of past experience "as a teenager, between the ages of 13 and 19." These correlations suggest that for men in this sample, past exposure as a teenager to use of physical force—whether one has been the "victim," the observer, or the "aggressor"—is related to greater use of more abusive types of conflict tactics in marital disputes. However, simple bivariate correlations can be misleading. To interpret them there is another fact that must be considered. Victimization, observation, and commission scores are significantly related to one another.[1] This means that someone who reported himself as having been spanked, slapped, shoved, and so on is also more likely to have observed such experiences happen to others and to have committed similar actions himself than someone who reports that he has *not* been spanked, slapped, shoved, and so on. If we look only, for example, at victimization scores in relation to later use of abusive conflict tactics in marital disputes, the correlation between them will be "contaminated" by the effects of observation and commission. We need a way to identify the effect of each type of past exposure independent of the others. The "partial correlation" is a statistic that helps us do this.

The second column in Table 12.2 lists the partial correlations between use of abusive conflict tactics in marital disputes and each type of past exposure to use of physical force, controlling for the effect of the other two types of past exposure. The partial correlations indicate that later use of abusive conflict tactics occurs with men who have been victimized or who observed use of physical force as teenagers primarily when they have also

TABLE 12.2

Correlations Between Different Types of Past Exposure to
Use of Physical Force (as a teenager) and Later Use of
Abusive Conflict Tactics in Marital Disputes

| | Correlation with Abusive Conflict Tactics | |
	Bivariate	Partial
Victimization	.30*	.03
Observation	.39**	.13
Commission	.52**	.37**
Past Exposure (combined score)	.49**	–

NOTE: p values represent the likelihood that a particular correlation could be obtained simply by chance. The statistical significance level of $\alpha = .05$ used in this study means that if the probability is only 5 times out of 100 or less that the observed correlation could be owing to chance, we will accept the correlation as "significant." In general, the larger the correlation, the less likely it is owing to chance.
*Statistically significant at alpha = .05, $p = .009$; **statistically significant at alpha = .05, $p = .001$.

committed similar acts themselves as teenagers. These findings differ somewhat from the results obtained by the author in an earlier study with a similar sample (Rouse, 1984). In that study, observation of violence in childhood or adolescence was significantly associated with later use of abusive conflict tactics in marital disputes, even when the effects of other types of past exposure to violence were controlled. In both samples, however, reported victimization, observation, and commission were intercorrelated, and partial correlations pointed to conclusions different from those suggested by a casual inspection of simple, bivariate correlations.

The precise manner that exposure to the use of physical force influences later behavior has yet to be determined by family violence researchers. One caveat for future research is the need to analyze more closely the effects of different types of past exposure on use of physical force in marital conflicts. Is use of force mainly a result of early observational learning? Is it a result of the negative effects of victimization on personal adjustment? Or is it a pattern established by positive reinforcement of violent acts committed? These are questions of practical concern for designing effective intervention strategies as well as questions of theoretical interest.

In the present report, to simplify further analyses, respondents' scores for each of the three types of past exposure are combined for a single summary statistic that will give an indication of the overall effect of such experiences on later use of abusive conflict tactics in marital disputes. The correlation obtained between overall past exposure to use of force in teenage years and later use of abusive marital conflict tactics is .49, as shown in Table 12.2.

Stress and Past Exposure

Both stress and the combined effect of different kinds of past exposure to use of force appear to be related to use of abusive conflict tactics in marital disputes for men in this sample. Yet, according to social learning theory, persons under stress will typically use abusive conflict tactics only if they have seen such behaviors acted out by others (models) or were rewarded for using such behaviors in the past (reinforcement). One might also consider whether persons exposed to use of force in teenage years will tend to be more abusive toward the female partner in marital disputes, whether or not they are experiencing other stressful life events.

For men in this sample, stress is in fact *not* significantly correlated with use of abusive conflict tactics when the degree of past exposure to use of force is held constant.[2] However, whether men have experienced few (0, 1, or 2) stressful life events in the past year or at least 3 or more, those who report greater past exposure to use of force are significantly more likely to use abusive conflict tactics in marital disputes.[3] *These data support the conclusions that: (1) stress itself does not generate abusive behavior, and (2) more abusive interpersonal conflict styles are learned through past experience, particularly in connection with earlier use of physical force ("commission").*

Family Background

In family violence literature, particular attention has been paid to early exposure to use of abusive behaviors within the family itself. Men in this study were asked how often there were conflicts between their parents that they knew of when they were growing up in which one or both parents physically or verbally "attacked" the other. Of the 65 men in this sample, 8 (12.3%) reported having observed their fathers using physical force[4] against the mothers at least once; 7 (11.8%) reported the mother using physical force against the father at least once. In four of these cases both parents had used physical force against the other[5]; in another 4, father only; in the remaining 3, mother only. However, for men in this sample, the reported use of physical force between parents was not significantly related to their own use of abusive conflict tactics in marital disputes. Men who remembered parents' using physical force were as likely to report using no abusive conflict tactics themselves as to report using at least one abusive conflict tactic in marital disagreements during the past year.

Rates of reporting at least one incident between parents that could be construed as verbal abuse were higher. For father's behavior toward mother (he "insulted her, yelled at her, or threatened her verbally"), only 26 men (42.6%) reported that they were aware of no such incident when they were growing up. For mother's behavior toward father the corresponding figure was 49.2% "never" happened. Fathers were slightly more likely to be reported as having been verbally abusive "6-20 times" or more (32.8%) than were mothers (26.2%), but only the mother's verbal behavior toward the father was significantly related ($r = .26$, $p = .021$) to men's later use of abusive conflict tactics in their own marital relationships.

Men in this study were also asked questions concerning the degree to which they were themselves targets of parental behaviors involving use of physical force or verbal "abuse." Interestingly, the number of spankings reported from both mother and father were related to later use of abusive conflict tactics in marital disputes.[6] For both mother and father, spanking was significantly correlated with using "other kinds of physical force, like punching, shoving, kicking, throwing things at you, and so on" ($r = .44$ and $r = .39$, respectively) and with the verbal behavior, "insulted you, yelled at you, or threatened you" ($r = .32$ and $r = .34$), as recollected by men in this sample. There was also a tendency for mother's and father's reported actions to be related for the same type of parental behavior. In other words, if a respondent reported that father spanked, he also reported that mother spanked ($r = .23$); if father had used other physical force, mother had used other physical force ($r = .47$); and, if father had insulted, yelled, or threatened verbally, mother had also ($r = .49$).[7]

As shown in Table 12.3, mother's reported actions were more strongly associated than were father's actions with differences among men in this sample in their use of abusive conflict tactics. Even father's spanking is not significantly related to use of abusive conflict tactics when its association with mother's spanking is taken into account.[8] The measures of family background used in this study are too crude to justify any elaborate theoretical interpretations of this finding but do strongly suggest a *difference in the impact of mother's and father's actions.* This may simply reflect the fact that mothers typically spend more time interacting with their children than do fathers, or may be the result of a more involved psychodynamic in which mother's and father's actions have different meanings for a boy in childhood, with different consequences for later styles of dealing with conflict in marital relationships.

Sex-Role Orientation

The concept of a sex-role orientation as used here refers to an individual's belief about how persons of each sex, male and female, should behave, especially in a marital relationship. There are at least two lines of argument suggesting that for men in our society stronger traditional sex-role orientations are related to greater use of abusive conflict tactics in

TABLE 12.3

Correlations of Recollected Parental Actions with Men's
Own Use of Abusive Conflict Tactics in Marital Disputes

	Correlation with Use of Abusive Conflict Tactics
Father's actions toward you	
— spanked	.24*
— used other kinds of physical force, like punching, shoving, kicking throwing things at you, and so on	.16 ns
— insulted you, yelled at you, or threatened you verbally	.002 ns
Mother's actions toward you	
— spanked	.44**
— used other kinds of physical force, like punching, shoving, kicking, throwing things at you, and so on	.30**
— insulted you, yelled at you, or threatened you verbally	.34**

NOTE: Scoring: 0 = never; 1 = once; 2 = twice; 3 = 3-5 times; 4 = 6-10 times; 5 = 11-20 times; 6 = more than 20 times.
ns = not statistically significant at alpha = .05; *statistically significant at alpha = .05, p = .03; **statistically significant at alpha = .05, p = .01.

marital disputes. One comes from clinical assessments made by counselors and psychologists who have seen battering men as clients. Battering men are typically described by such professionals as holding rigid, traditional sex-role orientations. In the eyes of the batterer, his abusive behavior is precipitated by his female partner's inability or unwillingness to live up to his expectations for her in her role as a wife or girlfriend. Additionally, a sense of inadequacy or failure on his part if he cannot be the kind of man he thinks he should be may generate anger, which he takes out on his female partner.

Feminist theory of patriarchy (male dominance) connects the physically assaultive behavior of severely battering men with male-female relationships in our society as a whole. In a patriarchal society, sex-role expectations favor male dominance in the family. Masculinity is traditionally defined in terms of independence, toughness, competitiveness, aggressiveness, and being in control. The man is head of the household and has the final say in family decisions. The woman's primary task is to look after the needs of her husband and children. The man's primary legal and social obligation is to provide financial support, in return for the rights of consortium—his wife's love, companionship, sexual availability, housework, and child care services. If traditional sex-role expectations promote and serve to justify male dominance, then men who are more traditional in their own individual attitudes may be more likely to use abusive conflict tactics, sometimes including use of physical force, to maintain control in the family.

The 12 questions used in this study as a measure of sex-role orientation were drawn from Mason (1975). In Table 12.4, the first column, the percentage of men who answered "somewhat agree," "agree," or "strongly agree" is presented for each item. For all items except 3, 7, and 10, agreement represents a more traditional (patriarchal) sex-role orientation. The majority of men in this sample agreed that it is the duty of the husband to be earning a living for his family and that the husband is the head of the family. Three-fifths of the men also agreed that the woman, more than the man, should have the responsibility for taking care of children. Just under half agreed that in a marriage the major responsibility of the wife is to keep her husband and children happy. There was less reported agreement with traditional ideas about a woman's place being in the home and not in the workplace.

To construct an overall index of sex-role orientation, only the seven items that were most strongly intercorrelated with one another were selected. These items all appear to be measuring a common underlying orientation and reflect sufficient difference of opinion among respondents to be potentially useful in explaining differences in use of abusive conflict tactics. Column 2 in Table 12.4 presents the correlations of each original item with the final seven-item sex-role orientation index. As shown at the bottom of Table 12.4, scores on the sex-role index are *not* significantly related to use of abusive conflict tactics. The third column in Table 12.4 shows the consistently negligible correlations found in this sample between individual sex-role items and use of abusive conflict tactics.

Among possible interpretations for this finding are the following:

(1) Sex-role orientations are related to use of abusive conflict tactics only in the most extreme cases. As noted earlier, the upper limit of "abusiveness" reported by men in this sample is well below the frequency and severity of abuse typically involved for men who are seen in batterers' counseling programs. The sex-role orientations of men in this sample may likewise not be as rigid or extreme as those observed among identified batterers.

(2) Questionnaire items of the kind used in this study may be subject to social desirability effects. Respondents may answer as they think they "should" answer (e.g., in keeping with more "liberated" ideas), not necessarily what they actually believe or practice on a day-to-day basis.[9] Other, less "obvious" item wordings, additional scales to estimate strength of social desirability effects, or measures of the female's perception of her male partner may be necessary to demonstrate a link between sex-role

TABLE 12.4

Correlations of Sex Role Orientation Items[a] with
Sex Role Index[b] and with Use of Abusive Conflict Tactics

Items	Percent Who Agree[c]	Sex Role Index	Use of "Abusive" Conflict Tactics
It is more important for a wife to help her husband's career than to have one of her own.*	32.3	.71	−.05
A woman's place is in the home.*	23.1	.72	−.004
Men should share the work around the house with women, such as doing the dishes, cleaning, laundry, and so on.	90.8	−.09	.13
It is the duty of the husband to be earning a living for his family.*	86.2	.63	.008
The husband is head of the family.*	75.4	.68	.20
Sometimes a man might have to hit his wife to remind her who is boss.	3.1	.31	.003
A wife should work if she wants to, even if her husband is not personally in favor of it.	83.1	.35	−.04
If a wife earns more money than her husband, the marriage is headed for trouble.	21.5	.29	−.21**
In a marriage, the major responsibility of the wife is to keep her husband and children happy.*	47.7	.62	−.08
A wife should be able to say no if her husband wants sexual intimacy and she does not.	93.8	.15	.11
The man should have the final say in major family decisions.*	43.1	.75	−.06
The woman, more than the man, should have the responsibility for taking care of children.*	60.0	.63	−.09
Sex Role Index	−	−	−.01

a. Responses scored: 1 = strongly disagree; 2 = disagree; 3 = somewhat disagree; 4 = somewhat agree; 5 = agree; 6 = strongly agree.
b. Sex Role Index scores are the result of adding up scores on the seven starred items.
c. All who responded "somewhat agree," "agree," or "strongly agree."
*Items included in Sex Role Index; **statistically significant at alpha = .05 (but barely, p = .046).

orientation and use of abusive conflict tactics.

(3) Another consideration, tentatively suggested by a cross-tabular analysis of these data, is that if there is a relationship between sex-role orientation and use of abusive conflict tactics, it may not be a simple linear relationship. Men "in between" in sex-role orientation (falling in neither the clearly traditional nor nontraditional score ranges) were the most likely to report use of abusive conflict tactics. This is the group of men that includes those who might be characterized as having more inconsistent attitudes or more ambivalent feelings about sex roles. The most abusive men in this sample were twice as likely to have "in-between" sex-role orientation scores as to be either traditional or nontraditional, and the percentage of "in-between" sex-role index scores was highest among men aged 26-35 (who had the highest reported use of abusive conflict tactics). Effects of this nature will be masked by correlational statistics that assume linear relationships.

Self-Esteem

Self-esteem is another factor that has been associated with spouse abuse. Specifically, both female victims and male batterers are described as being low in self-esteem. The extent to which low self-esteem is a consequence of abusive behavior versus a cause and the different implications of low self-esteem for female victims versus male batterers remain open to question.

To test whether self-esteem is correlated with use of abusive conflict tactics for men in this study, Rosenberg's (1965) measure of self-esteem was used. A self-esteem index was constructed by summing responses on a set of interrelated items worded as follows:

(1) I feel I am a person of worth, at least on an equal basis with others.
(2) I feel I have a number of good qualities.
(3) All in all, I am inclined to feel that I am a failure.
(4) I am able to do things as well as most other people.
(5) I feel I do not have much to be proud of.
(6) I take a positive attitude toward myself.
(7) On the whole, I am satisfied with myself.
(8) I wish I could have more respect for myself.
(9) I certainly feel useless at times.
(10) At times I think I am no good at all.

For each statement, respondents indicated their level of agreement, from strongly disagree (1) to strongly agree (6). Items 3, 5, 8, 9, and 10 were recoded so that higher scores reflected higher self-esteem. Self-esteem scores for men in this sample ranged from a low of 23 to a high of 60. The majority of men (89.2%) reported basically positive self-regard, and for about half of the men in this sample, scores were 50 and above.

The self-esteem index scores were *not* significantly correlated with use of abusive conflict tactics for men in this sample (r = .02). Level of self-esteem was related to level of educational attainment (r = .26, p = .017) but not related to age, stress, or past exposure to use of physical force, except certain aspects of family background. Self-esteem index scores did tend to be lower for men whose father or mother had used physical force other than spanking against them in childhood (r = .39 and r = .21, respectively) or had been physically abusive toward the other parent (for father's actions, r = .34; for mother's actions, r = .27).

Summary and Conclusion

In an effort to understand more about the social problem of domestic assault, we have been looking at the conflict tactics used in marital disputes reported in a sample of 65 men who completed and returned a mailed questionnaire. We have considered some of the factors possibly related to use of more abusive kinds of conflict tactics: age; stress; past exposure to use of physical force; family background; sex-role orientation; and, level of self-esteem.

In this final section, these factors will be considered all together as they relate to the conflict tactics used in marital disputes. Neither sex-role orientation, as measured by the questions used in this study, nor level of self-esteem were significantly correlated with use of abusive conflict tactics. The summary table (Table 12.5) presents the correlations that were found in this study for the variables most strongly related to reported use of abusive conflict tactics.

Note that stress is *not* related to use of abusive conflict tactics when the effects of age, past exposure, and family background are taken into account. This is primarily because men in this sample did not use abusive conflict tactics under stress unless they had some previous exposure to use of physical force or verbal "abuse"—specifically, in mother's actions toward them in childhood or in their own behavior during teenage years. Moreover, given such past exposure, they were more likely to use abusive conflict tactics whether they were experiencing stressful life events or not.

The simple demographic variable of age remains significantly (inversely) related to use of abusive conflict tactics when the effects of stress, past exposure, and family background are controlled. Partial correlations in the summary table also indicate that though past exposure and family background are somewhat related to one another, each has a separate effect on the later use of abusive conflict tactics in marital disputes. Thus it is appropriate to consider both early home environment and wider exposure to use of physical force outside the home in efforts to explain the use of abusive conflict tactics.

TABLE 12.5
Summary of Final Bivariate and Partial[a] Correlations

	Stress	Past Exposure	Family Background	Use of Abusive Conflict Tactics	
				Bivariate	Partial
Age	−.31	−.45	−.29	−.46	−.27*
Stress		.36	.33	.30	.07ns
Past exposure			.37	.49	.26*
Family background[b]				.47	.33**

a. Partial correlations controlling for the other three variables in summary table.
b. A summary index of mother's action toward respondent: that is, spanking, use of other physical force, and verbal "abuse."
*Statistically significant at alpha = .05, p = .025; **statistically significant at alpha = .05, p = .005; ns = statistically significant at alpha = .05.

Overall, we can "explain" a considerable part of the variation among men in this sample in their reported use of abusive conflict tactics by considering together, age, past exposure to use of physical force, and family background. Multiple regression analysis shows a multiple R^2 value for this sample of .39. This means that 39% of the variation in the use of conflict tactics among men who participated in this study can be accounted for simply by differences in age, past exposure to use of physical force, and family background.

To the extent that efforts to deal with the social problem of spouse abuse (specifically, "wife beating") include a concern with the conflict styles men generally use in domestic disputes, one approach suggested by the findings reported here is to target younger men (roughly, up to age 35) for educational and social service interventions. Teenage boys, particularly, might benefit from high school programs designed to teach positive skills in resolving interpersonal conflicts without use of physical force. Better awareness and understanding of family dynamics as they affect male children's developing styles of conflict resolution will also be helpful in generating specific suggestions, for counseling adult men who are abusive, and for developing family education programs.

Notes

1. Victimization with observation, r = .45; victimization with commission, r = .49; and, observation with commission, r = .56.

2. For men with lowest, intermediate, and highest past exposure, correlations of stress with use of abusive conflict tactics drop to .09, .14, and .15, respectively.

3. The correlation between overall past exposure and abusive conflict tactics remains r = .45 for men experiencing few stressful events during the past year and r = .44 for men experiencing three or more stressful life events.

4. Such as slapping, hitting, pushing, kicking, throwing things, and so on.

5. Though not necessarily of equal intensity or frequency.

6. Spanked by mother, r = .44 (p = .001); spanked by father, r = .24 (p = .031).

7. Mother's and father's actions were not significantly related for *different* types of behaviors; for example, father's spanking not related to mother's verbal "abuse"; mother's use of physical force not related to father's spanking; and so on.

8. The partial correlation drops to r = .18, p = .084.

9. If so, this would apply particularly to younger men. The older men in this sample were more traditional in sex-role orientation as well as less likely to report using abusive conflict tactics. Controlling for age, however, produced only a slight and statistically not significant correlation between sex-role orientation and use of abusive conflict tactics. The partial correlation coefficient was .14 (p = .126).

References

Mason, K. (1975). *Sex-role attitude items and scales from U.S. sample surveys.* National Institute of Mental Health.

Rosenberg, M. (1965). *Society and adolescent self-image.* Princeton, NJ: Princeton University Press.

Rouse, L. (1984). Models, self-esteem and locus of control as factors contributing to spouse abuse. *Victimology, 9*(1), 130-141.

Straus, M. (1979, February). Measuring intrafamily conflict and violence: The conflict tactics scales. *Journal of Marriage and the Family, 41*, 75-88.

13

Correlates of Early Violence Experience Among Men Who Are Abusive Toward Female Mates

Mildred E. Johnston

After years of selective inattention, spouse abuse has been accepted as a serious national problem. The White House Conference on Families (1980) stated that violence within the family is a serious national problem of epidemic proportions. In 1981 the Maryland State Police documented 9,028 spousal assaults, and 89% of the victims were female. Straus, Gelles, and Steinmetz (1980) reported that 1 of 26 American wives get beaten by their husbands every year, or a total of almost 1.8 million per year.

Public attention has not only prompted researchers to take a closer look at the "problem" of spouse abuse but has influenced several states to develop criminal justice programs, including court ordered treatment programs for the male abuser. While information gathered from individuals who have been coerced into treatment is not, necessarily, the most representative data, such programs do provide an available population from which to begin studying spouse abuse from the abuser's perspective. Firsthand information about the male abuser/batterer is scarce, primarily because in the past battering males have seldom presented themselves for treatment or even acknowledged that they have a problem (Steinmetz, 1977, Straus et al., 1980; Walker, 1979).

Unanswered questions pertaining to the association of spouse abuse and characteristics of the abuser are of social importance. Although the literature reports that family violence is more prevalent among the young, poor, and uneducated; violence and spouse abuse cut across all socio-economic levels; all educational, racial, age, and occupational categories (Gelles, 1980; Roy, 1977; Straus et al., 1980).

One of the greatest blocks to dealing with the widespread problem of wife-beating/spouse abuse has been the tacit acceptance and covering up of the crime. In 1983, only 43 states provided a woman with the legal option of an Order of Protection, and only 41 states allowed eviction of a violent husband as a part of the legal protection of the wife (Lerman, Livingston, & Jackson, 1983). In October 1983, Oregon became the first state to rule that a battered woman could sue police for failure to enforce her protection order (Civil Order of Protection) under the mandatory arrest provision of the state Abuse Prevention Act (Oregon Supreme Court, 1984). Police agencies traditionally have viewed family problems as noncriminal "disputes" or "disturbances," essentially verbal in nature, not serious, and causing no one injury (Fields, 1978); the police share society's view that domestic violence is an individual problem and not a public issue (Bannon, 1975).

There is evidence in the literature that men who observed or experienced violence in the home as children are more likely to physically abuse their spouses. Studies by Carlson (1977) of 101 women; Gelles (1972) of 80 families; Hilberman and Munson (1977-1981) of 60 women; Roy (1982) of 4,000 women; and Straus et al. (1980) of 2,143 families (960 men and 1,183 women) support the view that violence is a role-modeled behavior passed through socialization. All of the above studies reported that a large percentage of men who were spouse abusers observed or experienced violence as children. Straus et al. (1980) reported observed or experienced violence as children, and found that men who had seen parents physically attack each other were almost three times more likely to have hit their own wives. Male children from violent families are learning the correct way to behave or act.

Rosenbaum and O'Leary (1981) suggest that children of couples where the wife is abused may be especially predisposed to the development of behavioral and emotional problems. While efforts have been made to analyze the impact on children who witness family violence, empirical findings remain equivocal. However, there is some indication that conflict and tension between parents is associated with low self-esteem in children (Cooper, Holman, & Braithwaite, 1983; Rascke & Rascke, 1979).

The male batterer is characterized as holding traditional and sex-stereotyped values and possessing low self-esteem (Coleman, 1980; Gelles, 1980; Walker, 1981). Rosenbaum and O'Leary (1981) reported in a comparative study of 60 couples that the abusive men were significantly more conservative/traditional in their attitudes toward women. Straus (1976) posits that socialization patterns in society that are entrenched in sexism and violence against women both initiate and sustain violence within the family. Ganley (1981) suggests that men who batter have learned certain cultural and social values about masculinity and their roles in families that support their aggression and violence; males are socialized into roles that encourage both dependence on and aggression toward females. Socialization and sex-role conditioning appear to be instrumental in defining the attitudes that males have toward violence, and are major factors in determining the power relationship between men and women that allows battering behavior to take place.

Abusive men who hold sex-stereotypic views—men are supposed to be strong and dominant, superior, and successful—may find their already low self-esteem attacked even more if there are any feelings of inadequacy in these areas (Coleman, 1980). Boyd (1978) reports that low self-esteem among batterers is evidenced in perceived unachieved goals for self and disappointment in careers, even if successful by others' standards.

Several authors (Boyd, 1978; Gayford, 1975; Labell, 1979; Martin, 1976; Walker, 1979) suggest that many batterers have low self-esteem, and use violence to compensate for feelings of inadequacy and to prove their masculinity. Kaplan (1972) suggests that individuals who lack self-esteem are seen as prone to adopt deviant patterns of behavior as a means of receiving attention from others and achieving a positive self-attitude. Violence provides such a vehicle because of the individual's experience in cultural or social settings that covertly or overtly permit or condone violence. Thus men are seen likely to choose a path of violence/spouse abuse in order to establish a positive identity (Kaplan, 1972).

The problem of spouse abuse appears to be very complex and does not fit a simple explanation. It is becoming increasingly clear that marital violence/spouse abuse, once thought to be relatively rare, or perhaps just ignored, is a "serious problem of epidemic proportions" (White House Conference on Families, 1980). Since there are no laws mandating the reporting of spouse abuse, investigators have to make use of indirect measures of reported marital violence/spouse abuse. Michael Flaherty, Chief of Police of Prince George's County, Maryland, states that spousal abuse statistics are low because reports of spousal assault are made only when: (a) injury is readily apparent; (b) ambulance personnel treat or transport the victim; or (c) the victim is treated by other personnel. Misdemeanor assault and battery cases must occur in the presence of a police officer before an arrest can be made (Flaherty, San Felice, & Linnell, 1984).

Of the 180 clients at a Montgomery County (Maryland) Abused Persons Program (1979), only 54% had been reported to the police. In a survey of 150 cases of female victims of spouse abuse, Roy (1977) reported that only 50% were reported to the police. Hilberman & Munson (1977-1978) reported that in one year, half of all women referred by the medical staff to a mental health clinic were found to be victims of severe marital violence. Of these 60 women, only 4 were known to have a history of marital violence despite the fact that most of these women and their children had received medical care at the clinic. Fowler (1981) suggests that when assisting patients or clients, agencies such as hospitals and social service agencies often appear not to be sensitive to the existence of spouse abuse, which may be owing to a lack of training in recognizing the existence of a violent home situation.

The present study investigated the relationship between spouse abuse and attitudes toward women, self-esteem, and observing or experiencing violence as a child. Comparison groups were used; however, the men in each group were not matched or randomized; therefore covariates (age, education, and income) were designated as a substitute for experimental control.

Research Design

The instruments used to assess characteristics of the male batterer were: (a) A sociodemographic questionnaire, (b) the Tennessee Self-Concept Scale (Fitts, 1965), (c) the Attitudes Toward Women Scale (Spence & Helmerich, 1972), and (d) the Conflict Tactics Scale (CTS) (Straus, 1979).

Since the present study modified the instructions of CTS, relating to time span, it was necessary to do a pilot study on the test-retest reliability of the instrument. The CTS has been used previously for a period of time involving only one year; however, the present research used the instrument for a time span that either covered the entire time of the partner relationship or during the first 18 years of an individual's life.

In the pilot study, the CTS was given to 67 graduate students a week apart; the resulting r's were as follows: .95 for husband to wife violence, .70 for mother to child violence, and .79 for father to child violence.

Subjects

Subjects were solicited from four different sources. The sources were: men from two mental health treatment centers in Prince George's County and Montgomery County, Maryland, men who were enrolled in University College of the University of Maryland, and men from economically diverse communities in Prince George's County.

Men who were participants in the clinic programs were either court ordered or self-referred abusers. Questionnaires given to the court ordered men were included in a packet of questionnaires that was required by the clinic as a part of the court ordered First Offenders Program. These men were solicited by the researchers and informed of the addition of the research questionnaires, and were asked to sign a consent form. The men who referred themselves to the clinics and the men from the University of Maryland classes were solicited by the researcher. The men who responded from the neighborhoods were informed of the research study via a door-to-door solicitation. The door-to-door solicitation involved leaving the questionnaire at the door with an appropriate cover letter.

The men who responded to the questionnaires were classified into three groups:

- Group A—Known Abusers: This group consisted of a sample of 27 men who had been court ordered into therapy programs in Montgomery and Prince George's County. Their mean age was 33.6 years, with a range of 20 to 67.
- Group B—Self-Reported Abusers: This group consisted of 34 men who were solicited from the two clinics, university classes, and communities in Prince George's County. Their mean age was 42.4 years, with a range of 22 to 65 years.
- Group C—Nonabusers: This group consisted of 44 men who were solicited from university classes and communities in Prince George's County. Their mean age was 42.6 years, with a range of 25 to 63 years.

Because of an overriding interest in differences between abusive and nonabusive men, the men in this study were also classified as abusive (known abusers and self-reported abusers) and nonabusive.

Discussion of Results

The present study had subjects with a range of income of $0 to $175,000; education of 5 to 24 years; and age of 20 to 67 years, 40% were college educated, and 51% had an income over $25,000. With the exception of three men, one in each group, all men were married to their partners. Three men in Group A and six men in both Groups B and C had been divorced previous to the present marriage. The known abusive and self-reported abusive men did not differ significantly on scores measuring spouse abuse, self-esteem, attitudes toward women, observing violence, or experiencing violence.

The abusive men in this study did not fit the "typical" abuser as described in the literature. Even though the literature suggests that abusive men come from all age, educational, and socioeconomic levels, it is suggested that abusive men are more prevalent among the young, poor, and uneducated. Some of the abusive men in this study fit the above categories; however, they were also middle-aged, middle-class, and educated (see Table 13.1). The implications of the above finding is that men who abuse their spouses do come from all age, educational, and socioeconomic levels.

The literature reports that men who are more traditional in their attitudes toward women are more likely to become spouse abusers (Kalmus & Straus, 1982; Straus et al., 1980; Walker, 1981). However, this hypothesis was not validated in analysis of the current data. There were no differences in scores measuring attitudes toward women among abusive, self-reported abusive, and nonabusive men, nor were there differences between abusive

TABLE 13.1

Sociodemographic Characteristics of Known Abusive
and Self-Reported Abusive Men

	Known Abusive		Self-Reported Abusive	
	Range	*Mean*	*Range*	*Mean*
Age	20-67	33.6	24-65	42.4
Education	8-24 years	13.5	5-22 years	14.9
Income	0-35,000+	20.4	0-35,000+	28.3

(known abusive, and self-reported abusive) and nonabusive men (see Table 13.2). Previous research appeared to use subjective data and did not use comparison groups when reporting that abusive men have more traditional values toward women. The Attitudes Toward Women Scale has been used successfully to separate persons favoring traditional roles for women from those favoring nontraditional roles for women (Collins, 1974; Smith & Bradley, 1980; Spence & Helmerich, 1972). Therefore, for the current sample of men, it can be inferred that abusive and nonabusive men do not differ significantly on attitudes toward women.

Several authors (Carlson, 1977; Gelles, 1972; Hilberman & Munson, 1977-1978; Roy, 1982) support the view that violence is a role modeled behavior passed on through socialization. The results of a regression analysis indicated that a significant ($p < .007$) positive relationship exists between observing or experiencing violence and spouse abuse (see Table 13.2). Male children who observe father-to-mother violence or experience parent-to-child violence may be learning how to control and get what they want; consequently, if they do not get their way as adults, they may resort to violence to communicate their needs.

Another bivariate relationship suggested by several authors (Boyd, 1978; Gayford, 1975; Labell, 1979; Martin, 1976; Walker, 1979) is that batterers have low self-esteem. While many of the abusive men and nonabusive men in the present study did have low self-esteem scores, the study did indicate that a significant ($p = .007$) negative relationship exists between self-esteem and spouse abuse (see Table 13.2). This relationship is consistent across both minor and severe spouse abuse.

Given the strong relationship between the exposure to violence in childhood and spouse abuse and the strong relationship between self-esteem and spouse abuse among men, it is important to examine the relationship between these three variables. Table 13.3 examines the correlations between attitudes toward women and self-esteem on spouse abuse only for men who were exposed to violence as children. Among these men, there is a strong relationship between self-esteem and spouse abuse.

TABLE 13.2

Correlation Matrix on All Variables

	MS	SS	SE	AWS	EXPM	EXPS	EXPOV	OBM	OBS
SS	.75*								
SE	-.28*	-.23*							
AWS	-.11	-.14	.24*						
EXPM	.37*	.36*	-.18*	-.00					
EXPS	.35*	.41*	-.25*	-.04	.71*				
EXPOV	.38*	.42*	-.25	-.03	.70	.71*			
OBM	.57*	.46*	-.24*	-.14	.46*	.36*	.44*		
OBS	.73*	.70*	-.20*	-.11	.44*	.38*	.45*	.91*	
OBOV	.71*	.67*	-.19**	-.11	.45*	.38*	.47*	.93*	.99*

NOTE: MS = minor spouse abuse; SS = severe spouse abuse; SE = self-esteem; AWS = attitudes toward women; EXPM = experienced minor abuse; EXPS = experienced severe abuse; EXPOV = experienced minor or severe abuse; OBM = observed minor abuse; OBS = observed severe abuse; OBOV = observed minor or severe abuse.
$*p < .007$; $**p < .03$.

TABLE 13.3
Planned Comparison on Self-Esteem and Attitudes Toward Women
for Abusive and Nonabusive Men

Statistic	Abusive Men			Wilks F	Univariate F	Nonabusive Men		
	N	Mean	S.D.			N	Mean	S.D.
Variable								
Experience by Group Effect								
Self Esteem	43	46.04	11.66	4.85*	9.78**	18	58.27	9.57
Attitudes Toward Women	43	51.06	11.96		.68	18	53.27	14.03

$*p < .01$; $**p < .002$.

There is a need for more extensive multivariate analysis of this relationship, but these results are suggestive.

The inference is that men who are abused as children may develop low self-esteem. If self-esteem is defined as one's own self-worth, which develops as the result of achieving a status commensurate with one's conception of one's self-importance (Ausebel, 1952), being abused as a child could confuse one's conception of self-importance. Individuals with low self-esteem may degrade others to increase their own self-worth. Spouse abuse may then be seen as a function to an exhausted ego importance that the male would hope to maintain. If one accepts that experiencing violence leads to low self-esteem, an immature way of loving, and an unhealthy way of venting frustration, the addition of observing violent role-modeling behavior may indeed increase the potential of a man becoming a spouse abuser.

Conclusion

The conclusions based on the present research are that men who abuse their spouses come from all age, educational, and socioeconomic levels. There appears to be a relationship between being abused as a child and levels of self-esteem and minor or severe spouse abuse. The study infers that observing or experiencing violence is predictive of spouse abuse and that a combination of factors, rather than a single factor, is the most predictive.

Limitations and Implications

The study has limitations in generalizing to men in lower income brackets. Only 11 (15%) of the men had incomes below $15,000, while 52%

of the men had incomes over $25,000. The abusive (known abusive and self-reported abusive) men had an income of $23,721. However, the true mean is unknown because 11 of the abusive men had incomes of $35,000 plus.

Even though there was some control of age, education, and income by designating these variates as covariates, it was a limitation of the study; there is suggestion in the literature that these variables are related to spouse abuse. Another limitation of the study is that scores on spouse abuse for five known abusers had to be extrapolated from clinical records because these men denied abuse on the Conflict Tactics Scale.

The major implication of this study is that further empirical research is needed on men who batter, especially pertaining to the following: (a) levels of self-esteem and experiencing violence as a child; (b) differences in observing or experiencing violence between abusive and nonabusive men; and (c) issues around attitudes toward women and spouse abuse.

Recommendations

This study suggests a further investigation of the relationship between self-esteem and experiencing and witnessing violence. Both experiencing and witnessing violence as children appear related to spouse abuse at a bivariate level. However, their multivariate contribution to explaining spouse abuse is unknown, what is needed is a study with a larger number of men in order to estimate the separate effects of self-esteem, childhood exposure to violence, and spouse abuse.

Better methods of investigating and reporting spousal abuse are essential, not only to assess the severity of the problem, but to establish a need for services to both the abuser and the victim. Exposure to violence is related to spouse abuse; therefore, the therapeutic community must provide parents with techniques for coping with and resolving the inevitable conflicts of family life and develop comprehensive assessment and treatment approaches for abusive families. Otherwise, spouse abuse will continue to be passed down from generation to generation.

References

Ausebel, D. P. (1952). *Ego development and the personality disorder*. New York: Grune & Stratten.

Bannon, J. (1975, August). *Law enforcement problems with intra-family violence*. Paper presented at the annual convention of the American Bar Association, Montreal, Quebec.

Boyd, V. D. (1978, September). *Domestic violence: Treatment alternatives for the male batterers*. Paper presented at the annual meeting of the American Psychological Associates, Toronto, Canada.

Carlson, B. E. (1977). Battered women and their assailants. *Social Work, 22,* 455-465.

Coleman, K. H. (1980). Conjugal violence: What 33 men report. *Journal of Marital and Family Therapy, 6,* 207-213.

Collins, A. M. (1974). The Attitudes Toward Women scale: Validity, reliability, and subscore differentiation. (Doctoral dissertation University of Maryland, 1973). *Dissertation Abstracts International, 34,* 5036A. (University Microfilms No. 76-2351, 72)

Cooper, J. E., Holman, J., & Braithwaite, V. A. (1983). Self-esteem and family cohesion: The child's perspective and adjustment. *Journal of Marriage and the Family, 45,* 153-159.

Fields, M. (1978). Wife beating: Government intervention policies and practices. In United States Commission on Civil Rights, *Battered women: Issues of public policy.* Washington, DC: Government Printing Office.

Fitts, W. F. (1965). *Tennessee self-concept scale manual.* Nashville, TN: Counselor Recordings and Tests.

Flaherty, M. J., San Felice, J., & Linnell, D. (1984). *Prince George's County domestic violence task force.* Prince George's County, Maryland.

Fowler, J. (1981, February). *Spouse abuse: Research, federal activities and proposed legislation* (Report No. 81-59 EPW). Washington, DC: Congressional Research Service.

Ganley, A. L. (1981). Resource paper: Causes and characteristics of battering men. In A. L. Ganley (Ed.), *Participants' manual for workshop to train mental health professionals to counsel court mandated batterers.* Washington, DC: Center for Women Policy Studies.

Gayford, J. J. (1975). Wife battering: A preliminary survey of 100 cases. *British Medical Journal, 1,* 194-197.

Gelles, R. J. (1972). *The violent home.* Beverly Hills, CA: Sage.

Gelles, R. J. (1980). Violence in the family: A review of research in the seventies. *Journal of Marriage and the Family, 42,* 873-885.

Hilberman, E., & Munson, K. (1977-78). Sixty battered women. *Victimology, 2,* 460-470.

Kalmus, D. S., & Straus, M. A. (1982). Wife's mental dependency and wife abuse. *Journal of Marriage and the Family, 44,* 277-286.

Kaplan, H. B. (1972). Toward a general theory of psychosocial deviance: The case of aggressive behavior. *Social Science and Medicine, 6,* 593-617.

Labell, L. S. (1979). Wife abuse: A sociological study of battered women and their mates. *Victimology, 4,* 258-267.

Lerman, L. G., Livingston, F., & Jackson, V. (1983). State legislation on domestic violence. *Response, 6,* 1-27.

Martin, D. (1976). *Battered wives.* New York: Glide.

Montgomery County, Maryland (1979). *Psycho-social profile of the battered women in Montgomery County.* Montgomery County Community Crisis Center.

Oregon Supreme Court allows battered women to sue under mandatory arrest law. (1984). *Response, 7,* 3-4.

Rascke, H. J., & Rascke, V. J. (1979). Family conflict and children's self-concepts: A comparison of intact and single-parent families. *Journal of Marriage and the Family, 41,* 367-374.

Rosenbaum, A. R., & O'Leary, K. D. (1981). Marital violence: Characteristics of abusive couples. *Journal of Consulting and Clinical Psychology, 49,* 63-71.

Rosenbaum, A. R., & O'Leary, K. D. (1981). Children: The unintended victims of marital violence. *American Orthopsychiatry, 51,* 692-699.

Roy, M. (1977). *Battered women.* New York: Van Nostrand Reinhold.

Roy, M. (1982). Four thousand partners in violence: A trend analysis. In M. Roy (Ed.), *The abusive partner: An analysis of domestic battering.* New York: Van Nostrand Reinhold.

Smith, R. L., & Bradley, D. W. (1980). In defense of the attitudes toward women scale: An affirmation of validity and reliability. *Psychological Reports, 47,* 511-522.

Spence, J. T., & Helmerich, R. L. (1972). *The attitudes toward women scale.* Washington, DC: American Psychological Association.

Steinmetz, S. K. (1977). *The cycle of violence.* New York: Praeger.

Straus, M. A. (1976). Sexual inequality, cultural norms, and wife beating. *Victimology, 1,* 54-76.

Straus, M. A. (1979). Measuring intrafamily conflict and violence: the conflict tactics (CT) scale. *Journal of Marriage and the Family, 41,* 75-86.

Straus, M. A., Gelles, F. J., & Steinmetz, S. K. (1980). *Behind closed doors: Violence in the American family.* New York: Anchor/Doubleday.

Walker, L. E. (1979). *The battered woman.* New York: Harper & Row.

Walker, L. E. (1981). Battered women: Sex roles and clinical issues. *Professional Psychology, 12,* 81-91.

White House Conference on Families (1980). *The report: Listening to America's families.* Washington, DC: Government Printing Office.

14

Interpersonal and Intrapersonal Factors Associated with Marital Violence

Gayla Margolin

G rowing attention to the problem of spouse abuse over the past 10 years has led to three levels of explanation of this problem—intraindividual, sociopsychological, and sociocultural (Gelles, 1980). The intraindividual level attempts to explain marital violence by focusing attention on personality characteristics of the victim and the abuser. Representative data from this body of literature have shown, for example, that abusive men tend to be unassertive, jealous, depressed, prone to alcoholism, and have low self-esteem, and abused women tend to be suffering from depression, anxiety, and alcohol abuse (Douglas & Der Ovanesian, 1983; Faulk, 1974; Rosenbaum & O'Leary, 1981; Roy, 1982; Telch & Lindquist, 1984; Walker, 1984). The social psychological perspective considers the interactions of the individual with the social environment. This second level focuses on the relationship between the two spouses and on factors that affect the marriage. The data indicate that marital discord is a very important concomitant, if not predictor, of abuse (Rosenbaum & O'Leary, 1981) and that stressors on the marriage, such as financial difficulties or having many children, are associated with an increased risk of abuse (Straus, Gelles, & Steinmetz, 1980). Finally, the sociocultural perspective considers norms and values that contribute to spousal violence. As illustrated by Straus (1980), cultural norms regarding the subservient role of women and the privacy of the family have made the marriage license a hitting license.

The present study seeks to expand the available data base at the intraindividual and the sociopsychological levels.[1] The overall objective of this study is to identify factors that distinguish spouses who deal effectively with conflict versus those who embark on a destructive spiral of anger and aggression. Intrapersonal factors to be explored include overall susceptibility to anger, self-concept, attributional style, sex-role attitudes, psycho-pathology, and tendency to self-disclose. Interpersonal variables include actual and perceived styles of conflict resolution, apprehension about communicating with the spouse, assertiveness in the relationship, and relationship beliefs. It is assumed in this investigation that patterns of marital conflict are determined by the interaction between intrapersonal and interpersonal variables.

Data presented here are the preliminary findings of a larger, three-year investigation. This study differs from previous investigations on this question by including both the husband and wife in all aspects of data collection, including a group of withdrawing couples as well as a group of verbally abusive couples to help sort out whether physically abusive spouses are different from other types of maritally discordant spouses, and assessing couples who are not referred for therapy and who have not been publicly identified as abusive.

Method

Subjects

Subjects have been recruited from the greater Los Angeles area through radio announcements, newspaper stories, speeches at educational and religious gatherings, and word-of-mouth. The anticipated sample size is 80 couples, although only the 45 who have participated thus far are presented here. The study compares four types of couples: physically abusive (PA, n = 13); verbally abusive (VA, n = 12); withdrawn but nonabusive (WI, n = 10); and nondistressed and nonabusive (ND, n = 10). Categorization is based on the couple's scores on the Conflict Tactics Scale (Straus, 1979) and the Dyadic Adjustment Scale (Spanier, 1976). To be included in the study, couples needed to have at least one child between the ages of 3 and 17, to speak English as a primary language, and not to have been in marital or family therapy for more than three sessions.

Demographic characteristics of these couples are as follows: mean wife age, 35.7; mean husband age, 39.8; mean years married, 10.5; mean years of education for wife, 14.1; mean years of education for husband, 15.1; mean number of children from this marriage, 1.7; mean number of children from this marriage and previous marriages, 3.2. A total of 14 of the wives and 16 of the husbands had been married previously. Of the 45 couples, 13 were ethnic minorities. None of these demographic variables showed significant differences across groups.

Procedures

Participation in this study involved four laboratory meetings and one home meeting. The first three meetings consisted of individual spouse testing and interviewing, couple communication exercises that were videotaped for later coding, and spouse observation and rating of their own videotapes. The fourth meeting included children as well as the parents in order to examine patterns of family interaction, and the home visit focused on patterns of conflict resolution in the naturalistic environment. Between each meeting the spouses filled out a packet of questionnaires at home.

This write-up focuses on self-report questionnaire data.

Measures

Interpersonal measures include the Dyadic Adjustment Scale (Spanier, 1976), the Conflict Tactics Scale (Straus, 1979), the Spouse Specific Assertion Scale (Curley, undated) the Marital Status Inventory (Weiss & Cerreto, 1980), the Communication Apprehension Inventory (Powers & Hutchinson, 1979), the Relationship Beliefs Questionnaire (Eidelson & Epstein, 1982), the Areas of Change Questionnaire (Weiss & Perry, 1979), the PAIR Inventory (Schaefer & Olson, 1981) and the Conflict Inventory (Margolin, Fernandez, Gorin, & Ortiz, 1982). Although certain scores from the first two measures were used as screening criteria, other data from these measures serve as dependent measures.

Intrapersonal measures include a generalized anger scale (Novaco, 1975), a self-concept measure (Beck, 1978), a locus of control measure (Levenson, 1981), a questionnaire on sex-role attitudes (Mason, 1975), the MMPI (Dahlstrom, Welsh, & Dahlstrom, 1972), a self-disclosure measure (Jourard, 1971) and the Michigan Alcoholic Screening Test (Selzer, 1971).

Results

Separate one-way ANOVAs for wives and husbands were run, examining group differences on the screening criteria, and on interpersonal and intrapersonal variables presumed to be associated with couples' conflict management styles.

Screening Criteria

Although the Dyadic Adjustment Scale (DAS) and the Conflict Tactics Scale (CTS) were used for classifying couples, there are additional findings on these questionnaires that are not related to their being screening criteria. The DAS was used strictly to qualify couples for the ND group (ND spouses could not score < 97). Screening for the other three groups was unrelated to scores on the DAS. As the DAS data in Table 14.1 reveal, the ND couples do show higher overall marital satisfaction. Only the PA couples fall into what typically is considered the distressed range, and even their scores would be considered mildly distressed. Thus this may be viewed as a somewhat atypical group of PA spouses who are not particularly dissatisfied and are not seeking treatment. VA and WI couples fall into the low end of the satisfied range.

As anticipated, CTS scores show differences for the physical aggression, verbal aggression, and withdrawal items. There were no group differences, however, for reasoning. It can be noted that mean scores for physical aggression and for verbal aggression are approximately equal for husbands and wives in this sample. This does not mean that the impact of wife-initiated violence is equal to husband-initiated violence, but that the frequency of aggressive acts by men and women was approximately equal. As noted elsewhere, however, we suspect that self-defense and retaliation are the primary motives behind the women's use of violence (Margolin, 1987). PA spouses also score high on verbal aggression and withdrawal, in addition to their high scores on physical aggression. For spouses who occasionally resort to violence, the most common response appears to be some combination of withdrawal and verbal aggression.

Interpersonal Variables

As presented in Table 14.2, data on the interpersonal variables indicate that, when significant differences occur, ND couples show the highest marital adjustment while PA and WI couples show the lowest adjustment. VA couples often score in the midrange between these extremes. The pattern of differences on these variables is somewhat more pronounced for males than for females. The Marital Status Inventory, a measure of relationship stability, indicates that PA spouses have taken the most steps toward separation. However, their total scores are not all that different from VA or WI couples. The WI husbands and wives stand out in terms of their low assertion with the partner and their high communication apprehension. PA husbands and wives also are rather low on spouse-specific assertion. Only one of the five irrational relationship beliefs differentiates these couples. ND spouses, compared to the other three groups, are less likely to endorse the belief that "disagreement is destructive." There are no significant differences on other relationship beliefs, however.

Data from the Areas of Change Questionnaire indicate that PA and WI wives desire a lot of change from their partners. Although not a significant group effect, PA and WI wives also tend to assume that a lot of change is desired of them. PA husbands, more than other husbands, assume that their wives want a considerable number of changes from them. VA husbands, in contrast to their wives, want a high number of changes and incorrectly assume that the partner wants a similar number of changes in return.

Data from the Personal Assessment of Intimacy in Relationships (PAIR) indicate how much intimacy currently is perceived across five

TABLE 14.1
Screening Criteria

Variable	Wives					Husbands				
	PA	VA	WI	ND	F	PA	VA	WI	ND	F
Dyadic Adjustment Scale (DAS)	93.0	103.0	100.0	121.3	9.21***	91.1	106.3	102.2	117.9	6.93***
Conflict Tactics Scale (CTS)										
physical aggression (items k-s)	8.2	1.4	.4	.0	4.18*	8.7	1.8	.2	.1	5.04**
verbal agression (items d & h)	14.0	15.3	8.7	3.1	13.15***	14.7	14.5	8.6	2.9	19.42***
withdrawal (items e & f)	10.5	9.1	10.4	5.4	2.31	12.4	10.4	13.5	5.3	6.06**
reasoning (items a & b)	15.2	17.8	16.1	14.8	1.91	15.6	16.0	17.0	15.8	.23

NOTE: PA = physically aggressive (n = 13); VA = verbally aggressive (n = 12); WI = withdrawing (n = 10); ND = nondistressed (n = 10). The DAS was used as a screening criteria only for ND couples; no ND spouses could score 97. The CTS reasoning scale was not a screening criteria.
*p < .05; **p < .01; ***p < .001.

TABLE 14.2
Interpersonal Variables

Variable	Wives					Husbands				
	PA	VA	WI	ND	F	PA	VA	WI	ND	F
Marital status inventory	4.2	3.4	2.8	.5	5.04**	3.2	2.8	2.8	.8	3.68*
Spouse specific assertion	10.8	19.3	4.8	18.5	1.42	16.1	22.8	5.8	29.4	5.51**
Communication apprehension	82.6	76.5	90.6	65.0	4.00**	77.5	74.7	91.1	57.6	8.23***
Relationship beliefs										
disagreement is destructive	16.2	14.5	16.3	9.5	2.99*	13.5	14.2	11.3	7.6	4.37**
mindreading is expected	13.5	12.0	12.8	15.9	.91	14.4	13.3	12.8	12.9	.29
partners cannot change	10.2	12.8	14.0	9.5	1.04	11.0	14.9	13.5	10.0	1.97
sexual perfection	12.7	14.3	18.3	14.2	1.62	15.9	17.0	13.9	14.1	.78
the sexes are different	13.2	15.0	14.6	16.4	.37	13.8	17.8	15.0	16.0	.82
Areas of change										
desired change from partner	28.9	21.8	30.3	15.3	4.15*	24.7	28.1	19.6	10.7	2.42
perceived change on self	27.0	23.5	28.6	14.9	2.48	37.6	33.2	23.9	14.0	5.03**

Intimacy—Expected

	PA	VA	WI	ND	F	PA	VA	WI	ND	F
Emotional	88.6	84.3	85.6	93.7	1.92	82.0	77.7	72.4	92.0	5.44**
Social	75.7	68.0	77.6	83.6	1.74	68.0	64.0	64.4	80.8	2.70
Sexual	85.5	83.0	84.4	88.4	.32	85.0	80.0	75.6	87.6	1.26
Intellectual	81.5	68.3	80.4	86.4	3.19*	73.3	70.7	72.4	81.2	1.11
Recreational	83.4	74.3	83.6	85.2	1.65	79.1	79.3	65.2	87.2	4.87**

Intimacy—Perceived

	PA	VA	WI	ND	F	PA	VA	WI	ND	F
Emotional	43.1	49.3	40.4	73.6	8.22**	45.0	58.0	54.8	79.2	7.45**
Social	53.3	54.6	55.2	77.7	2.75	48.0	53.0	56.8	67.2	1.54
Sexual	61.8	66.3	50.4	75.6	2.78*	62.3	63.0	37.6	74.0	4.88**
Intellectual	52.0	49.8	48.0	74.4	4.28*	50.6	49.7	62.0	77.2	5.66***
Recreational	62.5	60.0	53.2	72.4	2.22	51.8	58.0	53.6	73.2	2.66

NOTE: PA = physical aggressive (*n* = 13); VA = verbally aggressive (*n* = 12); WI = withdrawing (*n* = 10); ND = nondistressed (*n* = 10)
*p < .05; **p < .01; ***p < .001.

relationship domains and how much intimacy is expected or desired. ND spouses show somewhat higher expectations for intimacy, particularly emotional and recreational intimacy for males. VA wives, compared to other wives, show fewer expectations for intellectual intimacy. Perceived intimacy tends to be highest for ND couples and lowest either for PA or WI couples, particularly in the areas of emotional, sexual, and intellectual intimacy.

The Conflict Inventory examines a spouse's perceptions of how: (a) he or she handles conflict; (b) how he or she would like to handle conflict; (c) how the partner handles conflict; and (d) how he or she would like the partner to handle conflict. For each of these questions, responses are clustered into three scales—aggression, problem solution, and withdrawal. Matching responses between current perceptions and desired levels provides a measure of satisfaction with oneself and the partner. As displayed in Table 14.3, higher discrepancies indicate more dissatisfaction. These data point to equally high dissatisfaction with how conflict is handled in the PA and the WI couples. PA and WI wives, compared to other wives, are dissatisfied with themselves in terms of inadequate problem-solving responses. Compared with VA and ND wives, these wives are dissatisfied with the husbands' use of aggression, problem solving, and withdrawal. PA husbands, compared to other husbands, are dissatisfied with their own aggression. PA and WI husbands are dissatisfied with the way problem solving is used by themselves and by their partners.

Intrapersonal Factors

Table 14.4 contains analyses on a number of individual characteristics that, based on previous research, may be related to patterns of abuse. These data reveal no group differences for wives. Husbands, in contrast, show several significant group findings. PA husbands are more likely than other husbands to have problems with alcohol. Wives' data on their husbands' drinking show significant differences, and husbands' data on themselves also support this finding. PA husbands also show higher SC and MA scores on the MMPI than do other husbands. Although internal attributions prevail over external attributions within all groups, PA husbands are more likely than other husbands to make chance attributions for causes of success and failure. Interestingly, there are no group differences for either men or women on sex-role attitudes, on self-concept, or on powerful other attributions on a generalized anger scale and on most MMPI scales.

The self-disclosure data consistently point to WI husbands as the least likely to self-disclose, particularly to their children. Relative to ND husbands, PA and VA husbands also are low in self-disclosure, for children and, nonsignificantly, for spouse.

TABLE 14.3
Conflict Inventory

Variable	PA	VA	WI	ND	F
Wife's perception of self versus wife's desired level for self					
aggression	7.4	6.7	7.5	4.3	1.76
problem solve	14.3	10.3	14.9	9.0	2.80*
withdrawal	12.1	9.3	12.3	7.5	1.91
total	40.9	34.0	44.5	26.3	2.86*
Wife's perception of husband versus wife's desired level for husband					
aggression	8.4	5.4	7.4	3.3	3.78*
problem solve	14.3	8.9	17.9	12.1	3.64*
withdrawal	11.5	9.2	18.7	8.9	5.97**
total	43.3	28.7	51.9	28.5	5.75**
Husband's perception of self versus husband's desired level for self					
aggression	7.7	4.8	5.5	3.2	4.55**
problem solve	12.0	10.0	12.9	6.3	2.80*
withdrawal	11.8	7.5	10.7	7.0	2.29
total	40.0	27.4	36.3	21.7	3.35*
Husband's perception of wife versus husband's desired level for wife					
aggression	8.9	4.9	6.4	2.8	2.64
problem solve	14.2	9.1	12.9	7.6	2.84*
withdrawal	12.3	8.0	10.6	6.1	2.34
total	45.5	30.7	39.2	21.0	3.67*

NOTE: PA = physically aggressive ($n = 13$); VA = verbally aggressive ($n = 12$); WI = withdrawing ($n = 10$); ND = nondistressed ($n = 10$).
*$p < .05$; **$p < .01$; ***$p < .001$.

Discussion

In interpreting these data, it should be noted that these are preliminary findings. The sample is yet to be completed. In addition, these findings represent only questionnaire data and do not take into account the behavioral samples of couples in the laboratory and at home (see Margolin, John, & Gleberman, in press). It also should be noted that this sample of physically abusive couples is somewhat different from subjects typically studied. These couples are strictly volunteers; they have not been referred for therapy nor have they been recruited through court order. The marital relationship is intact at the time of their participation and the couple must make a mutual decision to participate in the study. Although many of these couples would not label their own actions as physically abusive, all 13 PA

TABLE 14.4
Intrapersonal Variables

Variable	Wives					Husbands				
	PA	VA	WI	ND	F	PA	VA	WI	ND	F
Anger scale	326.2	326.3	342.4	313.1	.37	322.5	335.1	271.9	310.4	1.73
Self concept	82.8	79.9	84.4	86.3	1.67	84.7	84.2	84.3	88.9	1.32
Attribution										
powerful others	14.0	14.4	15.9	13.5	.08	17.6	18.3	11.7	17.0	1.33
chance	11.5	13.6	14.3	9.3	.50	18.0	12.2	7.6	10.4	3.58*
internal	34.9	33.3	38.7	34.2	1.37	34.6	42.0	40.4	35.8	3.77*
Sex role attitudes	87.0	93.5	88.1	79.8	1.73	83.8	88.4	85.8	80.7	1.55
MMPI										
HS	50.0	50.7	51.0	51.4	.06	58.8	55.8	54.0	48.8	1.60
D	56.7	55.2	53.2	52.4	.36	58.4	61.9	57.3	45.0	2.48
HY	57.7	51.2	53.3	52.9	1.11	62.4	57.7	57.3	54.2	1.23
PD	64.1	57.5	56.0	53.3	2.64	69.2	61.6	60.5	55.5	2.49

	PA	VA	WI	ND	F	PA	VA	WI	ND	F
PA	58.1	53.6	54.3	57.4	.88	58.1	61.2	54.3	56.6	1.83
PT	53.7	55.0	51.8	53.5	.40	57.5	56.4	51.6	49.4	1.83
SC	55.6	56.2	54.0	52.2	.64	64.7	54.7	54.4	52.0	4.25*
MA	55.2	53.4	50.5	51.3	.57	70.0	57.5	52.8	55.3	6.86***
SI	52.4	54.9	55.9	55.8	.27	52.3	49.6	52.0	49.3	.29
ego strength	60.4	50.6	59.3	55.2	1.40	53.3	53.3	55.8	48.9	.37
Self disclosure to:										
spouse	309.5	320.7	300.8	328.4	.40	304.3	309.0	268.0	341.4	1.67
children	113.8	153.3	174.4	185.6	2.24	114.5	138.0	99.6	184.7	2.85*
other relative	165.8	156.0	164.4	171.6	.09	124.9	145.3	103.2	150.8	.95
friend	213.8	179.0	222.0	188.8	.63	193.2	183.0	114.4	155.2	2.52
work associate	64.0	62.3	88.4	103.2	.75	135.7	96.3	89.3	115.6	1.30
Alcoholic screening test										
ratings by wife	3.2	4.1	4.3	2.6	.23	15.9	2.3	4.1	4.3	4.22*
ratings on husband	4.6	4.0	4.7	2.9	.13	14.5	3.5	6.0	4.8	2.42

NOTE: PA = physically aggressive ($n = 13$); VA = verbally aggressive ($n = 12$); WI = withdrawing ($n = 10$); ND = nondistressed ($n = 10$).
$*p < .05; **p < .01; ***p < .001$.

couples met Straus's criteria for serious abuse at some time in their relationship. Though different from subjects recruited from battered women's shelters or men's treatment groups, this sample may be quite representative of a large population of abusive couples that heretofore have not been studied. An important advantage found in this sample is that the couple is studied as a unit, allowing for the identification of interactional variables that differentiate abusive from nonabusive couples and for verification across spouses.

Based on these data, the following hypotheses regarding marital conflict and violence are entertained:

First, PA couples and WI couples appear to have certain interactional processes in common. The couples identified as withdrawing are clearly dissatisfied with their conflict resolution patterns yet still refrain from escalating to physically abusive conflict strategies. "Withdrawing" for these couples means walking out in the middle of a conflict or attempting to avoid discussion of problem areas altogether. Withdrawing spouses are characterized by low relationship assertiveness, high communication apprehension, the belief that conflict in relationships is destructive, and large discrepancies between ideal versus real conflict styles. Men in this group showed low self-disclosure. The group of spouses identified as physically abusive tend to engage in high frequencies of withdrawing actions and also report many of the same characteristics as the withdrawers. Although the data do not directly address this hypothesis, it is possible that a physically abusive couple engages in alternating patterns of withdrawing from anger and expressing anger. The withdrawing that occurs in PA couples, while perhaps not productive in the long run may, in the short run, cushion the couple from violence (Margolin, Baltazar & Gorin, 1984). Given their difficulties with conflict, it makes good sense that these couples would go to great lengths to avoid conflict situations. But, as is evident from data on the strictly withdrawing couples, withdrawal ultimately is not a satisfactory way of coping with marital conflict. Furthermore, the withdrawal may exacerbate the ultimate potential for violence if, in attempts to avoid conflict, there is an accumulation of frustrations, tensions, and hostile feelings.

A second hypothesis stemming from these data is that, as a group, verbally aggressive couples are not particularly dissatisfied with their relationships. Overall, these couples tend to score somewhere between PA and WI couples and ND couples. An exception, however, is found on the Areas of Change Questionnaire, which suggests that VA husbands do, in fact, want a considerable amount of change from the wife. Also, on the PAIR, VA spouses seem to expect less intimacy and to experience less intimacy. Overall, however, the VA couple seems to view their relationship as satisfactory, despite the fact that the relationship is different from the type of relationship experienced by couples labeled here as ND. If given further support, these data suggest that verbal displays of conflict and hostility are not necessarily destructive in marriage. Third, these data point to the suggestion that interpersonal more than intrapersonal factors differentiate physically abusive from nonabusive couples. In addition to their actual conflict behaviors, these data suggest that abusive couples experience substantially different levels of intimacy and communication. Whether these differences set the stage for abuse or are the outcome of abuse is not known.

Only moderate support was found for intrapersonal characteristics as mediating variables in abuse. Furthermore, despite the finding that there is wife-husband as well as husband-wife aggression in this sample, the significant intrapersonal differences that were revealed apply solely to husbands. Husbands in abusive relationships, compared to other husbands, tended to endorse chance attributions, show slightly more overall pathology, and have more problems with alcohol. Once again, it is unknown if these variables are precursors or concomitants of abuse. Furthermore, there is no evidence here that spouses who have trouble controlling their anger in the marriage also have problems controlling anger outside the marriage. In other words, for this particular sample of PA husbands, this mishandling of anger appears to be relationship specific.

One practical implication of these data is that, as concluded by others (e.g., Deschner, 1984; Mantooth, Geffner, Franks, & Patrick, 1987; Myers, 1984), there is a place for couple-oriented therapy in the treatment of spouse abuse. This is not to say that a couple-oriented approach necessarily is the best way to treat problems of violence or that it should be the only treatment. Based on the findings regarding husbands, there certainly is a need for specially designed programs for PA husbands (e.g., Saunders & Hanusa, 1984). However, for the type of couple represented here, in which spouses have not yet concluded that the marriage is too dangerous to continue, an adjunct treatment could be directed toward changing the interactional and communication styles that set these couples apart from other couples. This type of treatment could proceed only if there is a clear commitment to stop the violent behavior. This type of treatment should also proceed from the assumption that, while conflict and anger may be a function of faulty interactions, the violence is solely the choice of the individual (Sonkin, Martin, & Walker, 1985). In following such a course of action, it should be recognized that there is a tremendous amount of variability that characterizes men labeled as physically abusive. There is no one intervention that would fit all such individuals or couples. These data simply point to several variables that are worth assessing to determine whether or not they play a role in a given couple's nonproductive conflict pattern.

Note

1. This project has been funded by NIMH Grant RO1 MH36595, Gayla Margolin, principal investigator.

References

Beck, A. T. (1978). *Self concept scale.* Unpublished manuscript, University of Pennsylvania, Center for Cognitive Therapy.

Curley, A. (undated). *Spouse-specific assertion scale.* Unpublished manuscript, SUNY—Stony Brook, Department of Psychology.

Dahlstrom, W. G., Welsh, G. S., & Dahlstrom, L. E. (1972). *An MMPI handbook: Vol. 1. Clinical interpretation* (rev. ed.). Minneapolis: University of Minnesota Press.

Deschner, J. P. (1984). *The results of anger control training for violent couples.* Paper presented at the Second National Conference for Family Violence Researchers, Durham, NH.

Douglas, M. A., & Der Ovanesian, M. (1983). *A comparative study of battered and nonbattered women in crisis.* Paper presented at the 17th Annual Convention of the Association for the Advancement of Behavior Therapy, Washington, DC.

Eidelson, R. J., & Epstein, N. (1982). Cognition and relationship maladjustments: Development of a measure of dysfunctional relationship beliefs. *Journal of Consulting and Clinical Psychology, 50,* 715-720.

Faulk, M. (1974). Men who assault their wives. *Medicine, Science and the Law, 14,* 180-183.

Gelles, R. J. (1980). Violence in the family: A review of research in the seventies. *Journal of Marriage and the Family, 42,* 873-885.

Jourard, S. M. (1971). *The transparent self.* New York: Van Nostrand.

Levenson, H. (1981). Differentiating among internality, powerful others, and chance. *Research with the Locus of Control Construct: Vol. 1. Assessment Methods.* New York: Academic Press.

Mantooth, C. M., Geffner, R., Franks, D., & Patrick, J. (1987). *Family preservation: A treatment manual for reducing couple violence.* Tyler: University of Texas.

Margolin, G. (1987). The multiple forms of aggressiveness between marital partners: How do we identify them? *Journal of Marital and Family Therapy, 13,* 77-84.

Margolin, G., Baltazar, P., & Gorin, L. (1984). An interactional approach to marital violence. *Cognitive Behaviorist, 6,* 12-14.

Margolin, G., Fernandez, V., Gorin, L., & Ortiz, S. (1982). *The conflict inventory: A measurement of how couples handle marital tension.* Paper presented at the 16th annual meeting of the Association for the Advancement of Behavior Therapy, Los Angeles.

Margolin, G., John, R., & Gleberman, L. (1988). Affective responses to conflictual discussions in violent and nonviolent couples. *Journal of Consulting and Clinical Psychology.*

Mason, K. O. (1975). *Sex role items and scales from U.S. sample surveys.* Rockville, MD: NIMH.

Myers, C. (1984). *The family violence project: Some preliminary data on a treatment program for spouse abuse.* Paper presented at the second National Conference for Family Violence Researchers, Durham, NH.

Novaco, R. W. (1975). *Anger control: The development and evaluation of an experimental technique.* Lexington, MA: D.C. Heath.

Powers, W. G., & Hutchinson, K. (1979). The measurement of communication apprehension in the marriage relationship. *Journal of Marriage and the Family, 41,* 89-95.

Rosenbaum, A., & O'Leary, K. D. (1981). Marital violence: Characteristics of abusive couples. *Journal of Consulting and Clinical Psychology, 49,* 63-71.

Roy, M. (1982). *The abusive partner: An analysis of domestic battering.* New York: Van Nostrand.

Saunders, D. G., & Hanusa, D. R. (1984). *Cognitive-behavioral treatment of abusive husbands: The short-term effects of group therapy.* Paper presented at the second National Conference for Family Violence Researchers, Durham, NH.

Schaefer, M. T., & Olson, D. H. (1981). Assessing intimacy: The PAIR inventory. *Journal of Marital and Family Therapy, 7,* 47-60.

Selzer, M. L. (1971). The Michigan Alcoholism Screening test: The quest for a new diagnostic instrument. *American Journal of Psychiatry, 127,* 1653-1658.

Sonkin, D., Martin, D., & Walker, L. (1985). *The male batterer: A treatment approach.* New York: Springer.

Spanier, G. B. (1976). Measuring dyadic adjustment: New scales for assessing the quality of marriage and similar dyads. *Journal of Marriage and the Family, 38,* 15-28.

Straus, M. A. (1979). Measuring intrafamily conflict and violence: The conflict tactics scale (CTS). *Journal of Marriage and the Family, 41,* 75-88.

Straus, M. A. (1980). The marriage license as a hitting license: Evidence from popular culture, law, and social science. In M. A. Straus and G. T. Hotaling (Eds.), *The social causes of husband-wife violence.* Minneapolis: University of Minnesota Press.

Straus, M. A., Gelles, R. J., & Steinmetz, S. K. (1980). *Behind closed doors: Violence in the American family.* New York: Anchor/Doubleday.

Telch, C. F., & Lindquist, C. V. (1984). Violent versus nonviolent couples: A comparison of patterns. *Psychotherapy, 21,* 242-248.

Walker, L. E. (1984). *The battered woman syndrome.* New York: Springer.

Weiss, R. L., & Cerreto, M. C. (1980). The marital status inventory: Development of a measure of dissolution potential. *American Journal of Family Therapy, 8,* 80-85.

Weiss, R. L., & Perry, B. A. (1979). *Assessment and treatment of marital dysfunction.* Eugene: University of Oregon and Oregon Marital Studies Program.

15

Assessing Agreement
of Reports of Spouse Abuse

K. Daniel O'Leary
Ileana Arias

F ortunately, researchers from diverse
disciplines and backgrounds are now
beginning to devote attention to spouse
abuse or physical aggression between partners. Because reports of physical
beatings often come from one partner in clinical practice and research,
relatively little attention has been devoted to the interspousal agreement of
these reports. Most of the classic research to date in the spouse abuse area
has relied upon reports of one spouse, typically the wife, to assess the
prevalence and frequency of spouse abuse in marriages (e.g., Gayford,
1975; Straus, 1978; Straus, Gelles, & Steinmetz, 1980; Walker, 1979). A
potential problem in the research on spouse abuse is that spouses will not
agree on the reports of violence in their relationship. However, we need to
know the extent to which reports of aggressing against one's mate and
being victimized are accurate. *One* method of approaching this issue of the
veracity of reports of spouse abuse is to assess agreement on such reports
between spouses. Some check on the truthfulness of reports of spouse
abuse is necessary in order to develop reasonable theories about spouse
abuse. If the reports of spouse abuse are accurate, theoretical development
can proceed in a straightforward fashion. If the reports of spouse abuse are
inaccurate or systematically biased, then these inaccuracies or biases must
be understood for theoretical analyses to proceed unencumbered by
methodological problems.

Findings relevant to the reports of interspousal agreement on violence
come from examining agreements between spouses on daily behaviors in a
marriage, such as companionship activities, affection, and housekeeping

AUTHORS' NOTE: This report was supported by NIMH Grant MH35340. We thank Dr.
Susan O'Leary for helpful editorial and substantive feedback.

activities. For example, Jacobson and Moore (1981) found 48% overall agreement for 33 couples on a spouse observation checklist. Elwood & Jacobson (1982) found 38% overall agreement on couple behaviors for 10 couples beginning marital therapy. Christensen and Nies (1980) found occurrence agreement on reports of daily activities that ranged from 11% to 66% with a mean of 46%. In brief, with daily behavioral events that are more socially desirable than spouse abuse, interspousal agreement on the occurrence of these events is less than 50%.

There are a number of reasons why agreement regarding these daily behavioral events has been low. The daily behavior checklists are typically very long (ranging between 104 and 409 items), and these checklists are completed on a daily basis for one week. In our experience couples find the task of completing 104 items daily burdensome and demanding, and therefore may be careless in reporting events. Second, some of the items included in available checklists are not specific enough to be reliably assessed (Christensen, Sullaway, & King, 1983). Finally, some of the daily behavioral events typically assessed may seem mundane and trivial to partners completing the checklists. Therefore, they may lose their saliency and tend to be forgotten easily even within a 24 hour period. Certain errors in spouse reports of behavior are beginning to be understood. It has been reported that discordant couples agree less on the occurrence of behaviors than do happily married couples (Christensen & Nies, 1980; Jacobson & Moore, 1981). Also, individuals self-report engaging in more positive *and* more negative behavior than their partners do (a phenomenon called egocentric bias by Christensen et al., 1983). Even the two general results obtained in past investigations, namely, greater agreement in happily married than among discordant couples and egocentric bias do not result frequently enough to regard them as generalizable findings. It may well be that systematic errors or differences in reporting occur under quite specific situations, and that they have to be qualified by factors such as whether the behavior in question is generally viewed as positive, whether the behavior is highly specific, whether the behavior occurs frequently, and whether the behavior is seen as important by the person completing the evaluation.

Interspousal agreement regarding marital violence was assessed by Szinovacz (1983) on six items used to measure marital violence. Overall agreement ranged from 82% to 96% but such high agreements were largely due to agreement on the nonoccurrence of abuse. Agreement on the occurrence of the six physically abusive events ranged only from 0% to 38%. It is difficult to reach any firm conclusions regarding the reliability of reports of physical aggression between spouses from the Szinovacz study because the frequency of the six physically abusive behaviors ranged only from 0% to 15%.

Frequencies of behavior and reliabilities of those behaviors are inextricably intertwined. In order to address reliability or agreement issues regarding spouse abuse, it is necessary to know how prevalent spouse abuse is among various populations. If spouse abuse were a very, very infrequent event, then assessment of agreement on spouse abuse might prove very difficult. In fact, however, physical aggression between partners is quite common. Because of the interdependent nature of base rates of behavior and agreement about such behavior, it is necessary to discuss the prevalence or base rates of interspousal aggression.

In 1974, Gelles estimated that the prevalence of physical abuse among couples in the United States was as high as 60%. In 1978, Straus presented data that indicated that 30% of married women experienced physical abuse at some time in their marriage. Hornung, McCullough, and Sugimoto (1981), in one of the largest samples yet assessed (N = 1,553), found that physical aggression had occurred during the year preceding the survey in 16% of the couples and that the physical abuse generally was distributed in an equal fashion throughout all socioeconomic levels. Research with nonmarried dating partners (Cate, Henton, Koval, Christopher, & Lloyd, 1982; Makepeace, 1981) indicates that physical aggression occurs in approximately 20% of couples.

In our first study of agreements in reports of physical violence (Jouriles & O'Leary, 1984), we obtained reports of spouse abuse from 65 couples attending the University Marital Therapy Clinic at Stony Brook and 37 happily married couples from the community matched for age, SES, and years married. Our data source for the self-reports of physical abuse was the 18 item Conflict Tactics Scale developed by Straus (1978). In the happily married sample, we found that 9% of the women and 7% of the men reported that their spouses had been physically aggressive toward them at some point in their marriage. In the maritally discordant sample, we found that 36% of the women and 22% of the men reported that their spouses had been physically abusive to them at some point in their marriages. With regard to agreement that the spouse was aggressive we found the information contained in Table 15.1. These results indicate that when corrected for base rate frequencies using Cohen's Kappa (1960), agreement among clinic and nonclinic couples was remarkably similar. However, interpartner agreement for all couples was generally lower than those obtained in observational data in which a 70% agreement ratio between observers is often used as a cut-off for acceptable reliability (O'Leary, Kent, & Kanowitz, 1975).

Method

We are conducting a longitudinal research project designed to assess the development of marital discord and spouse abuse. We have assessed 369 of the 400 couples we intend to follow. These couples were given a battery of

TABLE 15.1
Agreement That the Spouse Was Aggressive

	Percentage Agreement (Occurrence & Nonoccurrence)	*Occurrence Agreement*	*Kappa*
Clinic Sample (N = 65)			
Husband was violent	72	50	47
Wife was violent	72	45	40
Community Sample (N = 37)			
Husband was violent	77	38	40
Wife was violent	80	36	41

personality, behavioral, stress, and family history measures, and a third of the couples were interviewed and completed a communication task. The couples were assessed and/or interviewed at four weeks prior to marriage and at 6, 18, and 36 months after marriage. The couples were paid $40 for each assessment, which took approximately one and a half hours.

Participants were recruited by newspaper and radio announcements in Suffolk and Onondaga counties in New York. They represent a fairly typical sample of young couples from these two counties. They were approximately 24 years old; 78% of the participants were employed full-time; 9% were employed part-time; 7% were unemployed; and 6% were students. The average income of those employed was $13,670; 57% of the population was Catholic, 22% Protestant, and 7% Jewish. The average educational level was 14.6 years of schooling. To our surprise we found that physical abuse occurred quite frequently prior to marriage. More specifically, using the overall violence index of the Conflict Tactics Scale, according to men's reports, 35% of the females were physically aggressive toward their fiancés prior to marriage, and according to female's reports, 30% of the males were physically aggressive (abusive) toward their fiancées prior to marriage. According to the women's reports of their partners and according to the men's reports of their partners, the rates of physical aggression were not different at Syracuse and Stony Brook.

Using reports from our sample of 369 couples about to be married, in which the rate of physical aggression was approximately 35%, we obtained the agreement data shown in Table 15.2. In short, interpartner agreement on spouse abuse with couples about to be married appears very similar to interpartner agreement both with distressed and nondistressed married couples (Jouriles & O'Leary, 1984). Further, these agreement rates or reliabilities are markedly similar to reliabilities obtained on spouse reports

TABLE 15.2
Agreement That the Partner Was Agressive
(couples about to be married; N = 369)

	Percentage Agreement	Occurrence Agreement	Kappa
Husband was violent	68	40	36
Wife was violent	72	39	32

of daily relationship events (e.g., Christensen & Nies, 1980; Elwood & Jacobson, 1982). The reliabilities are much greater than chance agreement but low enough to suggest problems of agreement in reports of behavior by husbands about their wives and vice versa. The Conflict Tactics Scale is certainly psychometrically adequate enough to allow one to detect differences in rates of abuse across samples, but we need to address why spouses differ in their reports of interpartner violence.

Discussion

Why the Concern About Interspousal Agreement?

Some might question why it seems necessary at all to have agreement between spouses regarding interspousal violence. It can be argued that there are such cogent reasons why there would be lack of agreement between spouses that the usual application of reliability statistics to spouse abuse is ill-advised. For example, women who are abused by their husbands might choose not to indicate to an investigator or therapist that they were abused because they fear that their husbands would hurt them if they disclosed such information. This very concern was so great that when we received a site visit by an NIMH team three years ago about our proposal to investigate spouse abuse in newly married couples, some members of the evaluation team questioned whether there would be any reports by victims of their physical abuse. As we have pointed out, even individuals about to be married have abuse rates of approximately 30-35%. To our surprise, however, the reports of aggressing against a mate were approximately 5% higher than the reports of being abused by the mate for both males and females.

We now outline some reasons for systematic overreporting and underreporting of being abused by one's mate and some reasons for systematic overreporting and underreporting of aggressing against one's mate. In presenting such reasons, we assume that under certain conditions, it is possible to obtain a reasonably accurate report of spousal violence. At the outset, however, we want to emphasize that the reasons proffered are simply *possible* factors that might influence underreporting and over-reporting. The reasons given certainly do not have equal status; some now seem much more important than others.

Reasons for underreporting abuse or victimization include (1) fear of reprisal by one's mate, (2) protect partner from looking bad, and (3) protection of one's self; concern that the data collector would view the person negatively if he or she tolerated repeated victimization. Reasons for overreporting victimization include (1) make the partner look bad in order to increase alimony payments if a divorce proceeding is imminent, (2) dramatize to the therapist how bad the relationship is and how strongly professional help is needed, and (3) exaggerate negative events because of depression or paranoia. Reasons for underreporting aggressing against one's mate include (1) it is socially undesirable to abuse a mate, and (2) memory for negative events is often poorer than memory for positive events. Reasons for overreporting aggressing against one's mate include (1) wish to be strong and in control of the relationship, and (2) egocentric bias, that is, a tendency to report both more positive and more negative events than one's partner reports about an individual. We believe that the reasons for underreporting victimization and aggressing against one's mate noted above are more cogent than the reasons for overreporting victimization and aggressing against one's mate, but we recognize that potential reasons both for overreporting as well as underreporting should be examined.

In addition to the factors listed above, which could produce systematic biases in reports of spouse abuse, there are methodological factors that could lead to *unsystematic* disagreements such as misinterpretation of items, different interpretation of items by husband and wife, and unclear recollection of events occurring approximately one year ago. Differences in agreement of both an unsystematic and a systematic nature have to be explored. It is premature to say that all we have to do is to concern ourselves with reports of abuse by the person reporting abuse as long as those reports are stable, that is, have test-retest reliability. Even if we knew that spouses' reports of abuse were stable, and we do not know that they are, such retest reliability does not address the important issues of disagreement in reports of violence between partners. These disagreements are important to understand both for their own right as well as in order to better understand the true prevalence of spousal violence.

Spouses' Reasons for Disagreement

We are currently assessing sources of interpartner disagreement on the occurrence of physically aggressive behavior. We are interviewing couples regarding differences in their reports of aggression in an attempt to see if there are systematic reasons why men and women differ in their reports of spouse abuse. We will code reasons for the differences given by the men and women regarding why they think they differ in their reports and, in particular, why there may be underreports by one spouse. For example, we expect that reasons for disagreement will be distributed into categories such as the following:

Intention: The person not reporting aggression or spouse abuse would say that it was accidental.

Intensity: The person not reporting abuse would say that it was playful not an intense act.

Intoxication: The person not reporting abuse would say that he or she was intoxicated and was unaware of what happened.

Memory Loss: The person not reporting abuse would say that he or she did not remember such an event.

Self-Defense: The person not reporting abuse would indicate that he or she acted in self-defense.

The reasons given by spouses for differences in reports of violence between them may be quite different from the factors described earlier in this chapter that might account for systematic underreporting and overreporting of victimization and aggressing against one's mate.

Use of Kappa for Base Rate Corrections

We have reported agreement on nonoccurrence as well as agreement on occurrence of spouse abuse. It is often observed by clinicians that physical aggression between spouses occurs frequently before treatment and very infrequently while in treatment. If physical aggression between spouses does indeed occur infrequently during treatment, it is important to know the reliability of such a report. The overall Kappa does not yield a separate agreement measure for occurrence and nonoccurrence. Kappa is a measure that takes into account agreement with respect both to occurrence and nonoccurrence. However, corrections for chance for occurrence and nonoccurrence can be made using Kappa (see Table 15.3).

In situations in which there is no variability because there is perfect agreement that no physical abuse occurred, Kappa is not a useful statistic. In such a case, Kappa would be zero (see Table 15.4). In determining what statistic to use to report agreement, one has to consider the distributions of the scores and the psychological nature of the data. No single measure of agreement is best for all situations. For example, in item analyses of the Conflict Tactics Scale we have data indicating that there is very high agreement in spouses' reports that their partners did not threaten them with a gun. We simply do not reject these reports as spurious because the Kappas for this item were not high. When base rates of behavior are either very high

TABLE 15.3

		Husband (Observer A)		
		Yes	No	
Wife (Observer B)	Yes	25 A	5 B	30 A + B
	No	5 C	65 D	70 C + D
		A + C = 30	B + D = 70	100

NOTE: A = number of intervals in which both observers indicated that the behavior occurred; D = number of intervals in which both observers indicated that the behavior did not occur; B + C = disagreement cells, that is, where one observer indicated that the behavior occurred and the other observer indicated that the behavior did not occur.

occurrence agreement = A/A + B + C = 25/35 = .71

nonoccurrence agreement = D/D + C + B = 65/65 + 5 + 5 = .87

correction for chance agreement for occurrence;
chance agreement = (A + B) (A + C)/A + B + C + D = 900/100 = 9

correction for chance agreement for nonoccurrence:
chance agreement = (B + D) (C + D)/A + B + C + D = 4900/100 = 49

correcting occurrence agreement for chance

$$\frac{A - [(A + B) (A + C)/A + B + C + D] = 25 - 9}{A + B + C - [(A + B) (A + C)/A + B + C + D] = 35 - 9}$$
$$= .61$$

correcting nonoccurrence agreement for chance

$$\frac{D - [(B + D) (C + D)/A + B + C + D] = 65 - 49}{D + C + B - [(B + D) (C + D)/A + B + C + D] = 75 - 49}$$
$$= .61$$

or very low, the correction for chance with Kappa is very restrictive.[1] While Kappa is very useful in correcting for chance in situations in which there are very high or low base rates, it is necessary to consider whether the behaviors in question, for example, threatening with a gun, would have spuriously high agreement by chance, or whether in fact the behavior did not occur.

In situations like the one described here, that is, the presence or absence of an abusive behavior as perceived by a female and a male, it seems legitimate to present agreement data using several different agreement indices. Ultimately, the proof of the pudding is whether the reports of abuse can be consistently related to other variables. Fortunately, we already know that reports of partner abuse can be related to family-of-origin variables such as parental violence and to personality variables. However, we cannot ignore certain low agreement indices on occurrence of spouse abuse. With

TABLE 15.4

		Husbands			
		Yes	No		
Wives	Yes	0	0	0	
		A	B	A + B	
	No	0	20	20	
		C	D	C + D	
		A + C = 0	B + D = 20	A + B + C + D = 20	

$$D - (B + D)(C + D)/A + B + C + D = 20 - (20)(20)/20 = 0$$
$$D + C + B - (B + D)(C + D)/A + B + C + D = 20 - (20)(20)/20 = 0$$

greater agreement it is *possible* that we could obtain stronger relationships between reports of abuse and personality variables.

Future Work

We are now assessing how individuals interpret various aggressive behaviors between partners to analyze certain factors that may relate to differences in reports of aggressive behaviors by husbands and wives. We are assessing rates of aggression between dating partners to ascertain whether the intensity of love or positive feelings is related to physical aggression because we were surprised by the 35% rate of aggression between partners who are about to marry. We are assessing personality, stress, family history, and day-to-day behavioral interactions as these factors may relate to physical aggression and spouse abuse. Within two years, we expect to be able to tell you some of the reasons why young married persons hit one another, how they interpret their hitting, and why they often differ in their reports of hitting and other acts of physical aggression.

Note

1. Following the presentation of this paper, Spitznagel and Helzer (1985, *Archives of General Psychiatry, 42*, 725-728) also argued that Kappa is unduly restrictive. They proposed several other statistics which are stable over varying base rates.

References

Cate, R. M., Henton, J. M., Koval, J., Christopher, F. S., & Lloyd, S. (1982). Premarital abuse: A social psychological perspective. *Journal of Family Issues, 3,* 79-90.

Christensen, A., & Nies, D. C. (1980). The spouse observation checklist: Empirical analysis and critique. *The American Journal of Family Therapy, 8,* 69-79.

Christensen, A., Sullaway, M., & King, C. E. (1983). Systematic error in behavioral reports of dyadic interaction: Egocentric bias and content effects. *Behavioral Assessment, 5,* 129-140.

Cohen, J. (1960). A coefficient of agreement for nominal scales. *Educational and Psychological Measurement, 20,* 37-46.

Elwood, R., & Jacobson, N. S. (1982). Spouses' agreement in reporting their behavioral interactions: A clinical replication. *Journal of Consulting and Clinical Psychology, 50,* 783-784.

Gayford, J. J. (1975). Wife battering: A preliminary survey of 100 cases. *British Medical Journal, 1,* 194-197.

Gelles, R. J. (1974). *The violent home.* Beverly Hills, CA: Sage.

Hornung, C. A., McCullough, B. C., & Sugimoto, T. (1981). Status relationships in marriage: Risk factors in spouse abuse. *Journal of Marriage and the Family, 43,* 675-692.

Jacobson, N. S., & Moore, D. (1981). Spouses as observers of the events in their relationship. *Journal of Consulting and Clinical Psychology, 49,* 269-277.

Jouriles, E., & O'Leary, K. D. (1984). Interspousal reliability on the report of marital violence. Paper revised for the *Journal of Consulting and Clinical Psychology.*

Makepeace, J. M. (1981). Courtship violence among college students. *Family Relations, 30,* 97-102.

O'Leary, K. D., Kent, R. N., & Kanowitz, J. (1975). Shaping data collection congruent with experimental hypotheses. *Journal of Applied Behavior Analysis, 8,* 43-51.

Straus, M. A. (1978). Wife beating: How common and why? *Victimology, 2,* 443-458.

Straus, M. A., Gelles, R. J., & Steinmetz, S. K. (1980). *Behind closed doors: Violence in the American family.* New York: Anchor/Doubleday.

Szinovacz, M. E. (1983). Using couple data as a methodological tool: The case of marital violence. *Journal of Marriage and the Family, 45,* 633-644.

Walker, L. E. (1979). *The battered woman.* New York: Harper & Row.

16

A Multivariate Investigation
of Children's Adjustment
to Family Violence

David A. Wolfe
Peter Jaffe
Susan Kaye Wilson
Lydia Zak

T he child who witnesses physical violence between his/her parents or caregivers is exposed to confusing and upsetting events that often result in undesirable or stressful changes to his/her life. It is not surprising, therefore, that preliminary research in this area has reported that such children may demonstrate a wide range of behavior problems (Hughes & Barad, 1983; Porter & O'Leary, 1980; Rosenbaum & O'Leary, 1981; Wolfe, Jaffe, Wilson, & Zak, 1985). Children from violent homes deserve the attention of mental health professionals, since they appear to be a diversified and substantially large group that may be at risk for psychological and behavioral problems.

In light of the very recent attention to this problem from behavioral scientists and practitioners, investigators have not begun to account for a host of factors associated with family violence that are likely in themselves to affect children's adjustment. For example, battered women are likely to suffer from both physical and emotional disorders, to be exposed to other

AUTHORS' NOTE: We wish to thank the staffs of women's transition houses in Cambridge, Chatham, Guelph, London, Sarnia, and Woodstock, Ontario for their generous assistance and support. This research was supported by a grant from the Ontario Ministry of Community and Social Services and the Ontario Mental Health Foundation. This chapter represents a longer version of the article "Critical issues in the assessment of children's adjustment to witnessing family violence." by P. Jaffe, D. Wolfe, S. Wilson, and L. Zak, *Canada's Mental Health*, Vol. 33, No. 4, December 1985. Reproduced with permission of the Minister of Supply and Services, Canada.

life stresses, and to be hindered by a number of socioeconomic disadvantages (Walker, 1979) that may seriously affect the parent/child relationship. The impact of stressful life events on children (Sandler & Block, 1979), as well as the difficulties they experience in relation to maternal adjustment problems (Mednick & McNeil, 1968) and socioeconomic disadvantages such as poor housing, overcrowding, frequent home and school moves, and multiple separations (Rutter, 1979) have been documented with other child populations. These environmental and family stress factors may serve to potentiate one another over time and lead to child adjustment problems (Rutter, 1971; 1979). Thus research investigating the impact of family violence upon children must be increasingly sensitive to the negative influence of factors that are indirectly related to violence in the home. There are several important reasons why researchers and clinicians should be extremely interested in understanding the adjustment of children who have been exposed to family violence. Retrospective accounts of men who batter their wives indicate that the vast majority have witnessed similar behavior on the part of their fathers in their family of origin (Rosenbaum & O'Leary, 1981; Pagelow, 1981). Similarly, retrospective accounts of victims suggest that wives are less likely to seek refuge from their husbands' beatings if they have witnessed their mothers as victims of abuse (Lerman, 1981), and they rely upon more avoidant and less active coping responses (Mitchell & Hodson, in press; Rosenberg, 1984). These findings are only suggestive, yet they raise important questions regarding the effects of violence upon children and the mechanisms by which young children learn to resolve interpersonal conflicts.

The present study was designed to extend our knowledge about the effects of family violence upon children by investigating relationships among several important family variables. The relative contributions of parent conflict, ongoing negative life events, and degree of family sociodemographic disadvantage were used as predictors of the development of child and maternal symptomatology and adjustment. To add to our understanding of children who have been exposed to family violence, a nonclinic sample of mothers and children who had sought refuge from family violence and a comparison sample of nonviolent families were compared on several broad-spectrum measures.

Method

Subjects

Subjects were 50 mothers and children (ages 4 to 16) from transition houses (shelters for abused women and their children), and 50 mother-child pairs from the community. Mothers and children who were receiving psychological/psychiatric services (beyond assessment and diagnosis) were excluded from the sample.

Subjects were classified as members of violent families based upon independent ratings of responses to items on the physical aggression subscale of the Conflict Tactics Scale (Straus, 1979; see below), in addition to shelter residence. Subjects classified as members of nonviolent families had never sought refuge from a violent partner and reported no incidences of overt physical violence (e.g., kicking, hitting, slapping) between adult partners since the child was less than 24 months old. Table 16.1 depicts the demographic and descriptive characteristics of the two samples. Whereas the groups did not differ on demographic variables (child's age and sex, number of children in the family, income, or marital status) the sample from violent families had significantly more changes in residence, marital separations, and physical aggression scores than nonviolent families, $F(1,78)$ = 10.77, 5.00, and 37.93, respectively ($p < .01$). These latter descriptive differences were expected on the basis of sample selection.

Procedure

Each mother was administered a structured interview designed to obtain a thorough history and description of the family. Interviews with women at the shelter were conducted in a designated room at the transition house. The community comparison sample was solicited through newspaper advertisements, and interviews with these subjects were conducted in an office setting. Control subjects were paid $10 for their participation, and were informed that they were participating in a study of family relations. All interviews were conducted by research assistants and graduate students who were trained during a pilot phase of the project to achieve reliable, standardized administration and recording of the responses. Following the interview, the women were administered four psychometric instruments to assess maternal and child adjustment, life events, and family conflict. Each woman was offered feedback from the assessment findings and referral recommendations when appropriate.

Measures

Maternal health. The General Health Questionnaire (GHQ) (Goldberg & Hillier, 1979) was administered to mothers in the study to assess their emotional and physical functioning. This instrument measures somatic problems, anxiety and insomnia, social dysfunction, and depression in adults, as rated over the previous few weeks. The 28 items require the respondent to indicate the frequency of various symptoms on a 4-point scale (0 = not at all; 3 = much more that usual). The total score used for this study ranges from 0 (no symptoms) to 84 (extreme symptomatology).

Child adjustment. Children's behavior was measured using the Achenbach Child Behavior Profile (CBP) (Achenbach, 1979). This checklist is a parent rating of the child's competence (e.g., school performance, activities)

TABLE 16.1

Demographic and Descriptive Characteristics of Samples
from Violent and Nonviolent Families

Characteristics	Violent Families (N = 50)	Nonviolent Families (N = 50)
Child's age		
M	8.4	8.8
SD	2.3	2.2
Sex of child		
Male	29	27
Female	21	23
Number of children in family	2.4	2.4
Family income		
M	$12,582	$13,088
SD	$ 9,705	$ 6,838
Marital status		
single	12	22
reconstituted	12	9
intact	26	19
Changes in family residence since birth of first child		
M	8.5	3.8
SD	7.8	2.8
Marital separations		
M	3.4	0.2
SD	7.6	0.4
Physical aggression between adults[a]		
M	24.5	1.6
SD	16.2	2.1

a. Range = 0–54 (no aggression-high aggression) based on 9 items from the Conflict Tactics Scale, averaged between mother and father.

and behavior problems (e.g., refuses to obey, withdraws). Computer scoring compares children 4 to 16 years old to age- and sex-based normative data. In the present study, t-scores are reported for second-order factors (i.e., social competence, internalizing, and externalizing behavior problems) as well as first-order factors (e.g., withdrawn, aggressive, hyperactive; Achenbach, 1979).

Family Disadvantage Index. Seven sociodemographic variables were combined in a linear fashion from interview responses to obtain an estimate of family disadvantage (see Rutter, 1971; Dumas & Wahler, 1983). A disadvantage score of 1 was assigned to each of seven variables according to the following criteria: (a) three or more children living in the home; (b) family income less than $13,000 (1984 poverty level for family of four in Canada); (c) three or more changes in residence since the birth of the oldest child (excluding moves to transition houses); (d) children had lived with one or more aggressive male role models for more than six months; (e) the family had experienced a marital separation for at least three months in the past two years; (f) the family had received two or more community services in the past (e.g., counseling, child welfare); and (g) the family was headed by a single parent. Therefore, a family's Disadvantage Index score could range from zero to seven.

Life events. The Life Experiences Survey (LES) (Sarason, Johnson, & Siegel, 1979) was administered to assess the degree of stress related to life events over the past 12 months. The respondent was asked to rate the positive or negative impact of 47 events on a scale from -3 (very negative) to 3 (very positive), such as changes in income, divorce, or death of a family member. The Total Negative Score (range = 0 to 141) reported from this instrument reflects the adult's rating of negative events.

Conflict tactics. The Conflict Tactics scale (CT) (Straus, 1979) was administered verbally to the mother to measure the amount of physical aggression between partners over the last 12 months. Responses to each item were rated on a 7-point scale according to the frequency of their occurrence (0 = never, 6 = more than 20 times). Responses to nine items comprising the physical aggression subscale were then assessed independently by three raters to calculate interrater agreement of classifying groups into violent and nonviolent. Raters were given the nine items, ranging from throwing and hitting objects to using a knife or gun on the partner. The raters were asked to determine whether, in their opinion, the family was violent based on the frequency and severity of the reported items. Interrater agreement was calculated by dividing the number of correctly matched subjects by the total number of subjects for each pair of raters. Agreement ranged from 75% to 87% with a mean of 81%.

In addition to assisting in the classification of violent and nonviolent family groups, the Conflict Tactics scale was used to provide a continuous measure of physical aggression between partners. This measure was the average of ratings based upon "wife to husband" aggression and "husband to wife" aggression as reported by the mother.

Results

Pearson product-moment correlations were calculated for all pairs of variables for each subject group in order to examine relationships among the variables. Results of the simple correlations are presented in Table 16.2. Intercorrelations among the three predictor variables (family disadvantage, life events, and physical aggression between partners) were not of such magnitude as to violate assumptions of independence (Gordon, 1968).

TABLE 16.2
Correlations Among Family Predictors and Child Adjustment Variables

Variable	1			2			3			4			5		
	Total	V	NV	Total	V	NV	Total	V	NV	Total	V	NV	Total	V	NV
Disadvantage index															
Physical aggression between partners	.76	.68	.61												
Negative life events	.39	.35	.13	.36	.31	-.13									
General health questionnaire	.31	.17	.06	.43	.31	-.18	.53	.46	.34						
Child behavior problems	.38	.33	.24	.24	.16	-.04	.42	.45	.22	.46	.47	.23			
Child social competence	-.25	-.07	-.23	-.16	.17	-.26	.19	.42	.17	-.10	.05	.10	-.26	-.04	-.31

NOTE: V = violent families, N = 50; NV = nonviolent families, N = 50. Underlined values are significant at $p < .01$.

Predictors of Maternal and Child Adjustment

Since maternal adjustment is likely to influence child adjustment ratings as well as parental effectiveness, a stepwise multiple regression analysis was conducted in order to investigate the relationship between the three predictor variables and the outcome measure of maternal adjustment (General Health Questionnaire). The two measures of child adjustment (behavior problems and social competence) were then predicted by all four family variables. Tables 16.3, 16.4, & 16.5 depict results of the separate analyses, revealing that the amount of violence in the home contributed significantly to the prediction model of child adjustment. The result of the first regression analysis (Table 16.3) revealed that maternal adjustment was significantly predicted by a combination of the three predictor variables, $F(3,76) = 13.25, p < .001, R = .59$. Tests of the individual predictors revealed that negative life events and physical aggression variables contributed significantly to the regression equation, whereas the family disadvantage index did not add to the model.

The second regression analysis (Table 16.4) revealed that the measure of child behavior problems was significantly predicted by a combination of the four predictors, $F(4,75) = 9.07, p < .001, R = .57$. In this analysis, maternal health contributed significantly to the equation, as did two measures of family functioning: disadvantage index and physical aggression. The negative life events measure failed to contribute significantly to the equation.

The third regression analysis (Table 16.5) indicated that the measure of child social competence was significantly predicted by a combination of the four predictors, $F(4,75) = 5.64, p < .001, R = .50$. This analysis revealed a different order among the predictors, in comparison with child behavior problems. Two measures of family functioning, disadvantage index and negative life events, contributed significantly to the equation, whereas maternal health and physical aggression between partners were not significant predictors of child competence.

Comparison of Mother and Child Adjustment
in Violent and Nonviolent Families

To extend the descriptive comparison between children from violent and nonviolent families, stepwise discriminant function analyses were separately conducted for boys and girls using family status (violent versus nonviolent) as an independent variable. Dependent variables for each analysis were three social competence scales and nine behavior problem scales from the Child Behavior Profile.

For boys, six variables entered into the stepwise procedure to produce a significant function, Wilks's Lambda = .46, $X^2(6, N = 47) = 32.63, p < .001$. This function was associated with a canonical correlation of .74 and an

TABLE 16.3

Stepwise Multiple Regression Analysis: Maternal Health as a
Function of Family Disadvantage, Negative Life Events,
and Physical Aggression Between Partners

Entry Order	R	R^2	R^2 Change	Beta Weights	F of Inclusion	df
Negative life events	.513	.263	.263	.430	27.84*	1, 78
Physical aggression	.579	.335	.072	.391	8.31*	2, 77
Family disadvantage	.586	.343	.009	−.146	.99	3, 76

*$p < .01$.

TABLE 16.4

Stepwise Multiple Regression Analysis: Child Behavior Problems
(Sum T) as a Function of Family Disadvantage, Negative Life Events,
Physical Aggression Between Partners, and Maternal Health

Entry Order	R	R^2	R^2 Change	Beta Weights	F of Inclusion	df
Maternal health	.439	.192	.192	.342	18.57**	1, 78
Family disadvantage	.513	.263	.071	.460	7.38**	2, 77
Physical aggression	.552	.305	.042	−.323	4.60*	3, 76
Negative life events	.571	.326	.021	.176	2.35	4, 75

*$p < .05$; **$p < .01$.

overall correct classification rate of 89% of cases (violent = 96%, nonviolent
= 83%). Factor scales in the stepwise order of entry for boys included
behaviors labeled aggressive, social, obsessive-compulsive, hyperactive,
school, and withdrawn. The remaining six factor scales did not enter the
function. Between-group comparisons for all Child Behavior Profile factor
scales for boys are shown in Table 16.6.

For girls, no significant between-group differences on the CBP were
revealed (Table 16.7), and the discriminant function was nonsignificant.
Although the data presented in Table 16.7 reveal a trend for girls from
violent homes to show more problems than the comparison sample, the
differences are not as marked as those for boys (as shown).

The third discriminant function analysis involved the four factor scales
from the General Health Questionnaire, in order to compare maternal
adjustment between the two groups. The stepwise procedure entered only
the scale labeled Anxiety and Insomnia, which produced a significant

TABLE 16.5

Stepwise Multiple Regression Analysis: Child Social Competence
as a Function of Family Disadvantage, Negative Life Events,
Physical Aggression Between Partners, and Maternal Health

Entry Order	R	R^2	R^2 Change	Beta Weights	F of Inclusion	df
Family disadvantage	.281	.079	.079	−.520	6.17*	1, 72
Negative life events	.453	.206	.127	.480	11.31*	2, 71
Maternal health	.485	.235	.030	−.235	2.71	3, 70
Physical aggression	.496	.246	.011	.170	1.02	4, 69

*$p < .01$.

TABLE 16.6

Group Differences for Measures of Social Competence
and Behavior Problems for Boys (ages 6 to 11)

Variable	Violent Families		Nonviolent Families		F(1, 45)
	M	SD	M	SD	
Social Competence Factors					
activities	42.04	17.51	49.63	16.28	2.37
social	38.30	12.64	56.13	17.71	15.64***
school	47.35	15.45	63.08	22.94	7.54**
Behavior Problem Factors					
schizoid	61.39	10.18	55.88	7.50	4.50*
depressed	64.74	7.80	54.83	10.63	13.17***
uncommunicative	67.00	11.17	57.37	8.80	10.82**
obsessive-compulsive	63.48	11.74	52.46	8.90	13.22***
somatic complaints	62.30	10.28	57.58	6.61	3.54
withdrawn	62.65	11.67	54.88	9.73	6.18*
hyperactive	61.30	9.68	53.46	9.46	7.90**
aggressive	67.65	10.37	53.29	10.82	21.55***
delinquent	66.91	9.17	58.00	7.25	13.73***

NOTE: T scores from the Achenbach Child Behavior Profile. Boys (ages 6 to 11)
from violent families, N = 23; nonviolent families, N = 24.
*$p < .05$; **$p < .01$; ***$p < .001$.

function, Wilks's Lambda = .69, X^2 (1, N = 100) = 36.19, $p < .001$. This
function was associated with a canonical correlation of .56 and correct
classification rates of 72% of all cases (violent = 60%, nonviolent = 84%).
Between-group comparisons for the four maternal health factors are shown
in Table 16.8.

TABLE 16.7

Group Differences for Measures of Social Competence
and Behavior Problems for Girls (ages 6 to 11)

Variable	Violent Families		Nonviolent Families		F(1, 30)
	M	SD	M	SD	
Social Competence Factors					
activities	48.77	10.79	54.74	9.95	2.59
social	44.23	8.32	42.74	8.78	.23
school	44.46	15.50	55.26	19.46	2.79
Behavior Problem Factors					
depression	63.69	13.94	58.37	11.30	1.42
social withdrawal	62.15	13.15	62.84	11.26	.03
somatic complaint	61.38	12.19	57.47	10.26	.96
schizoid-obsessive	61.23	8.26	61.37	8.53	.01
hyperactive	58.08	12.89	56.05	12.01	.21
sex problems	57.62	8.38	61.21	10.70	1.03
delinquent	63.85	10.42	60.63	6.42	1.17
aggressive	58.54	13.47	56.95	11.32	.13
cruel	62.69	10.18	61.47	8.15	.14

NOTE: T scores from the Achenbach Child Behavior Profile. Girls (ages 6 to 11)
from violent families, N = 13; nonviolent families, N = 19.

Discussion

Results of the multiple regression analyses suggest that child behavior problems are strongly associated with maternal adjustment and amount of physical aggression in the home. These findings pertain to a nonclinic sample of children who have been brought to shelters, as well as children who have not experienced family violence. These results were congruent with findings from the divorce literature that implicate positive relationships with adults as important mediators of child adjustment (Emery, 1982; Rutter, 1971). Mothers who reported fewer symptoms and changes in their own functioning were more likely to report fewer child behavior problems as well. It is conceivable that maternal functioning is a significant moderator of children's adjustment to family violence, which supports attempts to provide supportive counseling services for women in shelters.

The sex differences in this research seem to be supported from a number of other studies that suggest that boys are more vulnerable to marital discord (Rutter, 1971) and parental separation (Wallerstein & Kelly, 1980). These findings are consistent with the view that boys appear more vulnerable from birth to a host of physical and psychological disorders (Brooks-Gunn & Mathews, 1979). Rutter (1971), in reviewing the differential impact of family discord on boys' socially deviant behavior,

TABLE 16.8

Group Differences on Maternal Health Questionnaire Subscales

Variable	Violent Families		Nonviolent Families		F(1, 98)
	M	SD	M	SD	
Somatic problems	7.38	5.24	3.30	2.96	23.01*
Anxiety and insomnia	10.22	5.77	4.10	3.05	44.05*
Social dysfunction	7.88	5.61	6.20	3.00	3.49
Depression	5.24	5.54	1.64	2.76	16.92*

*$p < .001$.

concluded that boys are biologically and psychologically more sensitive to stress.

Aside from a general notion of boys' increased vulnerability to stress, there may be other explanations for the present findings. From a methodological view, mothers' more negative reporting of their sons' adjustment relative to their daughters' may be part of a "negative bias" against males, related to the violence from their husbands (O'Leary & Emery, 1982). Future research may include independent sources of information about the children, such as teachers' ratings of their behavior, to avoid this possible bias.

There is some evidence that adjustment problems in girls have a later onset than boys (e.g., Reitsma-Street, Offord, Finch, & Dummitt, 1984), which may suggest that longer-term follow-up is required to identify the potential impact of family violence. Since some researchers suggest women who are battered and remain in the situation have witnessed similar behavior on the part of their mothers (Walker, 1979), the impact may not even be apparent in adolescence, but in later adult years.

Within a psychoanalytic, social-learning, or cognitive-developmental framework, one might predict that boys would have the greatest adjustment difficulties after witnessing their fathers' violence. Aside from obvious notions such as modeling and identification, boys may be in a more difficult position after parental separation. The divorce literature suggests that boys may blame their mothers for the separation irrespective of the reasons, since they cannot resolve the conflict with their absent father (Wallerstein & Kelly, 1980).

Although previous studies have suggested boys may exhibit more externalizing symptoms and girls may demonstrate internalizing symptoms (Hughes & Barad, 1983), the present research suggests that boys' behavior is elevated in both behavioral dimensions. One explanation may relate to the profile of the abusive male (father) who is likely to model both aggression and inadequate, immature, and depressive symptomology

(Ganley & Harris, 1981). Future research would need to replicate this finding and provide more psychological data on fathers aside from their violence.

We stress that no causal link between witnessing spouse abuse and child adjustment problems can be determined on the basis of this study. Family violence is clearly associated with innumerable family problems that potentiate the overall negative impact upon the child. Furthermore, the child's own characteristics may serve to moderate the impact of these events in either a positive or negative fashion. Future research may move us closer to an understanding of the most significant family events that attenuate or accentuate the child's adjustment, beyond the life events and disadvantage factors reported herein. Furthermore, we cannot determine from this one sample how many children seem to be "invulnerable" to the negative effects of severe family problems. An analysis of additional variables that may serve to "buffer" the effects of parental conflict may confirm our suspicions that positive parental relationships and social supports are significant mediators of child adjustment in such situations (Emery, 1982; Rutter, 1979).

The findings support the growing consensus that family violence affects children in many direct *and* indirect ways, and highlight the need for mental health professionals to be vigilant as to the impact of family violence on children. Besides inappropriate modeling of conflict resolution, these children are affected by their mothers' diminished effectiveness as a parent, negative changes in family status, and related factors that result from family violence. To arrest this cycle, public awareness and prevention programs are needed at all levels of involvement: treatment programs for children who show adjustment problems, prevention/educational programs for children who have been exposed to family violence but do not currently show symptoms of stress, family assistance and crisis intervention programs, and school- and community-based educational programs for children and parents.

References

Achenbach, T. (1979). The child behavior profile: An empirically based system for assessing children's behavior problems and competencies. *International Journal of Mental Health, 7*, 24-42.

Brooks-Gunn, J., & Matthews, W. S. (1979). *He & she: How children develop their sex-role identity.* Englewood Cliffs, NJ: Prentice-Hall.

Dumas, J., & Wahler, R. (1983). Predictors of treatment outcome in parent training: Mother insularity and socioeconomic disadvantage. *Behavioral Assessment, 5,* 301-313.

Emery, R. (1982). Interparental conflict and the children of discord and divorce. *Psychological Bulletin, 92,* 310-330.

Eron, L. D. (1982). Parent-child interaction, television violence, and aggression of children. *American Psychologist, 37,* 197-211.

Ganley, A. L., & Harris, L. (1981). *Domestic violence: Issues in designing and implementing programs for male batterers.* Paper presented at the annual meeting of the American Psychological Association, Montreal.

Goldberg, D. P., & Hillier, V. F. (1979). A scaled version of the General Health Questionnaire. *Psychological Medicine, 9,* 139-145.

Gordon, R. A. (1968). Issues in multiple regression. *American Journal of Sociology, 73,* 592-616.

Hughes, H. M., & Barad, S. J. (1983). Psychological functioning of children in a battered women's shelter: A preliminary investigation. *American Journal of Orthopsychiatry, 53,* 525-531.

Jaffe, P., Wolfe, D. A., Wilson, S., & Zak, L. (1986a). Emotional and physical health problems of battered women. *Canadian Journal of Psychiatry, 31,* 625-629.

Jaffe, P., Wolfe, D. A., Wilson, S., & Zak, L. (1986b). Family violence and child adjustment: A comparative analysis of girls' and boys' behavioral symptoms. *American Journal of Psychiatry, 143,* 74-77.

Lerman, L. G. (1981). *Prosecution of spouse abuse: Innovations in criminal justice response.* Washington, DC: Center for Women's Policy Studies.

Mednick, S. A., & McNeil, M. (1968). Current methodology in research on etiology of schizophrenia. *Psychological Bulletin, 70,* 681-689.

Mitchell, R. E., & Hodson, C. A. (in press). Coping with domestic violence: Social support and psychological health among battered women. *American Journal of Community Psychology.*

O'Leary, K., & Emery, R. E. (1982). Marital discord and child behavior problems. Paper presented at Middle Childhood Symposium, New Orleans.

Pagelow, M. D. (1981). *Woman-battering: Victims and their experiences.* Beverly Hills: Sage.

Porter, B., & O'Leary, K. (1980). Marital discord and childhood behavior problems. *Journal of Abnormal Child Psychology, 80,* 287-295.

Reitsma-Street, M., Offord, D., Finch, T., & Dummitt, G. (1984). *Antisocial adolescents and their non-adolescent siblings.* Hamilton, Ontario: McMaster University, Department of Psychiatry.

Rosenbaum, A., & O'Leary, K. (1981). Children: The unintended victims of marital violence. *American Journal of Orthopsychiatry, 51,* 692-699.

Rosenberg, M. (1984). Intergenerational family violence: A critique and implications for witnessing children. In H. Hughes (Chair), *The impact of marital and family violence on children in shelters.* Symposium conducted at the meeting of the American Psychological Association, Toronto.

Rutter, M. (1971). Parent-child separation: Psychological effects on the children. *Journal of Child Psychology and Psychiatry, 12,* 233-260.

Rutter, M. (1979). Protective factors in children's responses to stress and disadvantage. *Primary Prevention, 3,* 49-74.

Sandler, I., & Block, M. (1979). Life stresses and maladaptation of children. *American Journal of Community Psychology, 7,* 425-440.

Sarason, I. G., Johnson, J. H., & Seigel, J. M. (1979). Assessing the impact of life changes: Development of the Life Experiences Survey. *Series in Clinical and Community Psychiatry, 6,* 131-149.

Straus, M. A. (1979). Measuring intrafamily conflict and violence: The Conflict Tactics Scales (CTS). *Journal of Marriage and the Family, 41,* 75-88.

Straus, M. A., Gelles, R. J., & Steinmetz, S. K. (1980). *Behind closed doors: Violence in the American family.* New York: Anchor/Doubleday.

Walker, L. (1979). *The battered woman.* New York: Harper & Row.

Wallerstein, J. S., & Kelly, J. B. (1980). *Surviving the breakup: How children cope with divorce.* New York: Basic Books.

Wolfe, D. A., Jaffe, P., Wilson, S., & Zak, L. (1985). Children of battered women: The relation of child behavior to family violence and maternal stress. *Journal of Consulting and Clinical Psychology, 53,* 657-664.

PART IV

Elder Abuse, Sexual Abuse, and Dating Abuse

17

Elder Abuse:
Its Relationship to Other Forms
of Domestic Violence

David Finkelhor
Karl Pillemer

After two decades of research and intervention into the problem of abused children and one decade into the problem of abused wives, academics and policymakers have only recently turned their attention to the problem of abused elderly persons. Since the middle 1970s, there have been a small number of studies complemented by a growing number of policy papers, all directed to raising public awareness about the problem (Block & Sinnott, 1979; Douglass, Hickey, & Noel, 1980; Lau & Kosberg, 1979; Sengstock & Liang, 1982; Phillips, 1983; Wolf, Godkin, & Pillemer, 1984; Pillemer & Wolf, 1986; Quinn & Tomita, 1986). States have responded to this new interest with mandatory reporting laws and protective services programs (Salend, Kane, Staz, & Pynoos, 1984).

Even with the new research interest, very little is yet known about the causes and consequences of elder abuse. No definition of *elder abuse* has been generally agreed upon, no definitive profile of a "typical" abused elder has been established, and little is known about effective intervention. Knowledge extends little further than what has been observed by professionals in the course of their practice, and even these observations are heavily colored by stereotypes (see Pedrick-Cornell & Gelles, 1982; Crystal, 1986; Hudson, 1986; Pillemer & Suitor, 1988).

There has also been remarkably little conceptual thinking about the phenomenon. The empirical and descriptive studies of elder abuse for the

AUTHORS' NOTE: Research for this report has been supported by funds from the National Institute on Aging (1 R01 AG04333-01), the National Institute of Mental Health (MH15161), the Eden Hall Farm Foundation and a special Title IV-C grant from the Administration on Aging. We would like to acknowledge the assistance of Ruth Miller, Donna Wilson, and Sigi Fizz in the preparation of this work.

most part have relied rather uncritically on concepts drawn from the family violence literature. Researchers have made the assumption that the sociological and psychological explanations for those other forms of family violence apply to the phenomenon of elder abuse.

Such presumptions about the nature of elder abuse, however, need to be critically examined. The unreflective transfer of ideas from other types of family violence may cause the unique features of the problem to go unnoticed. Further, policy decisions regarding the nature of elder abuse intervention may be influenced by assumed parallels that are untrue. The purpose of this chapter is to question some of these assumptions. It is hoped that this discussion here will alert researchers to matters that possibly need to be studied rather than simply taken for granted.

Some Boundaries

There are three major boundaries we want to establish for purposes of our discussion. These are as follows:

(1) Our analysis is limited to *physical* abuse, and omits discussion of other forms of maltreatment. For the purposes of this chapter, *physical abuse* is defined as "an act carried out with the intention, or perceived intention, of causing physical pain or injury to another person," in this case, a person over the age of 65. Some studies have not differentiated adequately among forms of abuse, as Pedrick-Cornell and Gelles (1982) have noted, resulting in lack of clarity. We will exclude from the present discussion types of abuse that are primarily psychological or material, or harm that occurs to the elderly owing to neglect or acts of omission.

(2) We consider here only abuse that occurs in *domestic* settings. Our discussion does not include maltreatment that occurs in institutions.

(3) Data on elder abuse are still relatively scarce, especially in comparison to data on other forms of family violence. Thus many of the observations here will necessarily be speculative and remain to be confirmed.

Elder Abuse as a Special Category of Abuse

An important question has been raised as to whether the phenomenon of elderly who are physically abused deserves a unique classification and a special term. Callahan (1981) thinks not:

> The fact that violence and abuse exist and that older people are affected does not necessarily mean, however, that public policy is to be served by carving out that segment of abuse and developing specialized programs to deal with it. . . . In other words, does calling this behavior "elder abuse" help us move

along in solving the problem . . . ? My answer to that question is that the well-being of the elderly will not be increased by a focus on elder abuse. (p.1)

Unlike Callahan, we would argue that the phenomenon of abuse of the elderly does constitute a distinct category. Such classification is justified by the special characteristics of the elderly, which affect their vulnerability to abuse and the nature of the abuse they suffer, and also by the nature of society's relationship to older persons.

First, the aged as a group share characteristics that can create vulnerability to abuse. Some elderly (particularly persons over the age of 75) experience increased frailty, especially as measured by the ability to perform ordinary activities of daily living (ambulation, dressing, bathing, and so on). As Reichel notes, "The elderly generally show diminutions of physiologic capacities; in fact, the definition of aging is the decline in physiologic capacities or functions in an organism after the period of reproductive maturity" (1978, p. 17). Many other gerontologists (see Hickey, 1980; Ward, 1984) have chronicled the heightened physical vulnerability of the elderly, as well as their greater likelihood of suffering from neurological impairments. These physical vulnerabilities can exacerbate the risk for abuse as well as affect the nature and effects of the abuse that elderly suffer.

Second, the elderly can be specially vulnerable to abuse because of their devalued social status. Butler (1975) observes that "a systematic stereotyping of and discrimination against people because they are old exists" (see also Levin & Levin, 1980). This contributes to a loss of meaningful roles (Newell, 1961) and to what Atchley (1977) has termed the "atrophy of opportunity," whereby society isolates older persons and no longer seeks their contributions. Mandatory retirement, which brings about the loss of occupational roles, further contributes to this process. This devaluation of elderly people can be seen as increasing their vulnerability to abuse as a class of individuals.

Finally, the special categorization of elder abuse also makes sense because of the relationship society has to the elderly. A service system exists that includes institutions, such as old age homes, and specialized professionals who relate to the elderly and deal with their needs and problems. Concern about abuse of the elderly has developed within this context, and it has legitimately evolved as a distinct problem, separate from other forms of family violence. Research and solutions will all develop within this distinct social matrix.

Elder Abuse and Other Domestic Violence

Notwithstanding that elder abuse deserves special categorization, it is also important to recognize that it does indeed share features with other types of domestic violence, particularly child abuse and spouse abuse. Here we would like to outline what would appear from current knowledge to be some of these similarities. Later we will mention some of the contrasts.

(1) Elsewhere (Finkelhor, 1983), we have analyzed family abuse as violence that occurs toward socially vulnerable and powerless groups. Elder abuse certainly falls within this framework; what makes violence against the elderly "abuse" is the specially vulnerable status of the elderly.

(2) In addition, many of the empirical observations about those at risk for elder abuse correspond with our understanding about what creates risk for other forms of family violence as well. Elder abuse, for example, like other types of abuse appears at least from anecdotal evidence to be more common under conditions of family stress and economic deprivation (O'Malley, Segers, Perex, Mitchell, & Knuepfel, 1979; Sengstock & Liang, 1982).

(3) Those who commit elder abuse have been noted to share characteristics with perpetrators of other types of family violence. For example, such perpetrators frequently have drug or alcohol problems or histories of other types of antisocial behavior (Douglass et al., 1980; Wolf et al., 1984). Although the evidence is more speculative, there are suggestions that some elder abusers, like some other family abusers, may themselves have been victims of family violence and abuse (see Pillemer & Suitor, 1988). One may presume that earlier experience with family violence teaches that violence is both legitimate and efficacious in the family context.

(4) Elder abuse has many effects on its victims similar to those of child and spouse abuse. These effects include a lowering of the self-esteem and coping skills of the victim, a sense of stigma and associated attitudes of self-blame, and the isolation of the victim from peers and the general community. The experience of being abused seems to result in psychiatric symptoms such as despair, depression, sleep disturbances, phobias, and suicidal actions among the elderly as among other victims of family abuse (Lau & Kosberg, 1979; Phillips, 1983). Ironically, all kinds of abuse seem to increase the dependency of the victim on the perpetrator.

(5) Intervention in cases of elder abuse has posed many of the same dilemmas as in cases of other forms of family violence (Sengstock & Liang, 1982; Wolf et al., 1984). Victims of abuse are intimidated by their abusers, and are afraid to leave. Workers characteristically have a difficult time ascertaining the existence of abuse because victims and families do not readily admit it. Helpers have encountered great resistance to gaining entry into the family to deliver services or to provide protection for victims. The protection of victims has involved a coordinated effort on the part of many community agencies, some of which, like the police, have not always been cooperative.

(6) In its emergence as a social problem, elder abuse has gone through some of the same evolution as other forms of family violence. Like child

abuse and spouse abuse, it is a problem with a long history, which is just being acknowledged. It is a problem whose recognition has met with a great deal of resistance, because it challenges cherished beliefs about family life. In its initial stages, the problem has been minimized or ascribed only to particularly pathological family environments.

Comparison and Contrast with Child Abuse

Within the context of family violence, elder abuse has been compared to child abuse much more frequently than to spouse abuse, because of certain apparent similarities. There are some conspicuous cases of elder abuse in which a very dependent and frail elderly person is abused by his or her caretaker. The relationship between caretaker and elder in such cases is often thought to have a parent-child character in the extreme dependency of the elder. Moreover, the presumed dynamic in these situations is that of a caretaker who is unprepared for and frustrated by the burdensome and often unexpected demands of having to take care of a dependent person, and this frustration erupts into violence and abuse (Steinmetz & Amsden, 1983). Such a dynamic would have strong parallels to the child abuse situation.

The comparison of elder abuse to child abuse also arises from the social context of the two problems. Both elder abuse and child abuse were problems that were first identified by professionals who had responsibility for the care of these two populations. These professionals publicized the problems and proposed solutions. Moreover, the locus of responsibility for dealing with both problems was placed in public welfare agencies. In fact, in some states the same agencies that handle child abuse were nominated to take responsibility for the management of elder abuse as well. This contrasts strongly with the case of spouse abuse where the problem was first identified by the feminist movement, and where the main response has been through volunteer efforts and private agencies.

Elder abuse is also akin to child abuse in the extent to which both social problems have been medicalized. Both problems have received extensive attention from health professionals and have had intervention programs organized within the institutional context of health care institutions, something that is emphatically not the case in spouse abuse. One reason why child abuse and elder abuse have been medicalized, while spouse abuse has not, may relate to the relative willingness of the affiliated medical specialties (pediatrics and geriatrics versus obstetrics/gynecology) to accept within their purview a problem that is to a great extent a social rather than medical one. Whatever the reason, however, the involvement of physicians and hospitals is one similarity between elder abuse and child abuse.

However, the parallels between elder abuse and child abuse can be overdrawn. There are many respects in which elder abuse does not resemble child abuse, and where the comparison leads to erroneous assumptions. For example, much elder abuse does not occur by a caretaker against a dependent victim. In fact in many instances the *abuser* may be the dependent one, as in the case of a young son with a drug abuse problem who comes to live with elderly parents and ends up inflicting violence on them. The abuse may not be in reaction to the responsibilities of caretaking but may be a rebellion against the position of dependency.

Thus Lau and Kosberg (1979) refer to the problem of the "nonnormal" child (e.g., mentally ill or retarded) who has been cared for by parents all his or her life, who may lose control when the parents become aged. For example, one elder abuse intervention project encountered an elderly couple who were primary caretakers of their 35-year-old brain-damaged son. The son would occasionally "act out," but the father had been able to restrain him. As the father grew older and weaker, he was unable to control the son by force, and both he and his wife were severely beaten (Pillemer, 1985a).

Similarly, a 68-year-old multiple sclerosis victim was repeatedly assaulted by his middle-aged son. The son had been discharged from the military because of emotional problems, had been frequently hospitalized in psychiatric facilities, and had been unemployed for years. His visits to this father involved requests for food and money; when these were denied, he responded violently (Pillemer, 1985a). Abuse by such a dependent child, documented consistently in studies of elder abuse (Wolf et al., 1984; Pillemer, 1985b), thus does not conform to the parallelism between elder abuse and child abuse.

Even when the elder is the dependent party, the conditions of dependency for the older person are very different from those for children. In particular, parents have a clear legal responsibility for minor children. Almost all children in society live with their parents, and there is an expectation that this is the optimal arrangement. By contrast, in most cases, adult children do not have legal responsibility for their elderly parents. Older persons are considered to be independent, responsible individuals. Moreover, most elderly do not live with their children (fewer than 1 in 10 do so), and there is only a small and disappearing social expectation that they should do so. In summary, the elderly are in a very different structural relationship to their abusers than are children.

Third, a related difference concerns social institutions for the protection of abuse victims. There are few routes of permanent escape for abused children. There are institutions, such as foster homes and group homes, but these are generally regarded as inadequate and solutions of last resort. There is a large public and professional sentiment in favor of keeping families intact. The situation for elders is quite contrasting. There are a great many institutions for the care of elderly, such as nursing homes, rest homes, and less restrictive supportive living arrangements, such as congregate housing. These are regarded as socially acceptable solutions to the problem of dependent elderly. Moreover, there are state-supported payment mechanisms to facilitate the placement of elderly in these settings. Thus while parents and young children may stay together because no other option is available, many such options readily exist for elderly. This is another way in which the comparison of elder abuse with child abuse is insufficient.

Comparison with Spouse Abuse

Elder abuse is not often compared to the problem of spouse abuse. Yet some important insights are available from such a comparison, too. First, it is not sufficiently recognized that some elder abuse *is* spouse abuse that has sometimes been ongoing in a relationship for years. Spouse abuse is widespread (Straus, Gelles, & Steinmetz, 1980), and although in some violent relationships divorce occurs and in some the violence stops, in others it continues and even intensifies as the couple ages.

An example of such a situation is provided in a recent manual on elder abuse (University Center on Aging, 1984, pp. 56-57). An elderly husband and wife, aged 81 and 79 respectively, had by their own reports always had a "difficult relationship." The wife reported that her husband had struck her previously, but never repeatedly or severely. The situation became much worse when she suffered a severe stroke. She could not accept her new physical limitations, and complained about and insulted her husband. During arguments, she would throw food and objects at her husband, which infuriated him. He responded by pushing and striking her more severely than ever before.

In a recent study of elder abuse and neglect, Pillemer and Finkelhor (1988), provide convincing evidence of spouse abuse among the elderly. Their random-sample population survey of 2,020 elderly persons in the greater Boston area found that 3.2% of the elderly reported being victims of physical violence, verbal aggression, or neglect. In all types of abuse, the abuser was the spouse in 58% of the cases, and a child or other individual in only 42% of the cases. When physical abuse alone is considered, spouse abuse made up fully 60% of the cases.

But even when abuser and victim are not husband and wife, the elder abuse situation is often more akin to spouse abuse than to child abuse: both parties are independent adults; they are living with each other by choice; the elder is connected to the abuser by ties of emotional allegiance and perhaps economic dependence, but certainly has more social, psychological, and economic independence than a child would have.[1]

The implications of the comparison between elder abuse and spouse abuse have not been sufficiently explored. There are various possibilities for intervention in elder abuse that might be fruitfully adapted from the experience of dealing with spouse abuse. For example, intervention in spouse abuse has made use of self-help groups, battered women who get together to give each other support, to allay the sense of stigma and self-blame, and to help each other to cope with their abusers. Such groups might be effective with some groups of battered elderly.

One component of these groups that has been important in the battle against abuse of women has been consciousness raising. Battered wives and their advocates have taken considerable pains to communicate to other women and their mates that women have a right to be free from violence, and that no cause justifies its use. It is possible that such an approach directed toward elderly and their families might have a similar utility.

As still another possibility, workers in the spouse abuse field have relied heavily on safe houses and shelters as institutions for protecting victims. This model differs radically from the nursing home solution currently used in elder abuse in that it is temporary, and presumes that after a chance to escape the abuser, the victim can get back on her feet either independently or with the relative who now knows she will not tolerate abuse. Such safe houses for elderly might achieve similar goals.

The parallel to spouse abuse also suggests consideration of criminal justice sanctions in cases of elder abuse. There has been a traditional reluctance of police and prosecutors to intervene in family violence, but recent research suggests that such intervention is effective in reducing incidents of revictimization (Sherman & Berk, 1984). There may be a role for such sanctions against some elder abusers, as a deterrent to repeated abuse.

Conclusion

It is apparent from the preceding analysis that elder abuse can be fruitfully compared to other types of family violence. These comparisons can be extremely useful in trying to understand the nature of a phenomenon that has at the present been the subject of limited research. However, such observations must be made with caution and subjected to empirical examination. It would be very easy for misleading assumptions about elder abuse to be promulgated by overstating parallels to other forms of family abuse.

It is our impression that at the present time the parallels between elder abuse and child abuse are at risk of being overdrawn. Too many observers have borrowed uncritically from the model of child abuse without examining salient differences. For example:

> Yet just as the child is abused by his parent who resents the dependency of the child because the parent himself lacks satisfaction of needs, the adult child who must assume a caretaker role to his own parents may become abusive as

a result of his parents' dependency and the lack of need satisfaction. (Davidson, 1979, p. 49)

However, as we pointed out earlier, much elder abuse does not conform to the child abuse model, and elder abuse victims are not necessarily in a structural relationship to their abusers parallel to that of children.

We argue that it may be useful to start examining elder abuse for more parallels with the spouse abuse situation: legally independent adults, living together out of choice for a variety of emotional and material reasons. One obvious advantage of this comparison is that it does not infantilize the elderly, and emphasizes the initiatives they can take on their own behalf. Another advantage is that it allows for consideration of the dependency of the abuser on the abused.

The arguments presented in this chapter can also be useful in setting an agenda for future research on elder abuse. First, it is of great importance that investigators move beyond agency samples, and begin to conduct general population surveys. Agency samples may select for certain kinds of elder abuse, and thus give a biased view of the distribution of types of elder abuse cases. This approach will allow such questions as these to be answered: What is the incidence of elder abuse? How much elder abuse is spouse abuse? How much occurs at the hands of children? Second, specific attention should be paid to issues of dependency. Is the dependency of an older person a risk factor? Or is living with a dependent relative a better predictor of abuse?

Third, efforts need to be made to study abusers and the history of violent behavior. How often is the abuse really a "new" behavior, a response to recent stressful events? How frequently is it long-standing violent behavior? More specifically, it would be useful to determine the degree to which abuse is related to the ongoing strains of caregiving, as opposed to external stressors such as poverty or unemployment.

Fourth, attention should be paid to a more theoretical issue: How are various types of elder abuse best categorized? Attempts have been made to construct typologies of abused elders (Pillemer, 1985b); these could be refined. New categorization schemes could be attempted that classify abuse cases by the dependency status of the older person, by the family relationship between abuser and abused, or by the nature of the maltreatment that occurs. Data-based typologies for abused women should be attempted. This will aid in understanding the relationship between elder abuse and other domestic violence.

Ultimately, elder abuse will need to be acknowledged as being different from both child abuse and spouse abuse as well as similar in important ways. Our goal should be to gather the knowledge that makes the details of this comparison the source of valuable insights for those concerned about all forms of family violence.

Note

1. If many of the abused elderly are not as vulnerable and dependent as children, does this then undercut our earlier assertions about the special vulnerable status of the elderly in regard to abuse? In our view, special social and physical characteristics of the elderly make them, just like wives, who also suffer special social and physical disadvantages, at higher risk to abuse and also to the consequences of violence. These characteristics do not reduce them to the dependency status of children.

References

Atchley, R. C. (1977). *The social forces in later life: an introduction to social gerontology.* Belmont, CA: Wadsworth.

Block, M., & Sinnott, J. (1979). *The battered elder syndrome: An exploratory study.* College Park, MD: Center on Aging.

Butler, R. N. (1975). *Why survive? Being old in America.* New York: Harper & Row.

Callahan, J. J. (1981, March). *Elder abuse programming—Will it help the elderly?* Paper presented at the National Conference on the Abuse of Older Persons, Boston.

Crystal, S. (1986). Social policy and elder abuse. In K. Pillemer & R. S. Wolf (Eds.), *Elder abuse: Conflict in the family.* Dover, MA: Auburn House.

Davidson, J. L. (1979). Elder abuse. In M. R. Block & J. Sinnott (Eds.), *The battered elder syndrome: An exploratory study.* University of Maryland: Center on Aging.

Douglass, R., Hickey, T., & Noel, C. (1980). *A study of maltreatment of the elderly and other vulnerable adults.* Ann Arbor: University of Michigan, Institute of Gerontology.

Finkelhor, D. (1983). Common features of family abuse. In D. Finkelhor, R. Gelles, G. Hotaling, & M. Straus (Eds.), *The dark side of families: Current family violence research.* Beverly Hills, CA: Sage.

Hickey, T. (1980). *Health and aging.* Monterey, CA: Brooks/Cole.

Hudson, M. (1986). Elder mistreatment: Current research. In K. Pillemer & R. S. Wolf (Eds.), *Elder abuse: Conflict in the family.* Dover, MA: Auburn House.

Lau, E., & Kosberg, J. (1979, September-October). Abuse of the elderly by informal care providers. *Aging,* pp. 10-15.

Levin, J., & Levin, W. C. (1980). *Ageism: Prejudice and discrimination against the elderly.* Belmont, CA: Wadsworth.

Newell, D. S. (1961). Social structural evidence for disengagement. In E. Cumming & W. E. Henry (Eds.), *Growing old.* New York: Basic Books.

O'Malley, H., Segars, H., Perex, R., Mitchell, V., & Knuepfel, G. M. (1979). *Elder abuse in Massachusetts: A survey of professionals and paraprofessionals.* Boston: Legal Research and Services for the Elderly.

Pedrick-Cornell, C., & Gelles, R. (1982). *Elderly abuse: The status of current knowledge.*

Phillips, L. R. (1983). Abuse and neglect of the frail elderly at home: An exploration of theoretical relationships. *Journal of Advanced Nursing, 8,* 379-392.

Pillemer, K. (1985a). *Physical abuse of the elderly: A case-control study.* Unpublished doctoral dissertation, Brandeis University, Waltham, MA.

Pillemer, K. (1985b). The dangers of dependency: New findings on domestic violence against the elderly. *Social Problems, 33,* 146-158.

Pillemer, K., & Finkelhor, D. (1988). The prevalence of elder abuse: A random sample survey. *Gerontologist, 28,* 51-57.

Salend, E., Kane, R., Satz, M., & Pynoos, J. (1984). Elder abuse reporting: Limitations of statuses. *Gerontologist, 24*(1), 61-69.

Sengstock, M., & Liang, J. (1982). *Identifying and characterizing elder abuse.* Unpublished manuscript. Institute of Gerontology, Detroit.

Sherman, L. W., & Berk, R. A. (1984). The Minneapolis domestic violence experiment. *Police Foundation Reports, 1,* April.

Steinmetz, S., & Amsden, D. (1983). Dependency, family stress, and abuse. In T. Brubaker (Ed.), *Family relationships in later life.* Beverly Hills, CA: Sage.

Straus, M., Gelles, R., & Steinmetz, S. (1980). *Behind closed doors: Violence in the American family.* New York: Anchor/Doubleday.

University Center on Aging (1984). *Working with abused elders: Assessment, advocacy, and intervention.* Worcester, MA: University of Massachusetts Medical Center.

Ward, R. (1984). *The aging experience.* New York: Harper & Row.

Wolf, R. S., Godkin, M., & Pillemer, K. (1984). *Elder abuse and neglect: Final report from three model projects.* Unpublished manuscript. University of Massachusetts Medical Center, Worcester.

Pillemer, K., & Suitor, J. J. (1988). Elder abuse. In V. Van Hasselt, R. Morrison, A. Bellack, & M. Hensen (Eds.), *Handbook of family violence.* New York: Plenum.

Pillemer, K., & Wolf, R. S. (1986). *Elder abuse: Conflict in the family.* Dover, MA: Auburn House.

Quinn, M. J., & Tomita, S. K. (1986). *Elder abuse and neglect.* New York: Springer.

Reichel, W. (1978). Multiple problems in the elderly. In W. Reicher (Ed.), *The geriatric patient.* New York: HP Books.

18

Multiple Sexual Victimization: The Case of Incest and Marital Rape

Nancy M. Shields
Christine R. Hanneke

Exposure to family violence as a child has been hypothesized to be a causal factor in the development of adult family violence. Childhood exposure to violence has been thought to bring about both an increased likelihood of victimization, as well as greater likelihood of active participation in family violence (Gelles, 1976; Straus, Gelles, & Steinmetz, 1980; Gil, 1970; Gayford, 1975; Steinmetz, 1977; Herrenkohl, Herrenkohl, & Toedter, 1983). As more research on the intergenerational transmission of violence has been conducted, researchers have begun to address more refined questions regarding specific ways in which the use of violence in the family is passed from one generation to the next. For example, Owens and Straus (1975) investigated the relationship between experiencing violence as a child and approval of the use of violence as an adult, and Kalmuss (1984) investigated the question of whether or not the transmission of marital violence is role and sex specific.

Several explanations have been suggested for the process of the intergenerational transmission of violence. Most family violence researchers have argued that childhood victims are "socialized to violence." It is generally believed that victims of childhood violence eventually come to model the violence that they have experienced (Bandura, 1973), both in the role of aggressor (Carroll, 1977) and in the role of victim (Post, Willett, Franks, & House, 1984). Straus et al. (1980), have argued that the child victim learns certain lessons about the use of violence against family members. These lessons are that: (1) the people who love you are violent with you; (2) it is morally right to use violence against family members; and, (3) when all else fails, the use of violence is permissible (Straus et al., 1980). More recently, Herzberger (1983) has suggested three possible mechanisms by which violent behavioral patterns are passed from parent to child. These are: (1) teaching the victim that the use of violence is appropriate; (2) teaching an interpersonal perspective that supports the use of violence; and (3) failing to help the child internalize a morality.

In contrast to the interest in the intergenerational transmission of nonsexual violence, Lystad (1982) has noted that relatively little attention has been given to the issue of whether or not sexual abuse is passed on from one generation to the next. There is some evidence that sexually abused male children are more likely than nonabused males to become sexual abusers (Lystad, 1982); Frieze (1980), and Russell (1982) also found that adult female victims of marital rape were more likely than nonvictims to have been "sexually molested" as children. However, according to Frieze's data, marital rape victims were not more likely than nonsexually battered women to have been childhood sexual abuse victims (Frieze, 1983). MacFarlane (1978) argues that there exists a "cycle of sexual abuse," noting that the mothers of incest victims often report having been incest victims themselves. Finally, Lees (1981) found that adult rape victims were more likely than nonvictims to have been molested or raped as children. Based on this research, we hypothesized that marital rape victims would be more likely than nonvictims to have been sexually abused children. It also seemed likely that marital rape victims would have had childhood sexual abuse experiences more often than nonsexually battered women, although Frieze's (1983) finding made this prediction somewhat unclear.

If marital rape victims are childhood sexual abuse victims more often than nonsexually battered women, there seems to be at least three possible explanations for such an outcome. Reasoning from a "socialization to violence" perspective, one possibility is that victims of childhood sexual abuse are taught to tolerate sexual victimization of women in general, and their own victimization in particular. Tolerance of sexual violence against women might increase a woman's chances of adult victimization. There are several studies that support this view. Ulbrich and Huber (1981) found greater approval of the use of violence among men who had seen their fathers hit their mothers than among those who had not. Owens and Straus (1975) found that experiencing violence as a child led both to approval of the use of violence as an adult and actually using violence more often as an adult. Finally, Herzberger and Tennen (1982) found that perceptions of college students concerning the severity of child abuse also support the view that victimization leads to greater tolerance of violence. They found that students who had been abused as children held more tolerant attitudes regarding abusive treatment of children than did students who had not been abused.

A second possible explanation for the way that childhood sexual abuse victims might become adult marital rape victims has to do with the child's reactions to childhood sexual victimization. MacFarlane (1978) suggests that the child victim may be unable to disassociate childhood sexual experiences from adult sexual experiences, thus causing adult sexual problems, such as an inability to form a stable intimate sexual relationship (Lystad, 1982). Other researchers have also suggested the development of sexual problems as a response to childhood sexual abuse. The inability of the woman to function satisfactorily in an adult sexual relationship, sometimes resulting in withholding of sex from the partner (Shields & Hanneke, 1984), may trigger sexual violence in some men. However, as Groth (1979) and Frieze (1983) note, sexual violence probably results only when the partner views the sexual refusal as a loss of power or as a threat to personal worth.

A third way that a childhood sexual abuse victim might become an adult victim has to do with internalizing the victim role and taking on the identity of a victim. MacFarlane (1978) argues that incest victims often internalize their roles as sexual abuse victims, and take on the identity of sexual victim. Internalization of the role of victim might increase the likelihood of adult sexual victimization.

All of the above explanations for the way that child sexual abuse victims might become adult sexual abuse victims can be thought of as "contagious poison," multiple victimization models (Coleman, 1964; Sparks, 1981; Thissen & Wainer, 1983), and would not necessarily be mutually exclusive. According to the "contagious poison" model, after a person has been victimized once, his or her odds of being victimized again are increased. Initial victimization changes the person in such a way that his chances of additional victimization have increased.

The purpose of our research was to investigate these questions relating to models of multiple victimization and the intergenerational transmission of violence. Based on the arguments stated above, we hypothesized the following:

(1) Victims of marital rape would be more likely than victims of nonsexual battering or a nonvictimized comparison group to have been victims of childhood sexual abuse.

(2) There would be no difference between battered women and marital rape victims (who were battered) in experiences with childhood nonsexual violence, but both victimized groups would be more likely to have experienced childhood nonsexual violence than a nonvictimized comparison group.

(3) Victims of marital rape would hold more tolerant attitudes about the use of sexual violence against women than would victims of battering or the comparison group.

(4) Victims of marital rape would have significantly more "sexual dysfunction" problems (that existed prior to adult victimization and during the marital/cohabiting relationship) than victims of battering or the nonvictimized comparison group.

(5) Marital rape victims would have more experiences than victims of battering or nonvictims that might have caused them to be labeled as sexual abuse victims. Specifically, we predicted that they would have discussed their victimization with others (especially significant others) to a greater extent than nonvictims would have.

Methods

Preliminary data pertaining to the hypotheses are available to us from a larger project on marital rape (Victim Reaction to Marital Rape and Battering, Grant #5R01MH37102-02, National Center for the Prevention and Control of Rape, NIMH). In all, 137 standardized interviews were conducted (by the authors)—44 "raped and battered" women (women who had experienced both sexual and nonsexual violence), 48 "battered only" women (women who had experienced only nonsexual violence), and 45 nonvictimized comparison women. All women had been married or lived with their partners for at least six months, and had not been separated for more than three years. The original research design also called for a group of "raped only," victims, that is, women who had experienced sexual but not nonsexual violence in their marital or cohabiting relationships. However, because so few "raped only" victims (n = 15) were interviewed, this group was eliminated from the sample.

For sampling purposes, *sexual violence* was defined (by a panel of experts on domestic violence) as "moderate" or "severe" violence that had occurred on two or more occasions. Moderate or severe sexual violence included the following specific sexual behaviors: (1) forced objects into vagina; (2) forced sexual activities with children; (3) forced to eat urine; (4) forced objects into anus; (5) forced vaginal intercourse with partner; (6) forced to masturbate; (7) forced to pose in the nude or in sexual positions while partner took pictures; (8) forced to eat feces; (9) forced to have oral sex with other men; (10) forced oral sex with partner; (11) forced to eat sperm; (12) forced sex with animals; (13) forced anal sex with other men; (14) injury to sexual parts of woman's body; (15) forced to perform oral sex on partner; (16) forced anal sex with partner; (17) forced vaginal intercourse with other men; (18) forced to masturbate others; and, (19) forced to observe others having sex. Only acts that were physically forced or that were performed under the threat of physical force were included.

Similarly, *nonsexual violence* was defined by the panel as "moderate" or "severe" nonsexual violence that had occurred on 2 or more occasions. Moderate and severe nonsexual violence included: (1) kick; (2) hit with fist; (3) hit with object; (4) burn; (5) threaten with weapon; (6) throw an object at; (7) choke or strangle; (8) stab or cut; (9) shoot or shoot at; (10) try to smother; and (11) try to drown. Nonvictims were women who had not experienced either sexual or nonsexual violence (thus defined) in their current or any past marital or cohabiting relationships. "Battered only" victims were women who had experienced nonsexual violence but not sexual violence (as defined here) in their most recent marital or cohabiting relationship, and "raped and battered" victims were women who had experienced both sexual and nonsexual violence in their most recent relationships. Although rarely the case, any other pattern of victimization (e.g., moderate or severe nonsexual violence on two or more occasions, but sexual violence on only one occasion) was excluded from the sample on the grounds that a clear pattern of victimization had not yet emerged.

Respondents were recruited from 14 different referral sources—local shelter, self-help groups, social service agencies, advertising, "snowballing," and court records of women who had filed for restraining orders. For the most part, approximately equal numbers of different kinds of women (battered, raped and battered, comparison) were referred from different types of sources (shelters, agencies, programs), unless a particular agency or group did not serve a particular type of person, for example, some shelters did not serve women who had not experienced violence. Victims were more likely than nonvictims to be referred from shelters and agencies, whereas nonvictims were more likely to be referred by programs (chi-square = 16.48; DF = 6; p = .01). Race was not related to type of victimization.

Respondents ranged in age from 17 to 63, and the average age was 31.4. Using the Meyers and Bean Index of Social Class (based on level of education and the occupation held for the longest time during the relationship), the Index range for the women was from 1 to 6, with a mean of 2.7. For their partners, the range was from 1 to 7 and the mean was 2.7. Overall, 60 of the respondents were black and 77 were white; 56 respondents were living in shelters at the time of the interview, and 81 were not. Of these 81, 35 were still living with their partners and 46 were either living alone or with other family members. Respondents had been married an average of 8.9 years.

There were no differences between the battered and raped and the battered groups in the recency of the nonsexual violence (the most recent nonsexually violent episode was a mean of 1.2 years before), the severity of the nonsexual violence experienced, or the frequency of the violence. However (using ANOVA with a p level of .10 or beyond), comparison women had been married or lived with their partners significantly longer than had the victims (comparison women had been married an average of 12.9 years, raped and battered 5.9 years, and battered women 8.2 years). Raped and battered women were significantly younger (mean 27.8 years) than battered (mean 32.3 years) or comparison women (mean 34.0 years). Victims were significantly more likely than comparison women to be separated from their partners.

To measure childhood sexual abuse, two questions were included on the interview schedule—one regarding whether or not a parent, guardian, or other relative had ever had any kind of sexual contact with the respondent when she was age 16 or under. A second question asked if she had ever had sexual contact with an adult nonfamily member (strangers, acquaintances, authority figures, etc.) when she was 16 or younger. The specific kinds of sexual contact included were: (1) exposure of the perpetrator's genitals; (2) exposure of the victim's genitals; (3) stimulation of the perpetrator's genitals; (4) stimulation of the victim's genitals; (5) oral sex performed on perpetrator; (6) oral sex performed on victim; (7) attempted vaginal intercourse; (8) vaginal intercourse completed; (9) anal intercourse attempted or completed; and (10) forced to pose in pornographic pictures or films.

Four questions were used to measure childhood exposure to nonsexual violence—whether or not the respondent had seen her father become violent with her mother, whether or not she had seen her mother become violent with her father, whether her father had been violent with her, and whether her mother had been violent with her. The percentage of "yes" responses to these four questions that were applicable to the respondent was used as an index of exposure to nonsexual violence as a child.

Tolerance of sexual violence against women was measured by asking the respondent to rate each sexually violent behavior as minor, moderate, or severe (1, 2, 3) in terms of how humiliating or degrading it would be for the victim. The behaviors of: (1) forced to listen to descriptions of sexual violence; (2) touching of breasts and buttocks against the woman's will; and, (3) forced to look at pornographic pictures or literature (which were rated minor by the panel of experts), were rated by the respondents, as well as the moderate and severe sexually violent behaviors already discussed. The respondent's average response over all the behaviors became the respondent's tolerance score.

Several questions were used to measure the respondent's level of "sexual functioning" during her relationship with her partner. Most of these questions used 5-point Likert type frequency responses, ranging from "rarely or none of the time" to "most or all of the time." Respondents were asked how often: (1) they felt satisfied with their sexual relationship with their partners; (2) how often they had refused to have sex with their partners; (3) how often they had argued with their partners about how often they should have sex; (4) how often they had argued about engaging in particular sex acts; (5) how often they had argued about whether or not they should have sex during their menstrual periods; (6) how often the woman had been the one to start sexual relations with her partner; (7) how often she had had trouble having an orgasm; and, (8) how often she had had trouble performing sexually. Respondents were also asked how often they and their partners (individually) had wanted to have sex (on the average), over the entire relationship. Victims were also asked if the violence they had experienced had been preceded by: (1) an inability to perform sexually because of pregnancy or illness; (2) her not being interested in sex; and (3) her withholding sex from her partner.

Questions were also included relating to factors that might contribute to the development of a sexual victim identity. Following labeling theory (Lemert, 1951), we hypothesized that if victimization were discussed with others, making it more "public," this might contribute to labeling and the formation of a victim identity. Furthermore, help-seeking for victimization as an adult might also be an indication that a victim identity had formed. Finally, whether or not respondents report victimization as traumatic life events might be used as a general measure of the extent to which victimization has become a salient aspect of identity. Accordingly, childhood sexual abuse victims were asked: (1) if they had ever discussed their victimization with anyone before the interview; and (2) if they had told anyone about it at the time it occurred. "Raped and battered" and "battered only" victims were asked if they had ever sought help for the marital violence within 24 hours of victimization or if they had ever sought counseling for the marital violence from a psychologist or counselor. Respondents were also asked what they considered to be the three most stressful or traumatic time periods in their lives.

Findings

To test the hypotheses, all dependent variables were submitted to one-way analysis of variance, with group membership ("battered only," "raped and battered," and the nonvictimized comparison group) as the independent variable. All dependent variables were either interval level or dichotomous, and therefore suitable for use as dependent variables in the analyses. Duncan's Multiple Range test was used to detect differences between individual groups whenever the overall ANOVA was significant at .05 or beyond.

Relationship Between
Childhood Violence and Adult Victimization

Victims of marital rape were more likely than the comparison women and the "battered only" group to have had sexual contact with a family member as a child (F = 3.95; DF = 2; $p < .05$, N = 137). Although the difference between the "raped and battered" and the "battered only" groups were not significantly different at the .05 level, the differences between the groups were in the predicted directions and the "raped and battered" group was statistically significant from the "battered only" group at the .10 level. A striking 50% of the "raped and battered" victims had had sexual contact with a family member during their childhoods. Overall, 33% of the "battered only" victims, and 22% of the comparison women had had such contact. There were no differences between the three groups in experiences with childhood sexual contact with nonfamily members.

We had also predicted that there would be no differences between the "raped and battered" and the "battered only" victims concerning their experiences with childhood nonsexual violence, but that both of these groups would have more exposure than the comparison group. Although there were no differences between the two victimized groups, there were also no differences between these two groups and the comparison group (F = .7304; DF = 2; p = .48). The mean percentage of all the possible "exposure" variables for the "raped and battered" group was 34%, 27% for the "battered only" group, and 28% for the comparison group.

Tolerance of Sexual Violence Against Women

The first theory of multiple victimization had suggested that if adult victims of family sexual violence were more likely to have been childhood victims of family sexual violence, then one explanation for this finding might be that the childhood victims had been taught to tolerate sexual violence against women. *However, contrary to prediction, there were no differences between the three groups in terms of their mean ratings of severity (minor, moderate, or severe) of 23 sexually violent behaviors.* The mean rating of the comparison group was 2.66, the "battered only" group was 2.64, and the "raped and battered" was 2.68 (F = .3346; DF = 2; $p<.71$; N = 136).

Sexual Functioning

Several variables were included on the interview schedule in an attempt to assess the quality of the sexual relationship for victims (both "raped and battered" and "battered") before any violence had occurred in the relationship, and for all respondents over their entire relationships with their partners. *The three variables that were intended to tap the presence of sexual problems before any violence began in the relationship—whether or not the violence was preceded by a period of the woman withholding sex, her not being interested in sex, or her not being able to perform sexually—showed no differences between the two victims groups.* However, there were differences between the three groups (victims differed from the comparison women), on the average over the whole relationship, for having difficulty having an orgasm (F = 3.82; DF = 2; $p<.05$; N = 134), and having difficulty performing sexually (F = 4.51; DF = 2; $p<.01$; N = 135).

There were significant differences on some of the other sexual problem variables also. Regarding their satisfaction with their sexual relationships, *"raped and battered" and "battered" women were less satisfied with their sexual relationships than comparison women* (F = 9.29; DF = 2; $p<1.01$;

N = 133). *Both victimized groups had refused sex more often over their relationships than had the comparison group* (F = 6.37; DF = 2; $p < 1.05$; N = 136). The mean (on a 5-point scale) for the comparison group was 1.96, the mean for the "battered only" group was 2.44, and the mean for the "raped and battered" group was 2.81.

There were also variables that discriminated between the "raped and battered" and "battered" groups. *The "raped and battered" victims had argued about how often to have sex more often than either the "battered only" or the comparison women* (F = 13.62; DF = 2; $p < .01$; N = 137—means: comparison = 1.91; battered only = 2.25; raped and battered = 3.32). *The same pattern was found for how often they had argued about engaging in particular sex acts, with the "raped and battered" group arguing more often than either of the other two groups* (F = 19.36; DF = 2; $p < .01$; N = 137—means: comparison group = 1.56; battered only = 1.58; raped and battered = 2.88).

The "raped and battered" victims were significantly more likely than the "battered" only group and the comparison group to have argued more often about whether or not they should have sex during their menstrual periods (F = 6.75; DF = 2; $p < .01$; N = 137). The comparison group mean was 1.47; the "battered only" mean was 1.25, and the "raped and battered" group mean was 2.02. *The same pattern was found for how often the women were likely to initiate sexual relations—"raped and battered" women were the least likely of the three groups to initiate sex with their partners* (F = 4.27; DF = 2; $p < .01$; N = 137).

Victim Identity

Using ANOVA, most of the "discussion" variables were not significant at the .05 level or beyond. "Raped and battered" victims were not more likely to have discussed their victimization at any time prior to the interview, or at the time of childhood victimization. Nor were they more likely to have sought help from others for the violence. However, of those victims who did tell someone about their victimization at the time it occurred, the "raped and battered" victims were more likely to have told a parent about it.

Discussion

Methodological Limitations of the Data

Before discussing the findings of the study, methodological limitations of the data should be mentioned. First, the sample is clearly not representative of battering and marital rape victims in general. As with most research of this type, the sample was generated through advertising and from referrals from social service agencies. Nonvictims were obtained from the same and similar sources. Accordingly, the sample probably overrepresents those with more serious problems (financial, marital, personal, and so on) and those who are most willing to talk about their problems.

Regarding internal biases of the sample, compared with nonvictims, victims were more likely to have been living in shelters at the time they were interviewed, even though extensive efforts were made to recruit victims not living in shelters. The stress of daily living in a shelter may have influenced the victims' responses. However, regarding the data analyzed in this chapter, this is probably not a major bias since almost all relevant measures were retrospective rather than current. Of course, the fact that most of the relevant data are retrospective poses a problem in itself, primarily memory problems. To minimize this problem, retrospective questions concerned primarily major events and behavioral variables. Furthermore, only women who had been in marital or cohabiting relationships within the last three years were interviewed.

That the comparison women had been married longer than had the victims and the "raped and battered" women were more likely than the other two groups to have left their partners is consistent with research in general finding the disruptive effects of family violence (e.g., Gelles, 1976), and as such is probably not a sample bias. It is also consistent with other research that has found that marital rape is more likely than battering alone to lead to terminating the relationship (Bowker, 1983; Shields & Hanneke, 1984). That "raped and battered" victims were also younger than the other two groups might also reflect the fact that they were more likely to leave their partners at an early age.

Regarding the interview methodology of the study, it is possible that the "raped and battered" victims were more likely than the other two groups to report childhood sexual victimization because they had already admitted adult sexual victimization, and therefore might be less reluctant to discuss childhood sexual victimization. Furthermore, since they were younger, "raped and battered" victims might simply be more likely to recall such victimization and to remember it more accurately. However, although "raped and battered" victims were significantly younger, the differences in ages between the three groups is probably not great enough to have a significant effect on recall (group mean ages were 27.8; 32.3; 34.0). It is impossible to know if the comparison group or the "battered" group underreported or overreported childhood sexual victimization. However, given that the comparison women reported a level of victimization similar to the levels found by Finkelhor (1979) in a population of college students (225), and Russell (1982) in a general population in San Francisco (16%), this would seem to argue for the relative accuracy of reporting.

It should also be noted that in terms of the interpretation of the causal relationship between childhood and adult sexual victimization, the research design is reversed in the sense that it starts with adult victims and examines the percentage who were childhood victims, rather than starting with childhood victims and seeing how many became adult victims. The current design probably exaggerates the causal relationship between the two variables, but the findings can still be used as a tentative indication of the possible relationship between childhood and adult sexual victimization when differences between groups are interpreted.

Interpretations of the Data

With these methodological limitations in mind, the findings lend support to a "Contagious Poison" model of multiple family sexual victimization. Women who were victims of childhood family sexual victimization do seem to be more likely to become marital rape victims, and childhood victims do seem to be affected in a way that increases the odds of further victimization. "Raped and battered" victims were more likely than the "battered" victims or the comparison women to have experienced childhood sexual victimization in the family, and there was not a statistically significant difference between the comparison group and the "battered group." It is also interesting to note that the differences were found only for childhood *family* victimization—there were no differences between groups in nonfamily childhood sexual victimization, and there were no differences between the groups concerning nonfamily personal victimization. There were no differences between the groups in whether or not they had been mugged or raped by strangers as adults. Thus it appears that a particular context of victimization (the family), as well as a particular type of victimization (sexual) is likely to be repeated in later victimization.

We had also predicted that there would be no differences between the victimized groups in exposure to childhood nonsexual violence, but that both victim groups would have had more exposure than had the comparison women. The data indicated that there were no significant differences between the victimized groups in exposure to childhood nonsexual violence, but neither victim group had more exposure than the comparison women. The data indicated that there were no significant differences between any of the groups. However, when informant data concerning husbands' exposure to childhood violence were examined, the husbands or partners of the victimized women were significantly more likely than husbands of the comparison women to have been exposed to violence as a child. This finding suggests that for this sample, the partners' background experiences seem to be more important than the women's experiences in determining involvement in family violence as adults. However, with only half of the comparison cases available for the analysis, these findings and interpretations should be considered tentative.

Three major explanations for the connection between childhood and adult sexual victimization were explored. The first explanation was that childhood sexual victimization makes the woman more tolerant of sexual victimization of women in general, and therefore she might also see her own sexual victimization as more tolerable. However, we found no support for the hypothesis that marital rape victims would be more tolerant of sexual abuse of women. When the respondents were asked to rate the sexually violent behaviors as minor, moderate, or severe in terms of how degrading or humiliating they would be to the victim, there were no significant differences between the groups with almost all women rating most behaviors as "severe." It is possible that these responses were reactive, with women rating behaviors as more severe because they knew that the topic of the research was the sexual victimization of women. It is also possible that the tolerance scale itself did not allow sufficient variation in response, with most items (as rated by a panel of expert judges) being at the extremes (minor or severe) and few being "moderate." To explore this possibility, we plan to analyze each group of behaviors separately for possible group differences.

Sexual Functioning

Three variables that were related to the woman's sexual behavior prior to victimization did not show any significant differences between the three groups, and therefore do not seem to suggest that the victim's sexual behavior precipitated the violence. All three of these variables have to do with withholding sex or not being able to function sexually, and accordingly, the findings support the ideas of Groth (1979) and Frieze (1983) that suggest that by itself, withholding of sex will not explain the phenomena of marital rape. Both researchers suggest that the meaning of the victim's sexual behavior to the husband (e.g., as a threat to his power in the relationship) must be taken into account in order to explain why rape occurs.

Furthermore, the data do not seem to support the idea that victims of marital rape are more likely to have problems with "sexual functioning" in general as adults. There were no differences between the three groups in how often they had had trouble having an orgasm, and in how often they had had trouble performing sexually. Rather, the variables for which there were significant differences between the "raped and battered" victims and the other two groups all had to do with their sexual relationships with their partners rather than with their own sexual functioning per se. "Raped and battered" victims were more likely to argue with their partners about how often they should have sex, whether or not they should engage in particular sex acts, and whether or not they should have sex during her menstrual period. Of course, it is possible that these sexual difficulties in their relationships were reactions to the marital rape itself, and as such have nothing to do with the incest experience. However, the idea that incest victims have problems developing satisfactory adult sexual relationships is also consistent with theories and research on the long-term effects of the incest experience (MacFarlane, 1978; Lystad, 1982).

Finally, some of the findings about sexual behavior also suggest that it is possible that both nonsexual and sexual violence do affect the quality of the couple's sexual relationship. Both victimized groups were less satisfied with their sexual relationships, were having more problems performing sexually and were refusing to have sex with their partners more often than the comparison group.

Using variables related to the victim discussing her victimization (childhood and adulthood) with others as an indication of the formation of a victim identity, only one variable was related to victimization or nonvictimization in marriage. The "raped and battered" victims who were also incest victims were more likely than "battered only" incest victims to have discussed the incest experience with a parent. The parent being a highly "significant other," it is possible that the parent's reaction might have had a major impact on the victim's identity. It is also possible that an ambiguous response on the part of a parent might impede the childhood incest victim's normal sexual development, leading to difficulty in forming adult sexual relationships. Finally, the fact that victims are more likely than nonvictims to report victimization as a major life trauma lends some limited indirect support to the notion that those who are victimized repeatedly over time do tend to develop victim identities.

The indirect measures of "victim identity" that are currently available to us are probably not precise enough to provide a fair test of the "victim identity" hypothesis, and as such it is impossible to draw firm conclusions about victim identity at this time.

Overall Conclusions

In conclusion, the incest experience does seem to play a role in eventual marital rape victimization, but the mechanisms by which this occurs are still unclear. It is possible that the connection is somewhat indirect, for example, incest victims who become victims of battering are more likely than battered women who were not incest victims to experience marital rape. The data from this study suggest that childhood victimization does impair the victim's ability to develop a satisfying marital sexual relationship. The victim's emerging identity as sexual victim also seems to be involved in this developmental process. Importantly, the data also suggest that although the incest experience does have an impact on the odds that further sexual victimization will occur, this experience does not seem to be sufficient to produce further victimization by itself. Whether or not further victimization occurs may depend on reactions of significant others to childhood victimization and other aspects of the family environment.

References

Bandura, A. (1973). *Aggression: A social learning analysis.* Englewood Cliffs, NJ: Prentice-Hall.

Bowker, L. H. (1983). *Beating wife beating.* Lexington, MA: Lexington.

Carroll, J. C. (1977). The intergenerational transmission of family violence: The long-term effects of aggression behavior. *Aggressive Behavior, 3,* 289-299.

Coleman, J. (1964). *Introduction to mathematical sociology.* New York: Free Press.

Finkelhor, D. (1979). *Sexually victimized children.* New York: Free Press.

Frieze, I. H. (1980). *Causes and consequences of marital rape.* Paper presented at the 1980 American Psychological Association meetings in Montréal, Canada.

Frieze, I. H. (1983). Investigating the causes and consequences of marital rape. *Signs: Journal of Women in Culture and Society, 8,* 532-553.

Gayford, J. J. (1975). Wife battering: A preliminary survey of 100 cases. *British Medical Journal, 25,* 194-197.

Gelles, R. J. (1976). Abused wives: Why do they stay? *Journal of Marriage and the Family, 38,* 659-668.

Gil, D. (1970). *Violence against children: Physical child abuse in the United States.* Cambridge: Harvard University Press.

Groth, A. N. (1979). *Men who rape: The psychology of the offender.* New York: Plenum.

Herrenkohl, E. C., Herrenkohl, R. C., & Toedter, L. J. (1983). Perspectives on the intergenerational transmission of abuse. In D. Finkelhor, R. J. Gelles, G. T. Hotaling, & M. A. Straus (Eds.), *The dark side of families: Current family violence research.* Beverly Hills, CA: Sage.

Herzberger, S. D. (1983). Social cognition and the transmission of abuse. In D. Finkelhor, R. J. Gelles, G. T. Hotaling, & M. A. Straus (Eds.), *The dark side of families: Current family violence research.* Beverly Hills, CA: Sage.

Herzberger, S. D., & Tennen, H. (1982, August). *The social definition of child abuse.* Paper presented at the annual meeting of the American Psychological Association, Washington, D.C.

Kalmuss, D. (1984). The intergenerational transmission of marital aggression. *Journal of Marriage and the Family, 46,* 11-19.

Lees, C. A. (1981, March). *Do life events contribute to rape victim vulnerability?* Paper presented at the 8th Annual Conference for Women in Psychology, Boston.

Lemert, E. C. (1951). *Social pathology.* New York: McGraw-Hill.

Lystad, M. H. (1982). Sexual abuse in the home: A review of the literature. *International Journal of Family Psychiatry, 3,* 3-31.

Lystad, M. H. (in press). Family violence: A mental health perspective. *Emotional First Aid.*

MacFarlane, K. (1978). Sexual abuse of children. In J. R. Chapman & M. Gates (Eds.), *The victimization of women.* Beverly Hills, CA: Sage.

Owens, D. M., & Straus, M. A. (1975). The social structure of violence in childhood and approval of violence as an adult. *Aggressive Behavior, 1,* 193-211.

Post, R. D., Willett, A. B., Franks, R. D., & House, R. M. (1984). Childhood exposure to violence among victims and perpetrators of spouse battering. *Victimology, 6,* 156-166.

Russell, D.E.H. (1982). *Rape in marriage.* New York: Macmillan.

Shields, N. M., & Hanneke, C. R. (1984, August). *Marital rape—cause and impact: A preliminary report.* Paper presented at the American Sociological Association Meetings, San Antonio, TX.

Sparks, R. (1981). Multiple victimization: Evidence, theory, and future research. *The Journal of Criminal Law and Criminology, 72,* 762-778.

Steinmetz, S. K. (1977). *The cycle of violence: Assertive, aggressive, and abusive family interaction.* New York: Praeger.

Straus, M. A., Gelles, R. J., & Steinmetz, S. K. (1980). *Behind closed doors: Violence in the American family.* New York: Anchor/Doubleday.

Thissen, D., & Wainer, H. (1983). Toward the measurement and prediction of victim proneness. *Journal of Research in Crime and Delinquency, 20,* 243-261.

Ulbrich, P., & Huber, J. (1981). Observing parental violence: Distribution and effects. *Journal of Marriage and the Family, 43,* 623-631.

19

Assessing the Long-Term Impact of Child Sexual Abuse: A Review and Conceptualization

David Finkelhor
Angela Browne

Since the problem of child sexual abuse first came to the forefront in the 1970s, clinicians have been amassing observations about the impact of this type of child abuse on its victims. However, few efforts have been made to review and organize these observations in a way to advance scientific knowledge and clinical practice. In this chapter, we review the status of empirical research findings concerning the long-term effects of child sexual abuse and suggest a framework that might be applied for future research investigation and clinical assessment.

The idea that sexual abuse in childhood can have serious long-term impact is generally accepted by clinicians who work with the phenomenon. However, this assumption has been periodically attacked by skeptics who argue that the trauma is greatly overstated or that evidence for negative effects is meager (e.g., Constantine, 1977; Henderson, 1983; Ramey, 1979). It is true that until recently, the argument for long-term impact was based primarily on less than rigorous clinical studies. However, as evidence from empirical studies accumulates, it generally confirms the clinical impression that sexual abuse in childhood poses a serious risk to mental health, even into adulthood.

At least eight nonclinical studies have now found that women in the general population with a history of child sexual abuse have identifiable mental health impairment when compared to nonvictims. Three of these

AUTHORS' NOTE: We would like to thank Linda Gott and Ruth Miller for help in preparing this manuscript. This research has been supported by grants from the National Center on Child Abuse and Neglect (1R01AG04333-01), National Institute of Mental Health (MHI5161), and the Eden Hall Farm Foundation.

studies were sophisticated random sample, community surveys that compared sexual abuse victims with nonvictims in the normal population. Bagley and Ramsey (1985), using a variety of standard epidemiological measures—including the Coopersmith Self-Esteem Inventory, the Centre for Environmental Studies Depression Scale (CES-D), and the Middlesex Hospital Health Survey—documented significant mental health impairment among women with a history of sexual abuse, in a random sample in Calgary. Russell (1986) found victimized women in a random sample in San Francisco to be significantly impaired on a number of objective and subjective measures of adjustment. And Peters (1984), surveying a random sample of women in Los Angeles, found sexual abuse victims to have significantly more problems with depression and substance abuse than nonvictims. Five other studies, based on college student samples (Briere & Runtz, 1987; Finkelhor, 1984; Fromuth, 1983; Sedney & Brooks, 1984; Seidner & Calhoun, 1984), also found indications of impairment in victims. Only one study that looked for impairment in nonclinical samples failed to find it (Tsai, Feldman-Summers, & Edgar, 1979).

These findings of impairment in nonclinical groups challenge the objection that the problems clinicians observe in sexual abuse victims are simply a function of the clinical setting. These findings are also impressive in that the studies were looking at differences associated with an event that occurred from 5 to 25 years previously. Moreover, all of these studies used very broad definitions of sexual abuse that included single episodes, experiences in which no actual penetration occurred, and experiences with nonrelatives, as well as the more "serious" kinds of abuse. In the four studies in which multivariate analysis was used (Bagley & Ramsey, 1985; Finkelhor, 1984; Fromuth, 1983; Peters, 1984), sexual abuse remained associated with mental health impairment even after a variety of other background factors had been controlled. All of this provides increasingly strong evidence that sexual abuse may have long-term deleterious effects for a substantial number of people.

Unfortunately, research evidence is much less specific about what these effects may be. The list of problems that have been associated with a history of child sexual abuse is long (see reviews by Browne & Finkelhor, 1986; Gelinas, 1983; Jehu & Gazan, 1983; Tufts New England Medical Center, 1984). This list includes depression and self-destructive behavior, anger and hostility, poor self-esteem, feelings of isolation and stigma, difficulty in trusting others (especially men), marital and relationship problems, and a tendency toward revictimization. Many sexual difficulties, including frigidity, vaginismus, inability to tolerate sexual arousal, and flashbacks— have been linked to the experience of child sexual abuse. In addition, childhood molestation is frequently cited as a background factor in the etiology of drug and alcohol abuse, prostitution, multiple personality disorder, and borderline disorder. However, the connections between sexual abuse and most of these factors are based, once again, primarily on clinical observations. Few of them have been confirmed in more rigorous empirical studies. In this chapter, we will try to summarize which of these effects has received empirical support; that is, has been confirmed in a study either with a clinical or nonclinical sample, using some comparison group or formal measures of the effect in question.

One of the areas receiving the most attention in empirical literature on long-term effects is the impact of early sexual abuse on later sexual functioning. At least six studies, five using some kind of comparison group, have found more sexual problems in women who have been victims of child sexual abuse than in nonvictims (Briere & Runtz, 1988; Courtois, 1979; Finkelhor, 1984; Herman, 1981; Langmade, 1983; Meiselman, 1978). These studies show higher levels of specific sexual dysfunctions such as difficulty with arousal, vaginismus, and flashbacks; as well as emotional problems related to sex, such as sexual guilt, sexual anxiety, and low sexual self-esteem (Finkelhor, 1984; Langmade, 1983). However, the prevalent supposition that sexual abuse victims tend toward promiscuity has not been empirically confirmed. Two researchers (Herman, 1981; Meiselman, 1978) do report promiscuity in clinical samples. However, in conducting research with a college population, Fromuth (1983) found that, although many sexual abuse victims described themselves as promiscuous, the actual number of their sexual partners and sexual experiences did not differ significantly from those of their peers. This suggests the possibility that the so-called promiscuity of sexual abuse victims may be more a function of negative self-labeling, owing perhaps to their low self-esteem, than a representation of actual behavior patterns.

One of the most alarming findings in regard to long-term effects concerns the apparent vulnerability of women who have been sexually abused as children to revictimization later in life. Five empirical studies found higher rates of subsequent rape among sexual abuse victims than among nonvictims (de Young, 1982; Fromuth, 1983; Herman, 1981; Miller, Moeller, Kaufman, Divasto, Pather, & Christy, 1978; Russell, 1984), and two found higher rates of wife abuse (Briere & Runtz, 1988; Russell, 1986). In Russell's (1986) community survey of 933 women, for example, child sexual abuse victims were two to four times more likely to suffer subsequent sexual assault when compared to women who were not childhood victims. One possible explanation is that those who divulge sexual abuse feel more comfort reporting other types of abuse, and thus the finding is a methodological artifact. However, it is more likely that sexual abuse—through its impairment of self-esteem, self-protection, and trust—makes victims vulnerable to abusive individuals or unable to anticipate dangerous sexual situations.

Depression and related behavior are other hypothesized outcomes of child sexual abuse that have received empirical confirmation. In a study of sexual abuse victims in a community population, Peters (1984) found that victims of childhood molestation had experienced more episodes of depression and had been hospitalized more often for depression than nonvictims. In another community study, Bagley and Ramsey (1985) found a history of sexual abuse to be associated with current depression, psychiatric treatment for depression, suicidal ideation, and a history of deliberate suicide attempts. Similarly, Briere and Runtz (1988), studying a clinic population, reported child sexual abuse victims as more depressed than the comparison group, with a more extensive pattern of suicide attempts and self-mutilation. Two controlled studies of college populations (Briere & Runtz, 1987; Sedney & Brooks, 1984) also found the victims of child sexual abuse to report more depression than do their peers. At least three studies, however, were not able to confirm more depression among sexual abuse victims than nonvictims; perhaps because depression is such a widespread psychiatric symptom and occurs across a continuum with less severe symptoms more difficult to rate (Fromuth, 1983; Herman, 1981; Meiselman, 1978).

An assocation between child sexual abuse and later substance abuse has also received some strong empirical support. Peters (1984) found that a higher percentage of victims manifested symptoms of alcohol abuse than the comparison group. More of the victimized group abused at least one type of drug, as well. Two other studies (Briere & Runtz, 1987; Herman, 1981) also found a higher incidence of alcohol abuse and drug addiction among victims of child sexual abuse than among their nonvictimized counterparts. Other clinical observations confirmed by the results of empirical studies include high levels of anxiety in victims (Bagley & Ramsey, 1985; Briere & Runtz, 1987; Sedney & Brooks, 1984); feelings of isolation and stigma (Briere & Runtz, 1987; Courtois, 1979; Herman, 1981); poor self-esteem (Bagley & Ramsey, 1985; Courtois, 1979; Herman, 1981); hostile feelings toward parents, particularly toward mothers (de Young, 1982; Herman, 1981; Meiselman, 1978); and fear of others, especially men (Briere & Runtz, 1987; Courtois, 1979; Meiselman, 1978). A few studies also link the experience of child sexual abuse to later prostitution (Fields, 1981; James & Meyerding, 1977; Silbert & Pines, 1981); and to particular types of pathology, such as eating disorders (Oppenheimer, Palmer, & Braden, 1984). However, without adequate comparison groups, the results of studies conducted with such specialized populations are hard to interpret.

A currently popular question is whether sexually victimized children later become abusers themselves. A number of studies have looked at this hypothesis, but almost all have serious weaknesses, one of the most important being that most of these inquiries have been conducted with male incarcerated convicts. For example, researchers at the Bridgewater, Massachusetts Treatment Center (Bard, Carter, Cerce, Knight, Rosenberg,

& Schneider, 1983) found that 57% of male child molesters had been sexually molested as children, compared to 23% of the adult rapists. At least three other studies (Groth & Burgess, 1979; Langevin, Handy, Hook, Day, & Russon, 1983; Pelto, 1981) found more victimization in the background of male molesters than in some comparison group, although the comparison groups were not always clearly appropriate. In a study conducted with women, Goodwin, McCarthy, & Divasto (1981) found that 24% of a sample of mothers from families in which there was physical child abuse reported incest experiences in their childhoods, compared to only 3% of women recruited from community organizations (again, not the best comparison group). Such studies do suggest that sexual abuse may be an important etiologic factor on the route to later abusive behavior. However, they do not tell us how many sexual abuse victims actually take this route or what prevents others from doing so.

In general, most studies have been better at establishing the fact that sexual abuse constitutes a risk factor for later long-term effects than at ascertaining how great the risk is. This is in part because studies based on samples of individuals seeking help are likely to overstate risks. Thus surveys of nonclinical populations give us an opportunity to check this perspective against a wider population. For example, Bagley and Ramsey (1985) found clinical signs of depression according to the CES-D in 17% of Calgary community women who said they had suffered a serious sexual assault in childhood. A total of 5% were acutely depressed and 16% had been in psychiatric treatment in the past year for depression. As noted earlier, Peters (1984), in the Los Angeles community survey, found alcohol and drug abuse in 22% and 31% of child sexual abuse victims respectively. She also found a major depressive episode in the histories of 85% of the sexual abuse victims, as well as 66% of nonvictims.

Overall, then, when measured with standard epidemiological tools, most victims of childhood molestation show up as slightly impaired or normal. Victims as a group demonstrate impairment, compared to their nonvictimized counterparts, but less than one-fifth evidence serious psychopathology. This does not mean, however, that the rest are symptom-free. Standardized tests in general are not sensitive to more subtle forms of discomfort and difficulty, and are often ill-suited to measure some effects associated with the experience of sexual molestation as a child. How many victims have truly no negative long-term effects is difficult to establish.

Impact of Different Types of Abuse

The knowledge that some victims of child sexual abuse suffer serious impairment while others do not has sparked considerable speculation about what kinds of abuse are more or less traumagenic. Groth (1978), for example, based on his clinical experience, contended that the greatest trauma occurs in sexual abuse that (1) continues for a long period of time, (2) occurs with a closely related person, (3) involves penetration, and (4) is accompanied by aggression. Increasingly, there have been studies that looked empirically at these speculations. Unfortunately, however, these studies have not always come to the same conclusions.

For example, clinical speculation has generally been that experiences with close relatives are more traumatizing than experiences outside of the family. What empirical findings suggest is that sexual abuse involving fathers and stepfathers is indeed more traumatic (Finkelhor, 1979; Russell, 1986) However, not all studies have found a clear difference between experiences with relatives versus those with nonrelatives. This may well be because the distinction of family versus nonfamily does not always reflect the closeness of the relationship between the abuser and the child. Abuse by a trusted neighbor may actually be more betraying than abuse by a distant uncle or grandfather.

Clinical observation has also suggested that sexual abuse involving intercourse is more traumatic, and this observation has received empirical support. Russell (1986) found that 59% of those victims who had suffered completed or attempted intercourse, fellatio, cunnilingus, analingus, or anal intercourse said they were extremely traumatized by the abuse. This compared to only 36% of those who suffered manual touching of the breasts or genitals, or 22% who suffered simply from unwanted kissing or touching of clothed parts of their bodies. Similarly, Bagley and Ramsey (1985), in a multivariate analysis, found penetration to be the variable most predictive of impairment on a composite of standard epidemiological measures. Other empirical studies have also shown greater trauma associated with genital contact, but have not always been able to demonstrate a difference between intercourse and other types of genital touching (Fromuth, 1983; Landis, 1956; Tufts, 1984).

In assessing the empirical literature on the trauma of different kinds of abuse, one of the most prominent traumagenic factors seems to be the use of force. Five studies found strong associations between the degree of trauma and whether force occurred (Bagley & Ramsey, 1985; Finkelhor, 1979; Fromuth, 1983; Russell, 1986; Tufts, 1984). These findings cast doubt on a commonly heard speculation that victims who are forced have an easier time coping because they are less prone to attribute blame for the abuse to themselves (e.g., MacFarlane, 1978). Apparently, the fear and powerlessness created by being forced to comply act to increase, rather than decrease, the long-term trauma.

Another interesting finding concerns the effect of telling others about the abuse. Two studies have not found any relationship between whether the incident is disclosed and long-term trauma (Bagley & Ramsey, 1985; Finkelhor, 1979), and another finds children who do not tell, or at least do not tell right away, show fewer symptoms (Tufts, 1984). While it is true that in some cases silence may create isolation and suffering, it may also spare the child from the additional traumatic effects of parental and community reactions.

Research is also very equivocal in answering the ongoing controversy about whether children are more traumatized if the abuse occurs at earlier or later ages. Two studies (Courtois, 1979; Meiselman, 1978) found more serious impact associated with abuse at a younger age. Four other studies (Bagley & Ramsey, 1985; Finkelhor, 1979; Langmade, 1983; Russell, 1986) found no significant differences of effect according to age. The effects of age have not yet been studied in a sophisticated way, however. Few have tried to parcel out the effects of other aspects of the experience, such as intercourse, which tend to covary with age. In addition, not enough consideration has been given to the possibility that the relationship between age and trauma may be curvilinear, with the most serious effects occurring in preadolescence.

A small number of studies have looked at the specific traumatic impact of various other aspects of the experience. Two studies (Finkelhor, 1979; Russell, 1986) found that experiences with male perpetrators were more traumatic than those with female perpetrators. Three studies (Finkelhor, 1979; Fromuth, 1983; Russell, 1986) reported that experiences with adult perpetrators were more traumatic than experiences with adolescents. Two studies (Anderson, Bache, & Griffith, 1981; Tufts, 1984) found that negative parental reaction was associated with more severe trauma. And one study (Tufts, 1984) found that children removed from their homes following sexual abuse exhibited more overall behavior problems, particularly aggression, than did children who remained with their families.

From this review, then, it is apparent that there is still substantial work to be done before we fully understand the effects of different types of child sexual abuse. It would appear that sexual abuse by fathers and stepfathers is consistently more traumatic, as is abuse involving force or intercourse. Male perpetrators and adult perpetrators (as opposed to adolescents) also are associated with more trauma. And we might tentatively conclude that when families are unsupportive of victims or victims are removed from the home, the effects are more serious. However, in other matters about which there has been much controversy, no firm conclusions are available. It has not been demonstrated that abuse at any particular age is more harmful. And there are contradictory findings about the effects on victims of keeping the abuse a secret.

Traumagenic Dynamics

One of the shortcomings of research on the effects of child sexual abuse is the absence of any underlying conceptual framework. Researchers have tended to cast a wide net in a search for effects, without attempting to formulate a model of just how the experience of childhood molestation might lead to these effects. Such a model might help to focus the search for traumagenic factors, as well as clarify the different impact of various types of abuse. The remainder of this chapter is concerned with outlining such a model.

We would like to propose that the injury of child sexual abuse can be broken down into four components, which we call "traumagenic dynamics." These components are: (1) traumatic sexualization, (2) stigmatization, (3) betrayal, and (4) powerlessness. These are generalized traumatizing phenomenon that occur in other kinds of events as well, but their conjunction in one set of circumstances makes the experience of child sexual abuse somewhat unique.

The operation of these dynamics can be described in a general way: We suggest that they alter a child's cognitive and emotional orientation to the world, and thus create trauma by distorting a child's self-concept, worldview, and affective capacities. For example, stigmatization might distort a child's sense of his or her own value and worth. Powerlessness distorts a sense of ability to control critical events in life. When children attempt to cope with the world through these distortions, it may result in many of the problems commonly noted in victims of sexual abuse. Let us describe in more detail some possible components of each of these dynamics.

Traumatic sexualization is the process by which a child's sexuality is shaped in developmentally inappropriate and interpersonally dysfunctional ways. This may happen in a variety of ways in the course of sexual abuse. Traumatic sexualization can occur when a child is repeatedly rewarded by an offender for sexual behavior that is inappropriate to his or her level of development. It can also occur through the exchange of affection, attention, privileges, or gifts for sexual behavior so that a child learns sexual behavior as a strategy for manipulating others to get other developmentally appropriate needs met. It occurs when certain parts of a child's anatomy are fetishized and given distorted importance and meaning. It also occurs through the misconceptions and confusions about sexual behavior and sexual morality that are transmitted to the child from the offender. And it occurs when very frightening or painful memories and events become associated in the child's mind with sexual activity.

Sexual abuse experiences can vary dramatically in terms of the amount and kind of traumatic sexualization they provoke. Experiences in which the offender makes an effort to evoke the child's sexual response, for example, are probably more sexualizing than those in which an offender simply uses a passive child to masturbate with. Experiences in which the child is enticed to participate are also likely to be more sexualizing than those in which brute force is used. However, even with the use of force, a form of traumatic sexualization may occur as a result of the fear that becomes associated with sex in the aftermath of such an experience. The degree of a child's understanding may also affect the degree of sexualization. Experiences in which the child, because of young age or developmental level, understands few of the sexual implications of the activities may be less sexualizing than when a child has full awareness. Children who have been traumatically sexualized emerge from their experiences with inappropriate repertoires of sexual behavior, with confusions and misconceptions about their sexual self-concepts, and with unusual emotional associations to sexual activities.

Betrayal refers to the dynamic in which children discover that someone on whom they were vitally dependent has caused them harm. This may occur in different ways in a molestation experience. For example, in the course of abuse or its aftermath, children may come to the realization that a trusted person has manipulated them through lies or misrepresentations about moral standards. They may also come to realize that someone whom they loved or whose affection was important to them treated them with callous disregard. Children can experience betrayal not only at the hands of offenders, but also with family members who were not abusing them. A family member whom they trusted but who was unable or unwilling to protect or believe them—or who has a changed attitude toward them after disclosure of the abuse—may also contribute to the dynamics of betrayal.

Sexual abuse experiences that are perpetrated by family members or other trusted persons obviously involve more potential for betrayal than those involving strangers. However, the degree of betrayal may also be affected by how taken-in the child feels by the offender, regardless of who the offender is. A child who was suspicious of a father's activities from the beginning may feel less betrayed than one who initially experienced the contact as nurturing and loving and then is suddenly shocked to realize what is really happening. Obviously, the degree of betrayal is also related to a family's response to disclosure. Children who are disbelieved, blamed, or ostracized undoubtedly experience a greater sense of betrayal than those who are supported.

Powerlessness—or what might better be called disempowerment, the dynamic of rendering the victim powerless—refers to the process in which the child's will, desires, and sense of efficacy are continually contravened. Many aspects of the sexual abuse experience contribute to this dynamic. We theorize that a basic kind of powerlessness occurs in sexual abuse when a child's territory and body space are repeatedly invaded against the child's will. This is exacerbated by whatever coercion and manipulation the offender may impose as a part of the abuse process. Powerlessness is then reinforced when a child sees his or her attempts to halt the abuse frustrated. It is increased when the child feels fear, or is unable to make adults understand or believe what is happening, or feels trapped in the situation by conditions of dependency.

An authoritarian abuser who continually commands the child's participation by threatening serious harm will probably instill more of a sense of powerlessness. However, force and threat are not necessary: Any situation in which a child feels trapped, if only by the realization of the consequences of disclosure, can create a sense of powerlessness. Obviously, a situation in which a child tells and is not believed will also create a greater degree of powerlessness. On the other hand, when a child is able to bring the abuse to an end effectively, or at least exert some control over its occurrence, he or she may feel less disempowered.

Stigmatization, the final dynamic, refers to the negative connotations— for example, badness, shame, and guilt—that are communicated to the child around experiences of molestation and that then become incorporated into the child's self-image. These negative meanings are communicated in many ways. They can come directly from the abuser, who may blame the victim for the activity, denigrate the victim, or, simply through furtiveness, convey a sense of shame about the behavior. When there is pressure for secrecy from the offender, this can also convey powerful messages of shame and guilt. Stigmatization is also reinforced by attitudes that the victim infers or hears from other persons in the family or community. Stigmatization may grow out of the child's prior knowledge or sense that the activity is considered deviant and taboo. It is reinforced if, after disclosure, people react with shock or hysteria or blame the child for what has transpired. The child may be additionally stigmatized by people in his or her environment who now impute other negative characteristics to the victim (loose morals, spoiled goods) as a result of the molestation. Stigmatization occurs in various degrees in different abuse situations. Some children are treated as bad and blameworthy by offenders and some are not. Some children, in the wake of a sexual abuse experience, are told clearly that they are not at fault, whereas others are heavily shamed. Some children may be too young to have much awareness of social attitudes and thus experience little stigmatization from that source. Others may have to deal with powerful religious and cultural taboos, in addition to the usual stigma. Keeping the secret of having been a sexual abuse victim may increase the sense of stigma, since it reinforces the sense of being different. By contrast, those who find out that such experiences occur to many other children may have some of their stigma assuaged.

Making Use of the Model

The potential of separate kinds of traumagenic dynamics within the experience of child sexual abuse immediately suggests some hypotheses. For example, in analyzing the differential impact of different kinds of abuse, the main question asked has been: Was it more or less traumatic?

The conceptualization proposed here suggests that the question should not simply be the degree of trauma, but what kind of trauma has occurred? Different traumagenic dynamics should lead to different types of trauma. Thus we were encouraged to go back to the traumatic effects cited in the literature on child sexual abuse and see whether some might appear more likely to be associated with certain traumatic dynamics. Potential groupings are illustrated in Table 19.1. Obviously, there is no simple one-to-one correspondence, but there are some clear general clusterings.

It would be plausible to hypothesize that *traumatic sexualization* is particularly associated with impacts on sexual behavior. These effects would include sexual dysfunctions, promiscuity, sexual anxiety, and low sexual self-esteem. *Stigmatization,* we would hypothesize, might be most clearly related to such long-term effects as guilt, poor self-esteem, a sense of differentness and isolation; and secondary problems, such as drug and alcohol abuse, criminal involvement, suicidal ideation, and suicide attempts. *Betrayal* would seem most plausibly associated with effects such as depression, dependency in extreme forms, impaired ability to trust and to judge the trustworthiness of others, and anger. Some of the manifestations of this might be a vulnerability to subsequent abuse and exploitation, discomfort in intimate relationships, and marital problems. Finally, *powerlessness* would seem most likely to be associated with fear and anxiety, a lowered sense of self-efficacy, perception of the self as a victim, and sometimes an identification with the aggressor in an attempt to regain some sense of power. Manifestations here might include nightmares, somatic complaints, depression, running away, school problems, employment problems, vulnerability to subsequent victimization, aggressive behavior, delinquency, and becoming an abuser.

As mentioned earlier, these clusterings are not meant to suggest that there is any strict one-to-one correspondence between each traumagenic dynamic and each effect. Some effects, like depression, are undoubtedly associated with many dynamics. However, postulating associations between these general dynamics and specific effects can be useful in several ways. For instance, they suggest research hypotheses that might lead to an increase in our understanding of the effects of child sexual abuse. Instead of simply looking at sexual abuse in terms of whether abuse by fathers causes more general trauma, we might look at whether abuse involving more betrayal results in more subsequent marital and relationship problems. Likewise, instead of simply looking at whether intercourse has more negative impact than other types of sexual abuse, we might look at whether abuse involving more sexualization (perhaps more sexual involvement on the part of the child) results in more subsequent sexual dysfunctions. Testing these more specific hypotheses will yield much useful information about just how child sexual abuse causes injury.

The notion of traumagenic dynamics can also be used as a guide for developing assessment instruments. Up to now, research on child sexual abuse has been conducted primarily with broad psychological inventories like the Child Behavior Checklist (Tufts, 1984) or the California Psychological Inventory (Seidner & Calhoun, 1984). These instruments are not geared to detect trauma specifically associated with childhood molestation. Breaking down child sexual abuse into traumagenic dynamics suggests elements that might go into an instrument specifically designed to assess the traumatic impact of such abuse.

A third use of the idea of traumagenic dynamics, even in the absence of empirical research, is in making clinical assessments of sexual abuse victims. The model of four traumagenic dynamics reminds clinicians of the various ways that child sexual abuse may cause harm and encourages them to check for injuries in all of those areas. Thus clinicians might ask: How traumatically sexualizing was the experience; how betraying; how stigmatizing; how disempowering? This framework could then be used to guide planned interventions. If a clinician determined that one of the main traumas occurred in the area of stigmatization, for instance, this would suggest interventions designed to counteract the effects of stigma—for example, contact with other victims of child sexual abuse who could assuage the sense of differentness. If the trauma appeared to be primarily in the area of powerlessness, this would suggest therapy to restore the victim's sense of power and self-efficacy. Moreover, the framework may remind clinicians that recovery in one area may not mean automatic recovery in another. A victim may overcome the sense of stigma and still feel very powerless in the world, or may still have sexual dysfunctions stemming from traumatic sexualization.

Conclusion

The study of the effects of child sexual abuse is still in its infancy, but already the time has come for a change of emphasis. Early efforts have been directed at proving the seriousness, even the legitimacy, of sexual abuse as a problem of mental health and social policy. Thus we have endeavored to demonstrate that childhood molestation has long-term effects that can be identified years after the occurrence of the abuse. We have also tried to show that sexual abuse may be implicated in a host of other already recognized social and psychological problems, and research has tended to support these contentions.

What is needed now is research that gives more specification to prior findings; research that is not simply concerned with establishing that child sexual abuse can have serious consequences, but is designed to investigate: (1) how serious these consequences are, (2) to whom, (3) in what ways, and (4) under what circumstances. It is true that policymakers still need to be persuaded that this troubling problem deserves attention and resources. But other audiences must also be addressed. For example, victims and their families need reassurance that many victims recover well from the trauma of sexual abuse and go on to live happy and productive lives. Clinicians need to know how to guide interventions for victims, based on the dynamics of the victimization and victims' life circumstances. And social scientists need to be enticed to consider how sexual abuse articulates with general principles of human development, as well as with other pathologies of childhood, and encouraged to take a more sophisticated approach to the study of this particularly important and complex problem.

Note

1. Even though it is recognized that approximately one out of three or four abuse victims are boys, there are very few studies of its impact on them. (The exceptions are Finkelhor, 1979; Rogers & Terry, 1984; Wood & Dean, 1984.) All of the findings cited in this chapter, unless otherwise indicated, apply solely to women.

References

Anderson, S. C., Bach, C. M., & Griffith, S. (1981). *Psychosocial sequelae in intrafamilial victims of sexual assault and abuse.* Paper presented at the Third International Conference on Child Abuse and Neglect, Amsterdam, The Netherlands.

Bagley, C., & Ramsey, R. (1985). Disrupted childhood and vulnerability to sexual assault: Long-term sequels with implications for counselling. *Social Work and Human Sexuality, 4,* 33-48.

Bard, L., Carter, D., Cerce, D., Knight, R., Rosenberg, R., & Schneider, B. (1983). *A descriptive study of rapists and child molesters: Developmental, clinical and criminal characteristics.* (Available from Bridgewater, Massachusetts Treatment Center)

Briere, J., & Runtz, M. (1987). Post-sexual abuse trauma: Data and implications for clinical practice. *Journal of Interpersonal Violence, 2,* 367-379.

Briere, J., & Runtz, M. (1988). Symptomatology associated with childhood sexual victimization in a non-clinical adult sample. *Child Abuse & Neglect, 12,* 51-59.

Browne, A., & Finkelhor, D. (1986). The impact of child sexual abuse: A review of the research. *Psychological Bulletin, 99*(1), 66-77.

Constantine, L. (1977). *The sexual rights of children: Implications of a radical perspective.* Paper presented at the International Conference on Love and Attraction, Swansea, Wales.

Courtois, C. (1979). The incest experience and its aftermath. *Victimology: An International Journal, 4,* 337-347.

de Young, M. (1982). *The sexual victimization of children.* Jefferson, NC: McFarland.

Fields, P. J. (1981, November). Parent-child relationships, childhood sexual abuse, and adult interpersonal behavior in female prostitutes. *Dissertation Abstracts International, 42,* No. 5.

Finkelhor, D. (1979). *Sexually victimized children.* New York: Free Press.

Finkelhor, D. (1984). *Child sexual abuse: New theory and research.* New York: Free Press.

Fromuth, M. E. (1983, August). *The long-term psychological impact of childhood sexual abuse*. Unpublished doctoral dissertation, Auburn University, Auburn, AL.

Gelinas, D. J. (1983). The persisting negative effects of incest. *Psychiatry, 46,* 312-332.

Goodwin, J., McCarthy, T., & Divasto, P. (1981). Prior incest in mothers of abused children. *Child Abuse and Neglect, 5,* 87-96.

Groth, N. (1978). Guidelines for assessment and management of the offender. In A. Burgess, N. Groth, S. Holmstrom, & S. Sgroi (Eds.), *Sexual assault of children and adolescents*. Lexington, MA: Lexington Books.

Groth, N. (1979). *Men who rape*. New York: Plenum.

Groth, N. A., & Burgess, A. W. (1979). Sexual trauma in the life histories of rapists and child molesters. *Victimology, An International Journal, 4,* 10-16.

Henderson, J. (1983). Is incest harmful? *Canadian Journal of Psychiatry, 28,* 34-39.

Herman, J. L. (1981). *Father-daughter incest*. Cambridge, MA: Harvard University Press.

James, J., & Meyerding, J. (1977). Early sexual experiences and prostitution. *American Journal of Psychiatry, 134,* 1381-1385.

Jehu, D., & Gazan, M. (1983). Psychosocial adjustment of women who were sexually victimized in childhood or adolescence. *Canadian Journal of Community Mental Health, 2,* 71-81.

Landis, J. (1956). Experiences of 500 children with adult sexual deviation. *Psychiatric Quarterly Supplement, 30,* 91-109.

Langevin, R., Handy, L., Hook, H., Day, D., & Russon, A. (1983). Are incestuous fathers pedophilic and aggressive? In R. Langevin (Ed.), *Erotic preference, gender identity and aggression*. Hillsdale, NJ: Lawrence Erlbaum.

Langmade, C. J. (1983). The impact of pre- and postpubertal onset of incest experiences in adult women as measured by sex anxiety, sex guilt, sexual satisfaction and sexual behavior. *Dissertation Abstracts International, 44,* 917B. (University Microfilms No. 3592)

MacFarlane, K. (1978). Sexual abuse of children. In J. R. Chapman & M. Gates (Eds), *The victimization of women* (pp. 81-109). Beverly Hills, CA: Sage.

Meiselman, K. (1978). *Incest*. San Francisco: Jossey-Bass.

Miller, J., Moeller, D., Kaufman, A., Divasto, P., Pather, D., & Christy, J. (1978). Recidivism among sexual assault victims. *American Journal of Psychiatry, 135,* 1103-1104.

Oppenheimer, R., Palmer, R. L., & Braden, S. (1984, September). *A clinical evaluation of early sexually abusive experiences in adult anorexic and bulimic females: Implications for preventive work in childhood*. Paper presented at Fifth International Conferences on Child Abuse and Neglect, Montréal.

Pelto, V. (1981). *Male incest offenders and non-offenders: A comparison of early sexual history*. Doctoral dissertation, Ann Arbor, Michigan. (University Microfilms)

Peters, S. D. (1984). *The relationship between childhood sexual victimization and adult depression among Afro-American and white women*. Unpublished doctoral dissertation, University of California, Los Angeles, CA.

Ramey, J. (1979). Dealing with the last taboo. *SIECUS Report, 7,* 1-2, 6-7.

Rogers, C. M., & Terry, T. (1984). Clinical intervention with boy victims of sexual abuse. In I. Stewart and J. Greer (Eds.), *Victims of sexual aggression* (pp. 1-104). New York: Van Nostrand, Reinhold.

Russell, D.E.H. (1986). *Intrafamily child sexual abuse: A San Francisco survey*. Final Report to the National Center on Child Abuse and Neglect.

Russell, D. (1984). *Sexual exploitation: Rape, child sexual abuse, and sexual harassment*. Beverly Hills: Sage.

Sedney, M. S., & Brooks, B. (1984). Factors associated with a history of childhood sexual experience in a nonclinical female population. *Journal of the American Academy of Child Psychiatry, 23,* 215, 218.

Seidner, A., & Calhoun, K. S. (1984, August). *Childhood sexual abuse: Factors related to differential adult adjustment.* Paper presented at the Second National Conference for Family Violence Researchers, Durham, NH.

Silbert, M. H., & Pines, A. M. (1981). Sexual child abuse as an antecedent to prostitution. *Child Abuse and Neglect, 5,* 407-411.

Tsai, M., Feldman-Summers, S., & Edgar, M. (1979). Childhood molestation: Variables related to differential impact of psychosexual functioning in adult women. *Journal of Abnormal Psychology, 88,* 407-417.

Tufts New England Medical Center, Division of Child Psychiatry (1984). *Sexually exploited children: Service and research project.* Final report for the Office of Juvenile Justice and Delinquency Prevention, U. S. Department of Justice. Washington, DC: Government Printing Office.

Wood, S. C., & Dean, K. S. (1984). *Final report, sexual abuse of males research project.* Washington, DC: National Center on Child Abuse and Neglect (90 CA/812).

20

Date Abuse and Forced Intercourse Among College Students

John E. Murphy

F ew researchers in the past suspected that violence of any form was a normative pattern of family interaction and, concomitantly, little thought was given to its prevalence in the courtship process. However, the past two decades have been witness to an increasing awareness of various forms of family violence. Kempe, Silverman, Steele, Droegenmueller, and Silver (1962) first alerted the profession to the battered child syndrome, and others have continued to investigate this and other forms of violence and abuse within the family. Research during the decade of the 1960s tended to focus upon child abuse while in the 1970s attention shifted toward spouse abuse. Straus et al. (1980) used the first national representative sample to establish benchmark incidence rates of not only child and spouse abuse but other forms of family abuse also (sibling abuse, child-parent abuse, and so on). In the 1980s, while research on these forms of family violence and abuse continue, a new topic of concern, that of courtship violence, seems to be emerging.

While there seem to be a number of ongoing research projects currently studying courtship abuse, only four articles have been published on the topic. Three of these articles seem to be in approximate agreement regarding incidence rates. Makepeace (1981; 1983) and Cate, Henton, Kaval, Christopher, and Lloyd (1982) found the rate of courtship abuse to be between 168 and 228. These studies also suggest that, as in family violence in general, less severe forms of violence are the most common, and that males are more often the most serious aggressors. Their results also imply that violent behavior is more likely to be experienced later in a

AUTHOR'S NOTE: I would like to express my sincere appreciation to Judith Franklin, Assistant Director of Computer Services, St. Cloud State University, for her tireless assistance in data entry, analysis, and presentation.

relationship after commitment has been established rather than in the early stages of a relationship. The fourth article (Bernard & Bernard, 1983) reported a higher incidence rate (30%) than the above studies along with a tendency for respondents to be more abusive in their relationships if they were ever recipients of or observed forms of abuse in their own families.

Another aspect of courtship violence, date rape, has also received little research attention. Although some studies indicate that between one-third and one-half of all rapes or attempted rapes occur among acquaintances (Katz & Mazur, 1979; McDermott, 1979) few works have looked explicitly at the incidence of date rape. Some studies have looked at sexual aggression among the dating population (Kanin, 1957, 1967; Kanin & Parcell, 1977) but have tended to group all forms of sexually aggressive behavior together, making it difficult to estimate the actual incidence of rape among dating couples.

Although the above studies on date violence and sexual aggression are enlightening and provocative, their results are limited because of their general reliance upon convenience designs using convenience samples that make their results nonrepresentative of the population being studied. Attempts must be made to improve the quality of the data if a true incidence rate of courtship abuse and date rapes are to be developed, and if generalizations and predictions are to be drawn from the research. One of the purposes of the present research is to improve upon these earlier seminal works by incorporating a randomly selected sample within its design.

Method

As mentioned above, the results of previous studies on courtship violence have been limited because of their reliance upon nonprobability sampling techniques. Some have even expressed the opinion that obtaining a representative sample is not possible because the problems associated with probability sampling techniques are too numerous and onerous to overcome in research of this type. However, strong and convincing arguments have been made that representative samples are necessary in family research if we are to generalize to the larger population (Kitson et al., 1982; Miller, Rollins, & Thomas, 1982).

The telephone survey is one technique that lends itself well to research in which the accessibility of respondents is difficult. Telephone research is not only faster and more economical than traditional research methodologies but it also has the potential of reaching approximately 95% of all households (Miller, Rollins, & Thomas, 1982) and it can be an especially useful technique when studying low base rate family problems (Gelles, 1983). Previous thought suggested that the telephone could not be used in this type of research because of the topic's sensitive nature. Arguments were made that the response rate would be low and the data would suffer in reliability and validity. However, recent work has shown that telephone surveys not only have response rates similar to, or higher than, the more commonly used methods (Groves & Kahn, 1979; Harris & Associates, 1979; Gelles, 1983) but that the data obtained is high in reliability and validity (Hochstim, 1977; Bradburn, Sudman, & Associates, 1979; Gelles, 1983). In fact, Gelles (1983) argues that telephone surveys have several advantages over other methods when researching sensitive family issues: anonymity is assured, other persons cannot hear the questions being asked, and the respondent does not have to worry about reactions of other family members because they will have no knowledge of the topic of the interview. Therefore it was decided that a telephone survey would be used for the present study. Information regarding experience with family and courtship abuse was obtained by phone interviews with a random sample of single students enrolled at a medium sized university in the upper Midwest. It was estimated that some of the phenomena being investigated had low base rates, therefore, a sample size of approximately 500 students was determined to be necessary for relevant statistical analysis of these variables and to keep the sampling error as low as possible. Using a table of random numbers a sample of 750 telephone numbers was drawn from a list of 10,282 telephone numbers of students registered for classes in the spring of 1982. Since the present research was concerned only with single students, the oversampling of telephone numbers was necessary in order to compensate for those numbers that would be eliminated because of the respondent's marital status or for those numbers eliminated because of refusals or inaccessibility.

Phone interviews were carried out over a three week period. Each number was called up to six times, at varying times during the day, before it was eliminated from the sample (this was done to keep the sample as representative as possible by increasing our "odds" of getting the hard-to-get respondents). When a phone was answered, the answering person was asked if he or she was currently enrolled at the university and, if so, was immediately interviewed. If the person answering was not a student, he or she was asked to call to the phone the student registered at that number. If there was more than one student registered under a number, the interviewers were instructed to request that the student closest to the phone at the time of the call be interviewed. This procedure was necessitated because the interviewers had only the telephone numbers and not the corresponding names registered to them. The interview schedule consisted of 76 questions that gathered information on 198 variables and took between 15-20 minutes to complete. The Violence Scale from the Conflict Tactic Scale (Straus, 1979) was used to measure the incidence and levels of violence in the respondent's family and courtship relations. The Violence

Scale contains eight items that measure the actual use of physical force in interpersonal relationships and range along a continuum of severity from throwing something at another person to using a gun or a knife on another person. Questions regarding whether or not the subjects had experienced sexual intercourse with past or present dates and whether or not they felt they were forced psychologically or physically to do so were used to gather data measuring the incidence of forced intercourse among dating students.

The final sample consisted of 485 single students of which 230 were males (47.5%) and 255 were females (52.5%). This closely resembles the general composition of the single population of the university's student body (48.8% males; 51.2% females) as does the class composition of the sample (there was a very slight undersampling of freshmen (–1.7%), seniors (–1.5%) and graduate students (–0.4%) and a slight oversampling of sophomores (0.6%) and juniors (3.6%). In general it can be assumed that the sample is representative of the university's single student population. In all, 701 telephone numbers were called, of which 173 were either numbers of married students (101) or numbers at which no student resided (72). Of the 528 eligible respondents 43 refused to cooperate and 485 consented to the interview. This yielded a response rate of 91.8%.

Results

The overall rates of witnessed or experienced violence in family or courtship relations were rather high. In all, 22% indicated that some form of spouse abuse had occurred in their families of origin, 73.2% had witnessed or experienced some form of parent-child abuse, 28.5% had witnessed or experienced some form of child-parent abuse, and 87.7% had witnessed or experienced some form of sibling abuse. The overall rate of experience with at least one instance of courtship abuse, whether past or present, for those persons who had dated (N = 483) either as a victim or aggressor, was 40.4%. Specifically, 31.5% had experienced some form of abuse from their dates in past relationships, and 24.5% had abused a date in some manner during past relationships. Of those who were involved in a dating relationship at the time of the survey (N = 272), 15% reported that they had abused their partner in some manner, and 12.5% had been abused by their partner in some manner. The total percentage of those persons who were currently dating and who had experienced some form of abuse in this relationship within the last year, whether as victim or aggressor, was 19.1%.

Table 20.1 shows the major forms of abuse experienced as a victim, or used as an aggressor, tend to be those of throwing, pushing or slapping. Table 20.2 indicates that males tended to report greater rates of abuse (both past and present) and lesser rates of aggression (both past and present) than did women. It can also be seen in Table 20.2 that, for past relationships,

TABLE 20.1
Rates of Courtship Violence Experienced as Victims or
Aggressors in Past and Present Dating Relationships by Type

Types of Violence	Victim		Aggressor	
	Past (N = 472) %	Present (N = 269) %	Past (N = 472) %	Present (N = 269) %
Threw something	8.0	2.2	6.4	2.6
Pushed, grabbed or shoved	23.0	9.6	13.9	8.9
Slapped	16.5	5.9	13.8	9.6
Kicked, bit or hit with a fist	7.2	2.2	3.6	0.7
Hit or tried to hit with something	4.9	1.5	2.5	1.1
Beat up	1.5	0.0	0.0	0.0
Threatened with a gun or knife	0.6	0.0	0.0	0.0
Used a gun or knife	0.0	0.0	0.0	0.0

both men and women tended to report having received higher levels of abuse than the other person reports having given. However, while men tended to report higher levels of abuse in their present relationships than women reported having given, women, in contrast, reported *lower* levels of abuse in their present relationships than men reported having given. Women tended to use some forms of violence more than did men. These included throwing, slapping and kicking, biting, or hitting with a fist. Men tended to push, grab, or shove more (especially in present relationships) than did women.

In general the experience of violence had a negative effect on the relationships. Table 20.3 indicates that the majority of the relationships (64.3) worsened after the violent episode(s). Once again, however, there were important differences between men and women. Men were seemingly twice as likely as women to report that their relationship(s) had improved after a violent episode (14.8% versus 7.4%). Women, on the other hand, were much more likely to report that their relationship(s) had deteriorated after a violent incident (70% versus 56.4%).

Stepwise regression was used to determine what variables contributed to the overall variations in general courtship violence and date rape. These two dependent variables were coded either 0 or 1 with 0 indicating that date violence or date rape had not occurred and 1 indicating that date violence

TABLE 20.2
Rates of Courtship Violence Experienced as Victims or Aggressors in Past or Present Dating Relationships by Type and Sex

Type of Violence	Males				Females			
	Victim		Aggressor		Victim		Aggressor	
	Past (N = 222) %	Present (N = 118) %	Past (N = 222) %	Present (N = 118) %	Past (N = 250) %	Present (N = 153) %	Past (N = 250) %	Present (N = 153) %
Threw something	11.6	4.2	4.9	.08	5.2	.07	7.6	3.9
Pushed, grabbed or shoved	19.3	11.8	14.4	10.9	26.4	7.8	13.6	7.2
Slapped	20.7	10.1	4.9	4.2	12.8	1.3	20.4	13.1
Kicked, bit, or hit with a fist	10.3	5.0	2.2	0.8	4.4	0.0	4.8	0.7
Hit or tried to hit with something	6.0	2.5	1.4	0.8	3.6	0.7	3.6	1.3
Beat up	0.0	0.0	0.0	0.0	2.8	0.0	0.0	0.0
Threatened with a gun or knife	0.0	0.0	0.0	0.0	0.8	0.0	0.0	0.0
Used a gun or knife	0.0	0.0	0.4	0.0	0.0	0.0	0.0	0.0

TABLE 20.3

Differential Effects of Violent Experience on the Relationship

Effects on Relationship	Male (N = 108)	Female (N = 147)	Total (N = 255)
Relationship improved	14.8	7.4	10.5
Relationship stayed the same	28.7	22.4	25.0
Relationship got worse	56.4	70.0	64.3

or date rape had occurred. The independent variables dealt with the respondent's family structure, experience with various types of family or courtship violence, and their past and present sexual experiences. All regression analyses were involved in a stepwise procedure (BMDP2R, 1982). A probability level of .05 was used to stop the stepping procedure. Therefore, at each step an independent variable was entered into the regression equation if it explained a significant proportion of the dependent variable's variance, independent of the variables explained already in the equation.

Six variables accounted for 16% of the variation when looking at experience with courtship violence. These variables are listed below in order of importance (with their direction specified). They are:

(1) a higher number of persons an individual had gone steady with
(2) the individual had experienced sexual intercourse
(3) the perception of less affection expressed by the mother toward the individual
(4) being an older child in the family
(5) the individual's siblings abused their father
(6) the perception of less affection expressed by the father toward the individual

When sex was controlled for, three variables explained 14% of the variation for women's experience with overall courtship violence (listed in order of importance):

(1) the experience of sexual intercourse
(2) a larger number of persons the individual went steady with
(3) mother abused father

Five variables explained 17% of the variation for men's experience with violence (listed in order of importance):

(1) a higher number of coital partners
(2) a larger number of persons the man went steady with
(3) mother had spent low amount of time with the individual
(4) a larger family size
(5) experiencing abuse from mother

Violence also spills over into the sexual aspect of the dating relationship. Of those students who had experienced sexual intercourse with a past or present date, 19.8% reported having been forced to do so. A total of 12% of all men who had sexual intercourse with a date (both past and present) and 28.6% of all women indicated that psychological or physical force was used in gaining their compliance. With rates broken down by type of force, 9% of the men who had sexual intercourse with a date (both past and present) and 21.1% of the women said they were forced to do so under psychological pressure and 0.6% of the men and 9.5% of the women stated that they were physically forced to have intercourse with a past or present date. Stepwise regressions indicated that three variables accounted for 15% of the variation in women's experience with forced intercourse (listed in order of importance):

(1) mother spent low amount of time with the individual
(2) a larger family size
(3) a higher number of coital partners

For men, two variables accounted for 5% of the variation (listed in order of importance):

(1) father spent low amount of time with the individual
(2) the perception of less affection expressed by the mother toward the individual.

Discussion and Conclusions

The present research has uncovered higher rates of courtship violence in almost every category than have previous studies (Bernard & Bernard, 1983; Cate et al., 1982; Henton, Cate, Kaval, Lloyd, & Christopher, 1983; Makepeace, 1983, 1981) and the overall rate of 40.4% for persons who had been involved in some type of abusive relationship is almost twice as great as some of these studies have reported. The explanation for the differences in these rates may lie in the fact that the present study is the first to use a random, representative sample in its design. A representative sample is, of course, necessary before true rates of incidence can be determined, and the lower rates found in other works may simply reflect their potentially biased samples. A quick comparison of spouse, parent, and sibling abuse rates from the present study with those from Straus, Gelles, and Steinmetz (1980) national survey points to a great deal of similarity between the two, which lends support to the claim that the present results may be more representative than those of other studies. The anonymity of the telephone may also have contributed to the higher rates found. If, as Gelles (1983) argues, the telephone not only tends to increase response rates but also produces potentially more reliable data, then, once again, the rates found in this study may more accurately reflect the true incidence of violence.

Clear differences were illustrated when rates of abuse were analyzed by type and sex. As with other studies more persons perceived themselves as victims rather than as aggressors. Interestingly, though, with rates broken down by sex and type of violence, men perceived of themselves more often as victims, whereas women perceived themselves more often as the aggressor in violent episodes. This, once again, is contrary to current theory, and to other studies that have found men to be the aggressors and women the victims (Bernard & Bernard, 1983; Makepeace, 1981, 1983). Unfortunately, the aggregate rates by sex are not available so it is impossible to tell if a greater percentage of men as a whole experienced more violence than did women. It is quite possible that although a higher percentage of males reported being victims of specific acts of violence, a greater percentage of women reported having experienced violence as victims. The discrepancy between the present data and those from other works may also be a result, once again, of the fact that the present data comes from a representative sample and, therefore, gives a more accurate representation of the behavior being studied. If this is so, the differences illustrated by these data beg further explanation. These data may also reflect the acceptance of certain traditional sex-role stereotypes that support violent behavior on the part of males as normal and violent behavior on the part of females as abnormal in intimate heterosexual relationships. As a result women may be less likely to regard males' violent actions as deviant and, subsequently, less likely to remember them as such and report it. Concomitant men may also fail to consider some of their acts of violence as abusive, deviant, or out of the ordinary and, therefore, don't recognize and report these acts for what they are. Conversely, both sexes may perceive a woman's violent behavior as deviant and out of the ordinary and may be more likely to remember it as such and report it (even in situations in which the male is also abusive but neither reports it). Another explanation for these differences is that a woman's acts of defense may be interpreted by both males and females as acts of aggression (once again because the woman's actions are not consistent with her stereotypical role model of general passivity). Along this line, women may actually be intimidated into using more acts of violence in her defense than a male would be. A male's threat of violence may be more likely to produce a violent defensive move from a female than the reverse because of the male's greater strength and size, which would signal imminent danger unless appropriate defensive actions are taken. Therefore, women may actually use more violent forms of behavior but as a defense, not as an offense.

As with the other studies on courtship abuse the results of this research implies that violent acts had a negative effect on the relationships. Interestingly, the data suggests that men are more likely than women to feel that their relationship(s) improved after violent episodes and less likely to feel that their relationship(s) got worse. These differences may, once again, be owing to differing perceptions of violent behavior. Men may interpret acts of violence as an expression of commitment and as a way of "clearing the air," and thereby solidifying the relationship. Henton et al. (1983) support the idea that abuse may be interpreted as affection. Their data indicates that over one-fourth of victims and aggressors interpreted abusive behavior as "love," while only 4% saw these actions as acts of "hate" (Cate et al., 1982, also found similar results). Another explanation is that the male (and possibly the female too) may be perceiving a person's acquiescence, brought about by fear, as a sign of deeper involvement.

Central to the learning theory interpretation of violence is the belief that violent behavior is learned by being a member of a violent family, therefore, those persons who grew up in violent families tend to be more violent in their own relationships than those who did not. From this, one would predict that courtship abuse would be more prevalent among children from abusive homes than from nonabusive homes. Bernard and Bernard's (1983) research tended to support this assumption. Data analysis from the present study is at the moment too incomplete and too limited to draw any solid conclusions at this time. However, the stepwise regressions on courtship violence and date rape would seem to lend some support to this theory. Parent abuse, child abuse, and spouse abuse, along with the variables of family size, parental affection, and time spent with the subject tend to show up in the regressions for both violence and rape. Clearly these data indicate that something is occurring within the family environment that predisposes an individual toward experiencing physical and sexual abuse in his or her dating relationships.

A problem arises with this interpretation, however, when one tries to explain why the number of partners an individual has gone steady with along with one's experience with sexual intercourse and the number of coital partners show up as significant variables in the regression analysis. The results of a t-test analysis comparing those who experienced courtship violence with those who didn't may shed some light on this matter. The results indicate that those persons who experienced some form of courtship violence when compared to those who didn't tended to be younger when they had their first date ($\chi = 15.5857$, $\chi = 15.0471$, $t = 3.65$, $p < .000$), and were not only more likely to have engaged in intercourse ($\chi = 1.4185$, $\chi = 1.658$, $t = 6.23$, $p < .000$), but were also significantly younger at first coital experience ($\chi = 17.9484$, $\chi = 17.4934$, $t = 2.02$, $p < .05$) and had more coital partners ($\chi = 2.8969$, $\chi = 3.6154$, $t = 2.61$, $p < .01$). There are two possible explanations for this, both of which have their roots in family experience. First, as is commonly argued, early dating and coital experience may be the result of an individual's search for love and affection not found in the family. Second, and closely related to the first, these behaviors could be the result of negative family experiences that predispose an individual toward entering too quickly into a relationship that may place him or her at risk.

The data on forced intercourse also lend themselves to the above interpretation. Once again family factors tended to be significant variables in the regressions. Concomitantly, a t-test analysis of those who experienced forced intercourse with those who didn't tends to reinforce the regression data. Those who experienced forced intercourse, when compared to those who did not, tended to come from homes where the parent's marriage was seen as significantly less happy ($\chi = 7.9647$, $\chi = 7.4426$, $t = 2.45$, $p < .01$) and they tended to come from larger families ($\chi = 3.1955$, $\chi = 3.9516$, $t = -2.01$, $p < .05$).

In conclusion, analysis of the data seems to suggest that persons who experience courtship violence, whether physical, sexual, or both, tend to come from unhappy homes where abuse is either witnessed or experienced by the individual and where parental affection and attention is limited. There is also a demonstrated tendency for these individuals to become too involved too soon, both emotionally and physically, in their dating relationships. The question that needs to be asked at this point is, are these two sets of tendencies somehow linked together in a causal fashion that may predispose an individual to enter into a dating relationship that may place him or her at risk of physical or sexual violence? The present data analysis would suggest that this is so. If this, in fact, is the case then insight has been gained in explaining the etiology and dynamics of courtship violence (both physical and sexual) and for developing intervention strategies designed to prevent and stop such behavior from occurring.

References

Bernard, M. L., & Bernard, J. L. (1983). Violent intimacy: The family as a model for love relationships. *Family Relations, 32,* 283-286.

Bradburn, Sudman, & Associates (1979). *Improving interview method and questionnaire design.* San Francisco: Jossey-Bass.

Cate, R., Henton, J., Kaval, J., Christopher, S., & Lloyd, S. (1982). Premarital abuse: A social psychological perspective. *Journal of Family Issues, 3,* 79-91.

Gelles, R. (1983, October). *Parental child snatching: The use of telephone survey techniques to study a hidden family problem.* Paper presented at the National Council on Family Relations Theory Construction and Research Methods Workshop, Minneapolis.

Groves, R. M., & Kahn, R. L. (1979). *Surveys by telephone: A national comparison with personal interviews.* New York: Academic Press.

Harris, L., & Associates (1979). *A survey of spousal violence against women in Kentucky.* New York: Author.

Henton, J., Cate, R., Kaval, J., Lloyd, S., & Christopher, S. (1983). Romance and violence in dating relationships. *Journal of Family Issues, 4,* 467-482.

Hochstim, J. R. (1977). A critical comparison of three strategies of collecting data from households. *Journal of the American Statistical Association, 62,* 976-989.

Kanin, E. J. (1957). Male aggression in dating-courtship relations. *The American Journal of Sociology, 63*, 197-204.

Kanin, E. J. (1967). Reference groups and sex conduct norm violations. *Sociological Quarterly, 8*, 495-504.

Kanin, E. J., & Parcell, S. R. (1977). Sexual aggression: A second look at the offended female. *Archives of Sexual Behavior, 6*, 1.

Katz, S., & Mazur, M. (1979). *Understanding the rape victim: A synthesis of research findings.* New York: John Wiley.

Kempe, C. H., F. N. Silverman, B. F. Steele, W. Droegemueller, and H. K. Silver (1962). The battered child syndrome. *Journal of the American Medical Association, 181*, 107-112.

Kitson, G. C., Sussman, M. B., Williams, C. K., Zeehandler, R. B., Shickmanter, B. K., & Steinberger, J. L. (1982). Sampling issues in family research. *Journal of Marriage and the Family, 44*, 965-981.

Makepeace, J. M. (1981). Courtship violence among college students. *Family Relations, 32*, 101-109.

Makepeace, J. M. (1983). Life events stress and courtship violence. *Family Relations, 32*, 101-109.

McDermott, M. J. (1979). *Rape victimization in 26 American cities.* U.S. Department of Justice, Law Enforcement Assistance Administration. Washington, DC: Government Printing Office.

Miller, B. C., Rollins, B. C., & Thomas, D. L. (1982). On methods of studying marriages and families. *Journal of Marriage and the Family, 44*, 851-873.

Straus, M. A. (1979). Measuring intrafamily conflict and violence: The conflict tactics (CT) scale. *Journal of Marriage and the Family, 41*, 75-88.

Straus, M. A., Gelles, R. J., & Steinmetz, S. K. (1980). *Behind closed doors: Violence in the American family.* New York: Anchor/Doubleday.

21

The Severity of Courtship Violence and the Effectiveness of Individual Precautions

James M. Makepeace

Courtship and the Need for Precautions

The social science literature on mate selection exhibits two contrasting but perennial themes. On the one hand is the enormous inherent appeal of romantic love and the constructive potential of this force for society. On the other is the potential disruptiveness of inappropriate pairings for the individual and for society, and society's consequent implementation of measures of control. These two themes are evident in the following quotations:

> The mores formerly operated to produce a high rate of marriage at the proper age and at the same time protected most individuals from many of the possible traumatic experiences of the courtship period. (Waller, 1937, p. 728)

> This thrill dominated competitive process [i.e., campus dating] involving a number of fundamental antagonisms between the men and the women. . . . The men, who have been warned so repeatedly against coeds, are always afraid the girls are going to "gold-dig" them. The coeds wonder to what degree they are discussed and are constantly afraid of being placed on a black list of the fraternities. Then too they wonder to what extent they can take any man seriously without being taken for a "ride." Status in the one sex group depends upon avoiding exploitation by the opposite sex. (Waller, 1937, p. 731)

> One source of social control . . . is the individual's own teenaged companions. . . . Another source lies with the parents of both boy and girl. In our society, parents threaten, cajole, wheedle, bribe, and persuade their children to "go with the right people" during both the early love play and later courtship phases. Primarily, they seek to control love relationships by influencing the informal social contacts of their children: moving to appropriate neighborhoods and schools, giving parties and helping to make out the invitation lists.

... Since youngsters fall in love with those with whom they associate, control over informal relationships also controls substantially the focus of affection. (Goode, 1959, p. 46)

Force is still available as a male resource even in the modern middle class. A 1954-55 survey of girls at a midwestern college found that slightly more than one-half of them experienced sexual attacks, with the average number of reported experiences being six times in a year.... The more severe assaults usually came from steady boyfriends or fiances.... Thus, a mild use of force is taken into account in the dating system: women generally allow themselves to be made subject to force... after a tentative bargain has been struck. The availability of male force simply adds another element to the bargaining situation, and generally requires women to take the role of the sexually pursued, and thus to attempt to enforce an ideal of some degree of sexual inaccessibility except under the idealized condition of romantic love. (Collin, 1971, p. 17-18)

Most of the literature to date, including the sources of the foregoing quotations, has emphasized threats to socioeconomic endogamy, and sexual assaults as the principle mate selection contingencies to be guarded against. Recent research, however, has documented that American courtship is characterized by a range of abuse that goes far beyond sexual exploitation (Laner & Thompson, 1982; Makepeace, 1981). Indeed, in the present survey, only a minority of the reported cases of courtship violence included sexual assault.

In any case, it is clear that individuals, families, and community agencies have historically implemented a wide array of protective mechanisms to minimize the risk of intimate assault, whether sexual or nonsexual in nature. Examples of these mechanisms are numerous. Parents have used a wide array of control mechanisms, such as those indicated in the foregoing quotation by William Goode. The young themselves, particularly women, have sought to stay in groups and have avoided going off with strangers. Colleges, especially during the heyday of *in loco parentis* functioning (i.e., the period when campus officials were expected to act as substitute parents) implemented a wide variety of protective procedures including chaperonage, sex segregated dormitories, dorm "hours," curfews, bed checks, and weekend "sign outs." It is notable that these practices, common on American college campuses just 15 years ago, rarely applied to men. And all of the foregoing, of course, were in addition to the more general controls of the formal legal and justice systems.

The net effect of these measures has been a strategy of protecting against abuse by reducing opportunities for its occurrence. This has been achieved by preventing isolation of younger couples from the purview of social control, and by otherwise increasing the probability of apprehension and sanction of assailants. This popular understanding of courtship can be formulated using the conceptual tools of resource theory. From the perspective of resource theory, dating partners are assumed to make decisions on the basis of rational calculation; to analyze the various courses of action available to them, to estimate the relative reward/cost ratios associated with each, and to pursue the one that is perceived to offer the most favorable ratio of rewards to costs (what Thibault & Kelly, 1959, call the best comparison level for alternatives). With regard to the cost side of the equation, and other things being equal, there would appear to be an inherent economy in the use of violence by individuals who are larger, stronger, or more powerful than their partners. This is because, in the absence of social controls, violence is a more or less inexhaustible social resource (see Goode, 1971), the expenditure of which, as a result of the biological universal of pain, can yield large rewards at minimal cost (assuming, of course, the victim is not able to effectively retaliate).

To protect against the socially disruptive and personally harmful consequences of a "laissez faire" courtship system, however, society generally attempts to regulate romantic relationships by embedding them in the social structure of controls, described above, that weights the reward/cost ratio of abusive behavior below the comparison level for alternatives.

While society has thus clearly evolved mechanisms to curtail abusive courtship behavior, however, no evaluations of their effectiveness have been reported in the literature. In the remainder of this chapter, we will analyze the effectiveness of a series of precautionary measures that should, on the basis of theoretical and common sense reasoning, reduce the reward/cost ratios associated with courtship violence. The precautions that will be examined for effectiveness in reducing the injuriousness of courtship violence are: (1) presence of witnesses; (2) alcohol intoxication; (3) duration and intensity of relationship; and (4) the familiarity of the partners to one another's parents. The resource theory rationale for each of these factors is as follows:

Witnesses: Assailants (whether unilateral or bilateral) perceive that the observation of the infliction of injuries by witnesses constitute legal evidence sufficient to warrant official apprehension and sanction. Assailants should, then, be less likely to inflict serious injury in the presence of witnesses.

Alcohol intoxication: In popular values, alcohol intoxication is commonly believed to reduce personal moral responsibility. The rationalization, "He was drunk; he didn't know what he was doing," is widely subscribed to in American society, even though the social scientific literature suggests that intoxication may be more an excuse for violence than a cause of it.

Duration and intensity of relationship: Injuriousness of courtship violence is hypothesized to be greater in relationships of longer duration and greater seriousness. More advanced and serious relationships involve greater emotional intensity, the confronting of more serious and difficult issues, and presume the privilege of greater liberties in forms of interpersonal interaction. This theme of diminished accountability in advanced relationships underlies popular notions such as "crime of passion," "kiss and make up," "lover's quarrel," "love taps," and so on. These norms, however, shield assailants from detection, and thereby increase the probability of injury infliction.

Familiarity to parents: If an assailant is unknown to his partner's parents, the probability of escaping detection is increased. An assailant whose identity and whereabouts are well-known, by contrast, has a greater probability of apprehension and sanction, and should, therefore, be less inclined toward injurious courtship violence.

In the remainder of this chapter the seriousness of injuries resulting from courtship violence will be described and then compared for relationships of varying degrees of witness, alcohol intoxication, duration and intensity of relationship, and familiarity to parents. The data to be used for the analysis are from the College Premarital Abuse Project, a survey of 2,338 students from seven colleges and universities in varying regions of the United States. The data were collected in 1982 and 1983.

Throughout this chapter, the male pronoun is used to refer to assailants and the female pronoun to refer to victims. This convention is adopted in order to enhance the euphony of the text, and because research has, in general, found these to be the more common gender roles in courtship violence. This convention should not be understood to imply that the opposite roles do not also at times occur (i.e., that females are not sometimes the principal assailants and males the principal victims).

It should also be noted that the dependent variable here, the victim's injury level, is the injury level of those respondents who reported that either: (1) "I was the principal victim, the other person the principal aggressor"; or (2) "We were about equally victims and aggressors." The assumption was made that the respondent counted as a victim in both of these situations.

Results

The dependent variable in the present analysis is the degree of injury experienced by victims of courtship violence as reported by 2,338 American college students. Respondents were asked to indicate the degree of injury that was experienced by the victim in the worst incident of courtship violence they had experienced, regardless of whether they were the victim, assailant, or a cobelligerent. Naturally, the victim in an incident is better able to report accurately the degree of injury incurred, since: (1) the victim may experience pain that the assailant is unaware of; (2) injuries may be obscured from the assailant by clothing, hair, or glasses; and (3) injuries, such as bruises or miscarriages, may manifest themselves some time after the incident. In addition, the recall of injury is certainly subject to some memory lapse, and "motivated forgetting" may be especially pronounced for the assailant, since defense mechanisms of suppression or repression may operate. As a result, the injury figures reported here are probably underestimates.

The levels of injury from which respondents could select were as follows:

Using the 4 levels described below, how would you assess the extent of the harm or injury you and the other person experienced as a result of this incident?

(1) No injury or pain resulted.
(2) Mild—small cuts, lumps, bruises, minor pain, black eye, swollen lip, or similar injury.
(3) Moderate—lacerations requiring 1-4 stitches, extensive bruising and swelling, fractured extremities (nose, finger) outpatient emergency room treatment, or similar injury.
(4) Severe—injuries requiring hospitalization, fractured limbs, permanent disability or impairment, loss of consciousness, surgery, termination of a pregnancy, knife or gunshot wounds of any severity, death.

Effect of Witness Presence

The data on the relationship between witness presence and injury level are shown in Table 21.1. The data provide support for the general notion that being around other people provides some protection against courtship violence. The great majority (59.3%) of the incidents did occur in isolation. On the other hand, the severity of injuries that resulted from incidents that occurred in the presence of witnesses was not significantly less than for those that occurred in isolation. The implication of these results would seem to be that "Stay in a group" is good dating advice, but while there is some security in numbers, the presence of others will probably not inhibit the seriousness of violence should it occur anyway.

It is not clear from this data, however, just why the presence of witnesses does not lessen injuriousness. The finding is not entirely novel, of course. The "Genovese effect" of bystander passivity has been well-known since the 1964 slaying of a young woman of that name on a New York City (Queens) street in full view of several dozen witnesses, none of whom came to her aid (Milgram, 1970; Milgram & Hollander, 1964). Bystander passivity was also the subject of considerable public attention in a 1982 New Bedford, Massachusetts gang rape of a young woman in a barroom. Initial accounts indicated that 20 or more cheering patrons were present. These accounts were later revealed to be greatly exaggerated. Nevertheless, a few witnesses were present, and it appears that none of them made more than a feeble

TABLE 21.1
Courtship Violence Injury Level by Witness Presence

| | Witnessed by | | | | | | | |
| | Peers | | Parents | | Others | | Unwitnessed | |
Injury Level	%	N	%	N	%	N	%	N
None	45.5	30	42.9	3	32.1	9	59.8	128
Mild	50.0	33	57.1	4	60.7	17	35.0	75
Serious	3.0	2	0.0	0	7.1	2	3.7	8
Severe	1.5	1	0.0	0	0.0	0	1.4	3
(Subtotal	24.8	36	2.8	4	13.1	19	59.3	86)
Total	100.0	66	100.0	7	100.0	28	100.0	214

effort to intervene (see *New York Times* reports, February 6, March 1, and April 11, 1984).

In the present case we may propose several possible reasons why witness presence does not appear to inhibit injuriousness, although the data to evaluate them are not available at this time. Perhaps assailants had, indeed, assessed the probability of witness reportage or intervention, and had concluded that the particular witnesses present were unlikely to act. Perhaps the witnesses themselves felt, like witnesses to the Genovese slaying, that it was none of their business, and perhaps they themselves feared reprisal should they take action against the assailants. In some instances, witnesses may have been supportive of the assailant's behavior. A final possibility might be termed a "humiliation redress" factor. The most common type of disagreement to precede incidents of courtship violence in this study was "jealousy" (almost a third, 30.3%, of the incidents were preceded by a jealousy type disagreement). In some proportion of these incidents, assailants may have felt publicly humiliated by what they perceived as demeaning, flirtatious, or otherwise offensive behavior on the part of their partners, and may have felt that a public response was necessary to save face. In other words, assailants may at times actually prefer to inflict violence before witnesses.

Alcohol Intoxication

The influence of alcohol intoxication can be approached from the standpoint of the assailant or the victim. It is widely believed in American society that alcohol intoxication produces a "loss of control" and, thereby, reduces the individual's capacity to behave responsibly. Alcohol intoxication has been widely cited as a contributing factor to spousal violence in particular (Eisenberg & Micklow, 1977; Gelles, 1974; Langley & Levy,

1977). While some scholars feel that alcohol is a biochemical "trigger" for violent behavior, most literature interprets the link between the two as owing to the cultural meaning of intoxication. As Gelles (1974) has formulated this line of reasoning: "The drinker can use the period when he is drunk as a 'time out' when he is not responsible for his actions." For a review and assessment of deviance disavowal and other theories in this area, see Coleman and Straus (1981).

Victim intoxication might also be a predisposing condition in courtship violence. It is noteworthy that the victim's consumption of a considerable amount of alcohol in the New Bedford, Massachusetts rape case, previously referred to, was stressed by the defense and by the newspapers and other media. The implication seemed to be that as a result of her intoxication the victim was culpable for her own rape because she had willingly impaired her own judgment and self-restraint, and placed herself in a situation of unnecessary risk. The fact that she had bought drinks for one or more of her assailants was also cited, lending the impression that by such behavior she communicated to her assailants that she was sexually promiscuous (see *New York Times* reports, March 3, 16, and 20, 1984).

The relationship between alcohol consumption by self-reported victims and their offenders during the eight hours prior to the incident and the level of resulting injury is shown in Table 21.2. The following points seem noteworthy.

(1) All eight of the severe (level 4) injuries were perpetrated by individuals who had consumed some amount of alcohol prior to the incident. No alcohol-free individuals inflicted a severe injury.

(2) Light or moderate alcohol consumption (up to seven drinks) does not appear to contribute to a higher rate of occurrence of courtship violence. The relationship between amount of alcohol consumed and the percentage of respondents involved in incidents that produced physical injury is shown in Figure 21.1. The rate of injury is similar among respondents who had consumed between zero and seven alcoholic drinks.

(3) Heavy drinking (here defined as consuming eight or more drinks prior to the incident), however, does significantly contribute to seriousness of resulting injuries. The proportion of incidents that resulted in physical injuries was 66.7% among those who had consumed eight or more drinks, compared to 47.2% among those who had consumed seven or fewer drinks.

(4) While drinking does not appear related to the incidence of any injury, it is associated with increased severity. Thus the rate of serious injury (levels 3 and 4 combined) was 4.9% among alcohol free individuals, 5.4% among those in the one to three drinks group, 10.8% for the four to seven drinks group, and 11.2% for the eight or more drinks group. There is, then, a consistent increase in the rate of serious injuries as alcohol consumption increases.

TABLE 21.2

Courtship Violence Injury Level by Alcohol Consumption

	Alcohol Consumed (Prior 8 Hours)									
	0		1-3		4-7		8		All	
Injury Level	%	N	%	N	%	N	%	N	%	N
None	51.0	73	54.8	131	52.2	24	33.6	6	52.5	234
Mild	44.1	63	41.4	99	37.0	17	55.5	10	42.4	189
Serious	4.9	7	3.3	8	6.5	3	5.6	1	4.3	19
Severe	0.0	0	2.1	5	4.3	2	5.6	1	1.8	8
Total	100.0	143	100.0	243	100.0	46	100.0	18	100.0	450

The conclusion implied by these results is that alcohol use is a significant factor in the severity of courtship violence injuries. With heavy drinking, the proportion of incidents involving physical injuries significantly increased; the proportion of serious physical injuries increased consistently with increased use of alcohol; and virtually all severe injuries were alcohol related.

Duration of Relationship

Conventional wisdom is inconsistent with regard to what relationship prevails between degree of familiarity and the probability of hostile relationships. On the one hand, it cautions: "Be wary of strangers." On the other hand, we are told: "Familiarity breeds contempt." There are also conflicting clues to the relationship between familiarity and hostility in the professional literature. Straus, Gelles, and Steinmetz (1980) found that "The statistics from this nationally representative sample . . . leave no doubt that younger couples [and, therefore, those marriages of shorter duration] are more violent" (p. 142). Conversely, a concurrent study based upon the present data (Makepeace, 1984), as well as several previous courtship violence studies (Cate, Henton, Kaval, Christopher, & Lloyd, 1982; Laner & Thompson, 1982) found rates of courtship violence to be greater for relationships in the more advanced stage of steady dating (and presumably, therefore, of longer duration) than in more preliminary relationships such as first dates, just friends, or casual dating. And, a study by Yllö and Straus (1981) that compared married with unmarried but living together couples found that while violence decreases consistently with increasing duration of the marriage relationship, it was highest (50%) for living-together relationships of 3-10 years duration, lower for relationships of 2 years or less, and lowest for those over 10 years duration. Their analysis of this relationship was based upon a very small number of cases (n = 37), however, and was not reported to be statistically significant.

Which of these conflicting indications is best supported by the present

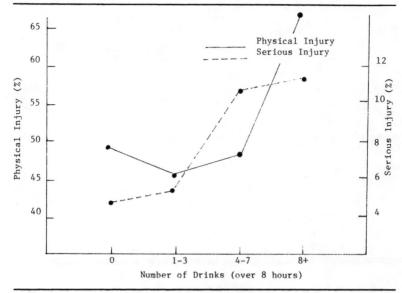

Figure 21.1. Courtship violence injury rate by alcohol use.

data? The advice: "Be wary of strangers" has the more support, particularly with reference to more severe assaults. The relationship between duration of relationship and occurrence of physical injury is shown in Figure 21.2, which exhibits a descending, although inconsistent trend. That is, the production of injuries was greatest between partners who had not known one another for very long, and was lowest for relationships of 13-24 months duration.

The rate of serious (level 3 and 4) injury was three times as great (33.3%) in relationships of less than one month duration than among all others combined (11.4%).

It must be concluded then that while familiarity may breed some contempt, any such effect is more than offset by the risks entailed in dating unfamiliar partners. The probability of encountering any violence appears somewhat greater, and the probability of experiencing serious injury much greater in relationships of brief as opposed to those of lengthy duration.

Familiarity to Parents

The relationship between familiarity of partners to respondents' parents and occurrence of injury is shown in Figure 21.3 (solid line). The relationship is curvilinear. The proportion of incidents that resulted in physical injuries was relatively low (41%) for relatively unknown partners, increased to 53.7% for those who were somewhat known, and declined

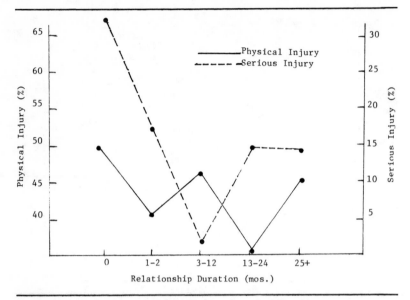

Figure 21.2. Courtship violence injury by duration of relationship.

again (40.7%) for those whose partners were very well known to their parents.

This result does not conform to the inverse relationship that was hypothesized. The higher rate of physical injury when the partner is somewhat familiar to the respondent's parents is not, however, difficult to explain. Violence is, after all, a form of intimate behavior. It involves the taking of liberties with and intrusion into the physical space of another person. Such behavior is both formally and informally sanctionable. We might reason, therefore, that a violently disposed individual would be more inclined to behave violently when: (1) he is so unknown/unfamiliar to the victim or the victim's family that they would be unlikely to be able to apprehend him; or, (2) he knows them well enough to know that they will probably not take action against him. In the latter scenario, gaining the victim's confidence, and gaining knowledge of her habits and dispositions and those of her family could be useful to a potential assailant in assessing the probability of being able to inflict violence with impunity.

There are also other reasons why violence might tend to erupt only after some degree of familiarity has been established between the partners and one another's families. It may be, for example, that families reduce their watchfulness when, after becoming familiar with an offspring's partner, they come to take him for granted.

For these reasons the curvilinear relationship between familiarity to parents and injuriousness should not be viewed as disconfirming the utility

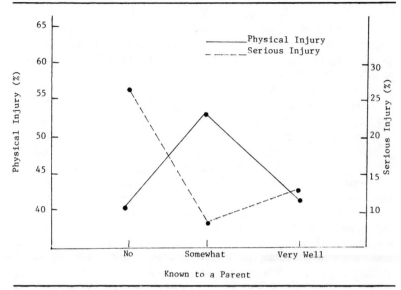

Figure 21.3. Courtship violence injury and familiarity to a parent.

of the resource perspective, although it does necessitate some modification in the present formulation.

The relationship between familiarity to parents and the infliction of serious injuries is shown by the dotted line in Figure 21.3. The relationship is clearly in line with the hypothesis, and is quite pronounced. Thus the proportion of courtship violence injuries that are serious (level 3 or 4) was two and one-half times greater (26.1%) among respondents whose partners were not known to their parents as it was for all others combined (10.0%). From the standpoint of avoiding serious injury, then, familiarity between parents and dating partners does appear to provide a significant measure of protection.

Conclusions and Discussion

The purpose of this study was to examine the effectiveness of several precautionary measures, which on the basis of both common sense and theoretical reasoning were hypothesized to be inversely related to the injuriousness of courtship violence.

"Violent acts" versus "violent effects." The methodology of this study involved the novel approach of defining the dependent variable not as what "acts" of violence (i.e., pushing, slapping, beating, and so on) occurred, as has been done with studies based on the Conflict Tactics Scales and similar

procedures, but as the degree of injury that resulted, whatever form was used to produce it. The use of a "violent acts" approach such as the Conflict Tactics Scales is essential for documenting one dimension of this form of family violence. It is insufficient, however, for obtaining a comprehensive understanding of family violence, since it provides no information on the effect of those acts on the victim.

The literature on family violence has been based largely on a "violent acts" approach to measurement, and lends the impression that all violent acts produce violent effects. Indeed, the very wording of much of the literature describes those acts as if they routinely involve maximum effects. But that is not so. Even common sense suggests that a substantial proportion of violent acts are more symbolic, postural, or intimidatory than injurious in intent. Some threats with weapons are bluffs, some punches are pulled, some pushes are so mild that they produce no sensation of pain and no observable injury. Such "submaximal effects" are legitimate and important parts of the subject matter of family violence and merit investigation in their own right.

They constitute important subject matter because, even though they may not produce serious injuries in any particular instance, they nonetheless contribute to the rate of serious violence. They do so because they are "precedents" for things that people have done to one another with impunity in the past and that, therefore, they come to expect can be enacted with impunity again in the future. They do so because a determinate proportion of acts of courtship violence that are not intended to produce injuries will, nonetheless, do so anyway. They constitute, in a sense, the reservoir of actions out of which a determinate incidence of serious incidents emerges, and, the larger that pool, the greater will be the absolute number of serious incidents. In a future paper, in fact, this author will show that the great majority of injurious incidents are not only intended to be injurious, but are not even perceived by the assailants to have been injurious.

Perhaps most importantly, such acts are important in the destructive and undignified tone that they impart to human relationships. Though they may not produce physical injuries, they constitute a defilement, a lowering of human conduct from civilized standards of discourse, reason, and negotiation. And, like the black spot on the Tao, they thereafter stand as reminders of those points in life when we were less than we could have been.

The exclusive use of a violent acts approach also results in a substantial overestimate of the extent of serious family violence. In the present research, not all of the incidents that involved violent acts produced violent effects. Only 56.5% of them did (according to victims' reports). And, only 7.9% of them were of a "serious" nature—that is, level 3 or 4, which in this study was judged to be a level that would merit professional medical attention.

The author is not a medical practitioner or medical researcher, and the scale of injuries used here can probably be improved upon. The important point, though, is that if a comprehensive understanding of family violence is to be obtained, research must shift to include a focus on "violent effects" as well as "violent acts."

The overestimation of rates of family violence that results from a "full effects" assumption may also constitute a strategic error in terms of enlisting social support for victims of family violence. To make a "full effects" assumption is to inadvertently sensationalize, and thereby undermine the credibility of the problem of family violence. The assumption that all violent acts are injurious is so transparent that it is probably more constructive for those of us with genuine concern for the problem to point this out than to allow detractors from the problem to do so. If we do not present a balanced view of the problem, we will appear as alarmists and prophets of doom rather than as objective professionals.

Furthermore, to overstate the problem as though all violent acts are physically injurious detracts attention from the minority of genuinely serious cases. It does so by spreading attention over the general pool of cases, many of which are not serious. Observers may then be more impressed by those cases that do not involve serious injury, and conclude that family violence, in general, is not very serious after all.

Effectiveness of precautions. The conclusion of this chapter with respect to the precautionary measures examined is that they are of some effectiveness in inhibiting injurious courtship violence, particularly serious courtship violence. From this analysis, it appears that there may be at least two major forms of courtship violence. One is that which occurs at the hand of a stranger or a relatively unfamiliar partner, and is relatively serious in its effects. Thus the average severity of injury was considerably greater among incidents that occurred in preliminary stages of relationships and at the hands of partners not well known to family members. On the other hand is the much more common, but on average less serious, courtship violence that occurs in relationships of longer duration and among couples more familiar with one another's families. These incidents seem to conform more with the stereotypic "lover's spat." While it thus appears, as other research has indicated (Henton et al., 1983; Plass & Gessner, 1983; Yllö & Straus, 1981); that courtship violence is more characteristic of advanced stages of relationships, such violence also appears, on the basis of the present research, to be less serious in the average severity of injuries sustained.

Finally, the proviso must be added that these findings do not, of course, imply that responsibility for the preventing of courtship or other intimate violence lies principally with individuals and their families. That assumption would come close to "blaming the victim," since it would imply that the victim was at fault for failing to take reasonable precautions. Responsibility for any violent assault lies with the assailant, not the victim (although varying degrees of aggravation may, of course, also exist). As far as dealing with the problem of courtship violence is concerned, society's legal, educational, social service, and criminal justice systems remain responsible for effective execution of their functions. Nevertheless, the exercising of good judgment by avoiding situations of risk and taking common-sense precautions is here documented to be an effective approach to the problem. Emphasis on the use of these measures could be of some help in reducing courtship violence and, thereby, permitting societal resources, which are currently inadequate and spread far too thin, to be more effectively used.

The tone of this chapter may seem somewhat neoconservative in that the results could easily be interpreted as implying the need for restricting the freedom of the young—for example, of raising drinking ages, or reinstating campus protective practices, such as chaperonage or dormitory hours. This would, no doubt, seem particularly disturbing to those who would view the renewed imposition of such controls as the loss of ground won at high cost. This is because if new or old restrictions are imposed, it seems likely that they would be imposed particularly upon women, since it is they who, in courtship violence as in sexuality, bear the brunt of the risk.

The author should not be misunderstood as advocating such increased controls on youth as an implication of this chapter. His penchant at this time is that freedom and self-determination in human relationships are of such fundamental primacy that they should be curtailed only for very compelling reasons. To deny it to the young might eliminate some courtship violence. It would, however, also deny the young many opportunities for experiences that could make important contributions to personal growth.

Freedom of association, then, has its costs, but the author, for one, would prefer that society bear that cost rather than restrict the freedom. This is not to say that the findings of the present research should be disregarded or that society should do nothing about courtship violence. On the contrary, the author's position would be that the findings of research on this and related issues ought to be heavily emphasized in educational and media materials on dating and interpersonal relations so that the young can see what risks and options are involved in human relationships, and what styles of behavior and what remedies are helpful, so they may themselves make enlightened decisions. These, of course, are preliminary comments on an issue that should be an important item for the future agenda of courtship violence theorizing and policy formulation.

References

Cate, R., Henton, J., Kaval, J., Christopher, F. S., & Lloyd, S. (1982). Premarital abuse: A social psychological perspective. *Journal of Family Issues, 3,* 79-91.

Coleman, D. H., & Straus, M. A. (1981, February). Alcohol abuse and family violence. *VA, 13,* 1-19.

Collin, R. (1971). A conflict theory of sexual stratification. *Social Problems, 19,* 3-20.

Eisenberg, S. E., & Micklow, P. L. (1977, Spring-Summer). The assaulted wife: Catch 22 revisited. *Women's Rights Law Reporter, 3-4.* (Rutgers University School of Law, Newark, NJ)

Gelles, R. J. (1974). *The violent home: A study of physical aggression between husbands and wives.* Beverly Hills, CA: Sage.

Goode, W. J. (1959). The theoretical importance of love. *American Sociological Review, 24,* 38-47.

Goode, W. J. (1971). Force and violence in the family. *Journal of Marriage and the Family, 33,* 624-636.

Henton, J., Cate, R., Koval, J., Lloyd, S., & Christopher, S. (1983). Romance and violence in dating relations. *Journal of Family Issues, 4,* 467-482.

Laner, M. R., & Thompson, L. (1982). Abuse and aggression in courting couples. *Deviant Behavior, 3,* 229-244.

Langley, R., & Levy, R. C. (1977). *Wife beating.* New York: Pocket Books.

Makepeace, J. M. (1981). Courtship violence among college students. *Family Relations, 30,* 97-102.

Makepeace, J. M. (1982). Life events stress and courtship violence. *Family Relations, 32,* 101-109.

Makepeace, J. M. (1984). *Courtship violence as resource exchange.* Unpublished paper.

Milgram, S., & Hollander, P. (1964). The murder they heard: Catherine Genovese and 38 uninvolved witnesses in New York. *Nation, 198,* 602.

Milgram, S. (1970). The experience of living in cities. *Science, 167,* 1461-1468.

Plass, M. S., Gessner, J. C. (1983). Violence in courtship relations: A southern sample. *Free Inquiry in Creative Sociology, 11,* 198-202.

Straus, M. A., Gelles, R. J., & Steinmetz, S. K. (1980). *Behind closed doors: Violence in the America family.* New York: Anchor/Doubleday.

Thibault, J. W., & Kelley, H. (1959). *The social psychology of groups.* New York: John Wiley.

Waller, W. (1937). The rating and dating complex. *American Sociological Review, 2,* 727-734.

Yllö, K., & Straus, M. (1981). Interpersonal violence among married and cohabiting couples. *Family Relations, 30,* 339-347.

About the Authors

ILEANA ARIAS received her M.A. and Ph.D. in clinical psychology from the State University of New York at Stony Brook. Her research focuses on the etiology and treatment of marital distress and family violence. More recently, her research efforts have been devoted to examining variables that contribute to the prediction of the occurrence of physical aggression in dating and married couples. She has been a Research Associate in the Marital and Family Studies Center at the State University of New York at Stony Brook and is currently in the Psychology Department of the University of Georgia at Athens.

F. G. BOLTON, Jr., is Coordinator of Psychological and Psychiatric Services at the Arizona Department of Economic Security. He is a practitioner, researcher, and author in the area of child maltreatment and other forms of family violence. He has published five books in the area, the most recent being *Working with Violent Families,* with Susan Bolton (Sage, 1987).

ANGELA BROWNE is a social psychologist specializing in family violence and abuse. She is currently a lecturer in the Department of Criminal Justice at Northeastern University. She is editor of the interdisciplinary journal *Violence and Victims,* has published articles on wife abuse and the consequences of child sexual abuse, and has recently published a book on women who kill their abusive mates, *When Battered Women Kill* (Free Press, 1987).

JAMES J. BROWNING received his Ph.D. in clinical psychology from the University of British Columbia. He has written extensively on male violence in interpersonal relationships. He is currently in private practice and is a cotherapist in the Assaultive Project at the University of British Columbia.

ROBERT L. BURGESS is Professor of Human Development at Pennsylvania State University. He is a recognized scholar in the area of child abuse and neglect. He has been awarded several grants to continue his studies in this area, most notably *Project Interat: A Study of Patterns of Interactions in Abusive, Neglectful, and Control Families* (National Center on Child Abuse and Neglect, 1978). He is currently exploring the intergenerational transmission of patterns of violence in the family.

PHYLLIS D. COONTZ is an Assistant Professor of Sociology in the Administration of Justice Program at the University of Pittsburgh. She received her doctorate in sociology from the University of Colorado at Boulder. In addition to her collaborative work with Dr. Judith Martin, she has conducted research investigating conditions of life for women under the sentence of death and has studied methadone treatment among heroin addicts. Her specific areas of expertise include female criminality, violent behavior, and the sociology of law, and she has published articles in all three areas. Her current work focuses on the international legal status of women.

DONALD G. DUTTON received his Ph.D. from the University of Toronto in social psychology and is currently an Associate Professor in the Department of Psychology at the University of British Columbia, Vancouver, and Director of the Assaultive Husbands Project. His research has focused upon the causes of assaultive behavior in males, effects on victims, and criminal justice policy. He is author of the forthcoming book *Wife Assault: Psychological and Criminal Justice Perspectives* (Allyn and Bacon, 1987).

KATHLEEN J. FERRARO is an Assistant Professor in the Center for the Study of Justice at Arizona State University, Tempe. She was a cofounder of a shelter for battered women, where she worked for 14 months. This work, along with other volunteer work and contacts with shelters, formed the basis for her dissertation and a number of articles on woman battering and the shelter movement. She is currently involved in research to determine the impact of police intervention on domestic violence. She is also collecting data on assaultive men through an educational group, Practical Alternatives to Violence.

DAVID FINKELHOR is Associate Director of the Family Research Laboratory at the University of New Hampshire. He has been studying the problem of child sexual abuse since 1977, and has published three books—*Sexually Victimized Children* (Free Press, 1979), *Child Sexual Abuse: New Theory and Research* (Free Press, 1984), and *A Sourcebook on Child Sexual Abuse* (Sage, 1986)—and many articles on the subject. He has been the recipient of research grants from the National Institute of Mental Health, the National Center on Child Abuse and Neglect, and the Conrad Hilton Foundation. His other research interests include elder abuse and sexual assaults in marriage.

RICHARD J. GELLES is Dean of the College of Arts and Sciences, Professor of Sociology and Anthropology at the University of Rhode Island, and Lecturer on Pediatrics at the Harvard Medical School. He directs the Family Violence Research Program at the University of Rhode Island and has published extensively on the topics of child abuse, wife abuse, and family violence. He is the author of *The Violent Home* (Sage, 1974) and *Family Violence* (Sage, 1979), coauthor of *Behind Closed Doors: Violence in the American Family* (Anchor/Doubleday, 1980) and *Intimate Violence in Families* (Sage, 1985), and coeditor of *The Dark Side of Families: Current Family Violence Research* (Sage, 1983) and *International Perspectives on Family Violence* (Sage, 1983).

ELLEN GRAY is Senior Research Associate for the National Council of Jewish Women Center of the Child. She was a Program Associate for Research at the National Committee for Prevention of Child Abuse, and was Director of the NCCAN-Funded Collaborative Research of Community and Minority Groups Action to Prevent Abuse and Neglect Project, which examined 11 prevention projects across the country to determine their effectiveness. She has worked in the field of child abuse for 13 years, in clinical, teaching and research positions. She won the Award of Merit in the category of Training in Child Abuse and Neglect for her report on a child abuse treatment project, and the Joseph B. Gavrin Memorial Paper Competition for "Childcare and Family Functioning." The author of *Evaluating Child Abuse Prevention Programs,* she recently conducted a research conference on the subject of the link between child abuse and delinquency, results of which are reported in this volume.

CHRISTINE R. HANNEKE is a Research Associate at Policy Research and Planning Group, Inc., in St. Louis, Missouri. Her areas of research interest include interpersonal violence, social psychology, and evaluation research. Her past work has appeared in several books and journals, including *Journal of Applied Social Psychology, Social Casework,* and *Law and Policy Quarterly.*

GERALD T. HOTALING is Assistant Professor in the Department of Criminal Justice at the University of Lowell, and Research Scientist of the Family Research Laboratory at the University of New Hampshire. He has edited two books on family violence and has been the recipient of a number of grants on violence and child sexual abuse.

CAROLLEE HOWES is Assistant Professor in the Graduate School of Education at the University of California, Los Angeles. Her research interests include the study of friendships and peer interactions among high-risk and normal children, and the social development of children within day-care settings.

PETER JAFFE received his Ph.D. from the University of Western Ontario, where he is currently an Adjunct Assistant Professor of Psychology. He has been the Director of the London (Ontario) Court Clinic since 1974, and has been active in the establishment of a family consultant service with the London Police Force to intervene effectively with domestic violence.

MILDRED E. JOHNSTON received her Ph.D. in community counseling from the University of Maryland. She is currently employed at the Family Crisis Center, a shelter for abused women in Brentwood, Maryland. She is also a cotherapist in a program for violent men at the Cheverly Outpatient Clinic of Prince George's (Maryland) Mental Health Department.

JOHN T. KIRKPATRICK is Associate Dean in the College of Liberal Arts at the University of New Hampshire. He received the doctorate in sociology from the University of New Hampshire in 1983. His research interests include interpersonal violence, gender roles and crime, and the epidemiology of violent crime in the United States.

JAMES M. MAKEPEACE is an Associate Professor and Chair of the Department of Sociology at the College of St. Benedict at St. John's University, St. Joseph, Minnesota. In 1981 he published the results of the first study of courtship violence and abuse and is currently analyzing the results of an eight-college survey on this topic. He is the author of numerous popular and professional articles, has lectured widely, and has appeared on national radio and television programs.

GAYLA MARGOLIN is an Associate Professor of Psychology at the University of Southern California. She is a coauthor of *Marital Therapy: Strategies Based on Social and Behavior Exchange Principles* and has written over 40 articles or chapters on the assessment and treatment of couples and families.

JUDITH A. MARTIN is an Associate Professor at the University of Pittsburgh School of Social Work. She is the coauthor of a study of transactional patterns in abusive families. With Alfred Kadushin, she has published *Child Abuse: An Interactional Event.* She is currently conducting research on the adult functioning of individuals severely maltreated as children, with Elizabeth Elmer. She has long been interested in the effect of sex-role expectations and sex differences in abusive situations, and has studied gender differences in the behavior of both abused children and their parents.

JOAN McCORD is Professor of Criminal Justice at Temple University, a Fellow of the American Society of Criminology, and a Fellow of the International Society for Research on Aggression. She is a member of the Steering Committee for the Society for Life History Research and an Executive Counselor for the American Society of Criminology. Her bibliography includes four books and numerous articles pertaining to family interaction and its effects on personality. She contributed to the article on family relationships and crime in the *Encyclopedia of Crime and Justice.*

JOHN E. MURPHY is Associate Professor of Sociology and Codirector of the St. Paul State University Survey Center at St. Cloud State University in Minnesota. He has conducted extensive research on dating and family abuse and child sexual abuse. He has also conducted workshops on child sexual abuse, nationally and regionally, and has served as a consultant in jury selection for prosecutors handling child and adolescent sexual abuse cases.

K. DANIEL O'LEARY, a clinical psychologist, is Professor and past Chairman of the Psychology Department of the State University of New York at Stony Brook. He was Editor of *Journal of Applied Behavior Analysis,* and is Associate Editor of *Journal of Abnormal Child Psychology.* He was President of the Association for Advancement of Behavior Therapy. His books include *Behavior Therapy: Application and Outcome* (with G. T. Wilson), *Classroom Management* (with S. O'Leary), *Mommy, I Can't Sit Still: Coping with the Aggressive and Hyperactive Child,* and *Assessment of Marital Discord.* He is among the top 100 cited psychologists in the English-speaking world.

KARL PILLEMER is an Assistant Professor in the Department of Sociology and Anthropology and a Research Associate of the Family Research Laboratory at the University of New Hampshire. He has published extensively in the area of elder abuse and neglect. He has recently published, with Rosalie Wolf, a collection of articles, *Elder Abuse: Conflict in the Family* (Auburn House, 1986).

JAMES PTACEK is working toward a doctorate in sociology at Brandeis University. His current areas of study include the family, critical social psychology, and political sociology. His chapter in this volume is taken from his master's thesis, "Wifebeaters' Accounts of Their Violence: Loss of Control as Excuse and as Subjective Experience." He received his M.A. in sociology from the University of New Hampshire. Along with his academic work, since 1981 he has been involved in counseling men who batter, community education, and research as part of Emerge, a Boston men's collective concerned with violence against wives.

LINDA P. ROUSE, Ph.D., is an Assistant Professor in the Department of Sociology, Anthropology, and Social Work at the University of Texas—Arlington. She has been involved in both teaching and research in the area of family violence. Her research interests have centered on the question of "why he hits." She has presented papers titled "Methods of Studying Male Assailants in Cases of Spouse Abuse," "Social Power and Family Violence," and "The Effect of Sex Role Orientation on Men's Abusive Behavior." Her published articles include "Models, Self-Esteem and Locus of Control as Factors Contributing to Spouse Abuse" (*Victimology,* 1984) and "Battered Women/Battering Men" (*Family Life Educator,* 1985). She served as Editorial Consultant for the *Journal of Sociology and Social Welfare* (1981-83) and Associate Director of the Center for Social Research at Western Michigan University (1981-82). She has also worked at a shelter for battered women and is the author of, *You Are Not Alone: A Guide for Battered Women* (1986). Currently she is analyzing data on acquaintance rape and courtship violence among college students.

NANCY M. SHIELDS is a Research Associate at Policy Research and Planning Group in St. Louis, Missouri. Her areas of research interest include interpersonal violence, social psychology, and research methodology. Her past work has appeared in several books and journals, including *Journal of Applied Social Psychology, Social Casework,* and *Law and Policy Quarterly.*

MURRAY A. STRAUS is Professor of Sociology and Director of the Family Research Laboratory at the University of New Hampshire. He has also taught at Minnesota, Cornell, Wisconsin, Washington State, York (England), Bombay (India), and University of Ceylon (Sri Lanka). He is a former President of the National Council on Family Relations, Vice President of the Eastern Sociological Society, and Member of the Council, American Association for the Advancement of Science. In 1977 he was given the Ernest W. Burgess Award of the National Council on Family Relations for outstanding research on the family. He is also the recipient of an American Sociological Association award for contributions to undergraduate teaching. He is the author or coauthor of over 125 articles on the family, research methods, and South Asia and of 10 books, including *Intimate Violence* (1988), *Social Stress in the United States* (1986), *Crime and the Family* (1985), *The Dark Side of Families* (1983), *The Social Causes of Husband-Wife Violence* (1980), *Behind Closed Doors: Violence in the American Family* (1980), *Family Measurement Techniques* (1978), and *Sociological Analysis* (1968).

LENORE E. WALKER is a licensed psychologist and President of Walker and Associates, a consulting firm in Denver, Colorado. She is an Associate Professor of Psychology at Colorado Women's College. She is also founder and director of the Domestic Violence Institute, a nonprofit private institute that conducts research on family violence. As a recognized authority in the area of family violence, she has given numerous lectures, testified before Congress, served as expert witness in numerous court proceedings, and has written extensively. She is the author of two books on battered women, *The Battered Woman* (Harper & Row, 1979) and *The Battered Woman Syndrome* (Springer, 1984). She was awarded the 1979 Distinguished Media Award for her work by the Association for Women in Psychology.

SUSAN KAYE WILSON is currently a graduate student in the child clinical program at the University of Western Ontario. Along with Lydia Zak, she has been interviewing mothers and children at shelters for battered women as part of the research study presented in the chapter in this volume, and is focusing her thesis research on social supports and coping abilities following exposure to family violence.

DAVID A. WOLFE received his Ph.D. from the University of Florida and is currently an Assistant Professor of Psychology at the University of Western Ontario. He is director of an early intervention program for parents who have shown indications of physical child abuse, and codirector (with P. Jaffe) of a research program investigating the impact of family violence upon children. He has written and researched extensively in the area of risk factors in physical child abuse.

LISE M. YOUNGBLADE is a doctoral candidate in the Department of Human Development and Family Studies at the Pennsylvania State University. She is currently conducting research on factors associated with peer rejection among children.

LYDIA ZAK received her honors B.A. in psychology from the University of Western Ontario, and currently is a Research Assistant in the Department of Psychology. Her honors thesis looked at changes in children's adjustment over time, following their stay in a shelter for battered women.

NOTES

NOTES